SIGNS AND WONDERS

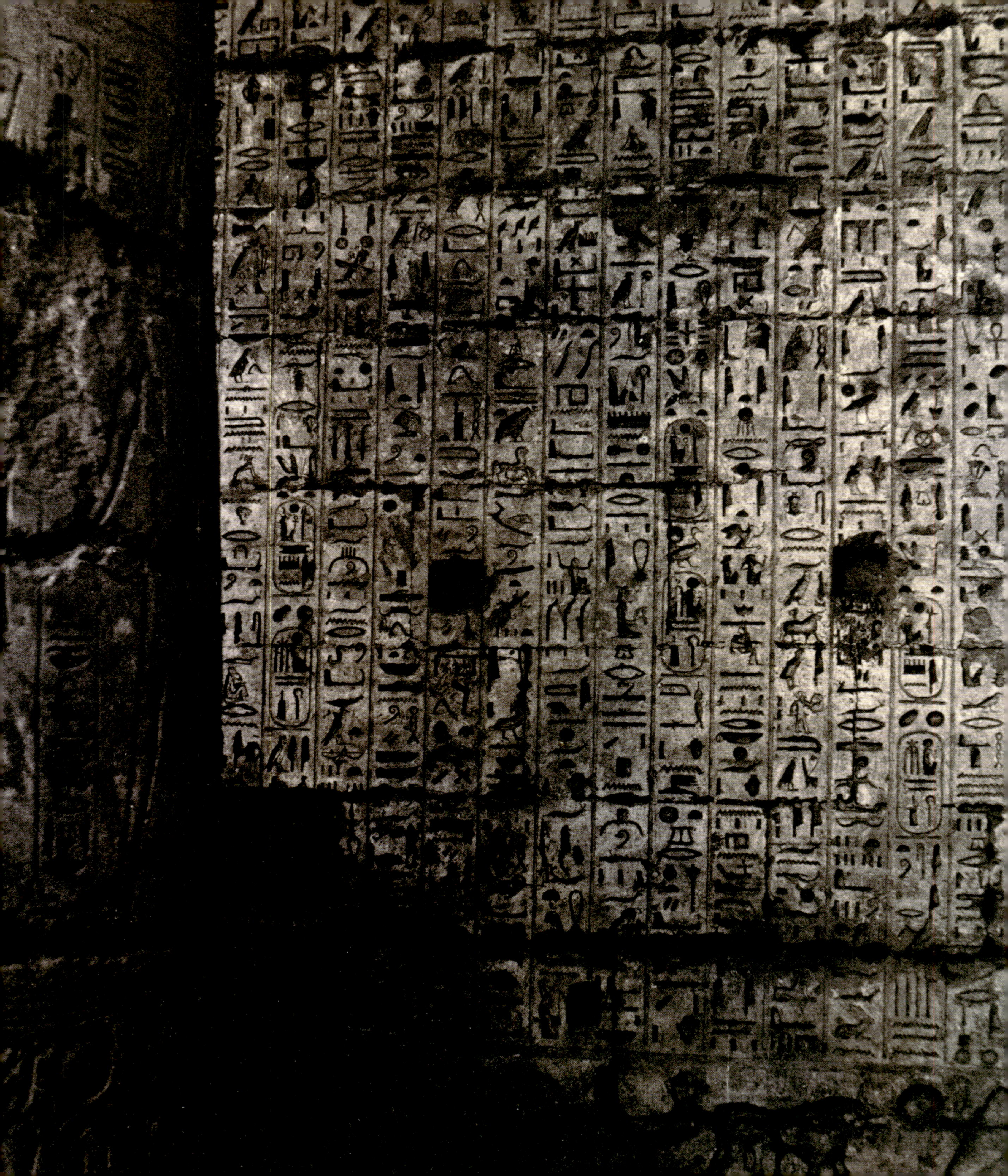

SIGNS AND WONDERS

The Photographs of John Beasley Greene

Corey Keller

DelMonico Books • Prestel
Munich London New York

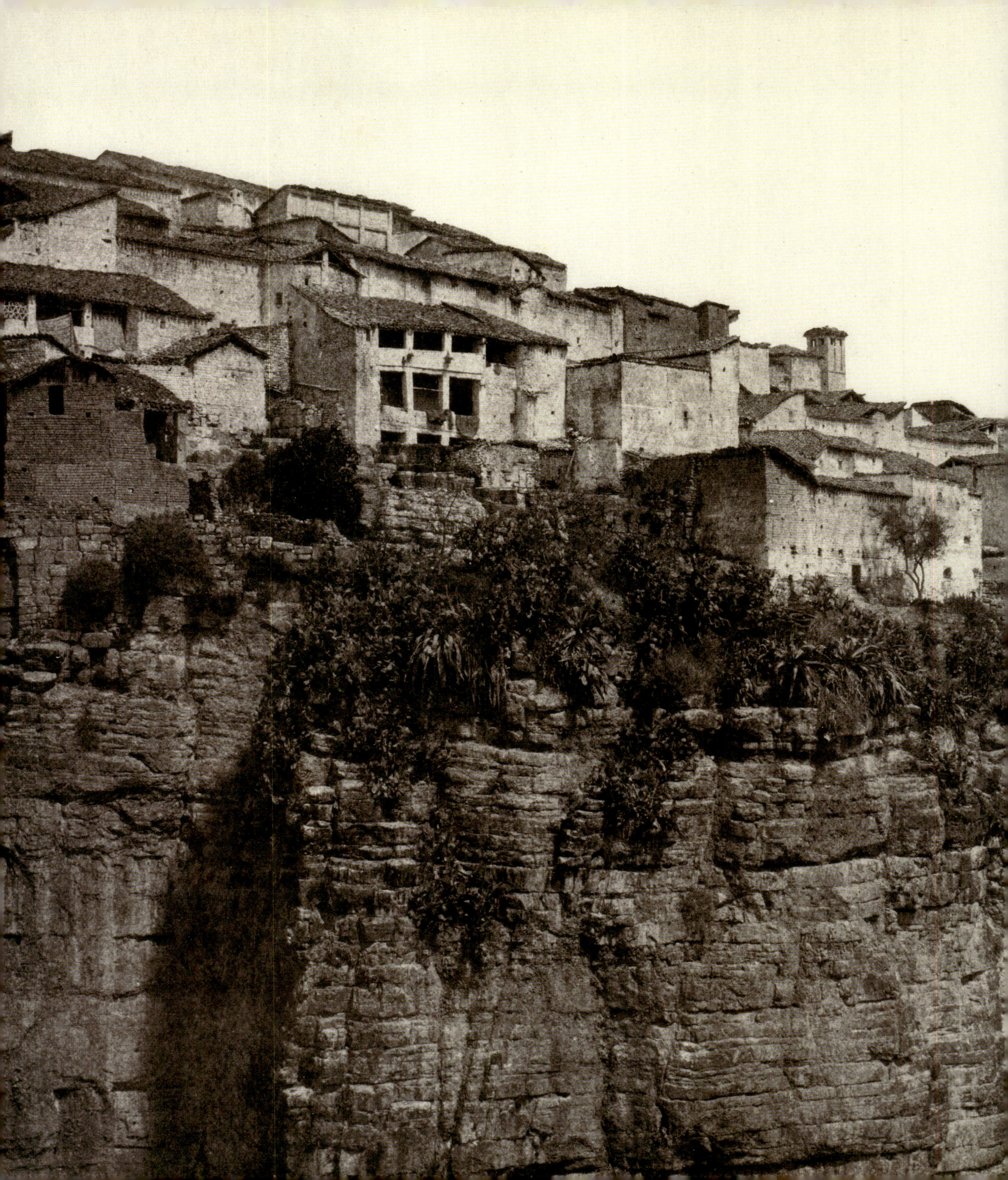

CONTENTS

ACKNOWLEDGMENTS

This exhibition and catalogue have been long in the making, and I have accrued innumerable debts over its gestation. I am deeply grateful to all those who have championed this project over the years.

I am above all beholden to the lenders who opened their collections to me for research and who so kindly agreed to share their photographs and Greene's legacy with a wider audience. I thank the current and former staffs at the following institutions for their generous assistance: Matthew S. Witkovsky and Elizabeth Siegel at the Art Institute of Chicago; Sylvie Aubenas, Flora Triebel, and Thomas Cazentre at the Bibliothèque Nationale de France; Louise Désy at the Canadian Centre for Architecture, Montreal; Jim Ganz, Virginia Heckert, Mazie Harris, and Karen Hellman at the J. Paul Getty Museum, Los Angeles; Françoise Bérard, Béatrice Delestre, and Mireille Pastoureau at the Institut de France, Paris; Robert Koch at Robert Koch Gallery, San Francisco; Hans Kraus, Shelley Dowell, Jennifer Parkinson, and Valentina Branchini at Hans P. Kraus Jr., Inc., New York; Janet Lehr at Janet Lehr, Inc., New York; Jeff Rosenheim and Bobby Walsh at The Metropolitan Museum of Art, New York; Thomas Galifot, Fabrice Golec, and Françoise Heilbrun at the Musée d'Orsay, Paris; Quentin Bajac, Sarah Hermanson Meister, and Tasha Lutek at The Museum of Modern Art, New York; Sarah Greenough, Diane Waggoner, and Andrea Coffman at the National Gallery of Art, Washington, D.C.; Ann Thomas and Lori Pauli at the National Gallery of Canada, Ottawa; Paul Sack and Cindy Herron of the Sack Photographic Trust, San Francisco; Paul-Louis Roubert, Vincent Guyot, Luce Lebart, and Carole Troufléau-Sandrin at the Société Française de Photographie, Paris; Michael Wilson, Hope Kingsley, Polly Fleury, and Stephanie Smith at the Wilson Centre for Photography, London. I would also like to thank private lenders Richard and Ronay Menschel, Gary B. Sokol, and those who wish to remain anonymous: without their help, this project would not have been realized.

It is nearly impossible for me to express my gratitude to Wes and Kate Mitchell, Sakurako and William Fisher, and Gary B. Sokol for their generous support. This long overdue presentation of Greene's work could not have taken place without their benevolence, passion, and friendship.

On behalf of my colleagues at SFMOMA, I also wish to thank the Art Institute of Chicago for its early interest in this exhibition. We are thrilled that the exhibition will be seen by a wider audience and at such an esteemed institution, and I thank James Rondeau, Matthew Witkovsky, Elizabeth Siegel, Megan Rader, and Jennifer Oatess for their enthusiastic support.

I have been the lucky recipient of a great deal of scholarly advice and research assistance, for which I am eternally grateful. Above all, I thank Anne Lacoste and Will Stapp, who so kindly and freely shared their immeasurable expertise with me. I would also like to thank Will for the chronology that enriches this volume. This project has also been greatly enriched by the intellectual generosity of many others who have shared (or at least entertained) my passion for Greene. For their invaluable help I would especially like to thank Susan Alison, Anne Flannery, W. Raymond Johnson, J. Brett McClain, and Foy D. Scalf, Oriental Institute, University of Chicago; Mari Nakahara, Library of Congress, Washington, D.C.; Elsa Rickal, Bibliothèque d'Égyptologie, Collège de France, Paris; and Benjamin Doizelet, Service Historique de la Défense, Vincennes. I likewise extend my thanks to Jessica Brier, Daniel Catan, Alexandra Courtois de Viçose, Melissa Cradic, Gary Edwards, James Hyman, Chuck Isaacs and Carol Nigro, Simone Klein, Hans Kraus, the late Gérard Lévy and his sons Daniel and Alex, Russell Lord, Flo Lunn and Christophe Lunn, Michael Mattis and Judith Hochberg, Anne de Mondenard, Douglas R. Nickel, Serge Plantureux, Catharine Roehrig, Michael Sachs, the late Howard Stein, Rachel Topham, and Jill Quasha.

The beauty of this catalogue is entirely due to the talents of the exceptional teams at DelMonico Books • Prestel and

Miko McGinty Inc. Special thanks are owed to Mary DelMonico, Karen Farquhar, Philomena Mariani, and Anjali Pala as well as Miko McGinty and Rebecca Sylvers for their superb interpretation of Greene's vision. I am deeply appreciative of their investment in the project, and this book is immeasurably improved as a result of their work.

I offer my gratitude to the outstanding staff at SFMOMA, particularly my current and former colleagues in the photography department: Sandra S. Philips, Clément Chéroux, Erin O'Toole, Margaret Ann O'Connor, and Adrian Martinez. For their research help and good humor, hearty thanks are due to Sally Martin Katz and Linde B. Lehtinen. I am particularly indebted to the ever-meticulous Matthew Kluk, without whose hard work this catalogue would not have materialized. I am grateful to Neal Benezra and Ruth Berson for their support of the project. I would also like to recognize my colleagues Theresa Andrews, Christina Brody, Olga Charyshyn, Sarah Choi, Kari Dahlgren, Steve Dye, Amanda Glesmann, David Funk, Tina Garfinkel, Jody Hanson, Brandon Larson, Emma LeHocky, Don Ross, Kimberly Walton, Greg Wilson, Jessica Woznak, and many others who contributed to its success.

For their wise counsel and unwavering friendship, I owe special personal debts to Janet Bishop, Malcolm Daniel, Jennifer Dunlop Fletcher, Sarah Kennel, Karen Levine, Wes Mitchell, Sarah Roberts, Sarah Schleuning, and Liz Siegel.

This catalogue, as with everything else, is dedicated to my family: to my mother and father, my brother, and with all my love to Craig, Zoë, and Theo.

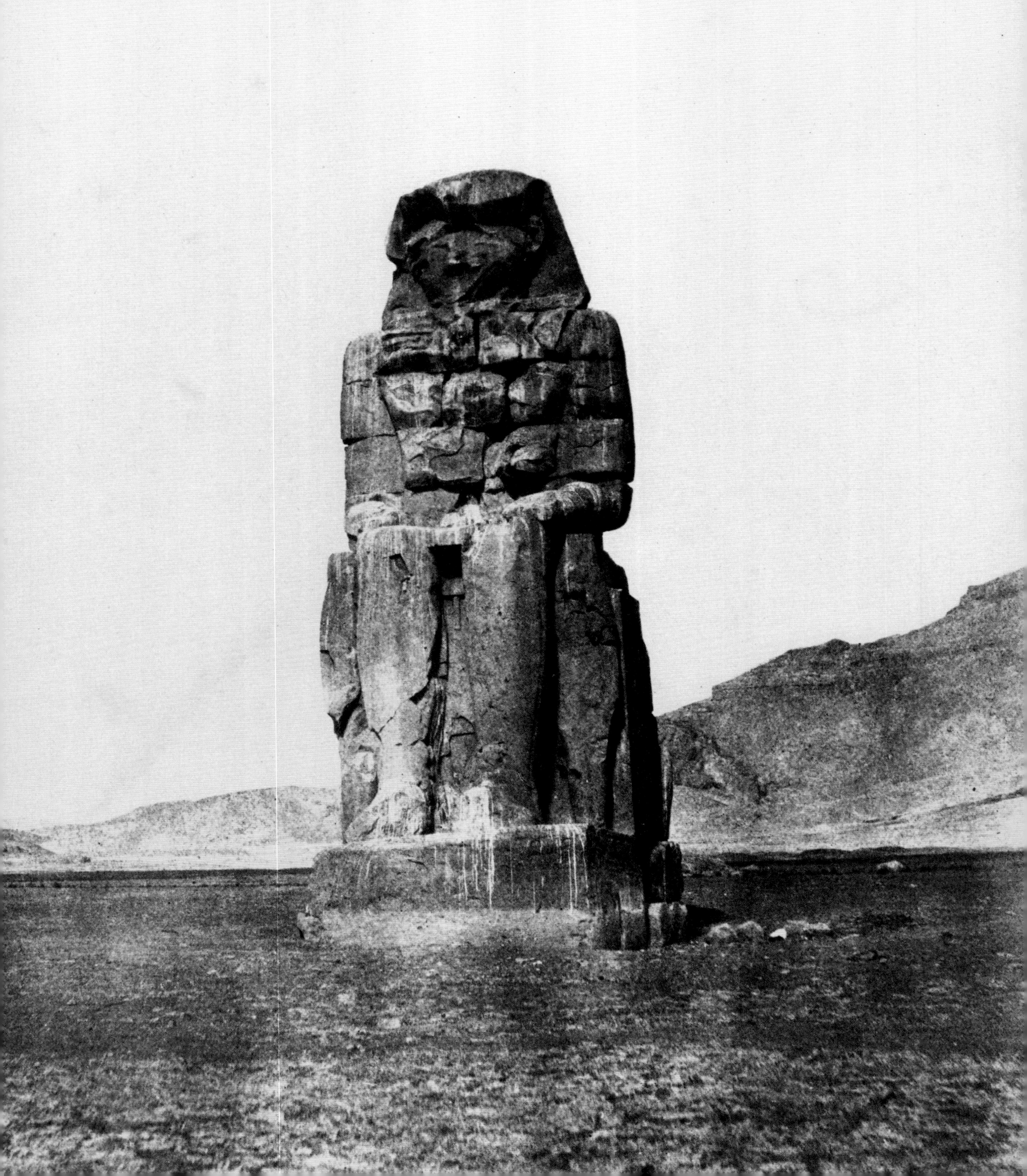

NOTHING BESIDE REMAINS

The Life and Work of John Beasley Greene

Corey Keller

When Napoleon's army in Egypt discovered the inscribed tablet that would be forever known as the Rosetta Stone in 1799, they discovered a key to a previously inaccessible past that would immediately change the way Egypt was studied and its history written. Though the French were deprived of the actual spoils of their find—the stone has been in the British Museum since 1802, confiscated as war booty by the British after their decisive defeat of Napoleon—they nonetheless took home an impression, a plaster mold made from the stone's surface, as well as drawn illustrations. From these copies, Jean-François Champollion would eventually crack the hieroglyphic code.[1] The text on the stela was written in three scripts: hieroglyphic (a priestly language), Demotic (used for more quotidian communication), and Greek. Familiarity with ancient Greek allowed Champollion and other scholars to bridge an otherwise insurmountable linguistic gap: the use of hieroglyphics had died out around the fourth century CE, and the language was forgotten in the intervening millennia. The archaeological possibilities opened up by the deciphering of hieroglyphic writing turned all of Egypt into a text to be read; its history was literally written on its walls. From that moment forward, the archaeologist's chief task was to record and translate those written narratives.

John Beasley Greene (1832–1856) would be among those drawn to Egypt in the nineteenth century, hoping to unravel the mysteries inscribed on its ancient monuments. He traveled there twice (in 1853–54 and 1854–55) equipped with a camera in order to take advantage of the speed and precision of transcription that the medium of photography seemed to promise. Yet Greene is himself something of a cipher. In addition to producing straightforward documentation of the hieroglyphic texts and monuments of most interest to archaeologists, he made some of the most evocative landscape studies ever produced in the Middle East. The pictorial economy of these views—all endless sweeps of desert sand and expansive, cloudless skies—is still stunning today. The work he made in Algeria in 1855–56 is similarly divided between archaeological investigation and visual studies whose concerns seem wholly aesthetic. From a historian's perspective, Greene represents a particular challenge: he died at the age of twenty-four and left behind very few written records that might help us to better understand either his biography or his oeuvre. Yet there is evidence to be gleaned in his surprisingly substantial body of work—hundreds of photographs made in Egypt as well as in Algeria—and in the albums in which he organized and presented them. Even Greene's earliest photographic efforts, produced while a student of Gustave Le Gray, provide information about his training, both technical and aesthetic, and the milieu in which he worked.

Greene came to both archaeology and photography at a moment of great excitement and change. In archaeology, a concerted effort was underway to build on Champollion's pioneering work in philology and to systematically record the texts of ancient Egypt—an enterprise seen as increasingly urgent as the monuments of Egypt deteriorated or were mined for materials and artifacts.[2] New tools were required for such an undertaking, and to adopt photography in its service was to declare oneself of the moment, modern. Indeed, Greene is considered the first to make photographic archaeological studies in both Egypt and Algeria.[3] He took up the camera when the possibilities of the medium were still being plumbed: though no longer in its infancy, photography in the 1850s was still a great experiment, as practitioners not only perfected its technical processes, but also consciously considered its potential applications and its relationship to other forms of representation. The twin prongs of Greene's photographic concerns, its use as a tool of science for objective recording and its potential as a form of artistic expression, mirror the poles of the critical debates that shaped photographic discourse at that time. In a sense, Greene's trajectory in photography thus also mimics the condition of the medium at the moment. Over the course of an exceptionally brief but productive career as an archaeologist and photographer, he produced a body of work whose complexities are still underrecognized and are worthy of further consideration.

Greene's photographic legacy is further complicated by the manner in which the history of photography, particularly that of its origins in the nineteenth century, has been written. His work, whose excellence was acknowledged by his peers, was exhibited regularly during his lifetime, both in small exhibitions for the photographic community and in large international shows such as the 1855 Exposition Universelle, where he was awarded a bronze medal, second class, for his views of Egypt. His photographs were last exhibited during his lifetime in 1856, at the Brussels Exposition des Arts Industriels. His work then languished in almost total obscurity for a hundred years—as did that of many of the medium's earliest practitioners—until it was "rediscovered" in the late 1970s and early 1980s as part of a resurgent interest in the medium's early history. The framing of that rediscovery also set the terms for how Greene's work is talked about today. His tragic death at a young age, the near-total blankness of his biography, and the absence of textual sources rendered Greene an ideal subject for romantic projection and historical revisionism. A consideration of his career is therefore also an invitation to revisit the historiography of nineteenth-century photography, and his positioning therein.

Beaumont Newhall—founding curator of the photography department at the Museum of Modern Art, New York, author of the earliest authoritative history of the medium in the United States, and champion of photographic modernism—was one of Greene's earliest twentieth-century admirers, and his assessment of the young photographer's career, written in 1981, typifies many contemporary responses to his work:

> Of John B. Greene we know but little, beyond the facts that he died in November 1856 at the age of twenty-four, that he was of American nationality and resident in Paris, that he was a founding member of the Société française de Photographie, that he voyaged up the Nile from Alexandria to the Second Cataract in the winter of 1854, that prints from the paper negatives he took on that trip were published later that year in album form, under the title *Le Nil: Monuments, Paysages, Explorations photographiques* by Louis Désiré Blanquart-Evrard at his celebrated *Imprimerie photographique* in Lille and that he also photographed in Algeria.[4]

Newhall goes on to describe Greene's work in formal and affective terms, commenting on his "sensitivity to the physical environment and the very lay of the land" in Egypt and noting the physical and emotional immediacy of his views of Algeria. He concludes by canonizing the young photographer: "Even though his life was inexplicably cut short, John B. Greene is to be numbered among the master photographers of all time."[5] This celebration of the artist as a romantic genius, a master of the medium—or even better, a previously unheralded master—was typical of such characterizations, and though Newhall's observations about the aesthetic qualities of Greene's photographs ring true, they also present an incomplete picture. Utterly absent from this narrative is any conjecture about Greene's motive for making such photographs, nor does it mention his scholarly engagement with Egyptology, or who the audience for his work might have been.[6] His pictures are figured as pure expression of his subjective vision, and the photographs Newhall chose to illustrate his essay support such a view.[7]

By looking more broadly and critically at Greene's entire body of work, we can understand that his approach to photography was self-consciously hybrid, guided by the aesthetic principles of paper photography elaborated in the 1850s as well as a strong sense of the needs of the archaeological field, and attuned to the distinct expectations of multiple audiences. Like much early nineteenth-century photography, Greene's work becomes far more interesting and rich when we consider the complex set of priorities that determined its production along with the conditions of its reception, both historical and contemporary.

BEGINNINGS

Only the broad outlines of Greene's biography are known, though far more can be stated with certainty now than when the first scholarly efforts began in the 1980s.[8] With so little biographical information, even Greene's name has suffered from orthographical inconsistencies. In the nineteenth century, the last name was frequently misspelled "Green," an error that is understandable given that members of his own family spelled the surname both with and without the final *e*. That he and his immediate family used the "Greene" spelling is certain, however, as we have abundant examples of his and his father's signatures. The French introduced into the historical record several additional typographical errors: on the roster of founding members of the Société Française de Photographie, he is listed as "Greenn," and in *La Lumière*, he appears once as Grenne but primarily as Green. As to Greene's middle name, it is spelled Beasley on his birth certificate and baptismal record but lacks the second *e* on the family tomb at Père Lachaise, which has resulted in some recent confusion.[9] As Greene's birthdate is also incorrect on the tomb (rendering him four years old instead of twenty-four at the time of his death), we can with reasonable confidence chalk this error up to an inattentive engraver. In earlier histories of photography, his name also appeared as John Baker Greene, a mistaken conflation of the American photographer with a British Egyptologist, and John Buckley or Bulkley Greene—the latter being the name of his prominent father.[10]

John Beasley Greene was born in France in 1832, the third child and only son of a successful New England businessman, John Bulkley Greene, and an American mother of French descent, Marie Regina Zélia Dejoye. As the son of Americans, he was a citizen of the United States, though he never set foot on American soil.[11] Greene senior managed the Le Havre branch of the important American commercial house and merchant bank Welles & Company (formerly Welles & Williams). With offices in Le Havre and Paris, it was founded by Massachusetts native Samuel Welles in 1815. Welles & Company in Paris was the first American bank in France. The branch in Le Havre later became Welles & Greene. The list of witnesses to the marriage of Greene's parents gives us a good sense of the family's stature among the wealthy bankers and merchants of Le Havre: signatories include Reuben Gaunt Beasley, American consul at Le Havre, and his wife Jenny (née Guestier, of the Bordeaux wine-producing family, whose relatives in the United States supplied wine to Thomas Jefferson); Samuel Welles and his wife, the former Adeline Fowle; and noted English merchant and president of the Le Havre chamber of commerce Charles Latham and his wife Pauline (née Delessert), herself the daughter of a powerful French banking family (Delaroche, Delessert and Company). From this list alone, it is clear that the Greenes were part of a close-knit, privileged community, with a powerful network and great resources at their disposal. Following the end of the War of 1812 and the lifting of the Napoleonic embargo, trade flourished during the Restoration—particularly between France and the United States—and Le Havre, one of France's two major ports, was the main point of entry for goods from America and the West Indies. Welles & Greene was particularly involved in the import of dry goods, especially cotton and rice from the southern United States.[12]

Greene's birth record shows that he was born in Ingouville, a suburb of Le Havre. The town was infamous for its poverty and ungovernability: it was where the working poor, prostitutes, and immigrants fled as the port of Le Havre gentrified and rent in the city center became unaffordable.[13] However, the heights of Ingouville, an area of the city along the coast and known as "La Côte," was a popular place for the wealthy to build summer homes with a sea view and cooled by ocean breezes. Many rich merchants of Le Havre lived in La Côte, only a short distance from the port, or retreated there for the summer. As one visitor described, "almost the whole upper part of Ingouville consists of such summer residences; and it would be difficult to find a more delightful situation."[14] As Greene was born in June, we might assume his well-to-do family came to Ingouville under similar circumstances. The family lived in Ingouville or Le Havre until Greene was nine.

In 1841, after Samuel Welles' death, the Greene family moved to Paris, where John Greene senior took over Welles & Company at 28, Place Saint-Georges, and the bank became Greene & Company (Greene et Cie.). Place Saint-Georges, an elegant square surrounded by splendid *hôtels particuliers*, was constructed in 1824, and was the heart of an area then known as *la Nouvelle Athènes*, in what became the ninth arrondissement.[15] The quartier was a lively, sought-after neighborhood, home to artists, writers, and wealthy entrepreneurs; among the Greenes' neighbors were the painter Eugène Delacroix, writer George Sand, pianist Frédéric Chopin, and many other intellectual and artistic luminaries of the Romantic Age. When Samuel Welles lived at No. 28, he was well known among American visitors and expats for his lavish parties and his wife's gracious hospitality.[16] There are no records of the Greenes' entertaining habits, but visiting Americans of means made a point of coming to call. When the Hunt family (whose sons included Richard Morris Hunt, the future American architect; William Morris Hunt, the artist; and Leavitt Hunt, who would photograph in Egypt) arrived in Paris in 1843, for example, their social entrée was smoothed by their connections with the Greenes and other prominent Americans:

> Arriving at Havre, where they had great difficulty in preventing the custom house authorities from taxing their six life preservers, which vessels apparently did not furnish in those days, they went by diligence to Rouen, and thence to Paris, where the Dyers, who knew Paris well, engaged a newly furnished small hotel for the two families in the Rue de Helder. Here Mrs. Hunt soon made friends with the Greens [*sic*], the family of their banker, and the Drapers, the American Consul's family, and others.[17]

The Greenes clearly belonged to an elite class of wealthy Americans in the city, a position that would have afforded them a unique kind of social mobility as well as a certain level of protection from the political unrest that troubled Paris for much of that time.[18] More importantly, their financial means (and perhaps social connections) would enable the young John Greene to pursue his two interests: photography and Egyptology.

AN EDUCATION OF THE EYE

Greene learned to make photographs from the most illustrious teacher in France, and its champion of photography on paper, Gustave Le Gray. Le Gray's studio, near the former Barrière de Clichy, an eighteenth-century toll gate in the city wall in northern Paris, was a short walk from Greene's home and was one of the most important centers of photographic activity and discourse in the city. From Le Gray, Greene would have learned the technical craft of the medium, particularly his innovative method for making waxed-paper negatives (calotypes), but would also have been schooled in the aesthetic debates that engulfed photography at that moment, specifically the nature of photography's relationship to art. Prints of only two of Greene's work from this very early period survive (they may be the only ones he printed), but a small group of negatives from this formative stage provide more information about the exercises of a nineteenth-century photography student and the subjects that drew the young man's attention. In these studies, particularly his landscapes in the Forest of Fontainebleau and a series of still lifes of a plaster figurine, we can see Greene developing the pictorial approaches he would master more fully in Egypt.

Le Gray began taking students as early as 1849, and although he did not keep formal rosters, many of his pupils can today be identified. Together they form a veritable "who's who" of early French photography as well as of the city's upper social echelons.[19] Le Gray's lessons did not come cheaply (the famed portraitist Nadar, for one, complained bitterly about the price), and so Le Gray's pupils were largely men (and a few women) of means.[20] Greene's membership in the cohort at the Barrière de Clichy is confirmed in a brief biographical essay on Le Gray written in 1860 by Léon Maufras:

> The most aristocratic hands from the capital and from abroad came, without compunction, to dirty themselves there with silver nitrate, among whom we must mention: Messrs. the comte Aguado, B. Delessert, the marquis de Béranger, the marquis de Rothschild, the marquis de La Beaume, the comte d'Haussonville, the duc de Montesquiou, the comte Branitski, the comtesse d'Essertein, Mlle Dosne, Badeigts de Laborde, Dumas de Lavince, et cetera, et cetera.

> Scientists and artists came there in droves as well: one encountered there Messrs. Maxime Du Camp, Piot, Bilordeaux, Greene, who succumbed to his ardor in Egypt; Le Dien, Nadar, Salzmann, Tournachon the younger . . .[21]

Though many of the aristocratic names are today unfamiliar, those of the "scientists and artists"—Du Camp, Nadar, Salzmann, among numerous others—are indelibly inscribed in the history of photography as some of its most important early practitioners.

Further evidence of Greene's association with Le Gray can be detected in certain photographs. Students sometimes accompanied the master on photographic outings, and there is evidence to suggest that Greene did so as well. In 1852, Le Gray received a commission to photograph the two bas-relief sculptures at the base of the Arc de Triomphe, one by Jean-Pierre Cortot (*The Apotheosis of Napoleon*) and one by François Rude, popularly known as *The Marseillaise*. Among Greene's negatives are two nearly identical views of the Arc de Triomphe: one of them, however, includes a camera—positioned closer to the monument than Greene's own—pointing at *The Marseillaise* (pl. 2). We might reasonably assume that he accompanied Le Gray on his shoot, and that the camera depicted is that of his teacher.[22]

More important, however, is the body of work Greene produced in the Forest of Fontainebleau (pls. 3, 4). Not only does this small corpus confirm his connection to Le Gray, it also demonstrates that the extraordinary aptitude the young photographer would later demonstrate for picturing landscape was shaped by the master's tutelage and theories. A former royal hunting ground, by the middle of the nineteenth century Fontainebleau came to be synonymous with the artistic representation of landscape in France.[23] Landscape painting, long exiled to the lowest rungs of the artistic hierarchy, assumed a new and unprecedented importance in the early decades of the century, spurred in large part by a group of artists in Barbizon and Chailly, small villages on the forest's edge. These artists—Théodore Rousseau, Charles-François Daubigny, and Jean-François Millet, among them—abandoned the tradition of mythological or idealized landscapes in favor of a new form of naturalism that embraced the direct and close observation of nature and sketching outdoors, *en plein air*. Fontainebleau's unique topography, characterized by sandy plains and limestone rock formations, and abundant flora despite extremely dry conditions (particularly its monumental oak and beech trees) offered artists a wild and varied terrain in which to observe and depict the changing effects of the seasons, shimmering light and velvety shadow, the tangled thickets of trees and the rough textures and otherworldly shapes of stones.

Photographers, too, came to Fontainebleau, their activity there encouraged by the forest's accessibility from Paris (vastly improved by the completion of a new train line in 1849) and the new portability offered by paper negatives.[24] Le Gray began photographing in the forest in 1849, and as it was common for groups of artists to venture to the area together, he brought students. In at least one of Le Gray's views, it is just

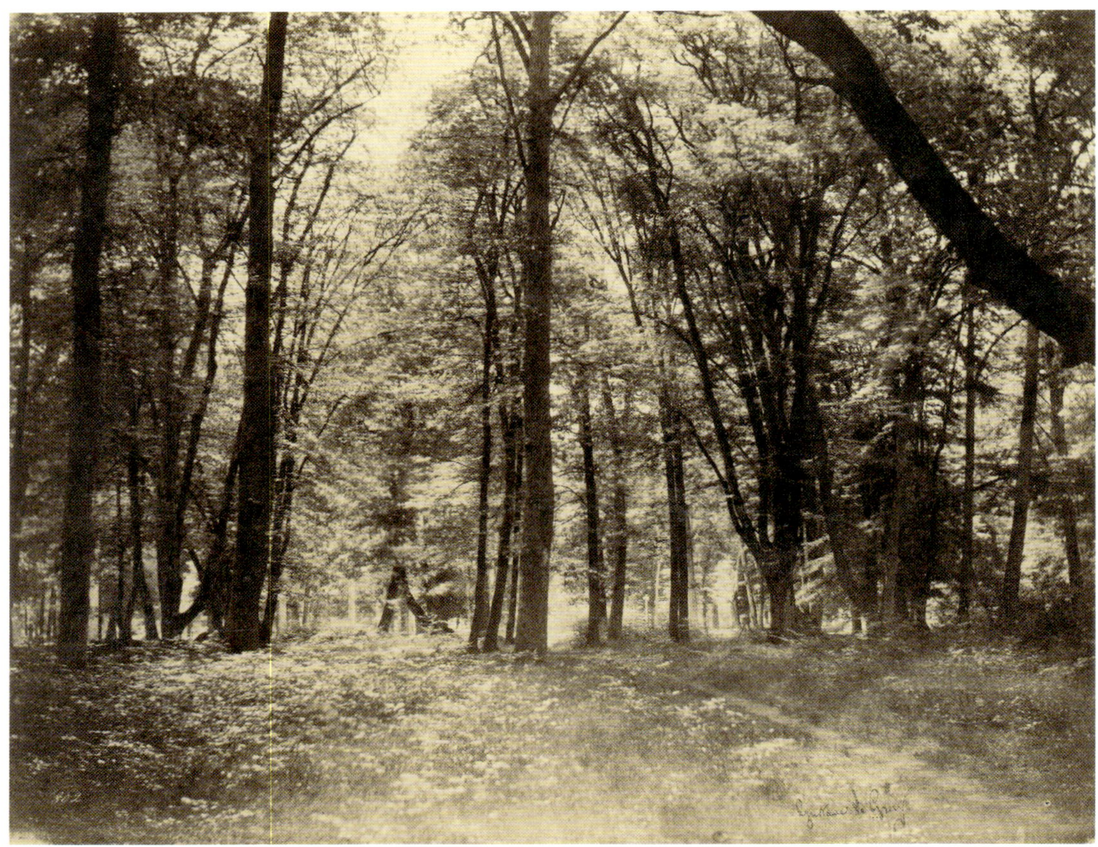

FIG. 1 Gustave Le Gray (French, 1820–1884), *Forest Scene, Fontainebleau*, 1852. Albumen print. The J. Paul Getty Museum, Los Angeles

barely possible to detect a camera on a tripod, camouflaged amidst the tall trees and dappled sunshine of the densely forested area known as the Bas-Bréau (fig. 1).[25] Greene made a similarly atmospheric view in a nearly identical location (pl. 5) and his image is so alike in form and feeling to Le Gray's that we might imagine the two men were working there together that day, and that the camera could well be Greene's. There is other evidence that Greene photographed on group outings: in another negative, for which no extant print is known, he recorded what appear to be photographers' tents along the road to Chailly (fig. 2). Such tents were used to prepare and process wet collodion glass-plate negatives in the field. Though Greene's negatives show that he regularly made pictures such as this one that documented the evidence of human presence or activity in the landscape (his negatives from Egypt even include a few portraits), he almost never chose those negatives to print.

The photographers in Le Gray's circle working in Fontainebleau were influenced by the subject matter and naturalistic approach of the painters, but they also used the representation of landscape to stake a claim for photography as an art. Their embrace of the calotype or paper negative, therefore, was not just a matter of convenience.

Unlike the minute detail of the daguerreotype, or, beginning in 1851, the descriptive precision of the wet collodion glass negative, the relative opacity of the calotype negative (resulting from the fibrous structure of the paper) produced pictures that were soft and atmospheric, that privileged tone and mass over line and emphasized the play of contrasts between light and shadow. These properties perfectly suited the natural textures and filtered light of Fontainebleau. Rejecting any form of photography that could be seen as mere slavish copy, the calotypists sought instead to interpret nature, by diffusing the purely descriptive or mechanical properties of the medium and exploiting the aesthetic effects paper negatives produced. As Le Gray, in the now famous "theory of sacrifices," asserted:

> The artistic beauty of a photographic print consists nearly always in the sacrifice of certain details; by varying the focus, the exposure time, the artist can make the most of one part or sacrifice another to produce powerful effects of light and shadow, or he can work for extreme softness or suavity copying the same model or site depending on how he feels.[26]

In Le Gray's theoretical formulations, and those of the critics who supported him, what distinguished the photographic artist from the lowly copyist or commercial photographer was the intelligence and imagination he brought to his craft.[27]

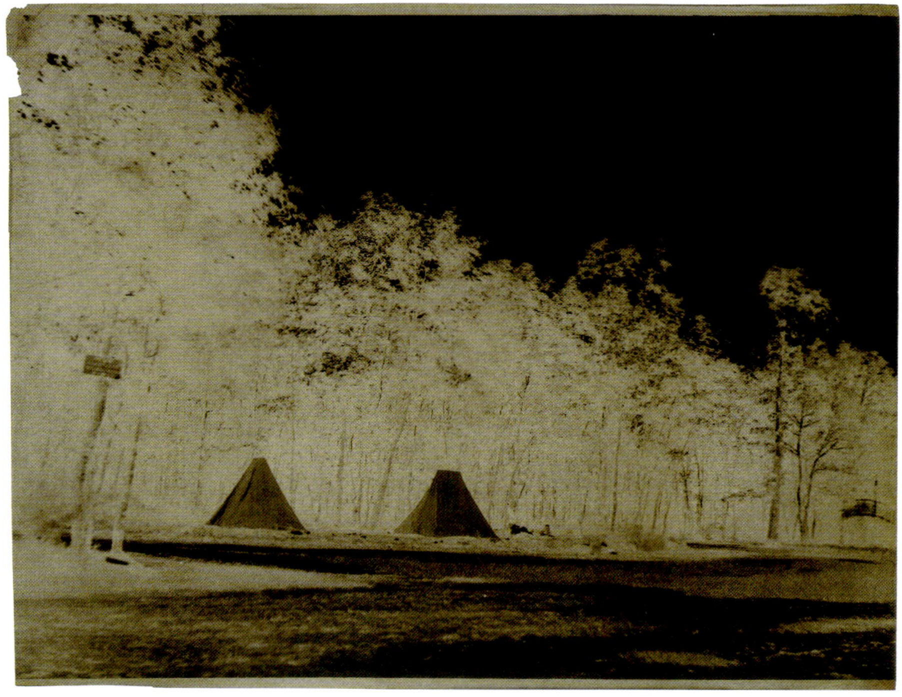

FIG. 2 John Beasley Greene, [Photographer's tents in Fontainebleau], 1852–53. Waxed paper negative. Hans P. Kraus Jr., Inc., New York, and Paul Kasmin, New York

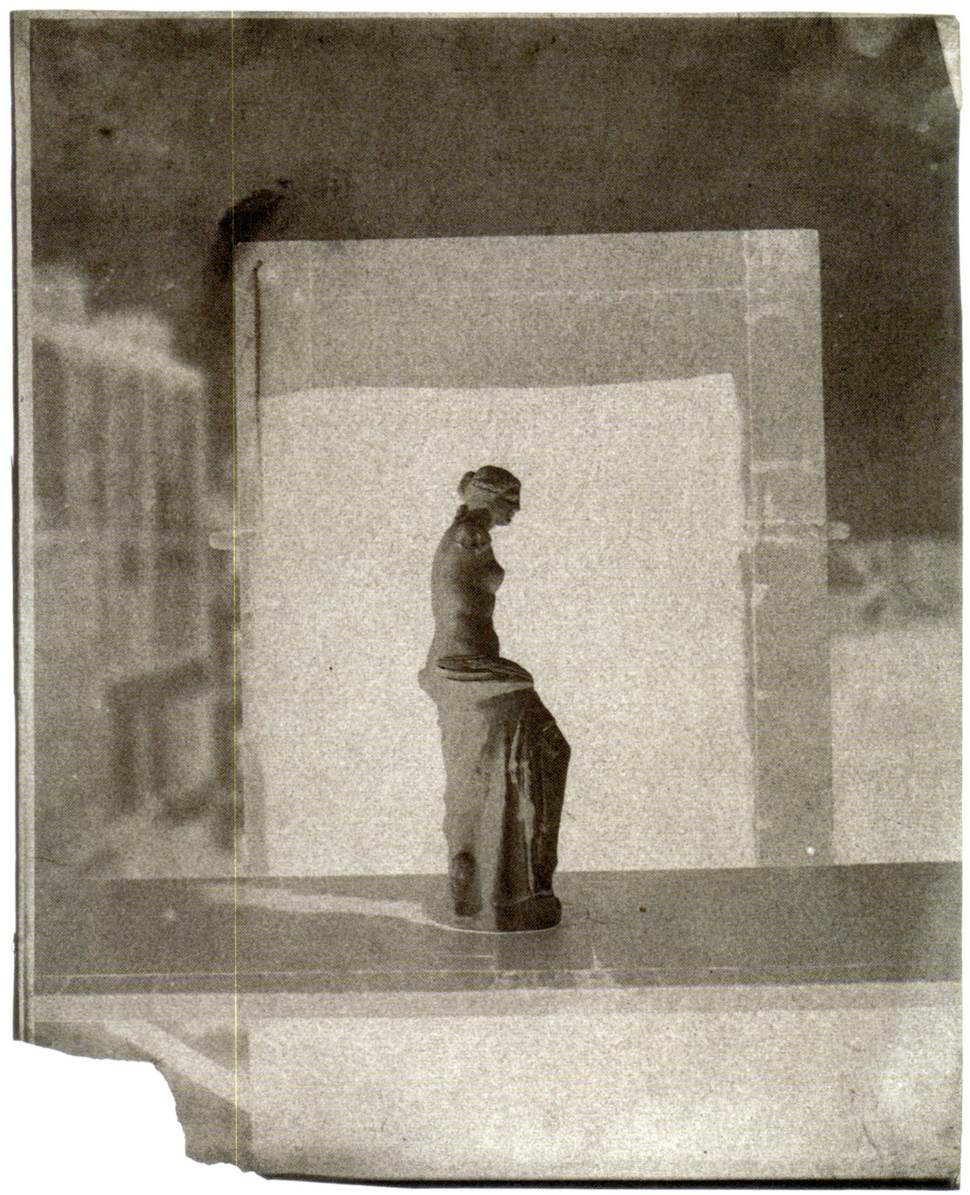

FIG. 3 John Beasley Greene, [Still life with a statuette of the Venus de Milo], 1852–53. Waxed paper negative. Michael G. and C. Jane Wilson 2007 Trust

Greene also honed his skills and trained his eye in the studio. Or more specifically, on its roof, where the light was better.[28] A series of four negatives depicting a small plaster statuette of the Venus de Milo shows the young photographer at work. He placed the figurine against a neutral backdrop and then rotated it to make photographs from multiple angles; seen together, they approximate the experience of looking at the sculpture in the round (fig. 3; pl. 6). Of all the very early negatives still extant, this is the only subject of which Greene made serial views in this manner.

Statues were ideal subjects for a photography student, if for no other reason than they were immobile, an optimal quality in a model at a time when exposures were lengthy.[29] Early photography is rife with such pictures of statues, an abundance that cannot be explained merely by the subject's practicality.[30] The English inventor of photography, William Henry Fox Talbot, for example, made dozens of views of a plaster cast of a marble bust of Patroclus in his own collection, singling out the properties of sculpture as an ideal arena for exploring the capacities of photography. He noted that its whiteness shortened exposure times by reflecting light strongly (Talbot failed to mention that it also neatly sidesteps one of photography's greatest shortcomings: the inability to reproduce color). Drawing from antique sculpture had long been a way to train the artist's hand; here Talbot imagined its parallel utility to the photographer: by changing the light or moving the camera, "it becomes evident how very great a number of different effects may be obtained from a single specimen of sculpture."[31] Talbot's suggestion of many pictures from a single source also obliquely conjures the reproducibility of the photographic medium itself.

The question of reproduction is at the very heart of this modest training exercise. The heated discussions around photography's relationship to art encompassed not only the question of whether photographs could *be* art, but also how they stacked up against other forms of art, especially engraving.[32] One of the earliest aspirations for photography was to make copies of works of art, throwing photographers into direct competition with printmakers, who by the mid-nineteenth century had found a brisk new market for reproductions of great artworks among the burgeoning middle class. Critic Francis Wey, for one, argued that photography offered a distinct advantage in this regard: an engraving relied upon an artist to first copy the painting, and then a second to translate that copy to the engraver's plate. The photograph, on the other hand, was imagined as a neutral copy: it seemed to transcribe the work without artistic intervention or possibility of error. Le Gray himself viewed photographic reproductions of artworks as one of the medium's most important contributions and made many of them—his commission to document Rude's *Marseillaise* is just one example. He also made numerous views of important exhibitions, believing that photography might thus expose a wider audience to good art and thereby refine public taste.[33]

But the work of art on which Greene trained his camera is not the marble Venus de Milo from the Louvre, but a miniature copy in plaster. Such statuettes—reproductions of the great sculptures of antiquity—were newly and widely available by the 1840s and 1850s, domestically scaled counterparts to the full-sized plaster casts collected by art museums and schools. Like engravings of paintings, they were enthusiastically collected by the bourgeoisie, who could not, perhaps, afford real works of art but wanted to demonstrate both their erudition and good taste. In a watercolor from 1860–65, Honoré Daumier shows a man in his study, the walls hung with paintings and a portfolio of prints on the floor beside his chair (fig. 4). The man's attention, however, is focused on a small figurine of the Venus de Milo nearly identical to Greene's. Daumier, who himself made a living from selling lithographs and drawings to such collectors, shows us a connoisseur in rapt contemplation. And though the Venus de Milo dates from the second century BCE, and is now one of the Louvre's most recognizable treasures, at the time Greene photographed it, the statue was a relatively recent addition to the collection. It was discovered on the island of Milos in 1820 by a Greek farmer, confiscated by the Turks, and acquired by a French diplomat, who donated it to the Louvre the following year.[34]

To a contemporary viewer, therefore, the statue not only stood for the aesthetic perfection of the sculpture of antiquity, but also spoke to a very active culture of archaeology in France, as well as to her rapacious collecting of artifacts in the name of national glory. Greene's unassuming series of student exercises thus opens up onto a whole set of far more nuanced nineteenth-century concerns. These conceptions of the photograph as a neutral and precise copy, a mode of reproduction and dissemination, and a substitute for a work of art would all come into play when Greene began to photograph the hieroglyphic inscriptions and monuments of Egypt. So, too, would the plaster copy as an interim step between the original object and photographic representation. Perhaps, when two years later he viewed the great Colossi of Memnon, which he likewise photographed in the round, since—unlike the Venus de Milo—they could not be transported to the Louvre, he took inspiration from these early efforts at the Barrière de Clichy.

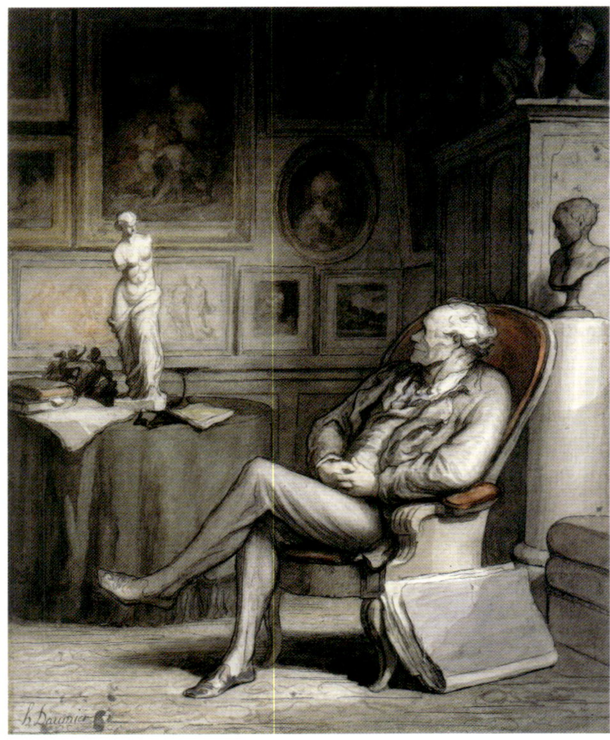

FIG. 4 Honoré Daumier (French, 1808–1879), *The Connoisseur*, ca. 1860–65. Pen and ink, wash, watercolor, lithographic crayon, and gouache over black chalk on wove paper. The Metropolitan Museum of Art, New York, H. O. Havemeyer Collection, Bequest of Mrs. H. O. Havemeyer, 1929

FRANCE

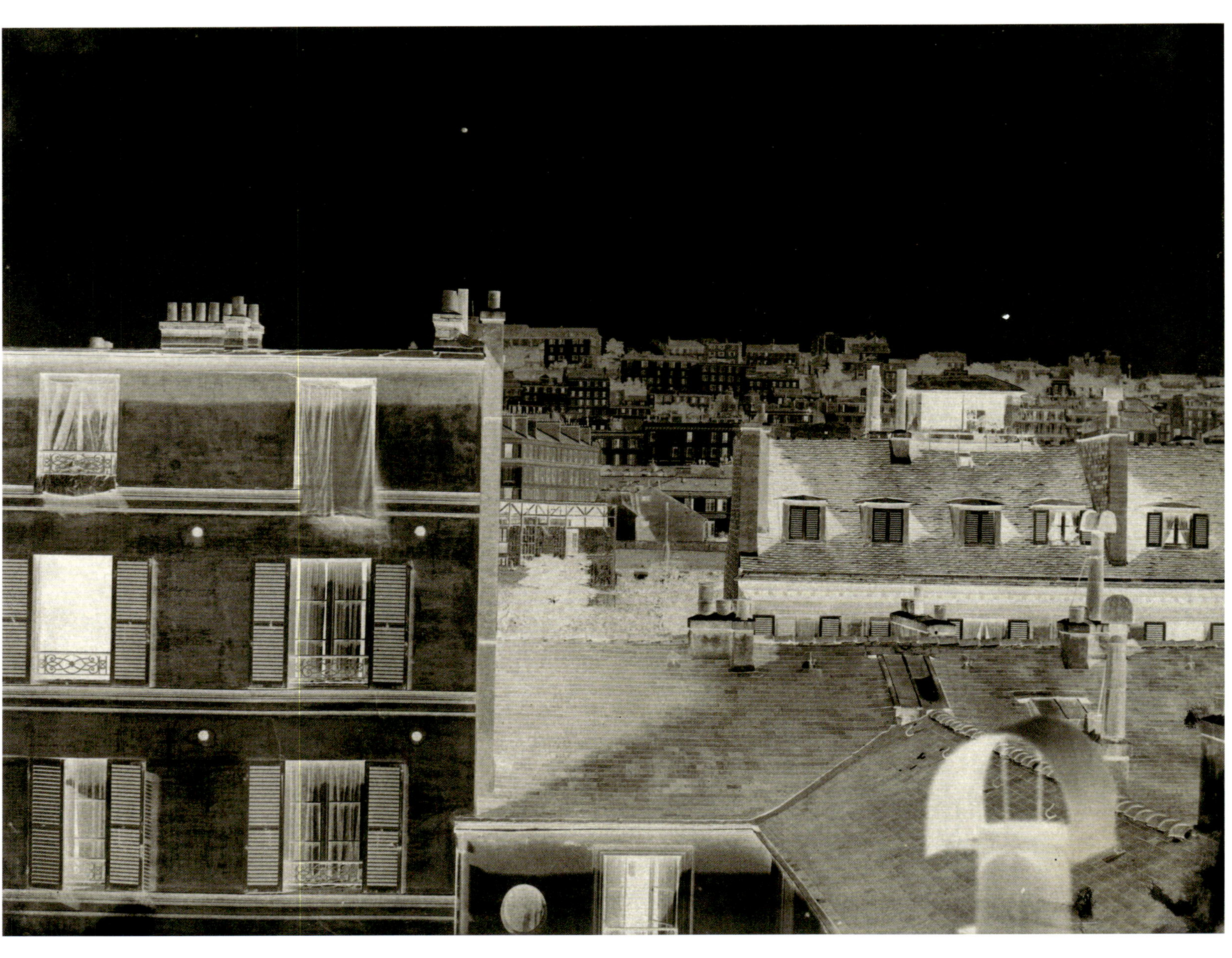

PLATE 1 [View of Paris rooftops], 1852–53

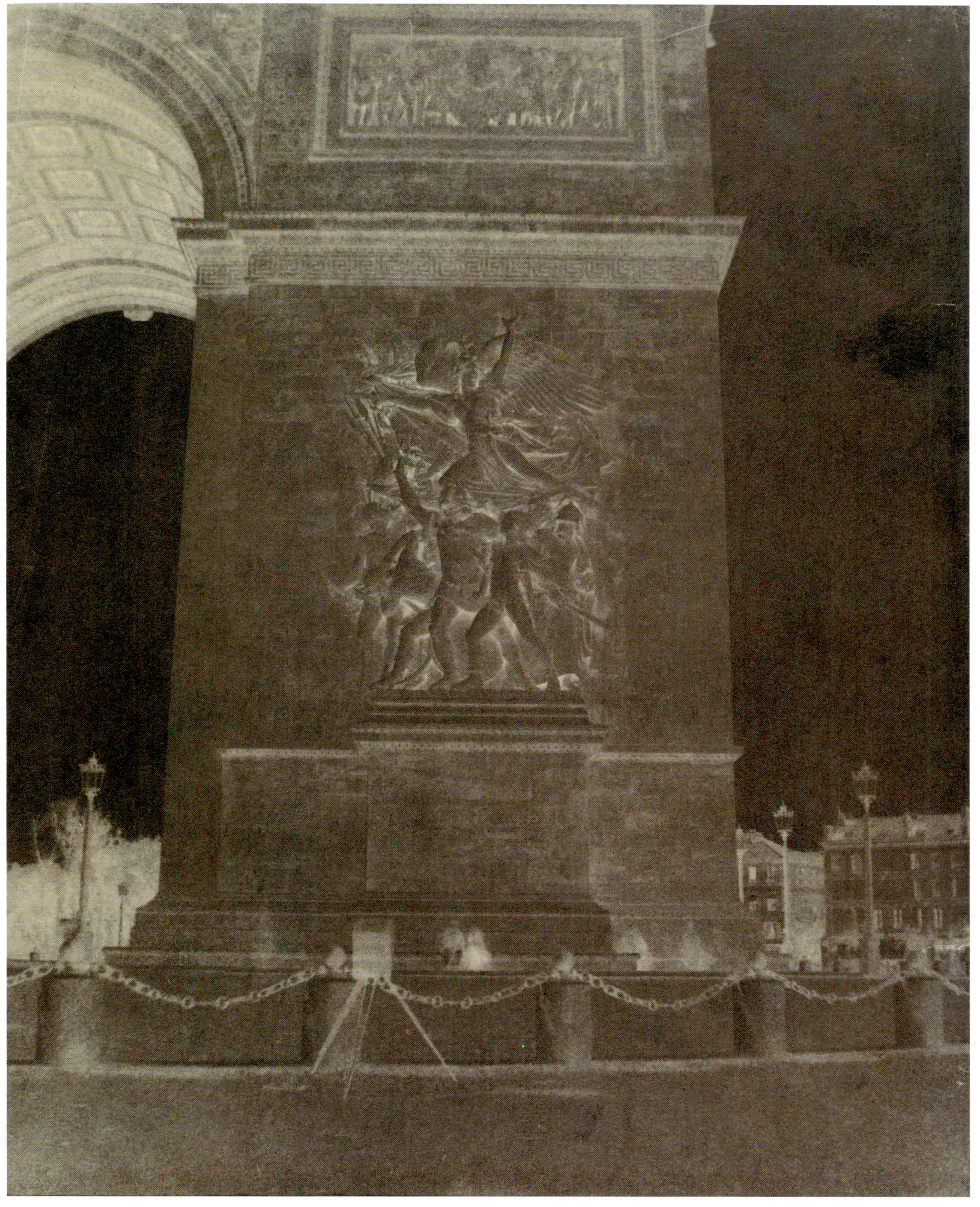

PLATE 2 [*La Marseillaise* by François Rude, Arc de Triomphe, Paris], ca. 1852

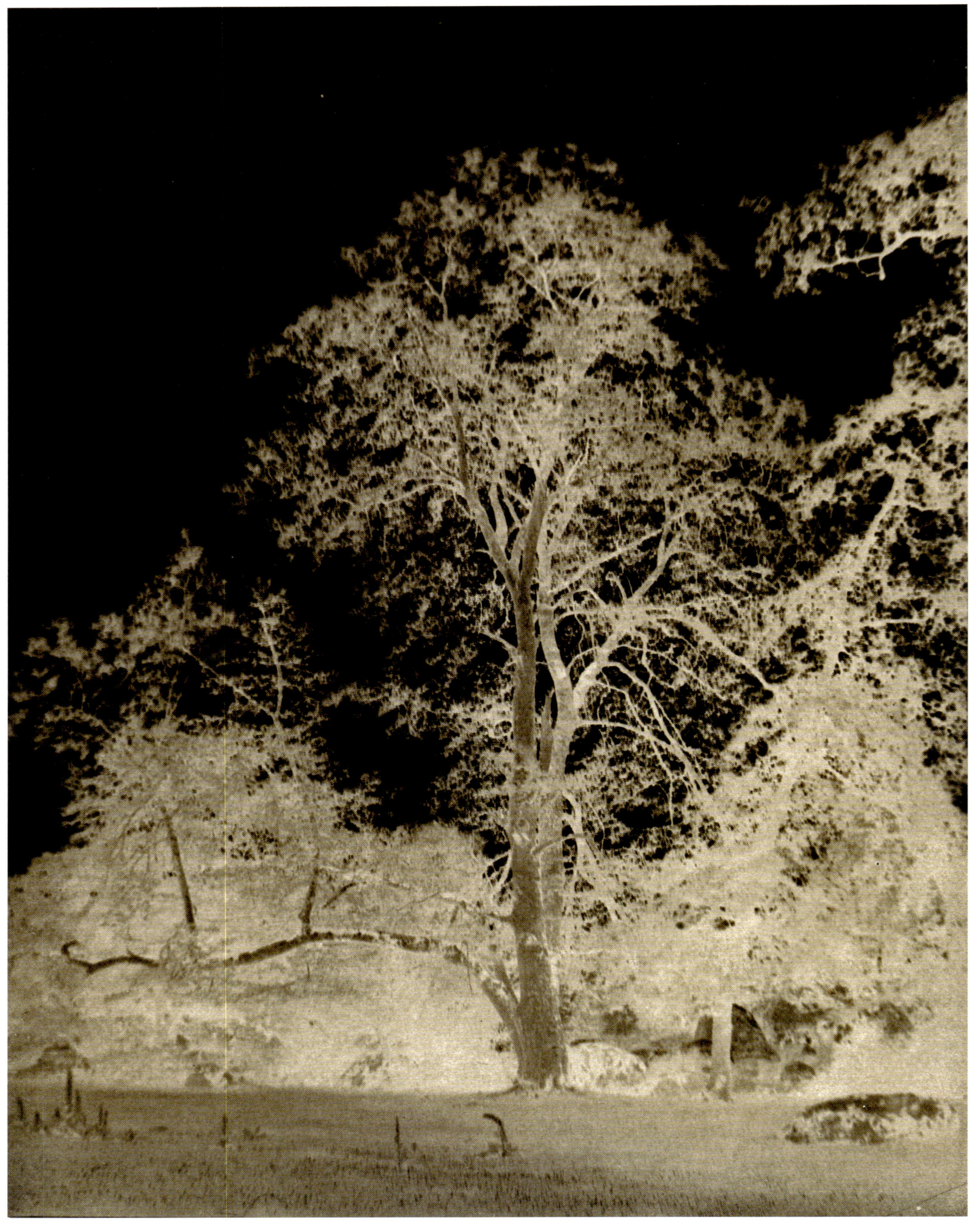

PLATE 3 [Forest of Fontainebleau], 1852–53

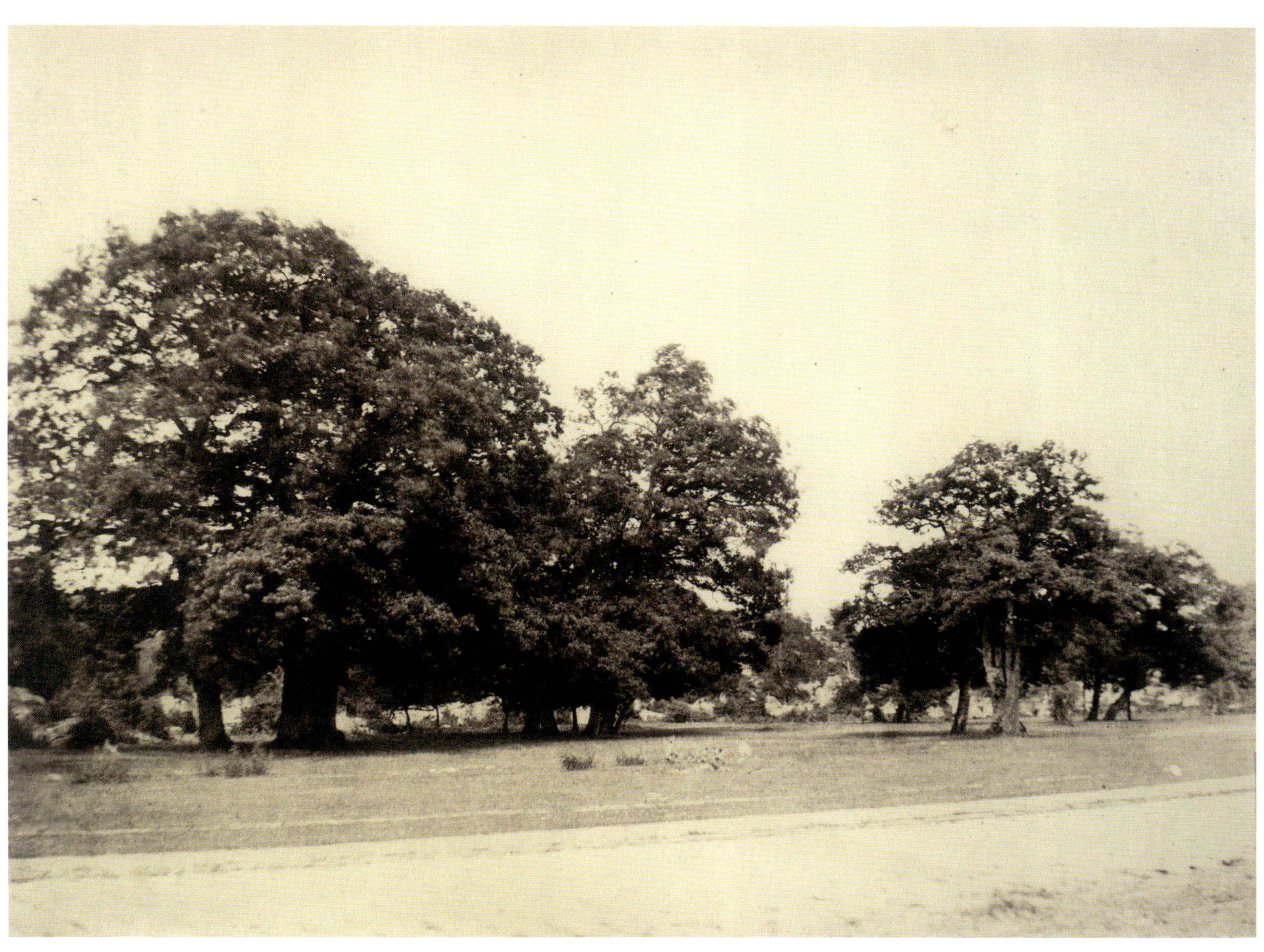

PLATE 4 [Road to Chailly, Forest of Fontainebleau], 1852–53

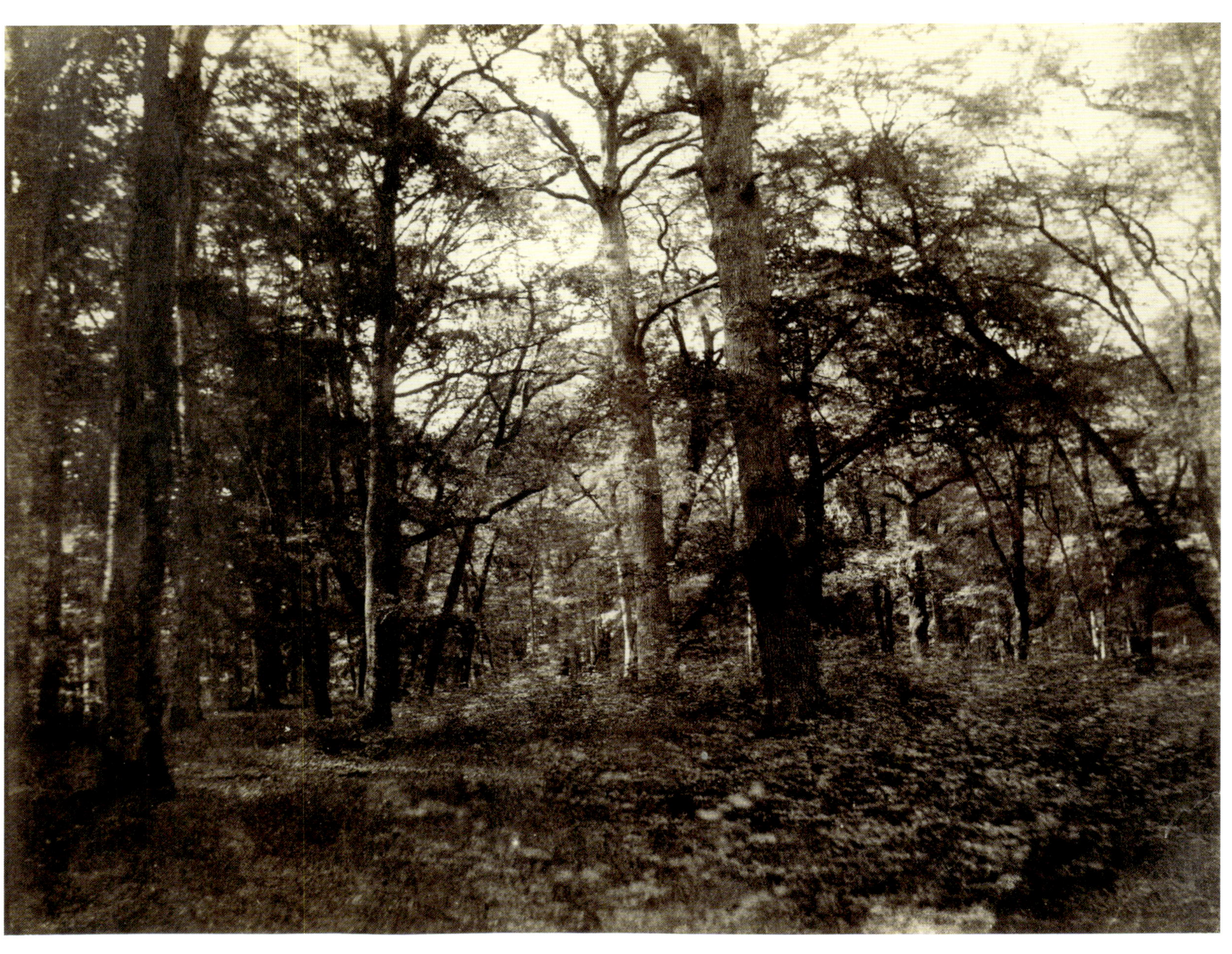

PLATE 5 [Forest of Fontainebleau], 1853

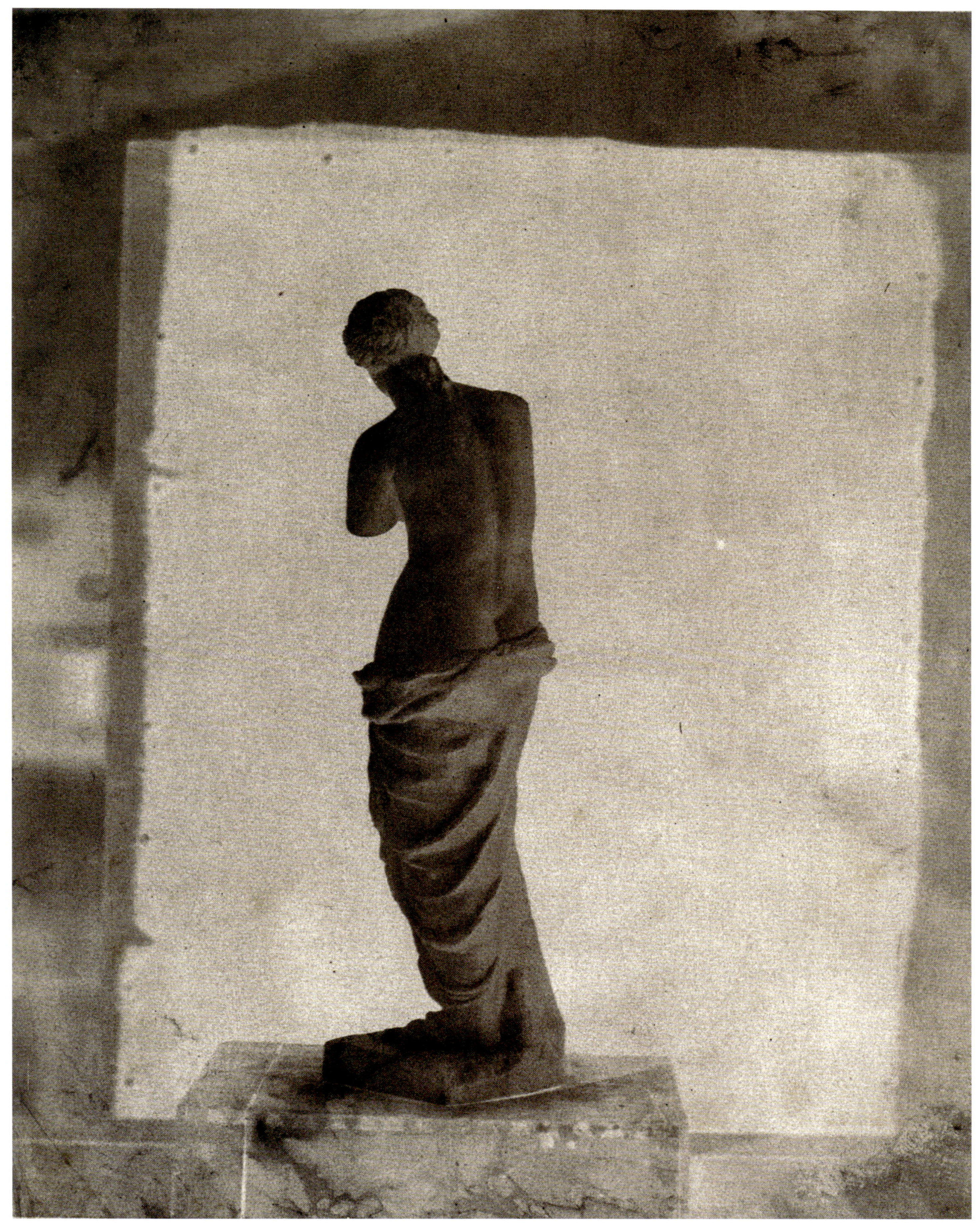

PLATE 6 [Still life with a statuette of the Venus de Milo], 1852–53

EGYPT

Greene was an ambitious young man. In the fall of 1852, he wrote to the Académie des Inscriptions et Belles-Lettres to inform that august body of scholars and scientists that he would shortly depart for Egypt: "I plan to set out from here in fifteen days' time on an expedition to Egypt and Syria, to collect archaeological, historical, and geographic information of interest, and I shall be trying to record the monuments I come upon by both photography and engraving." He offered his services to the academicians, and requested their guidance on how best to shape his work: "I should be delighted, Mr. President, if the Society would like to give me instructions which would allow me to be as useful to research as I can be."[35] The Académie des Inscriptions et Belles-Lettres, one of five learned societies at the Institut de France, was founded in the seventeenth century, and from the beginning of the 1800s devoted itself to the study of the monuments, inscriptions, and languages of antiquity through the classical age, and of the civilizations of the Orient. At the time, many archaeological expeditions were, like Greene's, undertaken on individual initiative and expense. Instructions from the Académie offered scholarly validation of an applicant's undertaking, but also provided much-needed direction to the still somewhat inchoate field of study. The Académie politely declined Greene's request, without supplying any particular rationale.[36] Moreover, although circumstantial evidence suggests that Greene did, indeed, make a trip along the Nile in the winter of 1852–53, there are no known photographs from this period.[37] He would not photograph in Egypt until late 1853.

It is important to note that Greene envisioned photography as a critical element of his projected activities in Egypt from the outset. What impelled him to learn to make photographs is not certain, but it seems likely that it was in order to better support his archaeological aspirations. In her study of early photography in Egypt, Kathleen Stewart Howe asserts that his two photographic predecessors there, Maxime Du Camp (1849–51) and Félix Teynard (1851–52), both learned photography expressly for their expeditions—Du Camp as a way of increasing his chances of getting official support, and Teynard (most likely) at the suggestion of a member of the Académie.[38] We may very well conclude that Greene's motivations were similar. By the time Greene left for Egypt, Du Camp's publication of his photographs, *Égypte, Nubie, Palestine et Syrie* (1852), the first such book produced on the subject, was enjoying widespread acclaim in the press and in photographic circles. Moreover, the Académie, whose approval Greene sought, had specifically endorsed Du Camp's use of the medium. However, Greene's engagement with photography also stands apart: neither Du Camp nor Teynard made any known photographs before their trips to Egypt, nor did they continue to practice the medium afterward.[39] Greene's small but important body of early work made in France, as well as the more significant group of pictures made in Algeria later, testify to his extended commitment to the medium. Howe also notes that neither Du Camp nor Teynard was a member of the Société Française de Photographie (founded in 1854, and the oldest photographic association in France after the short-lived Société Héliographique), but that Greene was a founding member, an indication that his interest in photography extended beyond its merely instrumental application for scientific research.[40]

There are few concrete details about how Greene came to be interested in Egyptology or what kind of training he may have had. We can, however, easily link him directly to a circle of France's most notable Egyptologists: philologist Emmanuel de Rougé (an expert in hieroglyphics, curator of Egyptology at the Louvre, and protégé of Champollion); archaeologist Auguste Mariette (famed for his discovery of the Serapeum at Saqqara, and whose excavations at the base of the Sphinx at Giza Greene photographed in late 1853) (pls. 7, 8); Émile Prisse d'Avennes, the great illustrator of Egypt (his papers at the Bibliothèque Nationale contain photographs by Greene); and Charles Lenormant, prominent archaeologist and member of the Académie des Inscriptions et Belles-Lettres (Greene thanks him personally in a letter for his advice and support). Greene also corresponded with notable philologist François Joseph Chabas.[41] And the young archaeologist was the subject of at least two letters to Chabas from Théodule Devéria (noted Egyptologist, epigraphist in the Department of Egyptian Antiquities at the Louvre, and photographer), one of which—a confirmation of Greene's death—refers to him as "our friend."[42]

It has been long assumed that Greene studied Egyptology with Rougé because of the very public support the eminent scholar lent the young archaeologist's projects, providing extensive translations and commentaries on the hieroglyphics Greene excavated and photographed in 1855. If so, it was done privately, as Rougé did not take up a public teaching post at the Collège de France until after Greene's death. Devéria studied Egyptology at the Collège, where Charles Lenormant became chair of archaeology and taught Egyptian languages beginning in 1849; it is certainly possible that Greene did as well, though there are no enrollment records to support this theory.[43] However he acquired his education, it is clear that Greene was no dilettante in the field. His membership in two societies, the Sociéte Orientale (joined 1852) and the Société Asiatique (joined 1853), is testimony both to the depth of his passion and to his official recognition as an Egyptologist.[44] Greene's admission—at the age of twenty-one—as a foreign member of the Société Asiatique, a learned society devoted to the study of philology and not open to casual amateurs, offers incontrovertible evidence of his seriousness and his likely linguistic abilities. Howe argues that it was probably through his membership in this society that he encountered Mariette. She further points out that Mariette's activities in Egypt were not widely known, and so Greene's awareness of them indicates a certain insider status in the field.[45] His familiarity with the central scholarly concerns of the field is also reflected in his choice of subject matter in Egypt, which distinguishes his project there from those of the photographers who preceded him.

Greene departed for Egypt in November 1853, a year after his letter to the Académie. His trip followed a well-established itinerary and timeline: he arrived in Alexandria in early winter, traveled from there to Cairo by sailboat or steamer, then hired a private *dahabiya* (a large houseboat with sails) or a cange (a smaller sailboat) from Cairo down to the Second Cataract—the farthest south that most Nile journeys ventured (pl. 66).[46] This was the most difficult part of the trip: traveling under sail, the boat had to fight the northward current, as well as traverse the first set of cataracts, usually by portage. Once the endpoint was reached, however, voyagers could

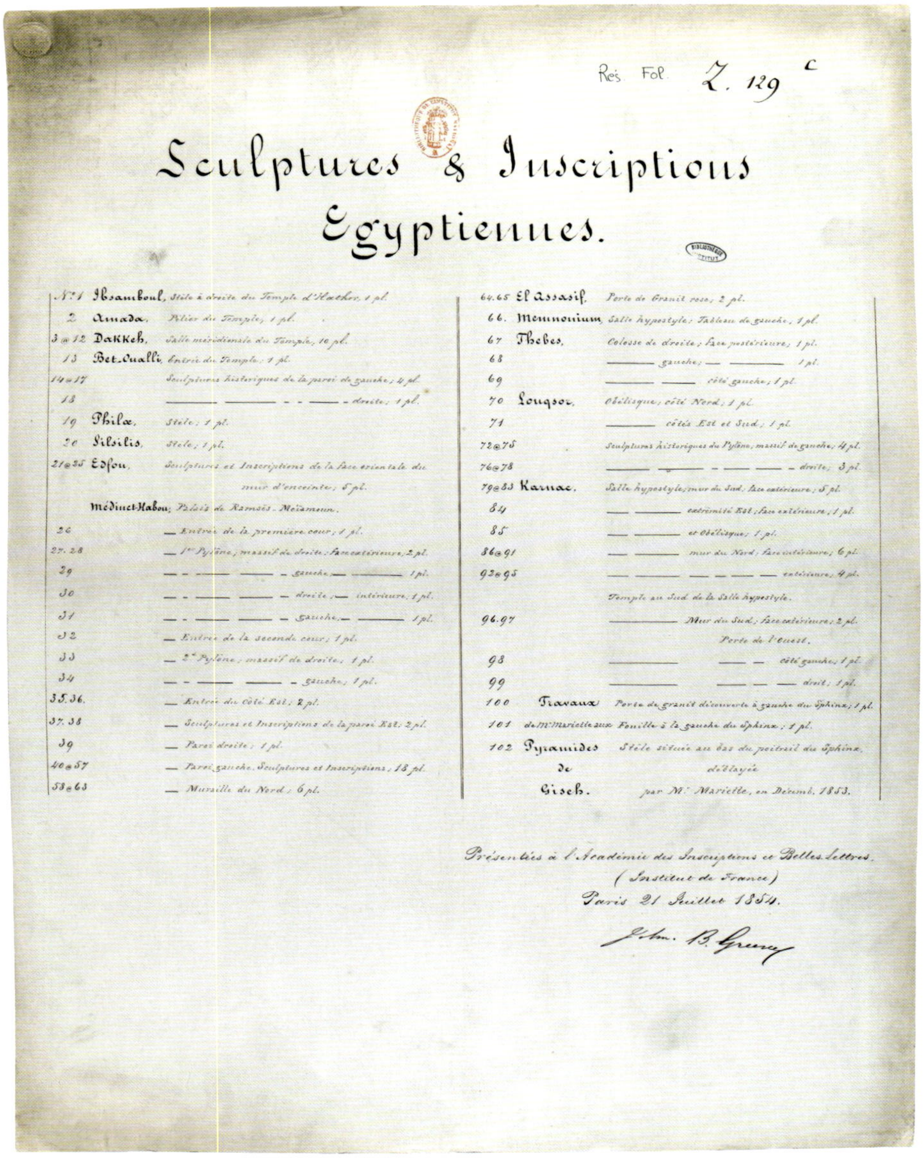

FIG. 5 Table of contents for John Beasley Greene's album *Sculptures et inscriptions égyptiennes*, 1854. Bibliothèque de l'Institut de France, Paris

turn around and travel up the Nile by oar, with the current, at their leisure.[47] Such trips could last two months, and frequently longer.

When Greene returned to Paris in the spring of 1854, he brought back more than 300 negatives. From these, he selected just shy of 200, which he categorized as either monuments, landscapes (*paysages*), or inscriptions—indicated on the negative by an M, P, or I—and numbered them, more or less in the sequence in which they were taken.[48] He bound the prints into two albums that he presented to the Académie des Inscriptions et Belles-Lettres a few months later. On July 21, 1854, he deposited *Sculptures et inscriptions égyptiennes* (Egyptian Sculptures and Inscriptions), containing 102 prints, each titled on the mount, and a detailed table of contents identifying both the sites and the particular features they record (fig. 5).[49] In October of that same year, he presented a second album, titled *Monuments et paysages de la Nubie et de la Haute Égypte* (Monuments and Landscapes of Nubia and Upper Egypt). This book included 83 hand-titled plates, divided almost evenly into discrete sections for monuments and landscapes, as well as a table of contents similar to that of *Sculptures et inscriptions*.

The manner in which Greene categorized his views, first dividing them by subject matter and then numbering them, thereby correlating the pictures to the chronology and geography of his journey as well as underscoring their relationship to one another, argues that he was deliberately considering the functions such photographs might serve. The albums he made—the two presented to the Académie, plus two others discussed below—offer a second clue as to how he conceptualized his work in Egypt and show that he was not only interested in the pictures' function, but also keenly attentive to the demands and interests of his intended audiences. In the case of the albums he gave the Académie, this was the scholarly community. Although Greene did not receive instructions from the Académie to guide his work in Egypt (it appears that he did not renew his appeal after his denied 1852 request), Du Camp, who traveled there a few years before him, did.[50] From the instructions the committee of scholars gave Du Camp, it is possible to see not only what they hoped a photographer might achieve in Egypt, but also how closely Greene's work seems to conform to their recommended program. In the letter that accompanied the album *Sculptures et inscriptions*, Greene thanked Charles Lenormant, president of the Académie, for "the benevolence that you have always shown me and the advice that you so kindly gave me before my departure,"[51] implying that he may have had some guidance from the Académie after all, even if unofficial.

In their instructions to Du Camp, the Académie asserted that the pictures produced through the convenience, speed, and accuracy of photography would offer "philology, archaeology, and art an immense resource."[52] Their language here echoes that of photography's first champion in France, Dominique François Arago, who in presenting Daguerre's invention to the Académie des Sciences in 1839 had encouraged his fellow scholars to imagine what might have come from the Napoleonic expedition to Egypt had it been equipped with cameras:

> To copy the millions of hieroglyphics which cover even the exterior of the great monuments of Thebes, Memphis, Karnak, and others would require decades of time and legions of draughtsmen. By daguerreotype one person would suffice to accomplish this immense work successfully. Equip the Egyptian Institute with two or three of Daguerre's apparatus, and before long on several of the large tablets of the celebrated work, which had its inception in the expedition to Egypt, innumerable hieroglyphics as they are in reality will replace those which now are invented or designed by approximation. These designs will excel the works of the most accomplished painters, in fidelity of detail and true reproduction of the local atmosphere.[53]

The Académie des Inscriptions et Belles-Lettres similarly saw Du Camp's expedition as an opportunity not only to add to the existing representations of Egyptian monuments, but also to correct them: "Although the principal monuments along the banks of the Nile have been copied with care and drawn with exactitude, it would be useful to have overall views made by daguerreotype [this term was still sometimes used as a synonym for photography writ large] as well as enlargements of architectural details."[54] The drawings they refer to are undoubtedly the illustrations for the *Déscription de l'Égypte*, eleven volumes of which contain some 1,000 plates and maps drawn and assembled by the scholars and scientists who accompanied Napoleon's army through Egypt. The committee urged Du Camp to photograph in a prolific but focused manner:

> . . . one would be tempted to recommend to the traveler to copy everything he sees. We leave to his zeal, to his desire to be useful, the responsibility to take advantage of every favorable moment while warning him to always apply himself, as much as location and time permits, to complete the general views and the details of a monument, whether an entire legend or a complete hieroglyphic tablet. Scattered, rough sketching, the all too common habit among travelers of jumping from one monument to another without having exhausted the attention and study which each of them requires, should be avoided; one does not obtain any serious results in this way. It is also not a question of charming our eyes by the seductive effects that light produces in the camera, but of faithfully and sequentially copying the texts claimed for science.[55]

In other words, they exhorted Du Camp to behave like a scientist, not a tourist or—worse—an artist. What they needed was methodical and comprehensive documentation; they required photographs that supplied enough legible information that they could be studied, at a distance, as substitutes for the subjects themselves. The committee also recommended that Du Camp supplement his photographs of hieroglyphics with "facsimile reliefs of inscriptions in their natural size," by which they most likely meant plaster castings.[56]

In the letter that accompanied *Sculptures et inscriptions*, Greene wrote that his aim was to "assemble several documents that might be interesting for science," and though he could not be sure of having attained this goal, he asked the Académie to accept the pictures in the spirit in which they were offered.[57] He also apologized for the uneven quality of the photographs, citing the difficulties he had encountered in making them:

> I sometimes had to overcome some rather great challenges in order to reproduce the totality of several walls; I note, among others, the left wall of the second court of Medinet Habu and the interior side of the northern wall of the hypostyle hall at Karnak. Also, I beg the indulgence of the Académie if my pictures seem to have been taken in an irregular manner. The terrain on which I was working did not permit me to do otherwise.[58]

As the temples had not yet been excavated, they were often filled with debris—fallen columns as well as the ruins of entire villages that had been built inside their courts during the intervening centuries. Such conditions obstructed clear vantage points. And yet Greene followed the committee's directives, making multiple, serial, detailed views of a single site. At the Nubian Temple of Dakka, for example, he made ten sequentially numbered views of the carvings on the walls of its southern court (pl. 26). Similarly, at Karnak, one of Egypt's most important temples, devoted to Amun-Re, king of the gods, Greene photographed the inscriptions of the Great Hypostyle Hall, an enormous space originally supported by more than a hundred massive columns. His photographs systematically record the exterior and interior walls of this sacred space, as well as details of the carvings on the massive stone pillars, many of which were toppled like so many felled trees (pl. 55). Amazingly, though he made seventeen detailed photographs of the hieroglyphs, he made not a single view that captures the magnificent geometry of the hall's architecture or its breathtaking corridors of standing columns.

One of Greene's chief challenges in photographing the inscriptions on the monument walls was the strong and contrasty Egyptian light. Raking sun yielded the best effects for illuminating the carvings, but the areas of bright highlight and deep shadow that such light produced made even exposures difficult.[59] In his 1851 treatise on photography, Louis Désiré Blanquart-Evrard specifically cited the pitfalls of such conditions for photographers of monuments: "The parts struck by light become excessively brilliant, while the masses in shadow become too strong and lack transparency. The shadows are hardly brought out in the print if one calculates the exposure only for the illuminated parts."[60] Additionally, many of the most interesting hieroglyphic texts were to be found on the interior of the temples, where the lighting was so somber it was essentially impossible to photograph at all. Greene found an ingenious solution for recording inscriptions in areas that did not receive enough sunlight

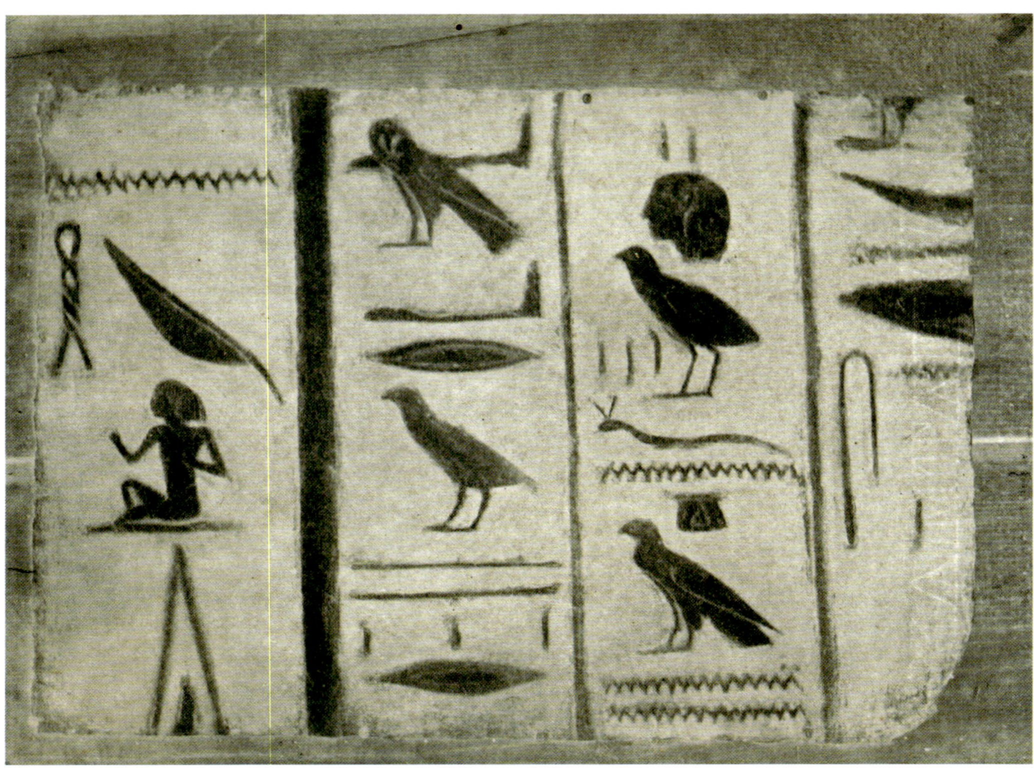

FIG. 6 John Beasley Greene, [Hieroglyphics], 1854. Waxed paper negative. Carnegie Museum of Art, Pittsburgh, Purchased with funds provided by the William Talbott Hillman Foundation

for a photographic exposure: He made papier-mâché impressions of the carvings and then used pigments to color the resulting molds to highlight the reliefs and darken the recessed areas. He then photographed the colored molds.[61] Though the process of making "squeezes," or direct impressions of the hieroglyphics, was regularly used by archaeologists (and sometimes by souvenir-seeking tourists—Du Camp complained that the face of the western colossus at Abu Simbel had been permanently whitened by a tourist's inexpert application of plaster),[62] Greene uniquely combined the practice of mold-making with photography. Such an approach not only made an extremely legible record of the text: the use of photography made it possible to make multiple copies of the inscriptions and also obviated the need to carry home the physical castings as earlier archaeologists had done. As Greene described:

> The process which is, as you see, one of great simplicity and easy application, allows photographic reproduction of all the bas-reliefs, without exception, that decorate the interiors of monuments; it adds to the importance that moldings already had in giving them a new usefulness, and at the same time ends up replacing them in an advantageous manner, because it gives perfectly exact reproductions that can be infinitely multiplied, that are more easily conserved, are infinitely less voluminous and more easily consulted.[63]

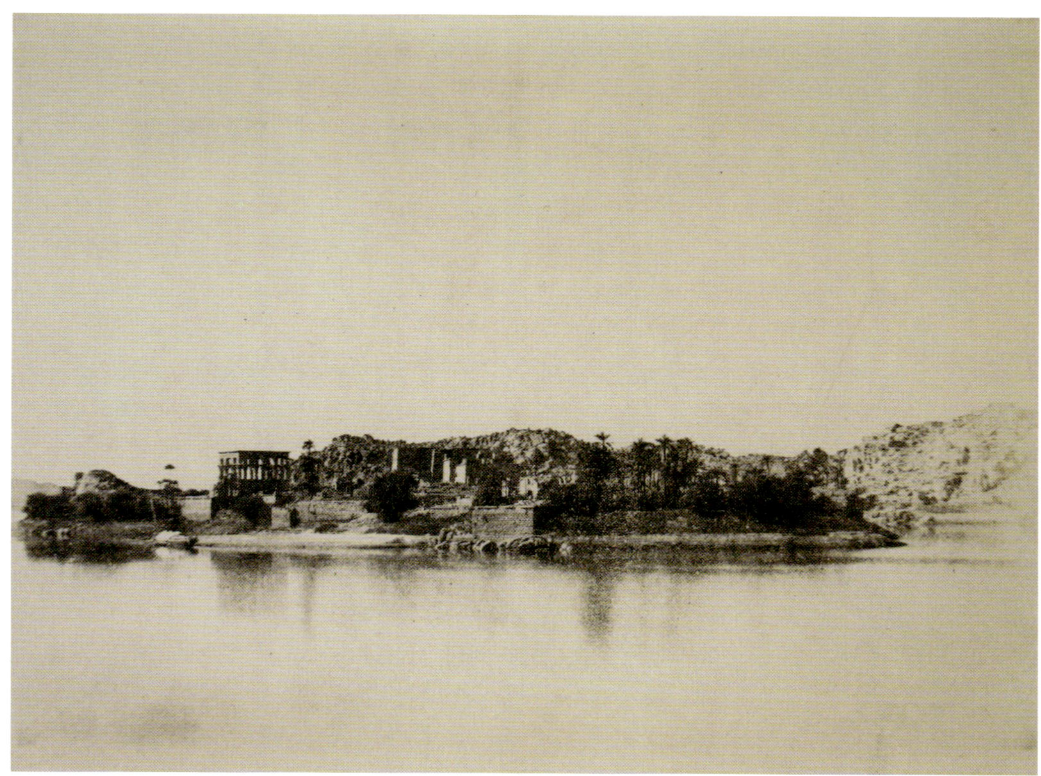

FIG. 7 John Beasley Greene, [View of Philae], 1854. Salted paper print. Janet Lehr, Inc., New York

Interestingly, Greene also mentions that this method could be used to make records of polychrome carvings by applying colored pigments on the mold. He does not address, however, how this would translate in a medium that could not reproduce color. The whereabouts of the photographs depicting the bas-reliefs of the sepulcher of Seti I at Thebes (opened by Giovanni Battista Belzoni in 1817, and commonly referred to as "Belzoni's Tomb") that Greene mentions as examples of his successful application of the method are unknown. Only a very small group of prints of hieroglyphic texts produced by Greene's innovative method are extant, but several surviving negatives attest to the clarity of the reproduction he was able to achieve (fig. 6).

Three months after donating *Sculptures et inscriptions* to the Académie, Greene deposited his second album in October 1854. The first forty-two plates are devoted to the monuments of Egypt, beginning with the enormous rock-cut temple of Ramesses II, Abu Simbel (pl. 16), and ending with the Great Pyramid of Khufu (Cheops) in Giza (pl. 10). As in *Sculptures et inscriptions*, Greene frequently included multiple views of the same temple, though in the monuments series he begins with a general overview, then moves (often in the round) to provide closer views. At Philae, for example, he made his most extensive series, which begins with the island temple as seen from across the river (fig. 7) so that it can be appreciated in its environment, then moves into the temple complex itself. The series of nine photographs concludes with carefully framed details, including a portal in front of the great temple (pl. 35) and a frieze of columns in the inner courtyard (pl. 36). Other series follow a similar formula, first showing the temple from afar so that the viewer can apprehend its dominant features or position in the landscape, then moving closer to focus on a particular aspect, like the two views he made of the Temple of Dendur. In the first of this pair (pl. 27), the temple is positioned low in the frame, almost camouflaged within the rock-strewn hillside. Only the top of the temple gate breaks the horizon, emphasizing the architectural flourishes at its crown. The second image (pl. 28) frames the temple's small sanctuary frontally, underscoring the simplicity and symmetry of its design. Over time, such pictures have acquired greater significance than Greene himself could have anticipated. Though archaeologists of his era felt pressure to record and preserve the rapidly deteriorating monuments of Egypt, efforts to modernize the country in the twentieth century frequently accelerated their disappearance. This particular temple, moved in pieces and reconstructed, is now housed in The Metropolitan Museum of Art, a 1963 gift from the Egyptian government to the United States in gratitude for its help relocating many of the monuments threatened by flooding after the construction of the Aswan Dam (including, astonishingly, Abu Simbel). A great many of Greene's photographs thus document an Egypt that no longer exists.

The subjects of *Monuments et paysages* frequently overlap with those in *Sculptures et inscriptions*, and it is useful to consider how Greene chose to divide them, and how their representations differ depending on which series the photograph was assigned to. In contrast to the abundant representations of Philae in the monuments section, for example, Greene devotes a single plate to the temple in *Sculptures et inscriptions*: a close-up view of a stela (fig. 8)—one of the subjects the Académie had specifically requested Du Camp copy. Greene similarly included in both albums photographs of one of the Colossi of Memnon—a pair of monumental sculptures, some 60 feet high, that once guarded the entrance to the Mortuary Temple of Amenhotep III and had been all that remained of the site for several centuries. In *Monuments et paysages*, one of the enormous statues is seen from a slight distance (pl. 41). It rises up—solitary, majestic, extraordinary—out of a great rocky plain, silhouetted in three-quarter profile against distant mountains and an immense blank sky. The same colossus is also the subject of plate 67 of *Sculptures et inscriptions* (pl. 42). Here is a completely different view: Greene centered the statue within the frame, top to bottom and left to right. Close to the camera and squared to the picture plane, the colossus is seen from the back, so that he could record the inscription written there. Viewed from this angle, the statue becomes nearly abstract: its sculptural qualities all but disappear, and its size and setting are indeterminate. The texts inscribed on the northern colossus were of great interest to scholars—Champollion himself made a squeeze there—and Greene's photograph was clearly intended to further that research by providing a clear copy of the inscriptions in situ.[64] Taken together, the two series, monuments and inscriptions, seem to fulfill the Académie's wish, "to complete the general

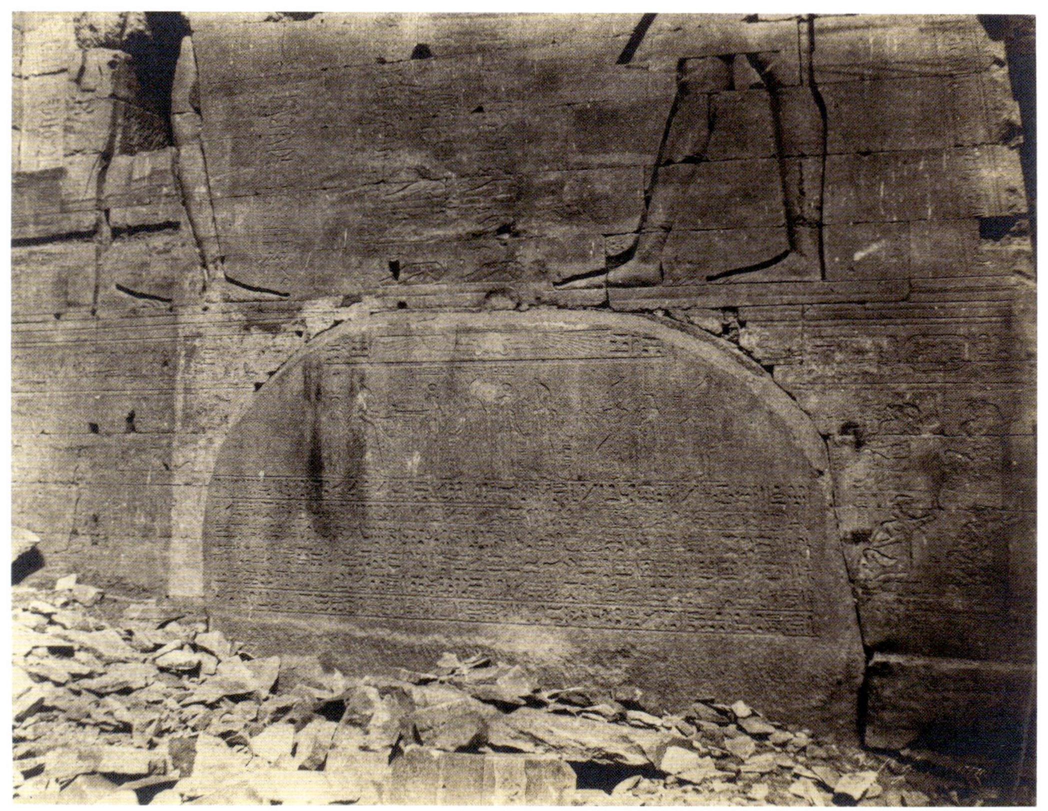

FIG. 8 John Beasley Greene, *Philae. Stèle (Philae. Stela)*, 1854. Salted paper print. Musée d'Orsay, Paris

views and the details of a monument, whether an entire legend or a complete hieroglyphic tablet."

The second half of *Monuments et paysages* is devoted to landscapes, and if here Greene seems to have deviated from the directions given to Du Camp, he adhered to the program laid out in his own appeal to the Académie "to collect archaeological, historical, and geographic information of interest." Photographs in this section depict the craggy rocks and treacherous shoals of the Second Cataract (pls. 13–15) and the wide variety of exotically shaped trees—the impossibly slender date palms, the gently curving branches of doum palms, and the dense, rounded crowns of gum trees (pls. 22, 23, 31, 32)—that grew along the river's fertile banks. The category of landscape was not, however, limited strictly to representations of the natural environment: some images show small villages along the Nile or other man-made structures, such as a small temple near Wadi Gyrshe, almost subsumed by the stony hillside on which it sits (pl. 19). A few of Greene's views of temples are also assigned to this category. In a picture of the Temple of el-Sebua, its top just breaking the horizon, it is not clear if the temple is emerging from the dune or on the verge of being engulfed by it. The colossus before it, its base entirely hidden by centuries of drifting sand, appears to walk toward us, as if through a mirage (pl. 20).[65] More strongly perhaps than either of the other two series of photographs Greene made, the pictures from the landscape group exude a sense of wonder and discovery, an almost visceral sense of the immensity of the Egyptian desert and the foreignness of its terrain. The temples, as yet unexcavated—as Gustave Flaubert, who accompanied Maxime Du Camp to Egypt, described one in 1850, "buried to its shoulders in the sand, partially visible, like an old dug-up skeleton"[66]—are part of the landscape itself, as old as eternity, tantalizing with the promise of the mysteries they conceal. The monuments depicted in this series are presented not as archaeological texts, precisely transcribed, but as marvels.

Greene's landscape photographs can hardly be described as mere geographical studies, though they are that, too. His views of the terrain around Gebel Abusir, a small hill (gebel) overlooking the rapids of the Second Cataract, are among the most compelling he made, balancing description of the region's inhospitable topography and the suggestion of a corresponding mood (pls. 11, 12). The hill offered the best view of the cataracts, but Greene turned his lens in the other direction, away from the clamor and drama of the rushing water. The barren, rocky landscape his camera captures in these pictures is as airless and unfamiliar as the surface of the moon. Without a monument or landmark to disrupt the expansive horizon or anchor the viewer to a particular point in space, Greene conjures seemingly endless fields of sand, stone, and sky, devoid of any trace of human presence. One traveler's description of Abusir echoes the atmosphere of Greene's photograph: "But the principal charm of the landscape consists neither in the savage rocks, nor in the eternal uproar and dashing of the waters; but in that utter solitude, sterility, desolation, which everywhere prevail, and suggest the idea, that in all that vast region you alone breathe the breath of life. . . . I have seldom experienced, in the presence of mere brute matter, emotions more powerful."[67]

In such views especially, Greene seems to return to the lessons of Le Gray in Fontainebleau, focusing as much on the experience as the appearance of landscape—its stillness and solitude, the play of light on sand or across rough limestone. Though the Egyptian landscape bore little resemblance to that of France, Greene applied what he had learned there to this strange new environment. There are some similarities in subject matter: his study of a row of sycamores at Korosko (pl. 23), for example, strongly recalls the trees he photographed along the road to Chailly (pl. 25). And just as the majestic oaks of Fontainebleau brought to mind a history of France that stretched back centuries, Greene's Egyptian gum trees seem to belong to a time and place equally remote (pl. 22). Such pictorial descriptions are underscored by the effects produced by the paper negative and the salted paper print. Though Greene's use of the process in Egypt was surely a product of his familiarity with it and, above all, its ease—paper, unlike glass, was lightweight, not subject to breakage, and, most importantly, could be prepared weeks in advance and developed at some delay from the exposure—the negatives and prints the process produced were ideally suited to the textures of gritty sand and coarse stone, and only amplified the picturesque

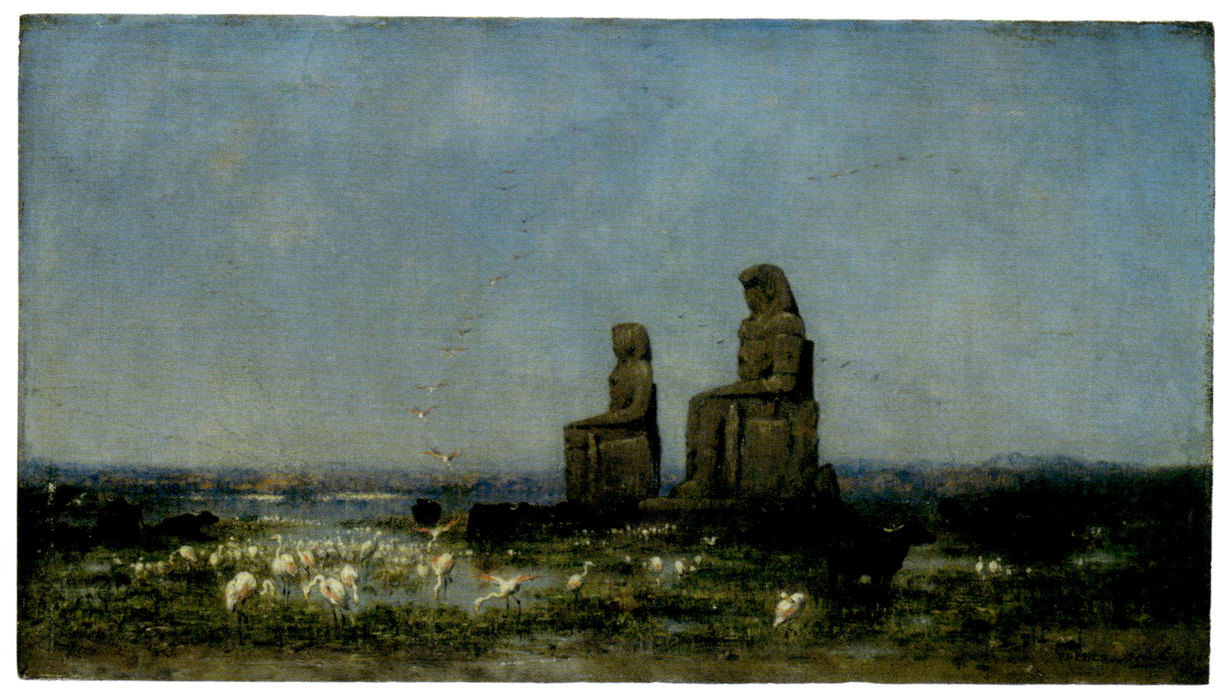

FIG. 9 Narcisse Berchère (French, 1819–1891), *The Colossi of Memnon at Thebes*, 1868. Oil on wood. The Metropolitan Museum of Art, New York, Gift of Kenneth Jay Lane, 2016

qualities of the crumbling, ancient monuments that punctuated the Egyptian landscape. It was in such circumstances, argued critic Francis Wey, that the paper negative was ideally deployed: "It is above all in the reproduction of abrupt sites, boulders and monuments, at which photography on paper excels and is superior to all."[68] Though the Académie had warned Du Camp about the dangers of indulging any impulse to privilege aesthetics over scrupulous recording ("It is also not a question of charming our eyes by the seductive effects that light produces in the camera, but of faithfully and sequentially copying the texts claimed for science"), in his landscape views Greene seems to have blended the two.

In looking at Greene's photographs, it is easy to forget that the world he encountered was both inhabited and in color. It is almost impossible to reconcile Flaubert's description of the vivid tones of the Egyptian landscape—"through holes in the temple walls we see the incredibly blue sky and the full Nile winding in the middle of the desert with a fringe of green on each bank"[69]—with Greene's austere studies in rich browns and cool grays. We only need compare his photograph of the Colossi of Memnon with Narcisse Berchère's nearly contemporaneous painting of the same subject to highlight the impact of the photographer's monochromatic palette and how different the kind of pictures the camera produced could be from the painted Orientalist fantasies to which European audiences had become accustomed (fig. 9). In Berchère's imaginative rendering, the stony field that surrounds the statues in Greene's photo is transformed into a lush floodplain, dotted with pale pink flamingos and placid grazing cattle. The flinty stone of Greene's imposing monument and the blank and forbidding sky are rendered in warm tones of brown against a cloud-studded field of rose-tinged blue. Berchère's colossi preside over an exotic landscape that has grown up around them, teeming with life, watered by the seasonal flooding of the Nile, and adorned with migratory birds. Greene's forbidding image, on the other hand, can be linked neither to season nor century; it seems utterly timeless.

Equally striking is the absence of people in Greene's views. Though a blurred figure can be spotted from time to time, their inclusion seems incidental. One or two

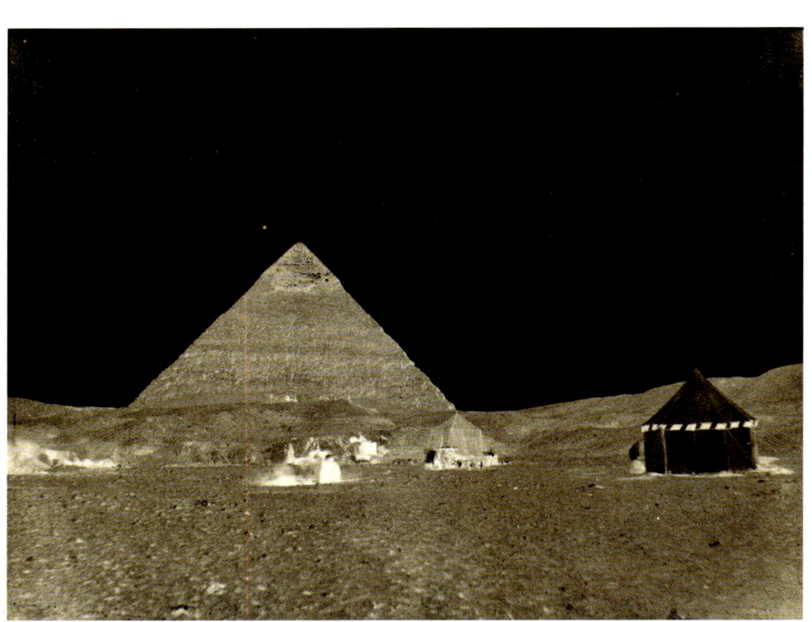

FIG. 10 John Beasley Greene, [Tent by the Pyramid of Khafre, Giza], 1853–54. Waxed paper negative. Musée d'Orsay, Paris

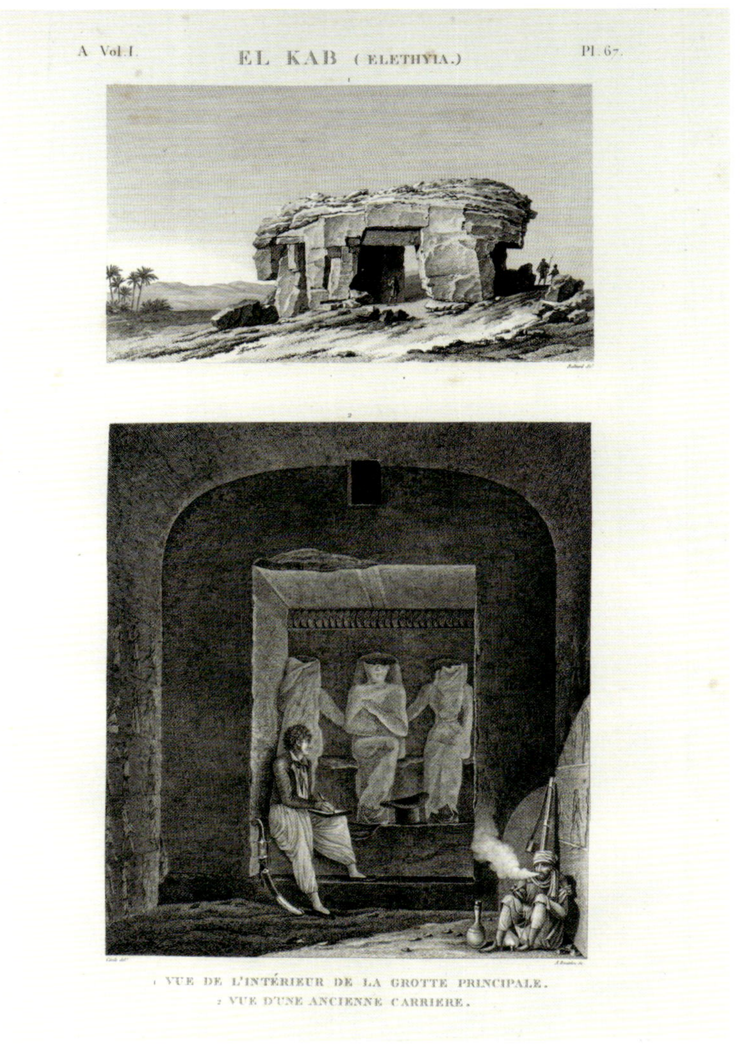

FIG. 11 *El Kab. (Elethyia). (1) Vue de l'intérieure de la grotte principale [View of the Interior of the Main Grotto]; (2) Vue d'une ancienne carrière [View of a Former Quarry]*. Plate 67 of the album *Description de l'Égypte, ou Recueil des observations et des recherches qui ont été faites en Égypte pendant l'expédition de l'armée française*, vol. 1, *Antiquités* (Paris: Imprimerie Impériale, 1809). New York Public Library

photographs show obvious signs of human activity; for example, an encampment in the second court of Medinet Habu—the laundry line offering a humorous juxtaposition between the mundane necessities of human existence and the grand achievement of the monument behind it (pl. 48). Even in this picture, however, the temple is clearly Greene's focus, and we are meant simply to ignore the encampment (though casual travelers usually slept on their boats, archaeologists frequently set up campsites inside the ruins). As at Fontainebleau, Greene's decision to exclude not just human bodies, but also most evidence of modernity, appears deliberate. Though portraiture was difficult due to the long exposures paper negatives required, it was not impossible. Several of Greene's negatives at the Musée d'Orsay depict people or clearly point to their presence: one view of the Pyramids at Giza shows a tent, its form mirrored by the peak of a pyramid and simultaneously dwarfed by it (fig. 10). Two other negatives depicting figure studies almost verge on portraiture, but Greene did not include any of them in his albums, and there are no known prints. It is notable that he repeatedly photographed people or recorded traces of their presence in his views, but that the body of photographs he ultimately produced conveys an image of an uninhabited land that belongs not to the present, but to ancient history. Whether a function of the medium's limitations or the product of artistic license, the overwhelming solitude of Greene's photographs is often at odds with the abundant written accounts by contemporary travelers, which describe festive encounters between fellow voyagers on the Nile, as well as the local population who catered to such tourists, providing services and entertainment of all sorts. The crew manning Greene's boat alone numbered at least six people, likely more.

Greene's photographs also depart from the kinds of representations of Egypt that preceded photography. Though he was himself encountering the landscape for the first time, he would have arrived in the country with some idea of what to expect, as well as a rich bank of visual imagery on which to draw for inspiration.[70] Chief among these visual precedents were the illustrations produced by Napoleon's army and reproduced in the multivolume publication *Description de l'Égypte*, whose thousands of pictures recorded the man-made monuments and natural landscape of Egypt. The pictures of *Description de l'Égypte*, intended to convey an aura of objectivity, provided not only a meticulous documentation of the country, but also signaled the French's conquest of that landscape—if their victory was not decisive in military terms, their self-proclaimed intellectual mastery is nonetheless very much on display in such imagery. These pictures are inevitably animated by two different kinds of human subjects: the French, dressed in Western clothes and armed with the accoutrements of the Enlightenment tradition—tools of recording, mapping, and measuring—and the natives, whose costumes, poses, and activities imply not only the primitive conditions of their lives, but also their moral inferiority (fig. 11). If in such pictures the European savants are emblems of modernity, the local peoples serve as their cultural and ideological foils, appearing to belong to another register of time altogether.[71]

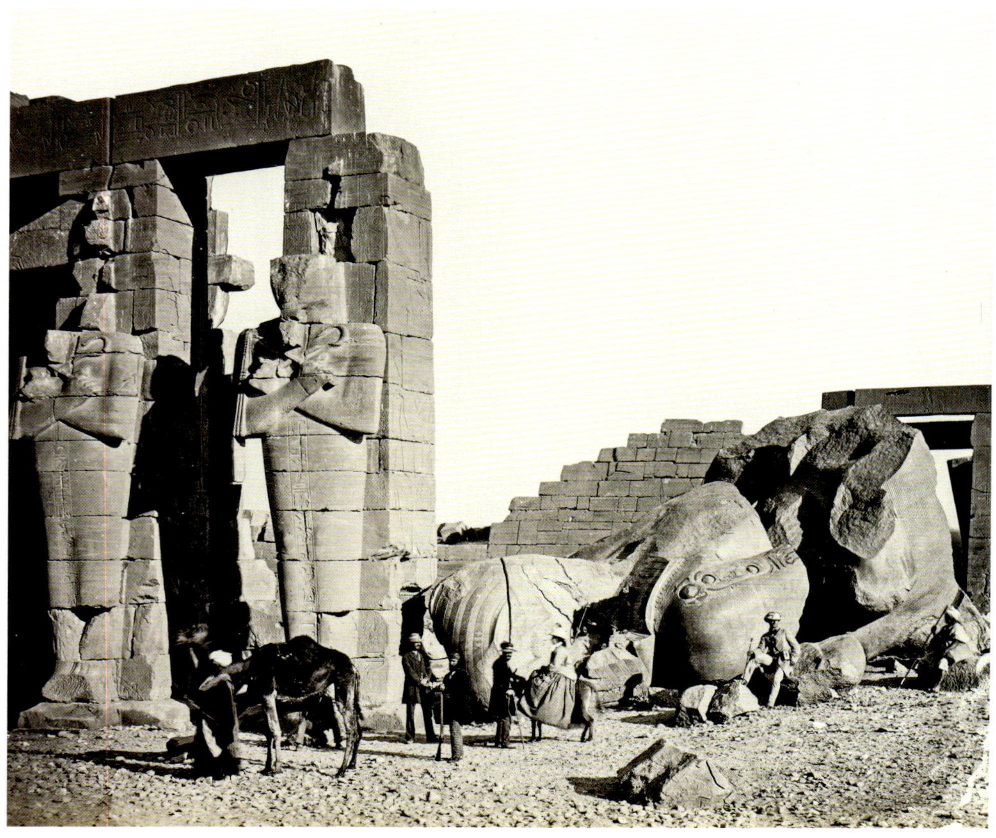

FIG. 12 Francis Frith (English, 1822–1898), *The Ramesseum of El-Kurneh, Thebes (First View)*, ca. 1857. Albumen print. San Francisco Museum of Modern Art, fractional gift of Paul Sack, 1995, and collection of the Sack Photographic Trust

Some of the early photographers fashioned their photographic projects as a deliberate response to such pictorial models. Teynard, for example, explicitly announced his album *Égypte et Nubie* as a complement to the illustrations in *Description de l'Égypte* and Franz-Christian Gau's *Antiquités de la Nubie* (1822). Francis Frith, working only a few years after Teynard and just after Greene, also looked to such illustrations, in his case the model provided by David Roberts' extremely popular series of lithographs, *The Holy Land, Syria, Idumea, Arabia, Egypt & Nubia* (1842–49).[72] Frith regularly inserted people into his photographic views of the Egyptian monuments: at first, tourists who could be seen as vicarious stand-ins for the European armchair travelers who purchased and viewed his pictures (fig. 12); and later, Egyptian natives, whose presence exoticized, rather than familiarized, the landscape and emphasized its geographical and cultural remoteness from Western civilization.[73] The inclusion of human figures in such representations, whether drawn or photographed, not only advanced the ideological or political agendas of their makers, but also had the practical effect of providing an immediately comprehensible measure of scale that is utterly absent in Greene's unpeopled views. For many nineteenth-

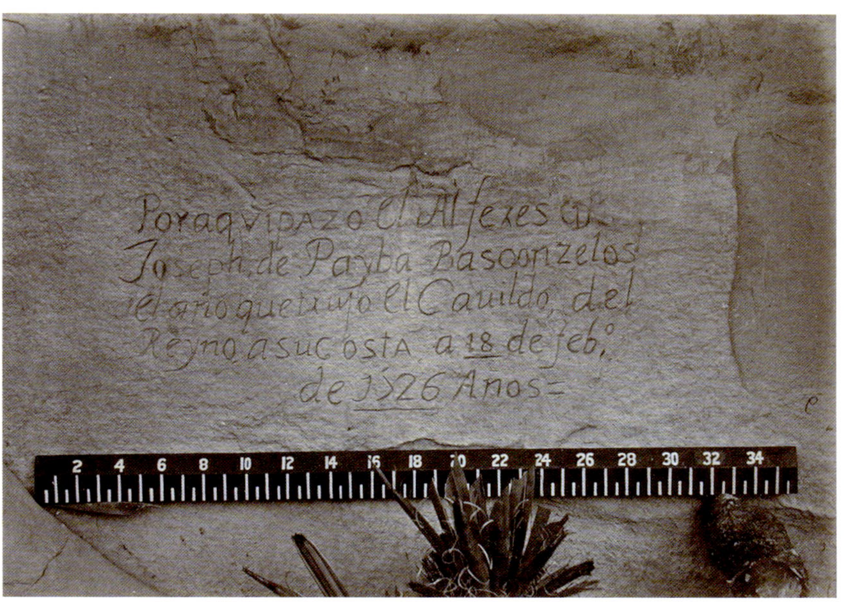

FIG. 13 Timothy H. O'Sullivan (American, born Ireland, 1840–1882), *Historic Spanish Record of the Conquest, South Side of Inscription Rock, N.M. No. 3*, 1872. Albumen print. San Francisco Museum of Modern Art, Accessions Committee Fund purchase, 1995

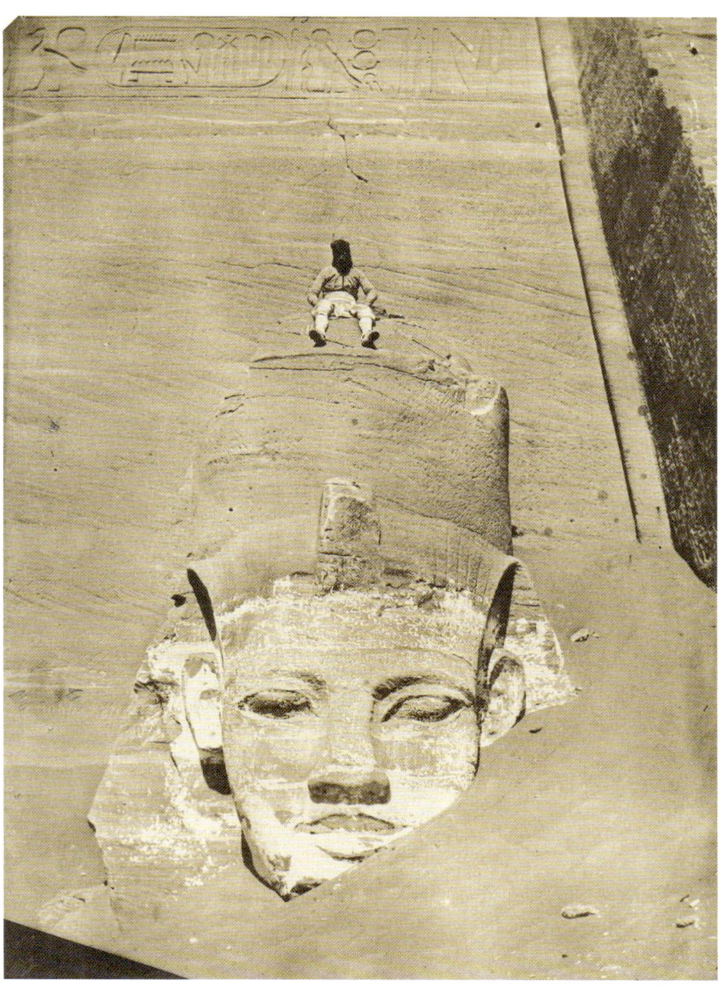

FIG. 14 Maxime Du Camp (French, 1822–1894), *Westernmost Colossus of the Temple of Re, Abu Simbel*, 1850. Salted paper print. The Metropolitan Museum of Art, New York, Gilman Collection, Gift of the Howard Gilman Foundation, 2005

century photographers, particularly those of a scientific bent, it became common practice to insert an object into the frame that would convey the relative size of the subject depicted. Timothy O'Sullivan, for example, who worked on the Wheeler Survey documenting the American West, frequently included familiar objects as a scale marker, though he also used more literal indicators of measurement, such as the ruler in his *Historic Spanish Record of the Conquest* (fig. 13). In Egypt, where the enormity of the ancient monuments would have been as unimaginable to European viewers as the grandeur of the American West must have been to denizens of the East Coast, a human figure could provide a sense of scale where the vast expanses of desert served only to disorient. Du Camp, for example, taking his cue from both the politics and tactics of the *Description de l'Égypte*, frequently employed his Maltese valet to this end, and also famously compelled one of the Nubian sailors working on his boat, Hajj Ishmael, to pose in many of his views, thereby providing "a uniform scale of proportions" (fig. 14).[74] Greene's photographs rarely provide any such point of reference, and as a consequence, his compositions impart an almost Romantic sense of both spatial and temporal infinitude. If his photographs do not evince the overt Eurocentrism of Du Camp's, Greene's near total erasure of the human presence nonetheless performs a fiction of its own, presenting Egypt as available terrain to be recorded, studied, and possessed without impediment or resistance.

ALBUMS AND AUDIENCES

It appears that Greene imagined that his photographs from the monuments and landscapes series would appeal to an audience beyond a scholarly one. In addition to the two albums he donated to the Académie des Inscriptions et Belles-Lettres, he made at least two others intended for rather different consumers. The first, and most significant, is *Le Nil: Monuments—Paysages. Explorations photographiques par John B. Greene 1854* (The Nile: Monuments—Landscapes. Photographic Explorations by John B. Greene), printed by Louis Désiré Blanquart-Evrard's Imprimerie Photographique de Lille. Of all the many mysteries surrounding Greene's life and work, *Le Nil* poses one of the greatest, at least in terms of understanding the conditions of its publication. There is but one known copy, a large-format, handsomely bound album in the collection of the Bibliothèque Nationale de France.[75] The album contains ninety-four plates, divided in two sections, monuments and landscapes, but no title page, text, or captions, either printed or handwritten, except for a single sheet that introduces each of the two sections. Though Greene is often described as having published the album, which would imply it was made in multiple copies and sold, this does not appear to have been the case. The copy at the Bibliothèque Nationale was certainly printed by the Imprimerie Photographique de Lille (the cover is debossed in gold with the company's crest), which functioned both as a photographic printing house and sometimes as a publisher. Yet this book was not deposited at the national library as part of the system of *dépôt legal*, as an actual publication would have been, but was purchased in the 1940s from a private collector. Nor do any of the individual pages bear the Blanquart-Evrard legend that the company's publications usually carried. The Société Française de Photographie owns what appears to be a title page for *Le Nil* (fig. 15) as well as nine plates bearing Blanquart-Evrard captions, all a donation from the Lille printing house in 1855. The pages on which these prints are mounted, all inscribed "J. B. Greene, phot." and "Imprimerie de Lille," are smaller than those at the Bibliothèque Nationale, and appear to be part of a sample album. No other copies of this particular title page, or similarly labeled plates, have been located in institutional or private collections. The most likely scenario is that Greene commissioned Blanquart-Evrard to print the album privately, in a quantity that cannot be determined, but must have been small.[76] There is no correspondence to shed light on the nature or terms of Greene's arrangement with the printing house. Perhaps he was inspired by Du Camp's *Égypte, Nubie, Palestine et Syrie*, which was both a financial and critical success.[77] Given Greene's family wealth, it seems unlikely he intended the album as a source of income, as Du Camp did, but his interest in producing pictures for wider distribution offers further evidence of the young man's ambition.

Le Nil and *Monuments et paysages* are similar in many ways, but their discrepancies are revealing. *Le Nil* is a somewhat larger book, containing ninety-four plates to *Monuments et paysages'* eighty-three, and as such contains a number of pictures not included in any of the groups Greene submitted to the Académie. Two of the additional plates are photographs that were included in the album *Sculptures et inscriptions*, though in *Le Nil* they are recategorized and assigned to the monuments section.[78] However, eight of the other nine additional prints are landscape views. These comprise more tree studies and views of the cataracts, as well as an extremely minimalist rendering of the wide river and a distant tree-studded island that has come to be one of Greene's best known works (pl. 63).[79] Several photographs give evidence of a more recent (relatively speaking) history, among them a type of well common in Egypt called a sakia (or Persian wheel), as well as two fourteenth-century mosques in Cairo. This enlargement of the landscape section demonstrates the importance Greene placed on this kind of picture, and also his awareness that such

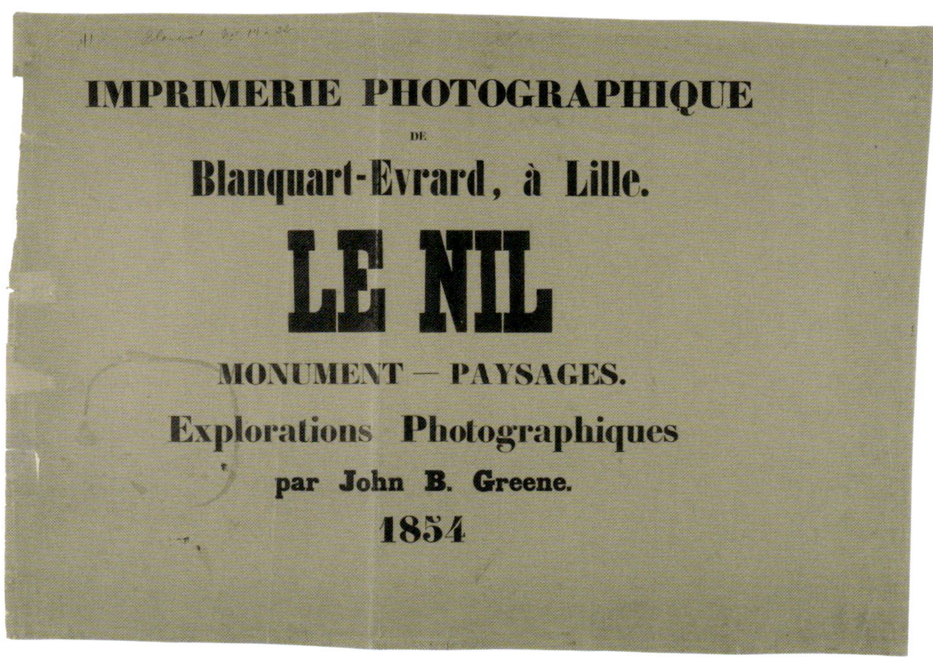
IMPRIMERIE PHOTOGRAPHIQUE
DE
Blanquart-Evrard, à Lille.
LE NIL
MONUMENT — PAYSAGES.
Explorations Photographiques
par John B. Greene.
1854

FIG. 15 Title page for *Le Nil: Monuments—Paysages. Explorations photographiques par John B. Greene 1854*. Imprimerie Photographique de Blanquart-Evrard, Lille. Collection of the Société Française de Photographie, Paris

imagery might have appeal for a broader audience, even if it did not conform to the interests or instructions of the Académie.

Like *Monuments et paysages*, *Le Nil* is divided into two sections, but another chief difference between the two books is the sequencing of the plates. *Monuments et paysages* is ordered from southern (Upper) Egypt to northern (Lower) Egypt, beginning with Abu Simbel, the southernmost monument on Greene's journey, following the path of Greene's travel.[80] Though he began his initial rapid descent of the Nile in Cairo and Giza, the pictures that he took there are the last ones in the sequence, as if he had first encountered them on his return. Both sections of *Monuments et paysages* are sequenced in this manner: the monuments section moves from Abu Simbel to Giza, followed by the landscape section, which similarly begins in the south, at the Second Cataract, and moves northward, ending at Alexandria, the port at which all Europeans entered Egypt, and from which they departed. *Le Nil*, on the other hand, begins with Greene's stunning views of the Pyramids and Sphinx at northerly Giza, and proceeds southward, ending at Abu Simbel. The landscape section, however, is not similarly reversed, and instead mimics the monuments section, from south to north. If *Monuments et paysages* gives the impression of two sequential northward journeys up the Nile, *Le Nil* offers a round-trip from north to south and back again.

Du Camp similarly produced two versions of his book of Nile photographs, one organized according to geography (north to south) and one that followed the actual path of travel. In her study of Du Camp's work, Julia Ballerini has argued that this sequencing was as much a philosophical choice as an aesthetic one, and that it reflects a larger problematic about the representation of Egypt:

> All travel accounts of Egypt throughout the nineteenth century follow two orders; formal books—such as Du Camp's luxury-edition photographic album with its scholarly introduction—are structured according to a "read" geography from north to south, rather than according to the sequence of the actual journey. Informal narratives—such as [Du Camp's] *Le Nil*—adhere to the chronology of the lived experience. The former an epistemological order, the latter an ontological one.[81]

According to Ballerini's logic, the armchair traveler would wish to share the photographer's experience of sailing south as quickly as possible and then leisurely traveling north. An expert in Egyptology, on the other hand, would be less concerned with an experiential approach and would be able to orient himself or herself more easily to the country as it was ordered geographically.[82] Though Greene's sequence does not follow exactly the same pattern as Du Camp's, nor does Ballerini's rubric seem to hold strictly true in his case, it is nonetheless apparent that Greene chose to present different versions to his scholarly and less specialized audiences.

The final album Greene produced is something of an outlier in comparison to the other three, yet it still offers useful information. We know very specifically the audience to which it was addressed. *Collection de photographies prises en Égypte en 1854 offerte à S.A. le Grand Duc de Bade en 1855* (Collection of Photographs Taken in Egypt in 1854, Offered to His Highness the Grand Duke of Baden-Baden in 1855) is a small album of only twenty-six photographs that was apparently assembled as a luxe gift from Greene, though his relationship to the recipient is unknown.[83] The logic guiding the selection of images is less clear than in his other three albums: they do not appear to follow particular themes—though the works are somewhat more concentrated around Cairo and Giza as well as Medinet Habu—nor are the plates organized according to any immediately apparent schema. Unlike the other albums, Egypt's geography—either imagined or experienced—plays little evident role in the sequence. Greene seems to have assembled a group of diverse views that provide a broad pictorial overview but lack an overarching narrative. Equally interesting: though the majority of the photographs were also included in the Académie albums, *Le Nil*, or both, six of the twenty-six pictures in this album appear only here, and at least three of them constitute the only known prints of those images. Several depict more contemporary or quotidian buildings in Cairo (pl. 67), a subject he did not include in any of his other groups of work. We know from the title of the album that the prints were taken in 1854 and given as a gift in 1855, but not numbered in the negative or included in any of the three albums assembled in 1854, so it seems likely that these six new photographs were made on the second trip to Egypt (1854–55) rather than on the first.

This hypothesis is supported by one photograph in particular: a view of Pompey's Pillar in Alexandria that is the opening plate of the album Greene gave to the grand duke (pl. 64). All visitors to Egypt from Europe arrived at that port city, and it was a rude introduction for many; one traveler observed that it required a good deal of imagination to picture it as the site of ancient wonders: "Nothing can be more barren or desolate than the situation of Alexandria. . . . Alexander must have been a far-sighted politician to conceive the idea of a great town ever flourishing in such a desert."[84] The area was not particularly rich in ruins or monuments, but Greene recorded the features that any visitor would have remarked: the so-called Pompey's Pillar (actually a monument to the Roman emperor Diocletian's suppression of an Alexandrian revolt in the third century CE), the adjacent large Arab cemetery that occupied the site of the city's former Serapeum, and some general views of the city, two of which include the famous obelisk popularly known as "Cleopatra's Needle."[85] Both *Le Nil* and *Monuments et paysages* include his view of the Arab cemetery in Alexandria. Though it is possible Greene took this photograph at the conclusion of his trip as he was about to depart Egypt for France, it seems far more likely that this is one of his very earliest views of the country, and as such reflects the impressions of a wide-eyed new arrival rather than the careful examinations of an Egyptologist. As all of the prints of the image are quite poorly preserved, and the negative appears to have been underexposed, it also suggests a young photographer finding his legs in an unfamiliar landscape and climate.

Greene also photographed Pompey's Pillar on this first trip, but did not make prints from those negatives. These early views of the iconic landmark are not particularly distinguished. The negatives feature several figures, who appear to lie on the ground in stereotypically Orientalist poses, a convention widely seen in earlier representations of Egypt and the Middle East more generally, but one that Greene appears to have jettisoned from the outset. Whether they are locals in native dress or fellow Europeans playing the part, it is impossible to say. The view Greene made on the second trip of the enormous granite monolith exhibits a completely different approach: the pillar, entirely isolated from the surrounding environment, is seen from a low vantage point so that it juts out into the open sky. It is a powerful picture, at once muscular and meditative, a far cry from the generally descriptive views Greene made on his earlier trip but chose not to print. Whether he made the photograph of Pompey's Pillar upon his arrival in Egypt for his second excursion or upon his departure we cannot know, but it seems clear that he left the country a far more confident and accomplished photographer than when he arrived.

SECOND EGYPTIAN SOJOURN, 1854–55

Greene returned to Egypt in the winter of 1854–55, this time with plans to excavate at the Mortuary Temple of Ramesses III (r. ca. 1184–1153 BCE) at Medinet Habu, an important New Kingdom site at the west bank of Luxor. Greene had photographed extensively at Medinet Habu on his previous trip: nearly half of the 102 photographs included in the album *Sculptures et inscriptions égyptiennes* were made at this important site. On this expedition, however, Greene did not merely photograph: he was able to obtain a firman, or permit, to excavate at the site from Egyptian ruler Sa'id Pasha, thanks to the intervention of former French consul Ferdinand de Lesseps.[86] Greene's activities on this voyage were far more focused than that of the previous year. From the photographic evidence, it appears he went directly to Medinet Habu, where he excavated in the first court of the Mortuary Temple and along its southern external wall.

Of all the sites in Egypt, few held more appeal to a student of Egyptian hieroglyphics than Medinet Habu. The large temple complex, where the pharaoh Ramesses III would come to participate in religious festivals, is one of the most impressive in Egypt and also one of the best preserved. Built out of commonly available sandstone, it had not been "quarried" for its precious materials and dismantled as so many other temples had been over the centuries, and thus stood relatively intact.[87] The central feature of this complex, the Mortuary Temple, or "House-of-Millions-of-Years of Ramesses III Possessed of Eternity" as the ancient Egyptians called it, was not just architecturally whole, but was also covered in inscriptions, many of which describe the feasts and rites associated with the king's death and resurrection.[88] The abundant inscriptions in the temple's first court and second pylon are complemented by those of the calendar on the temple's exterior wall, which expands upon the timeline of these festivals.[89] Champollion had described in great detail the visible inscriptions at Medinet Habu and their importance to advancing the state of Egyptology in his eighteenth letter, dated June 30, 1829.[90] It is clear that Greene envisioned his own archaeological work there as an extension of that begun by Champollion, as he turned his attention to two of the key features Champollion had identified as worthy of investigation. He also retained the elder Egyptologist's idiosyncratic nomenclature and spelling for many of the buildings, referring, for example, to Ramesses III as Ramsès-Méïamoun, as Champollion had done. Champollion's observations had been confined to the parts of the inscriptions visible above the rubble that filled the site; Greene's 1855 excavations at Medinet Habu constituted the first systematic effort to clear this debris and continue the earlier work by revealing inscriptions in their entirety and documenting them for study.[91]

Unlike the large and varied group of pictures Greene brought back from his first trip to Egypt, the photographic record of his second excursion was pictorially concise, the documentation of an archaeologist at work. He printed only twelve photographs from Medinet Habu (though his negatives demonstrate he made many more of the site), each depicting a particular discovery or significant inscription.[92] The photographs are direct and workmanlike, demonstrating the fruits of Greene's excavation in situ, as well as providing close-up documentation of the hieroglyphic texts he uncovered. He begins with an overview of the inscriptions on the second pylon, and then moves in to more closely examine his excavations at the pylon's base. The roof of the first court was supported by seven columns on the left side and seven pillars on the right, each of the latter adorned with a colossus nearly 30 feet tall, the heads of some of which were visible above the rubble (the ruins of centuries-old Coptic settlements) piled up in the courtyard. Greene was able to excavate one, and the next group of photographs systematically document the statue, both full-length and in close-up views that render fully legible the inscriptions on the statue's clothes and pedestal (figs. 16, 17). Two views of an ancient door discovered next to the Palace of Thutmose III (believed to be the only remaining trace of the building to which it belonged) function similarly: a long view to provide the larger context and a closer view to record the details (pl. 51). He deposited the twelve photographs, captioned by hand and bound in an album titled *Fouilles exécutées à Thèbes dans l'année 1855*, at the Académie des Inscriptions et Belles-Lettres.[93]

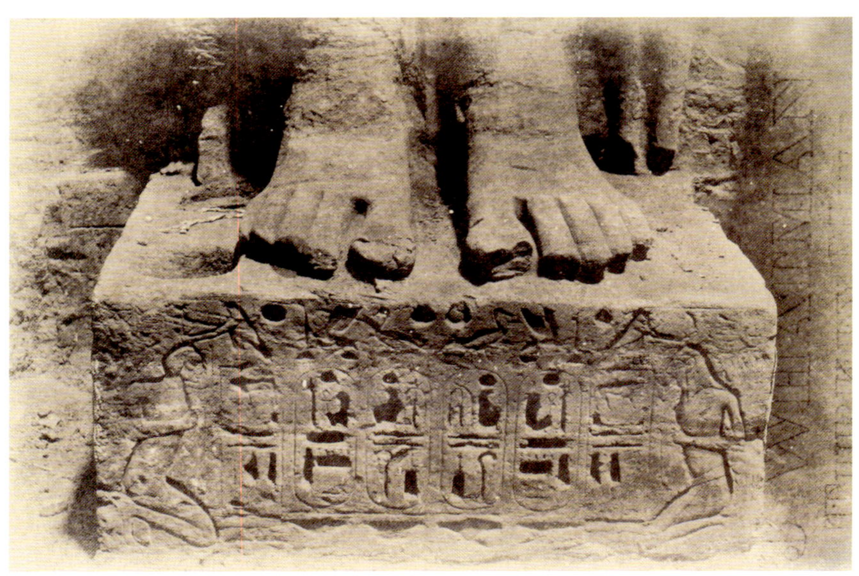

FIG. 16 John Beasley Greene, *Palais du Médinet Habou. Colosse de Ramsès III. Socle (Mortuary Temple of Medinet Habu. Colossus of Ramesses III. Pedestal).* Plate 5 of the album *Fouilles exécutées à Thèbes*, 1855. Salted paper print. Courtesy of the Oriental Institute of the University of Chicago

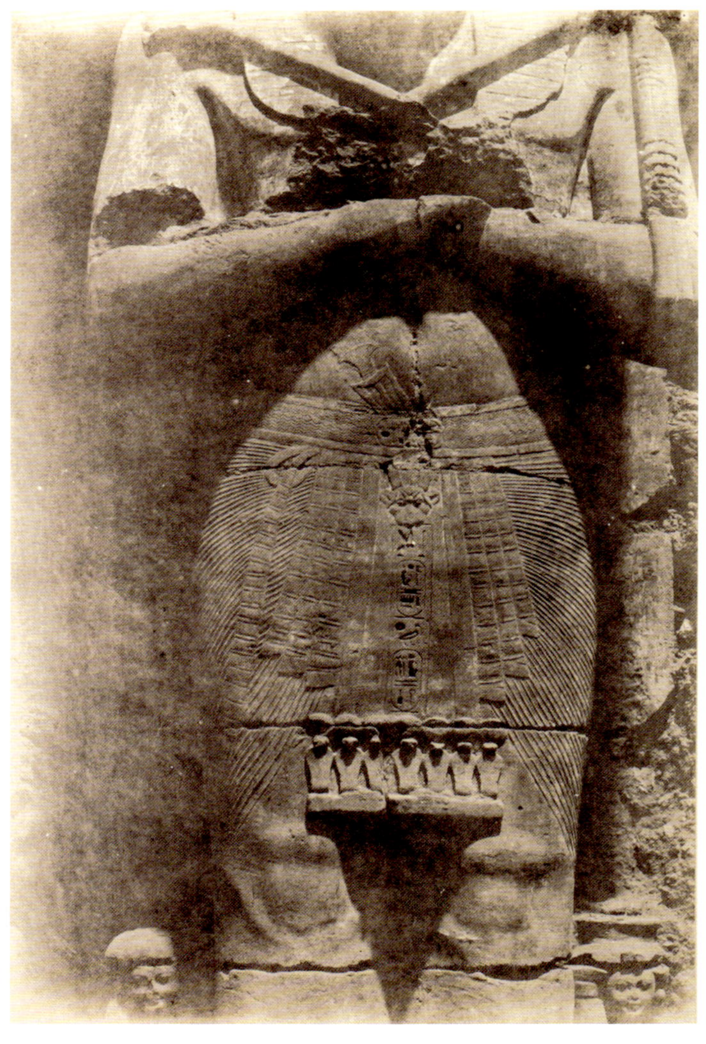

FIG. 17 *Palais de Médinet Habou. Colosse de Ramsès III. (Vêtement) (Mortuary Temple of Medinet Habu. Colossus of Ramesses III. Vestment).* Plate 4 of the album *Fouilles exécutées à Thèbes*, 1855. Salted paper print. Courtesy of the Oriental Institute of the University of Chicago

In addition to his excavations inside the temple, Greene cleared and recorded a large festival calendar inscribed on its southern outer wall. This calendar, which describes Egyptian rites and feasts, as well as lists of priestly offerings, is still considered one of the most important sources of information about Egyptian ritual practice, and is the longest single hieroglyphic text known.[94] In 1829, Champollion had transcribed the visible portions of the calendar, but only the upper third was accessible, beginning with line 553 (the text is inscribed vertically).[95] Greene was able to clear the whole calendar, nearly 275 feet in length, and transcribe the hieroglyphics with his camera.

Upon his return to Paris, Greene published the results of his excavations in a short tract titled *Fouilles exécutées à Thèbes dans l'année 1855: Textes hiéroglyphiques et documents inédits* (Excavations Executed at Thebes in 1855: Hieroglyphic Texts and Previously Unpublished Documents), illustrated with lithographs by Théodule Devéria based on Greene's photographs (fig. 18).[96] In his introduction, Greene thanked Rougé for his interest in Greene's work and for his study of and commentary on the hieroglyphics he transcribed. Though it is clear that Greene was up to date on the current scholarship and was well aware of the importance of the particular inscriptions at Medinet Habu, it seems that he was unable to actually read them independently and relied on his mentor and Champollion's scholarly heir Rougé for interpretation. The text blends Greene's voice describing the excavations and Rouge's textual explications.[97] At the end of the tract, Greene mentions that he also excavated and photographed two royal chapels at nearby Deir el-Bahri and planned to publish those results, but he never did.[98]

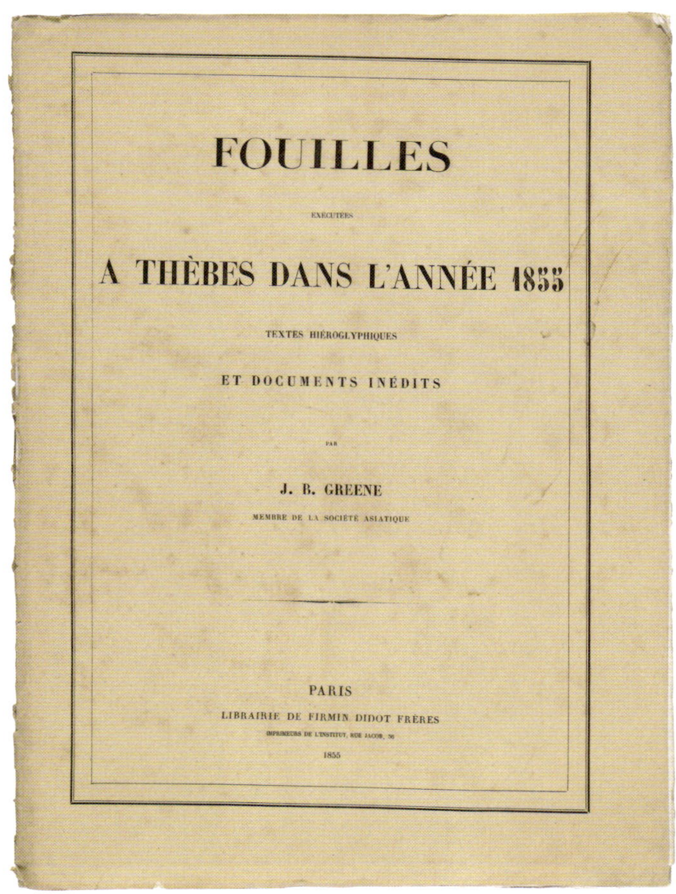
FOUILLES

EXÉCUTÉES

A THÈBES DANS L'ANNÉE 1855

TEXTES HIÉROGLYPHIQUES

ET DOCUMENTS INÉDITS

PAR

J. B. GREENE

MEMBRE DE LA SOCIÉTÉ ASIATIQUE

PARIS

LIBRAIRIE DE FIRMIN DIDOT FRÈRES

1855

FIG. 18 Cover of John Beasley Greene, *Fouilles exécutées à Thèbes dans l'année 1855* (Paris: Firmin Didot Frères, 1855). Private collection

Though Greene's work at Medinet Habu marked a substantial contribution to the decipherment of the texts at the site, photography did not solve all the epigraphers' problems. It did eliminate the need for copying the hieroglyphics by hand, as Arago had prophesied in 1839, but ultimately photographs could not replace drawings altogether. The Epigraphic Survey of the Oriental Institute of the University of Chicago, whose work, begun in 1924 (and still ongoing), resulted in the publication of the entire corpus of inscriptions at Medinet Habu, found that using photography and drawing in combination exploited the advantages of both media: "This facsimile combines three things: the speed and accuracy of the camera, the skill and clearness of the artist, and finally the reading ability of the epigrapher, who sees much which is not recorded by camera or artist."[99]

EGYPT

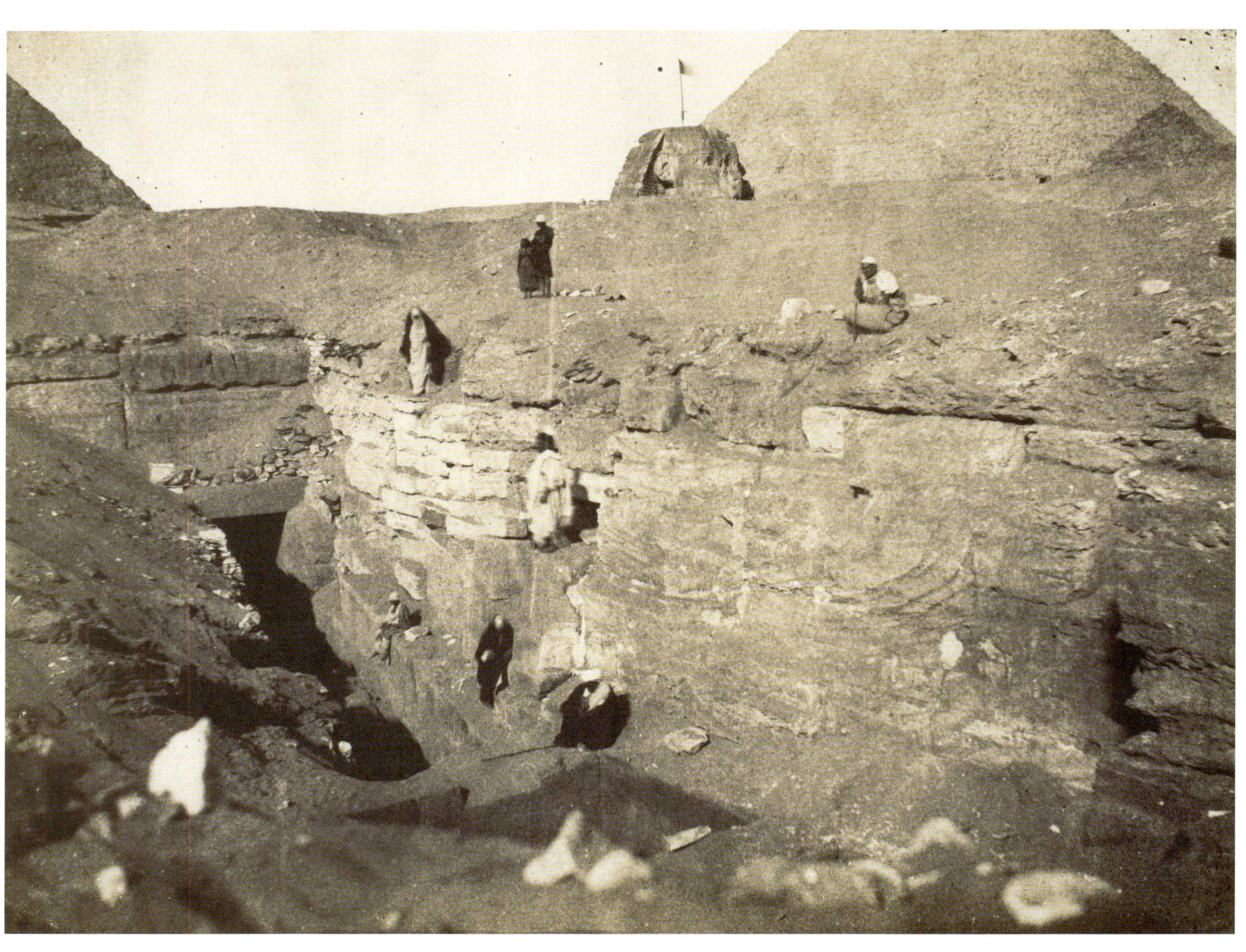

PLATE 7 *Pyramides de Giseh. (Travaux de Mr. Mariette). Fouille à la gauche du Sphinx (Pyramids of Giza. [Mr. Mariette's site]. Excavation to the left of the Sphinx)*, 1853

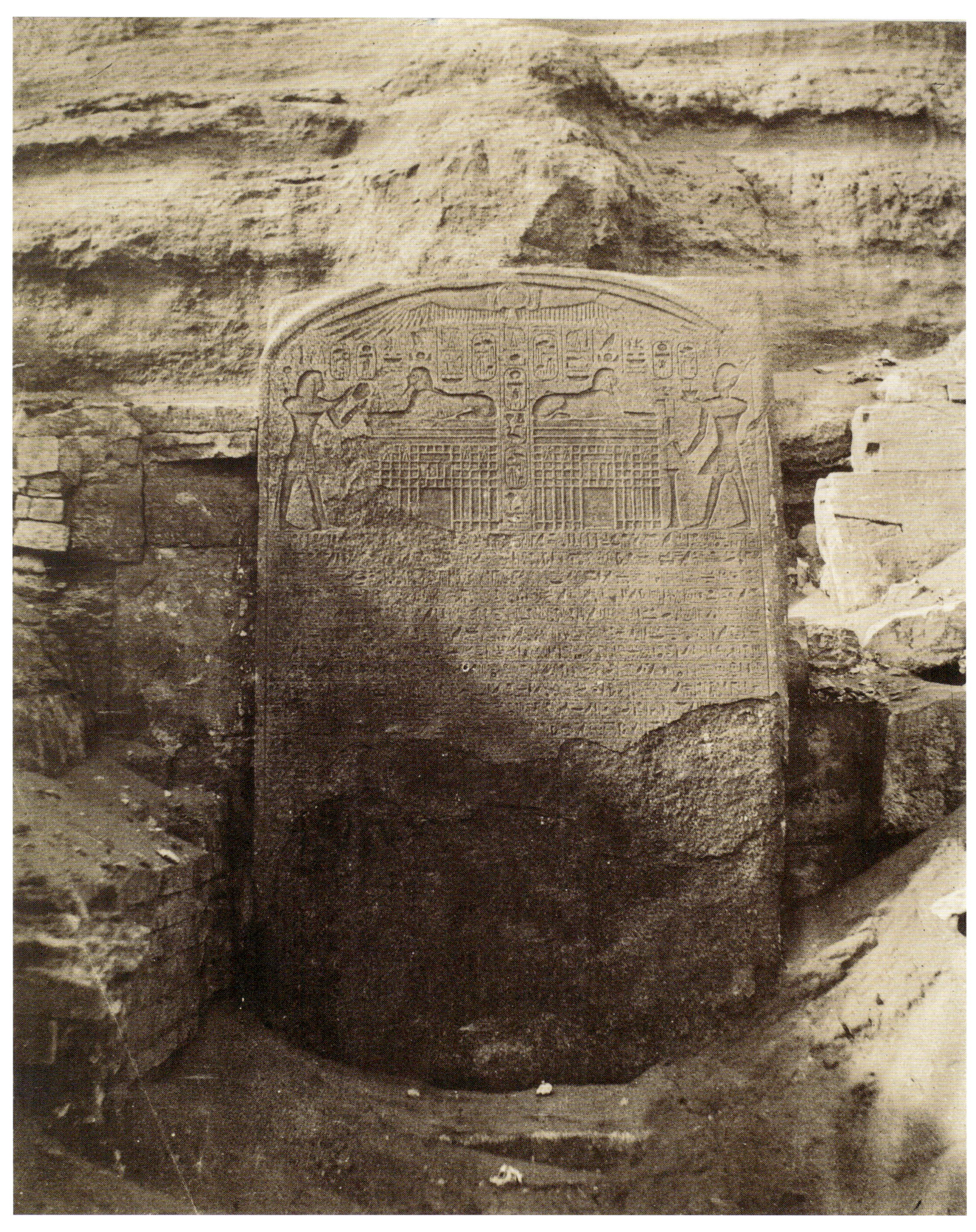

PLATE 8 *Pyramides de Giseh (Travaux de Mr. Mariette). Stèle au bas du portail du Sphinx deblayée par Mr. Mariette, décembre 1853 (Pyramids of Giza [Mr. Mariette's site]. Stela at the base of the Sphinx excavated by Mr. Mariette, December 1853)*, 1853

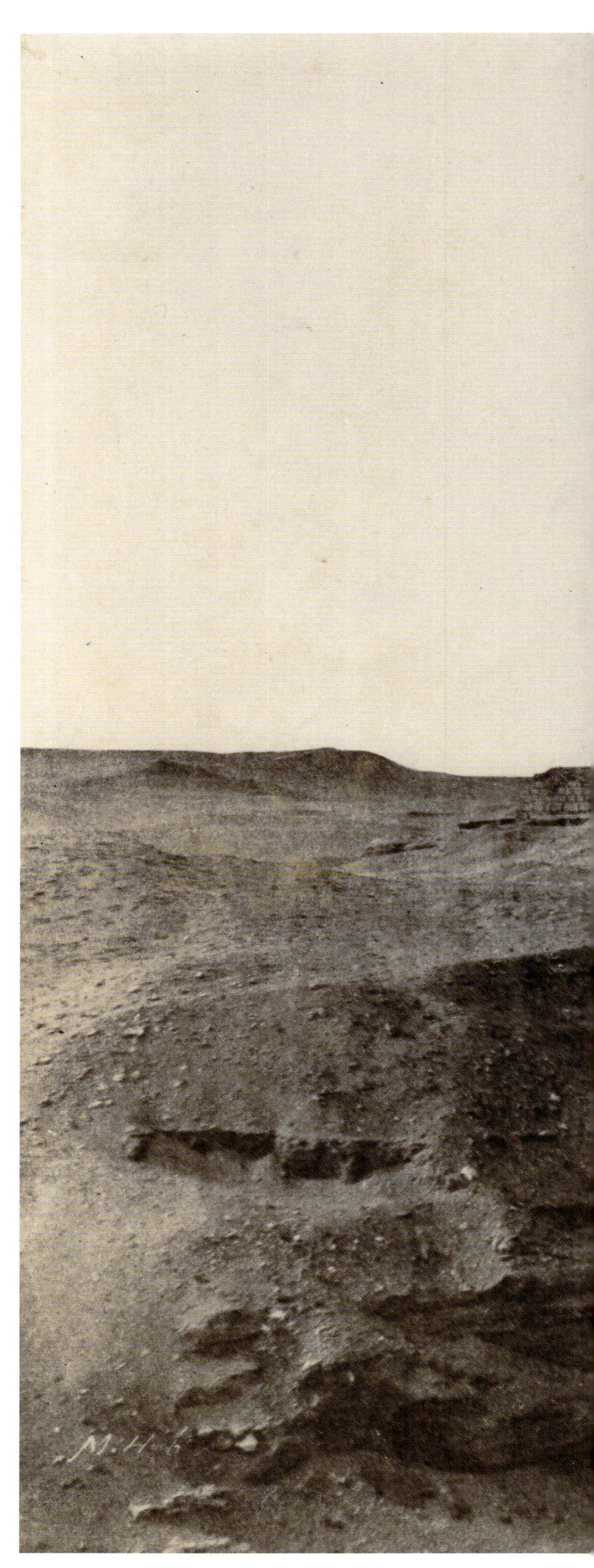

PLATE 9 *Giseh. Sphinx (Giza. Sphinx)*, 1853–54

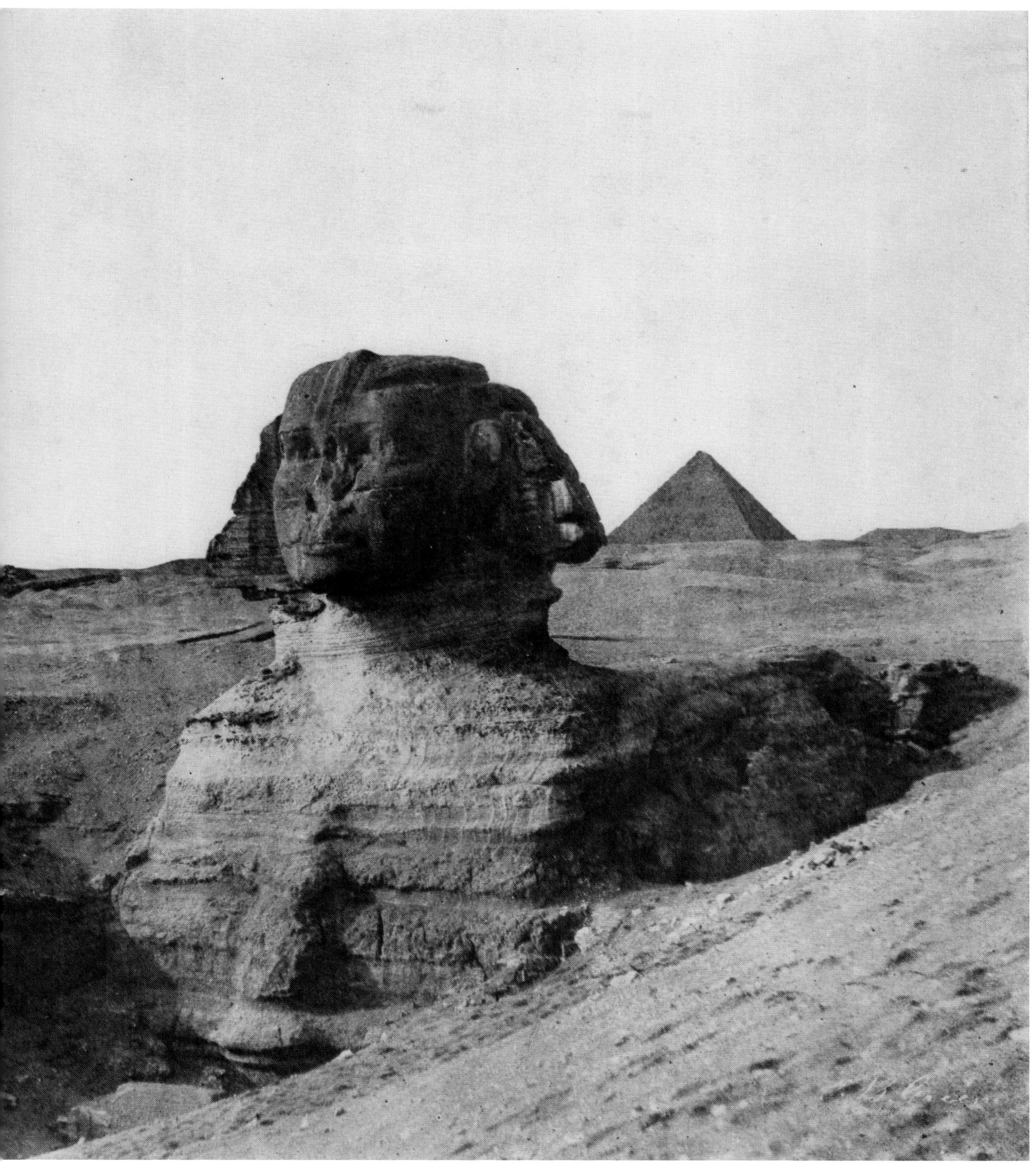

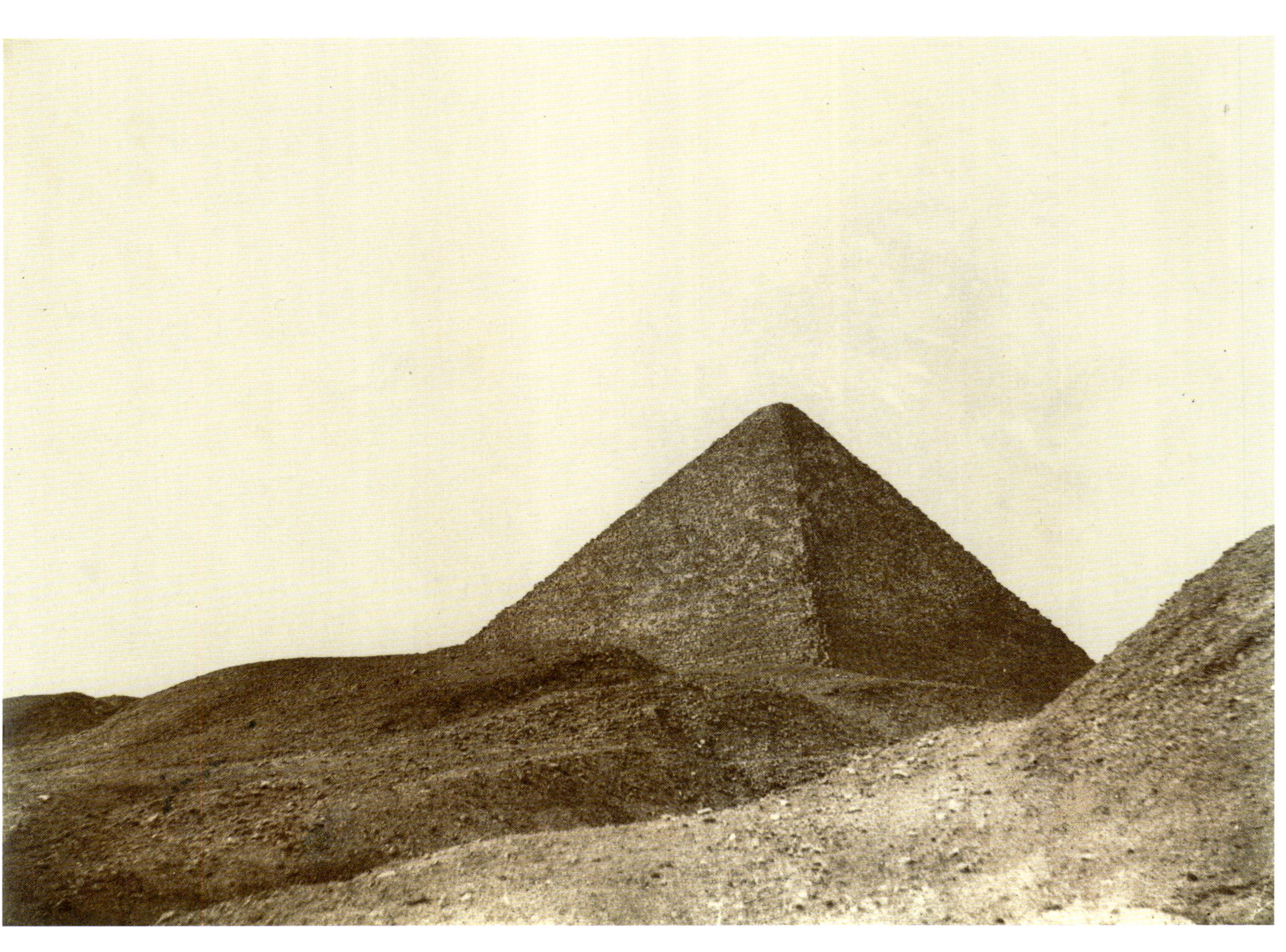

PLATE 10 *Giseh. Pyramide de Chéops (Giza. Pyramid of Cheops, or Khufu)*, 1853–54

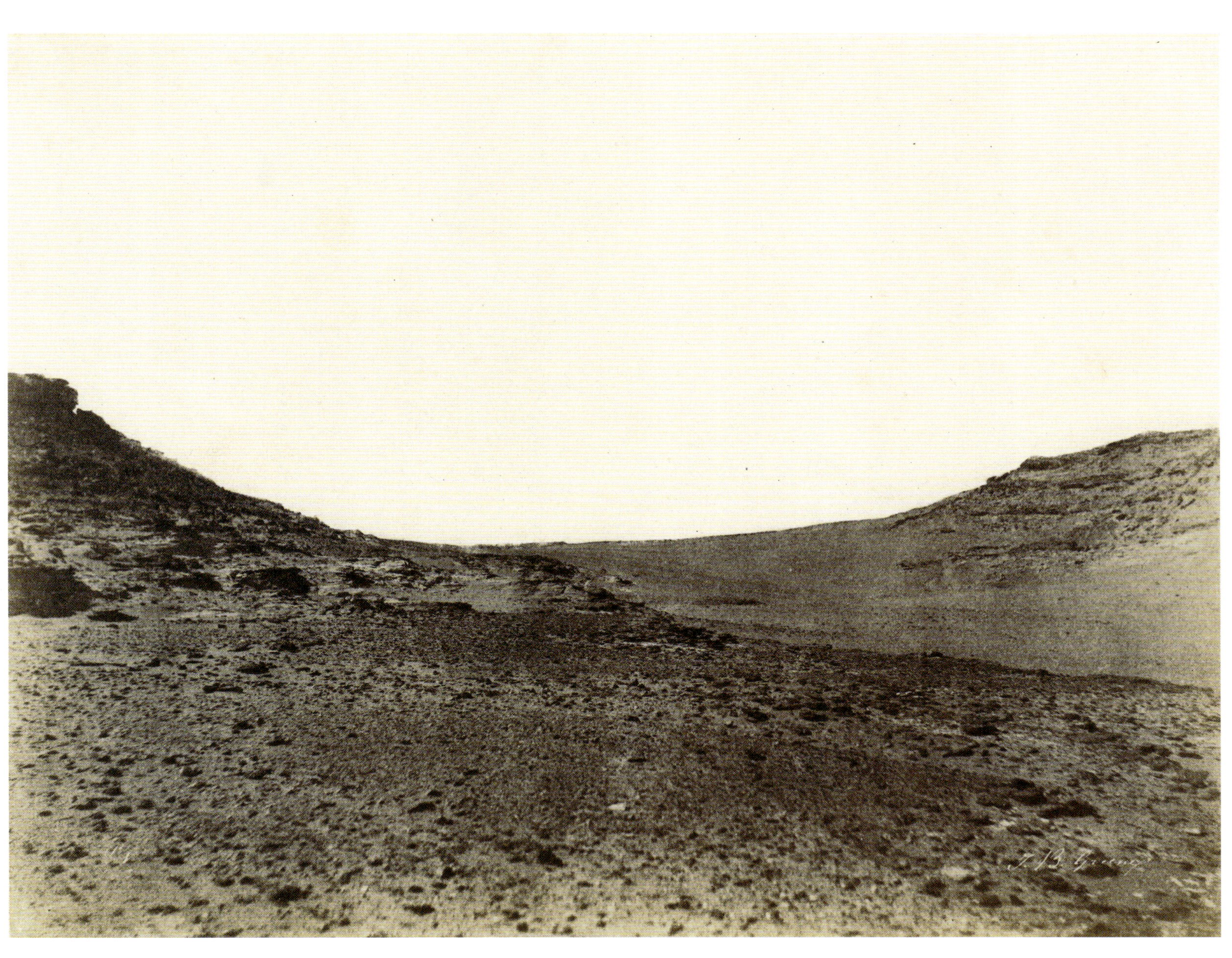

PLATE 11 *Études de terrain près de Gebel Abousir, 2e cataracte (Studies of the landscape near Gebel Abusir, Second Cataract)*, 1854

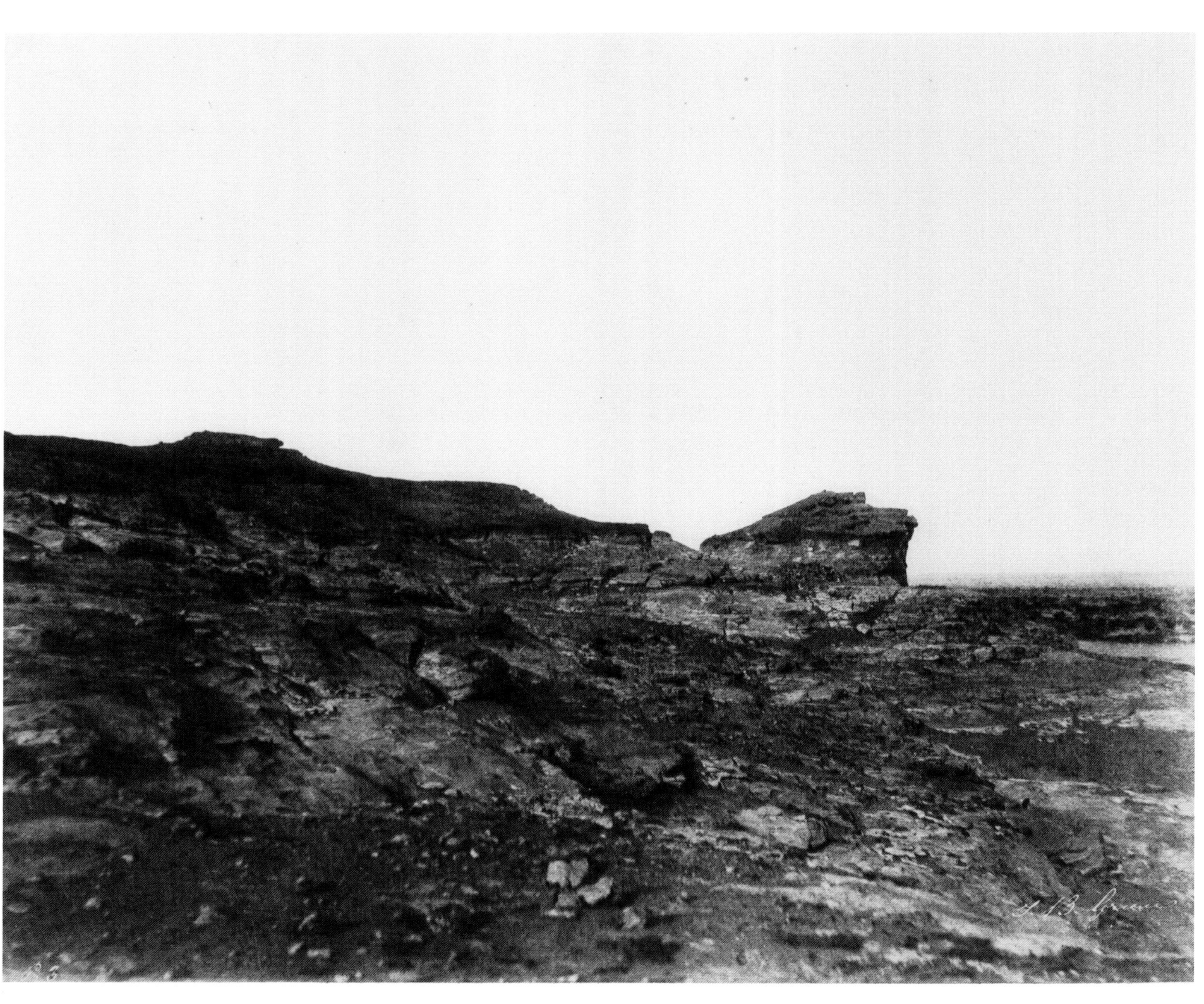

PLATE 12 *Études de terrain près de Gebel Abousir; 2e cataracte (Studies of the landscape near Gebel Abusir, Second Cataract)*, 1854

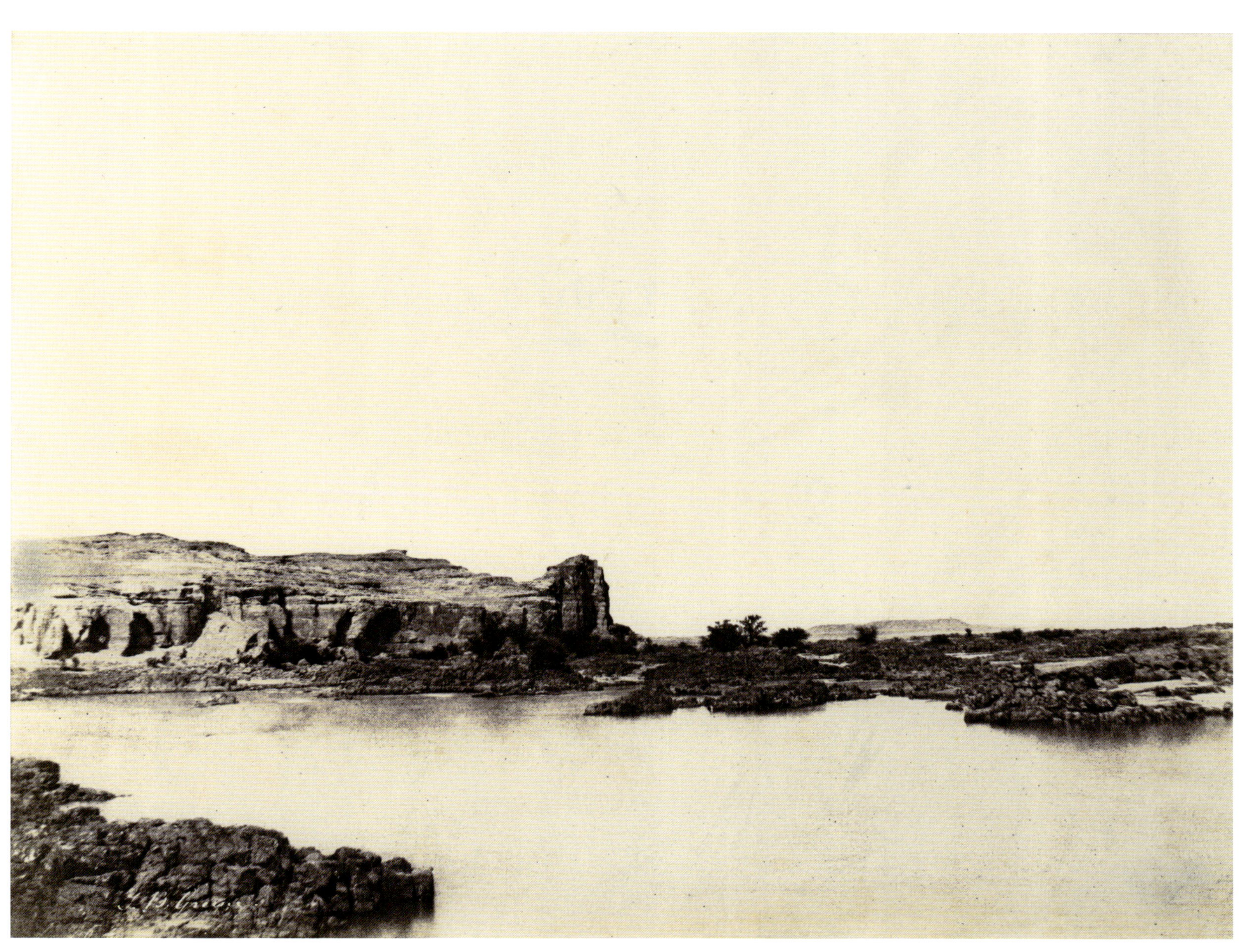

PLATE 13 *Seconde Cataracte, au dessus de Gebel Abousir (Second Cataract, above Gebel Abusir)*, 1854

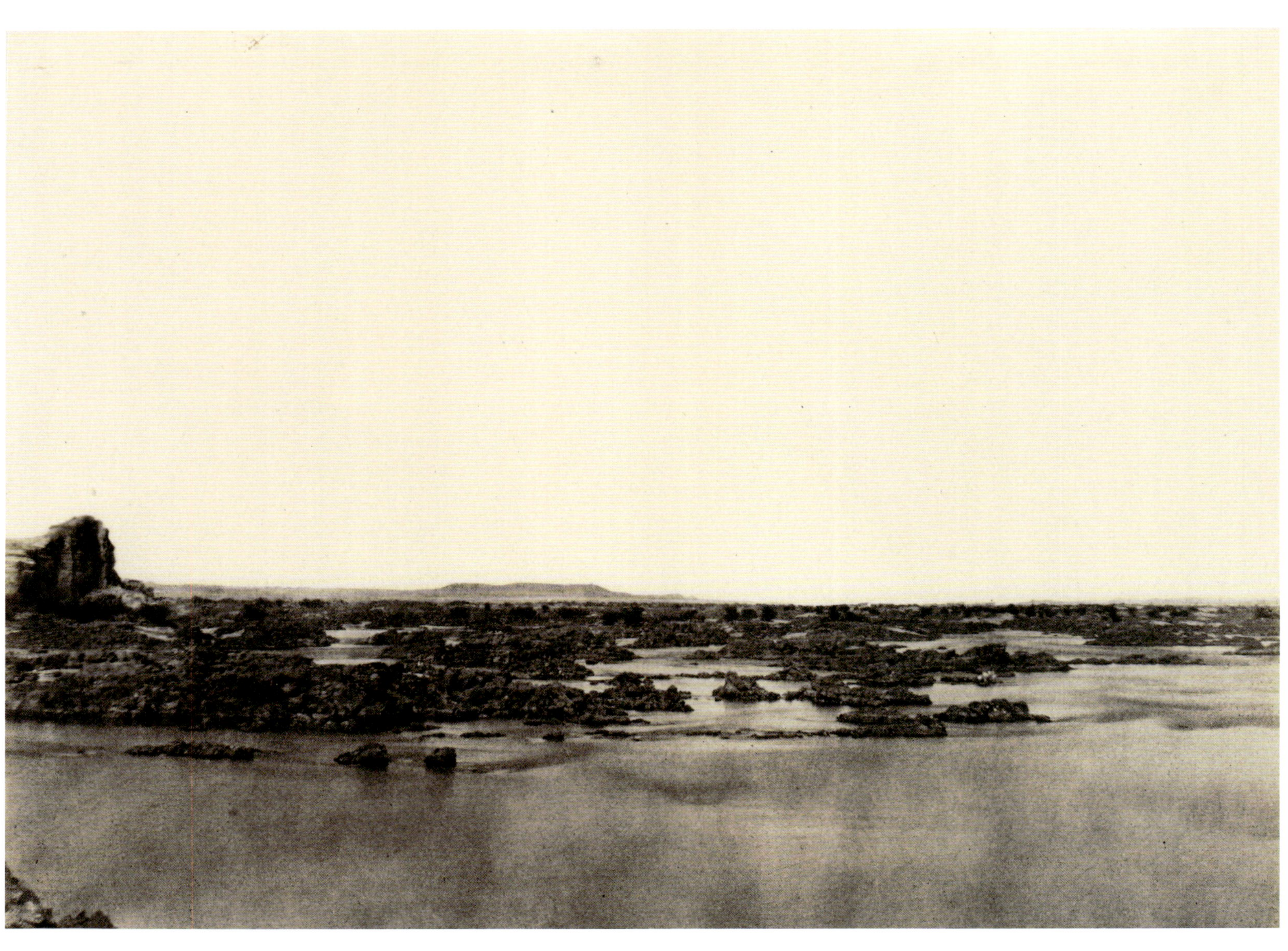

PLATE 14 *Seconde Cataracte (Second Cataract)*, 1854

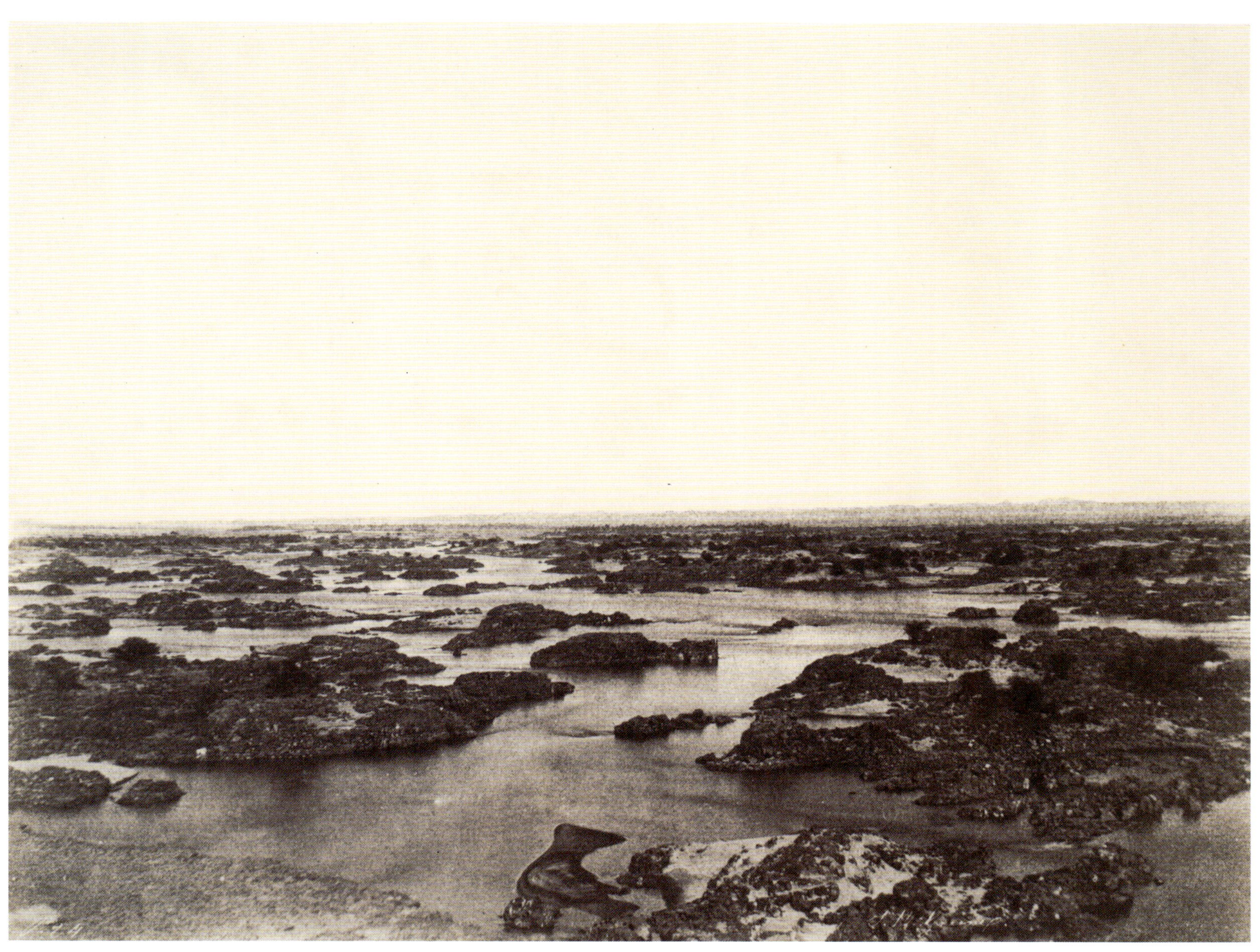

PLATE 15 *Seconde Cataracte (Second Cataract)*, 1854

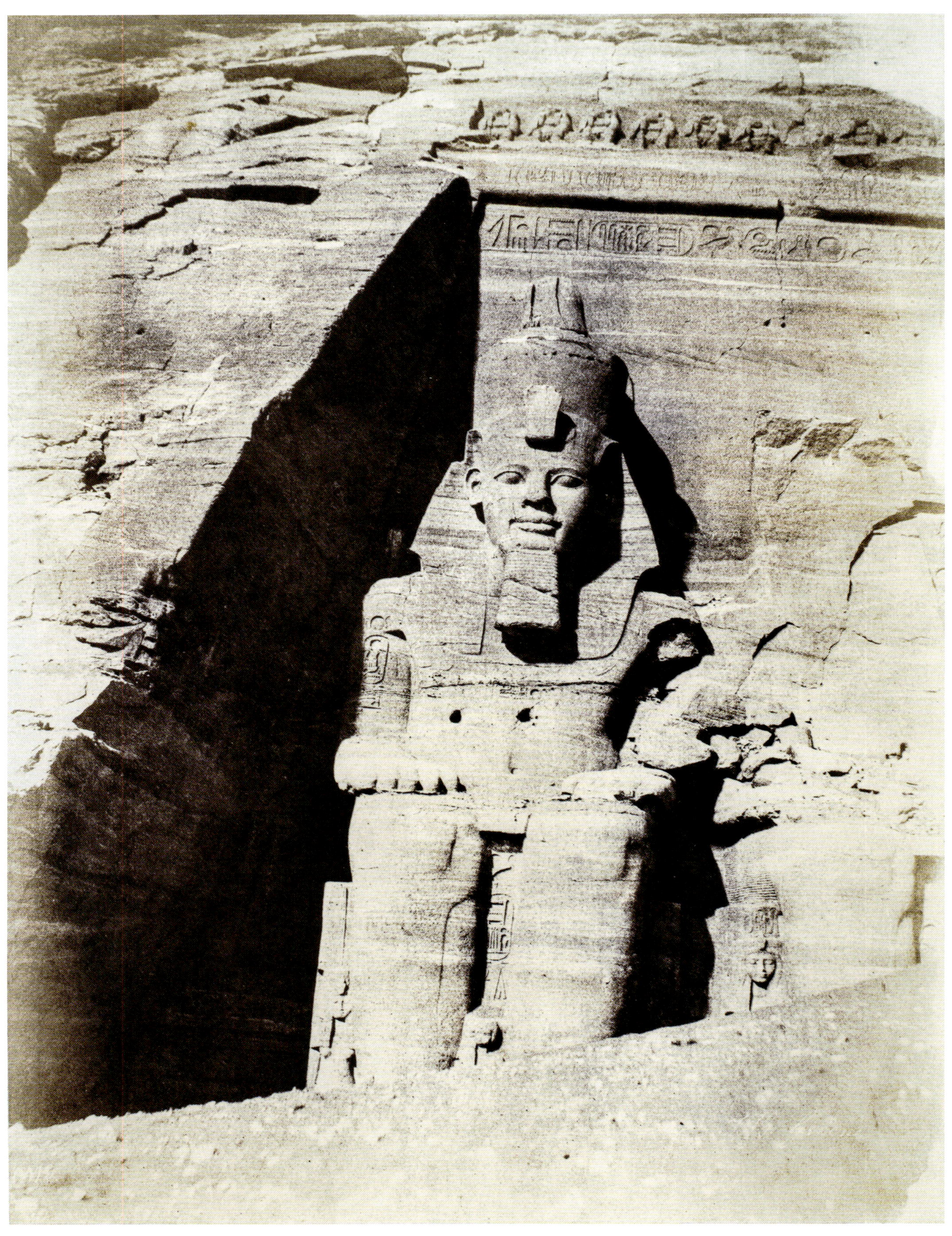

PLATE 16 *Ibsamboul. Colosse de l'Est (Abu Simbel. Eastern colossus)*, 1854

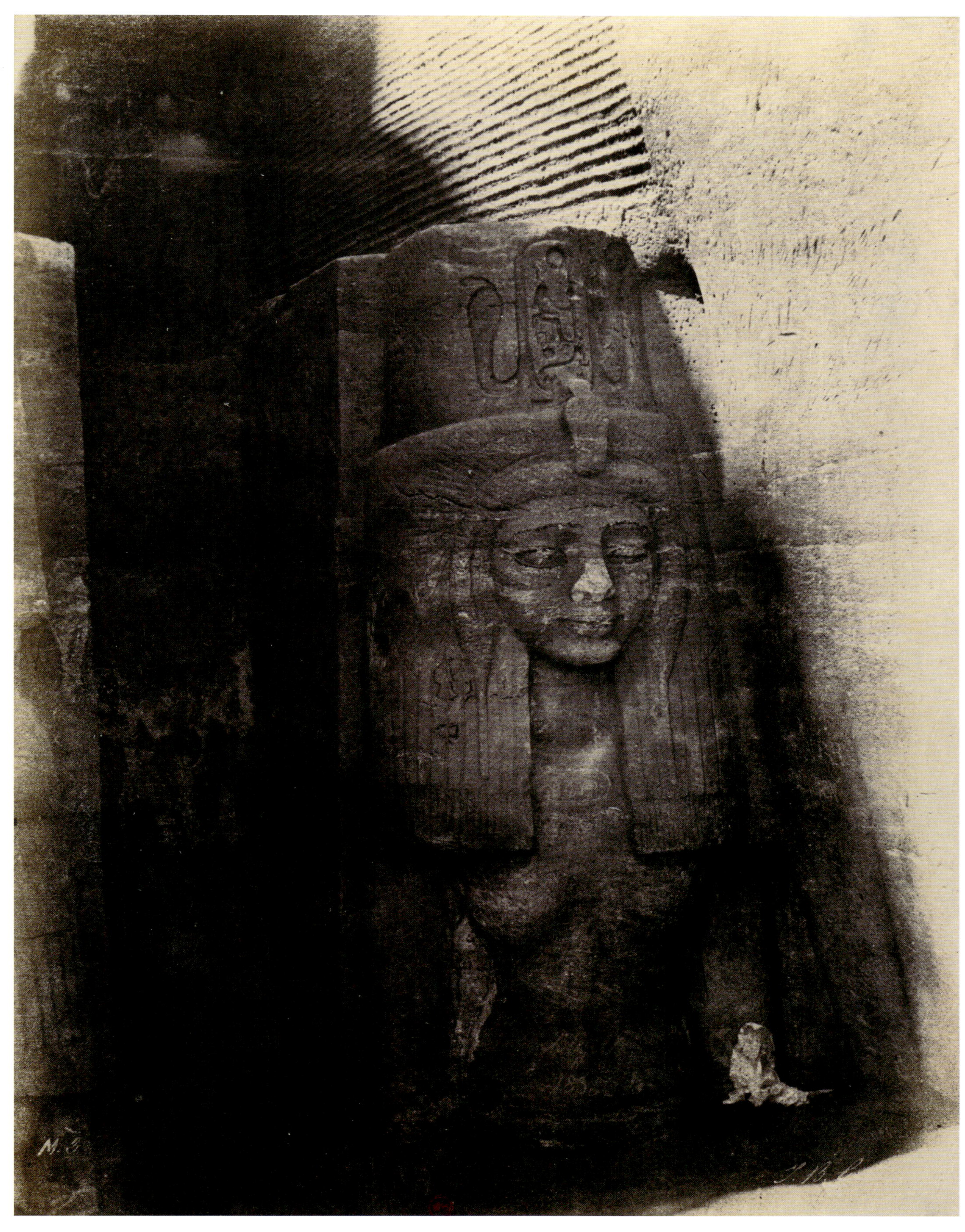

PLATE 17 *Ibsamboul. Statue de femme (Abu Simbel. Statue of a woman)*, 1854

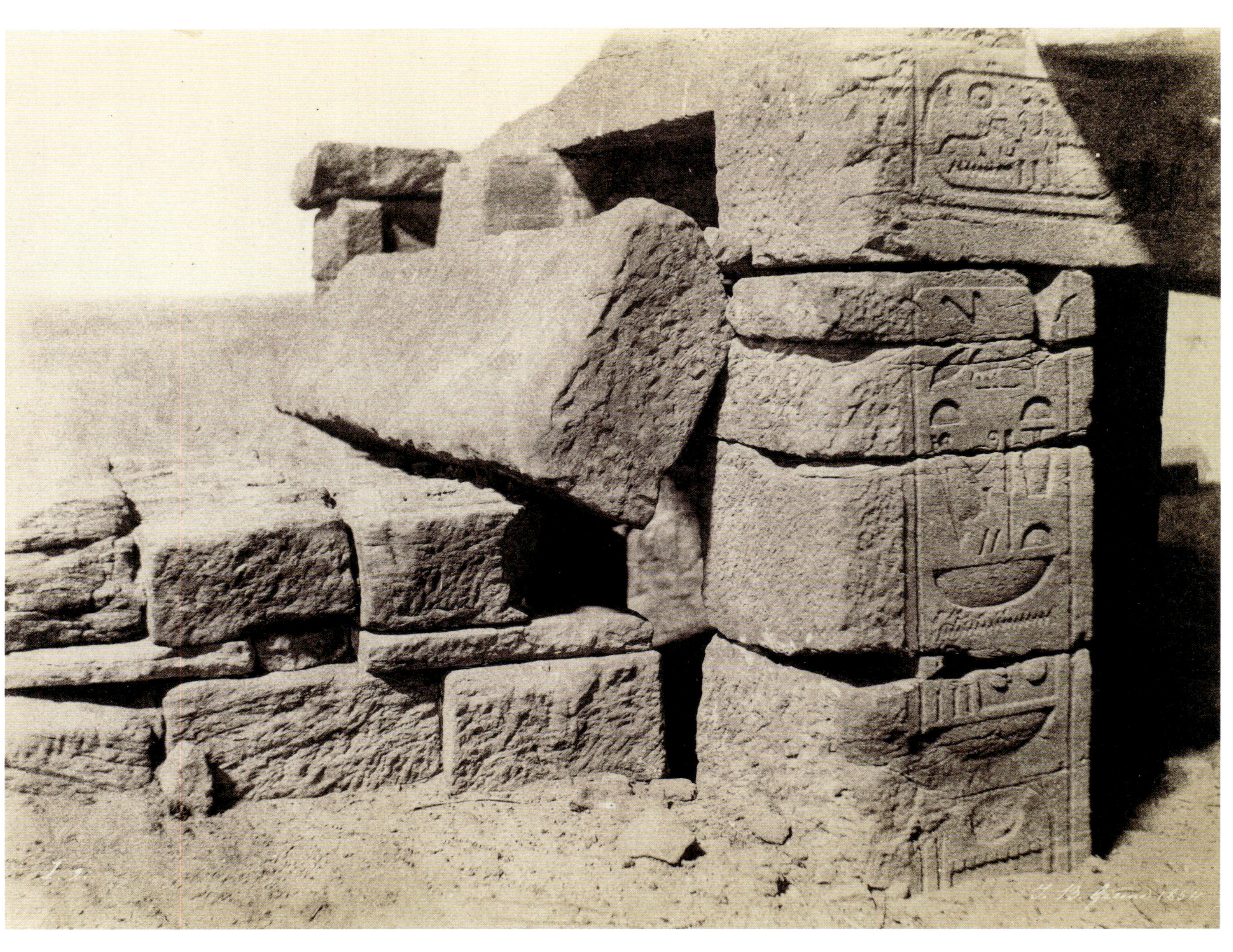

PLATE 18 *Amada. Pilier du temple (Amada. Temple pillar)*, 1854

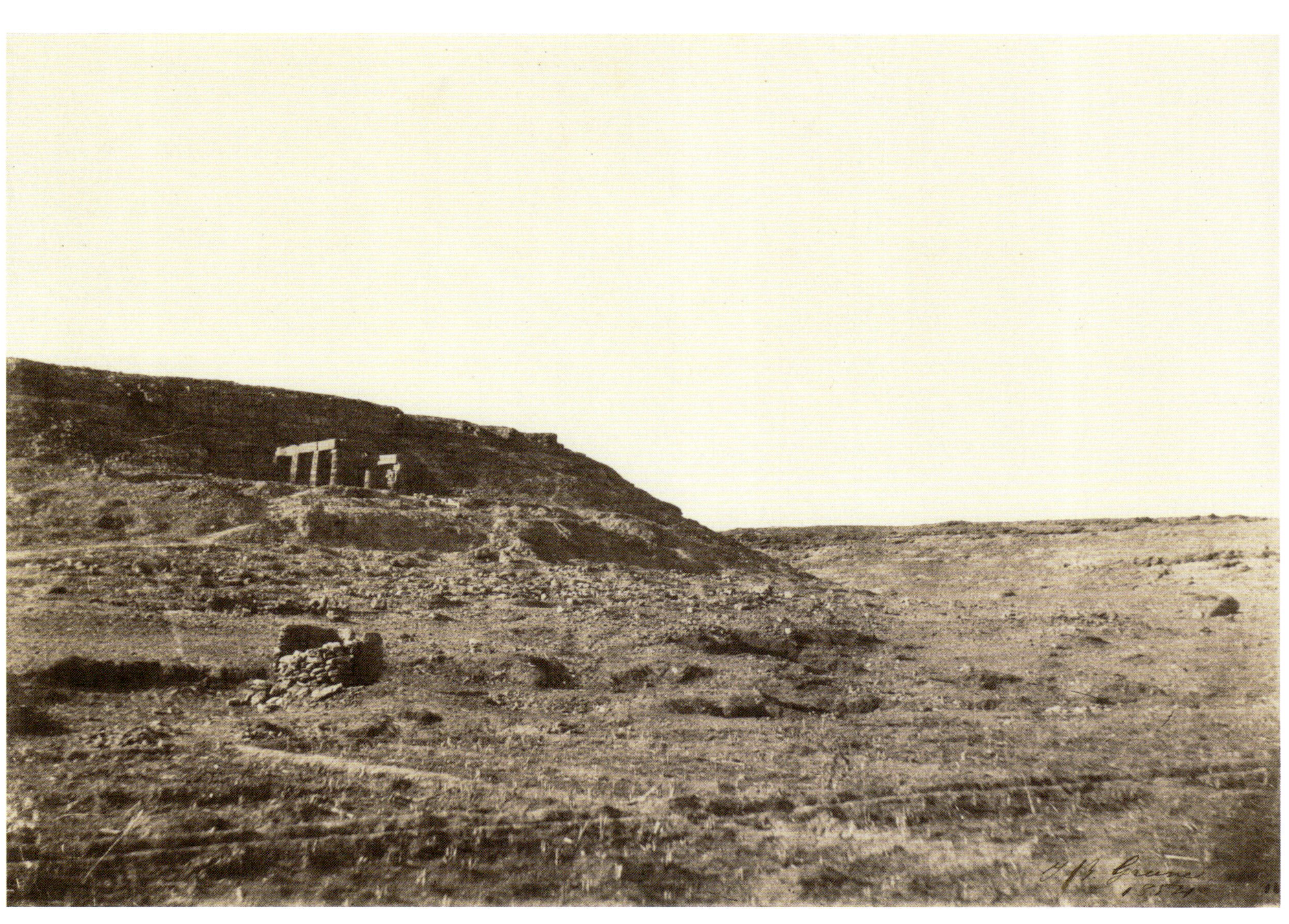

PLATE 19 *Montagne de Ghirché (Mountain of Wadi Gyrshe)*, 1854

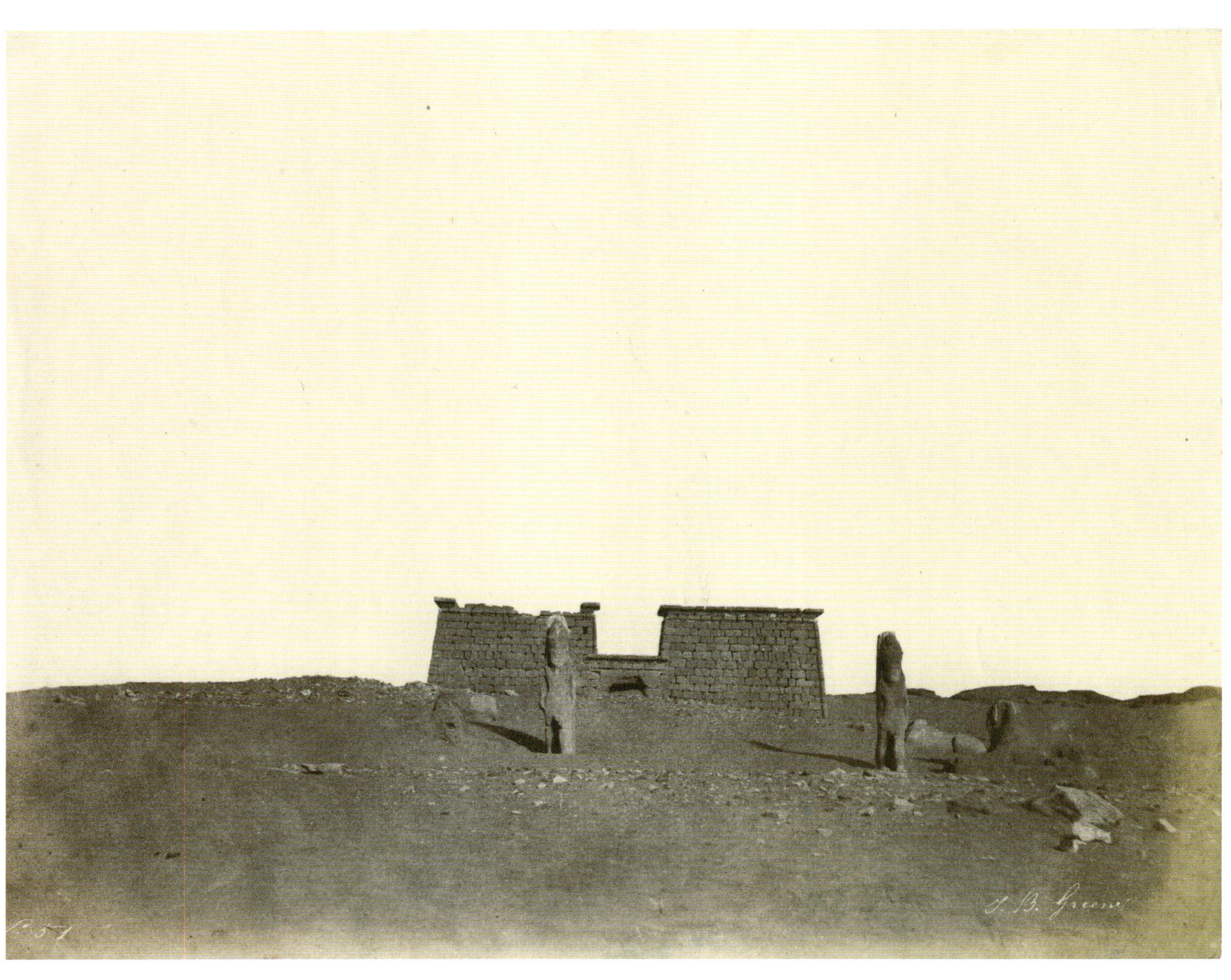

PLATE 20 *Ouadi Esseboua. Temple (Wadi es-Sebua. Temple)*, 1854

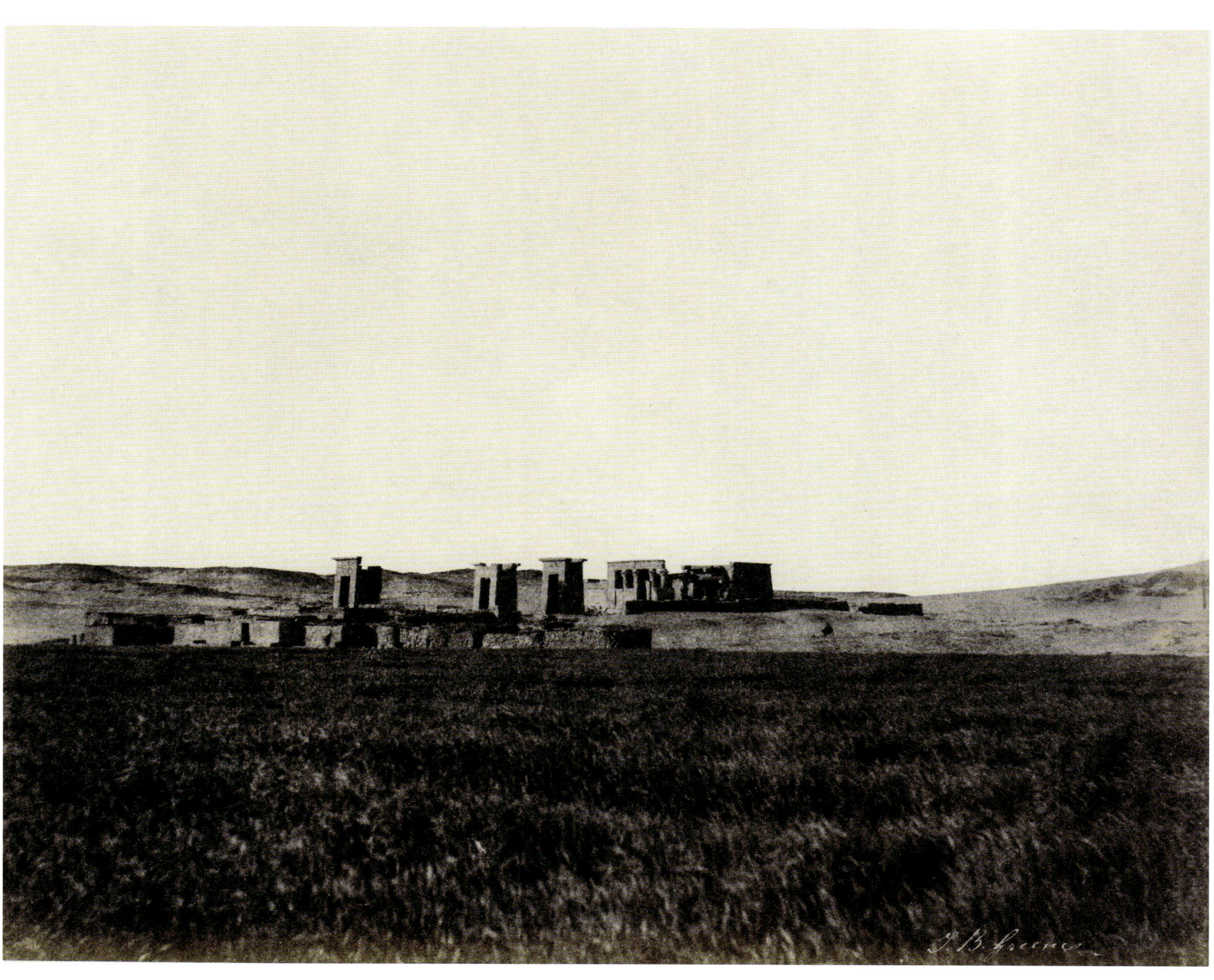

PLATE 21 *Deboud. Temple (Debod. Temple)*, 1854

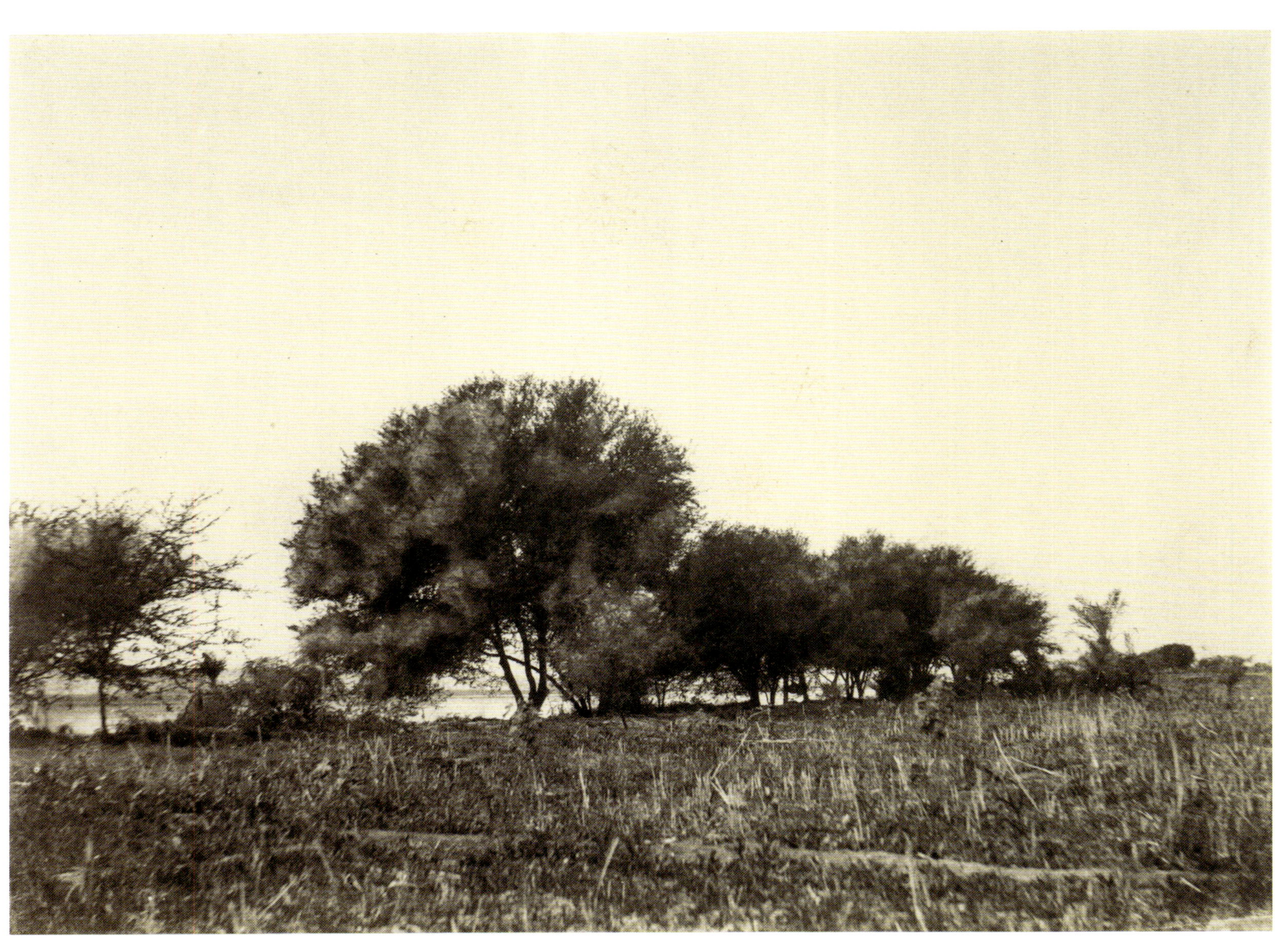

PLATE 22 *Étude de gommiers (Study of gum trees)*, 1854

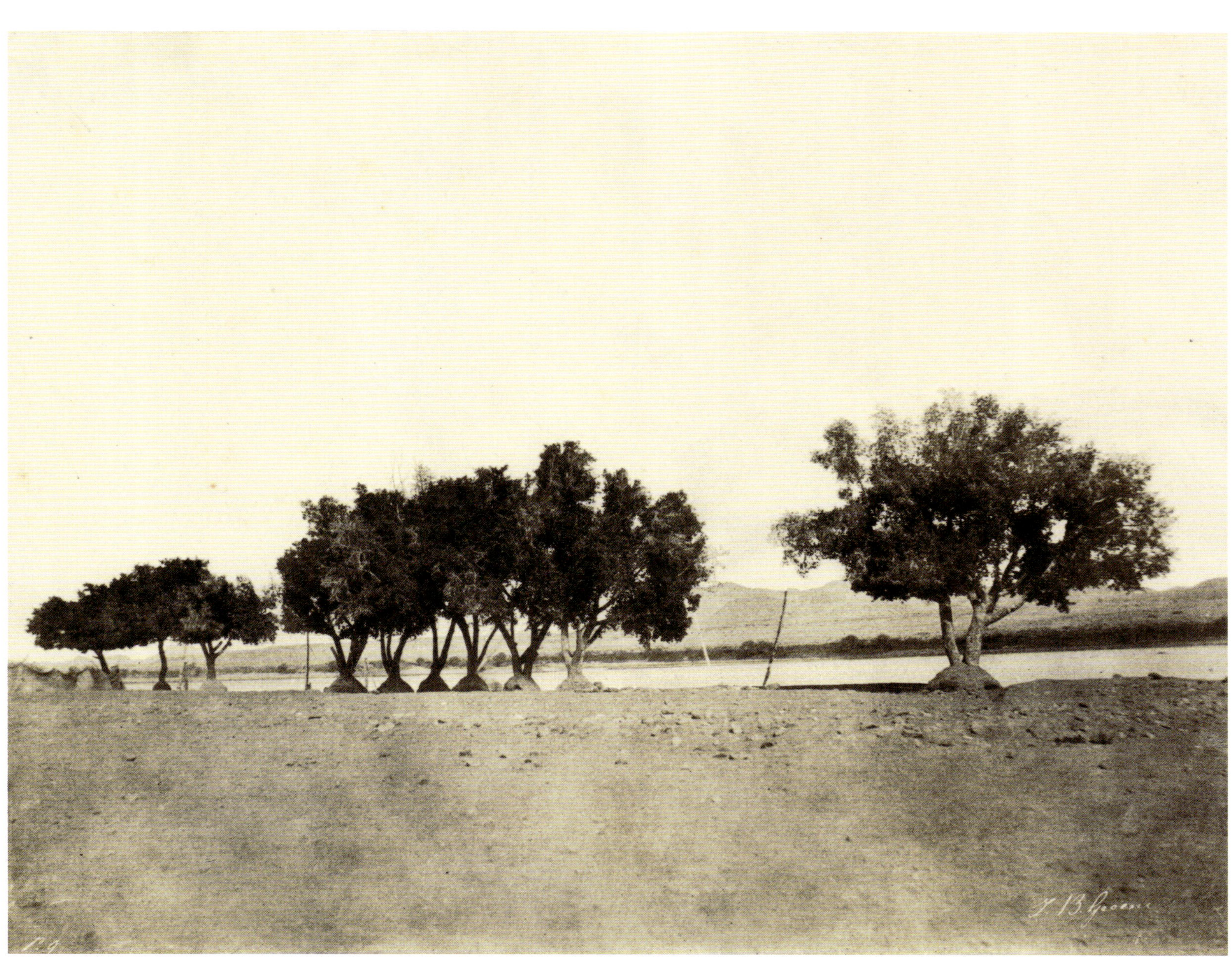

PLATE 23 *Étude de sycomores, Korosko (Study of sycamores, Korosko)*, 1854

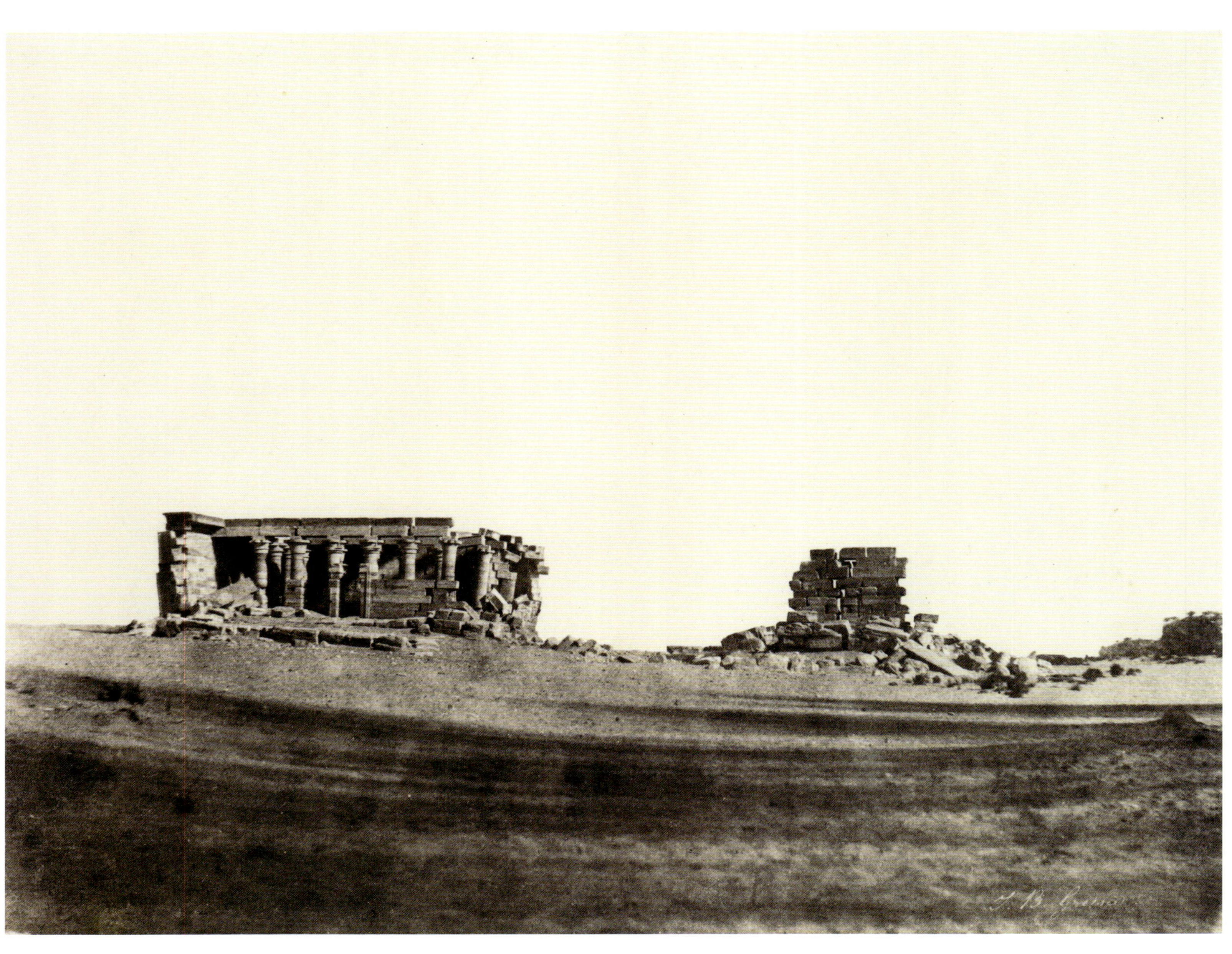

PLATE 24 *Meharraka. Temple (Meharraka. Temple)*, 1854

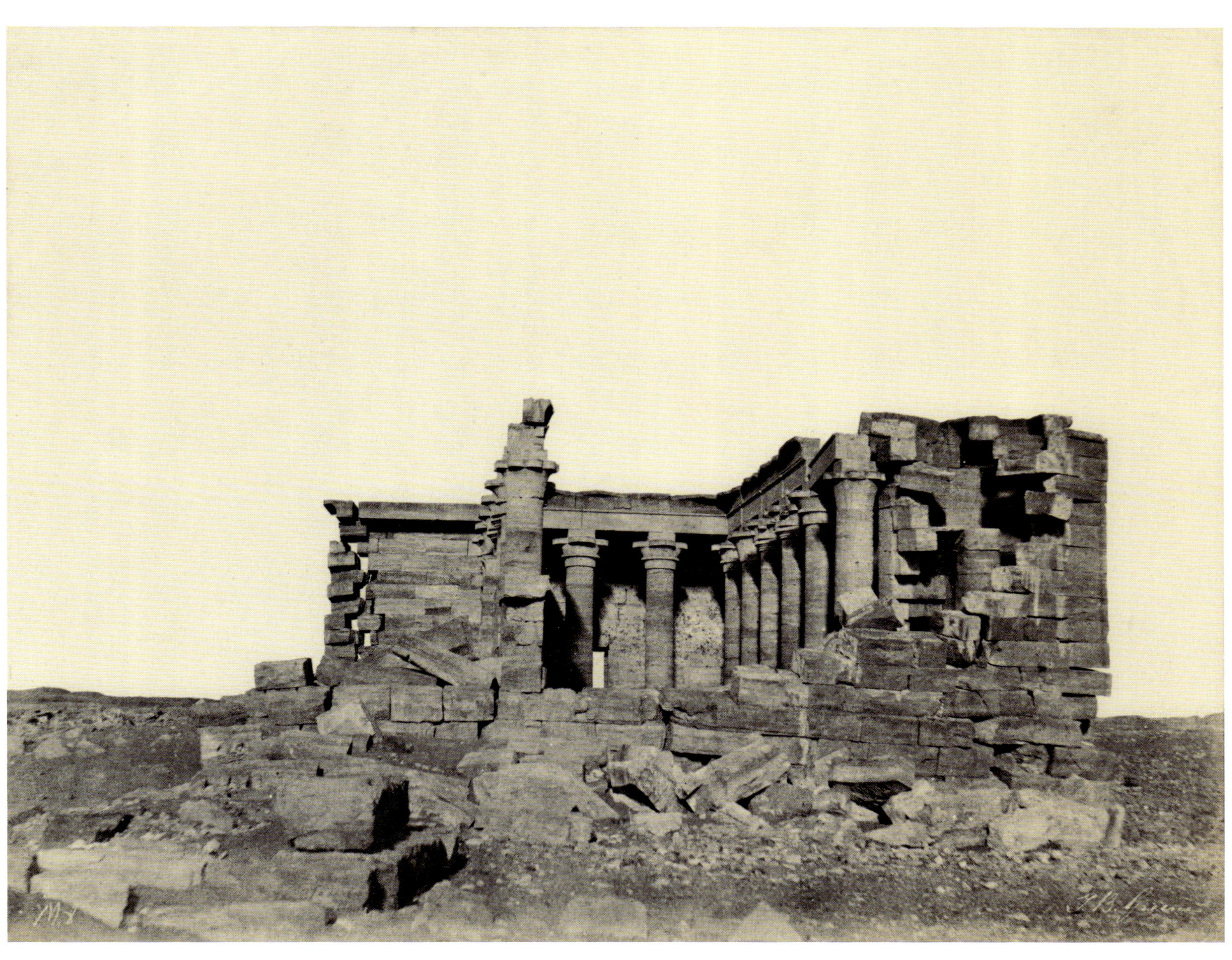

PLATE 25 *Meharraka. Temple (Meharraka. Temple)*, 1854

PLATE 26 *Dakkeh. Salle méridionale du Temple, No. 6 (Dakka. Southern chamber of the temple, No. 6)*, 1854

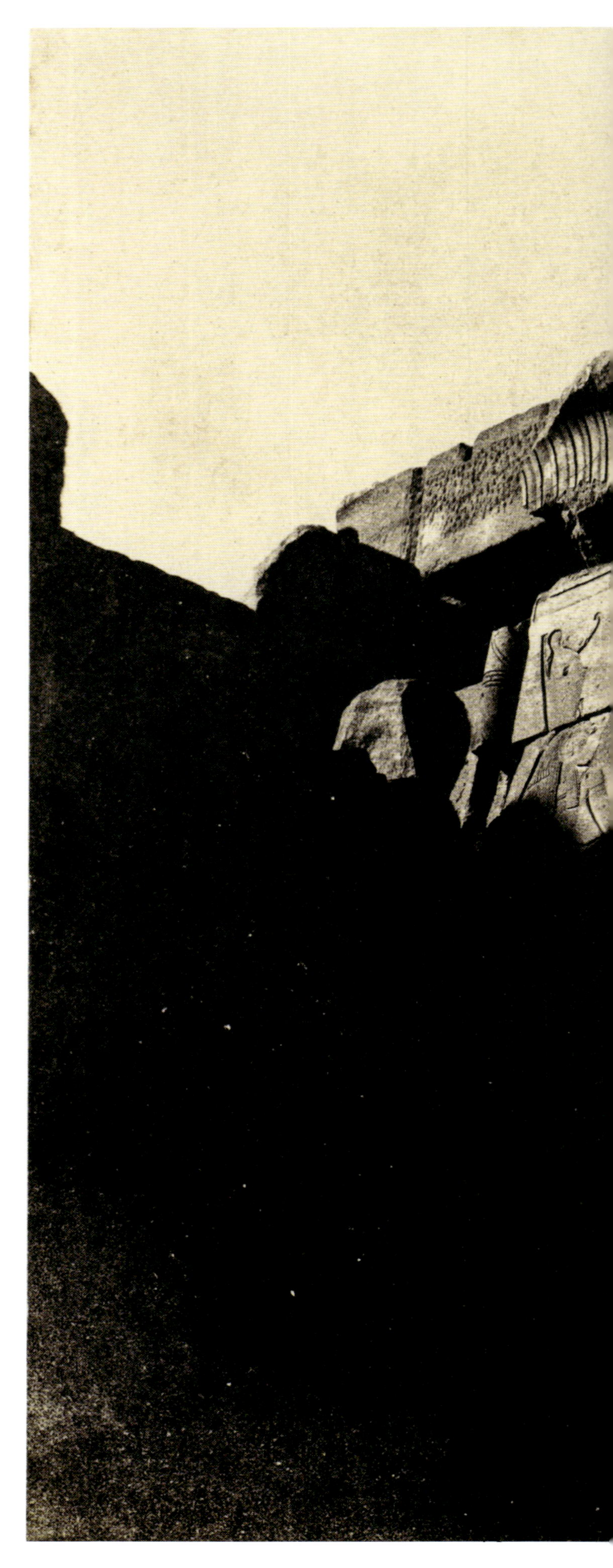

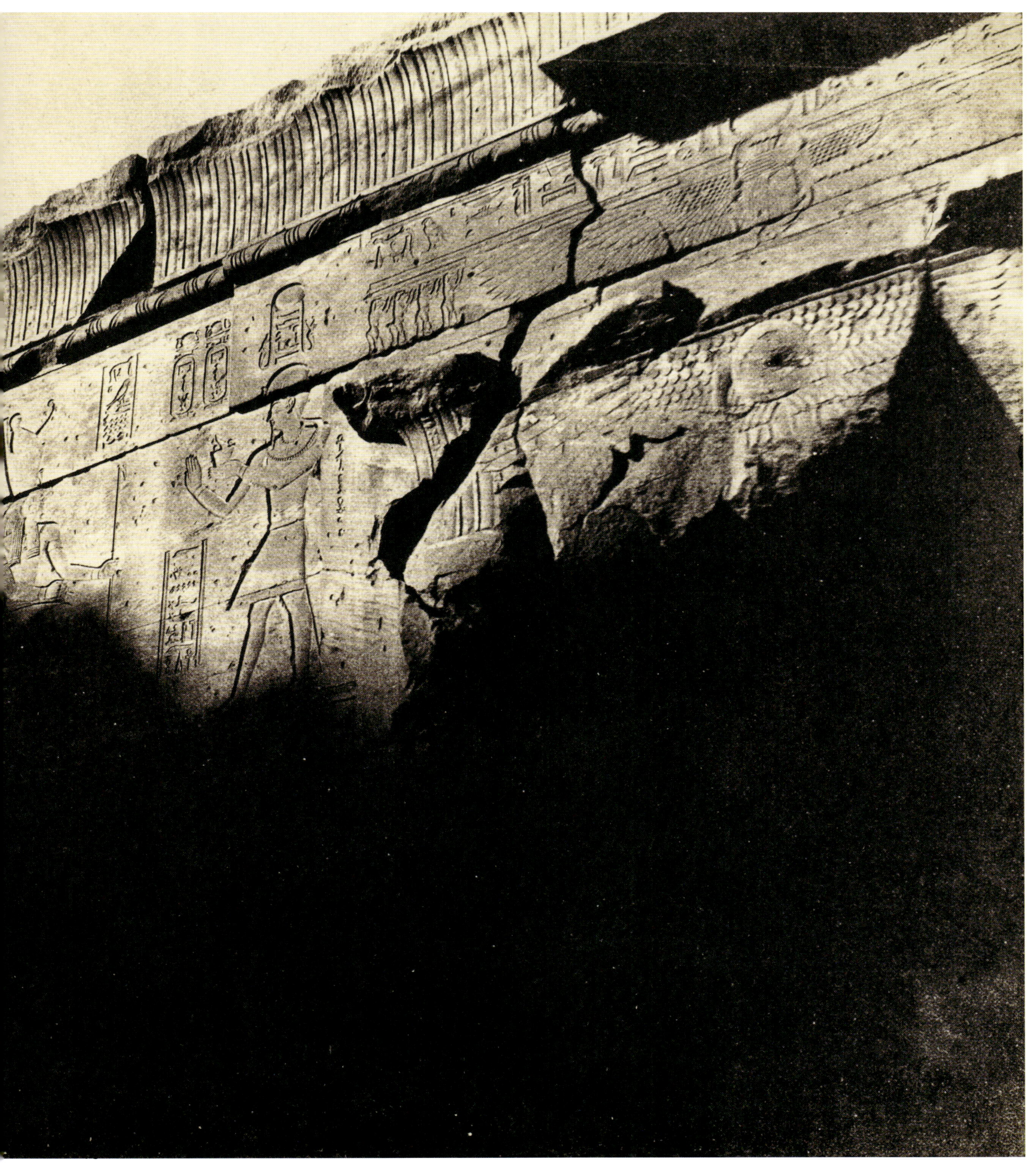

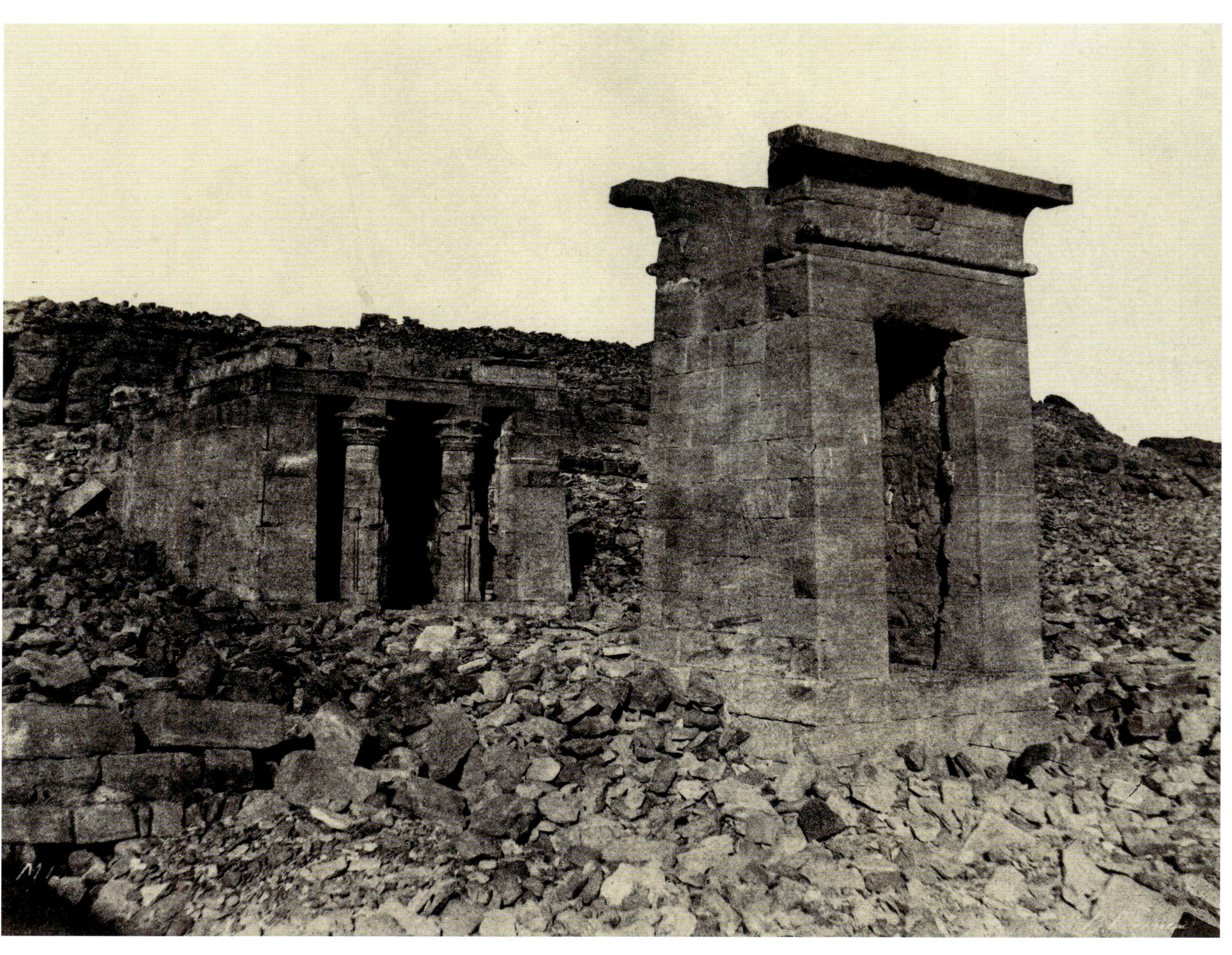

PLATE 27 *Dandour. Temple 1 (Dendur. Temple 1)*, 1854

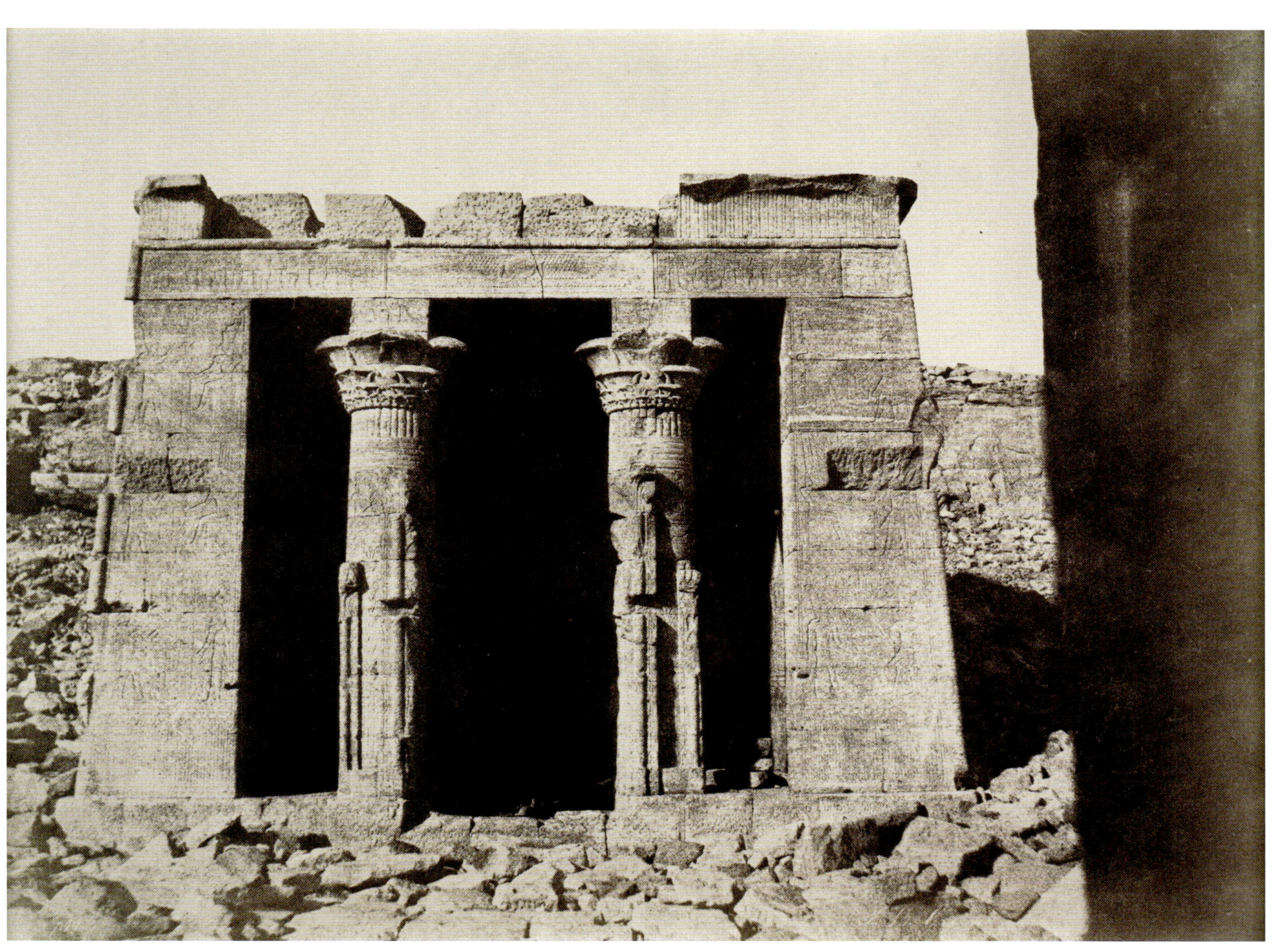

PLATE 28 *Dandour. Temple 2 (Dendur. Temple 2)*, 1854

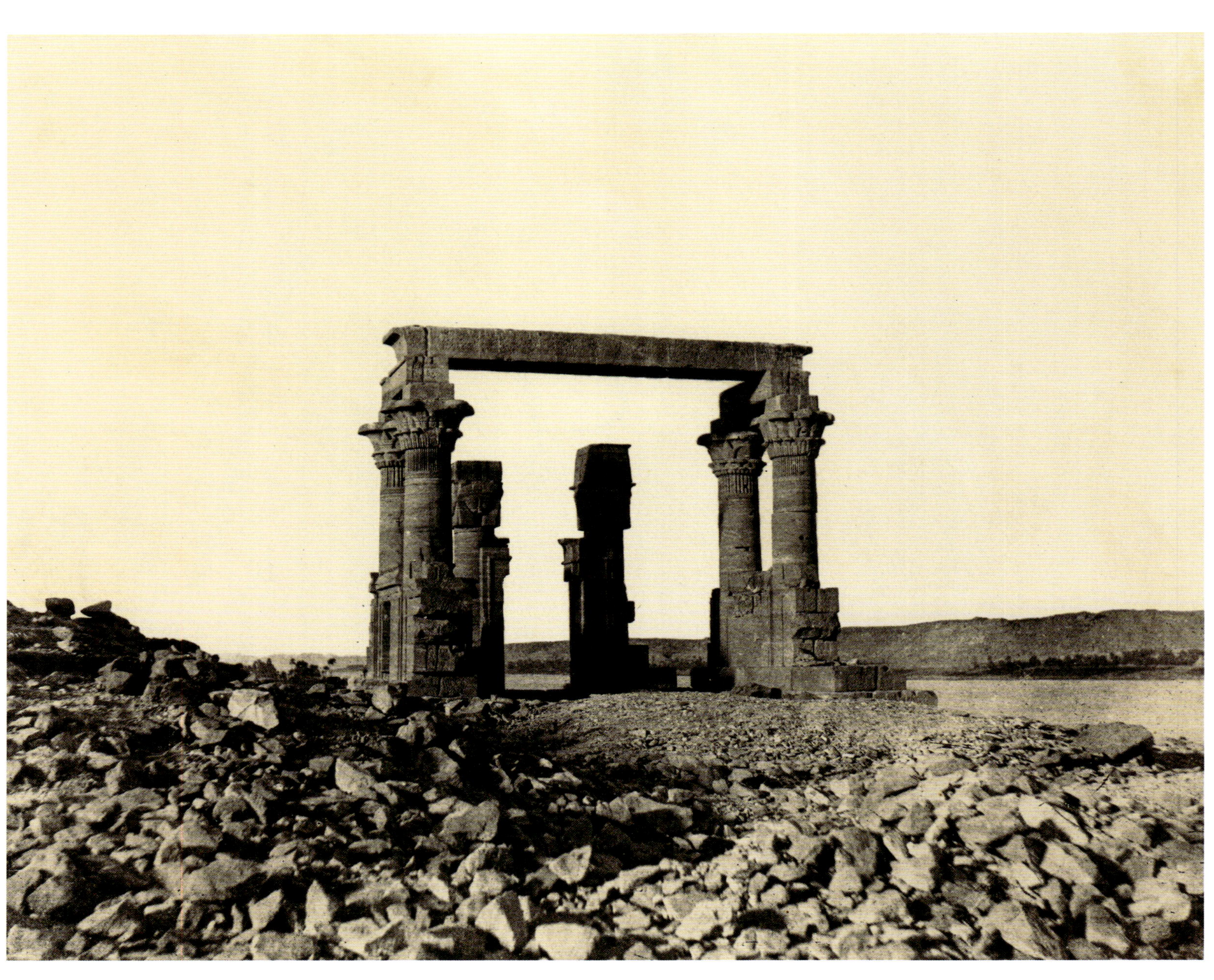

PLATE 29 *Qartas. Temple (Quertassi. Temple)*, 1854

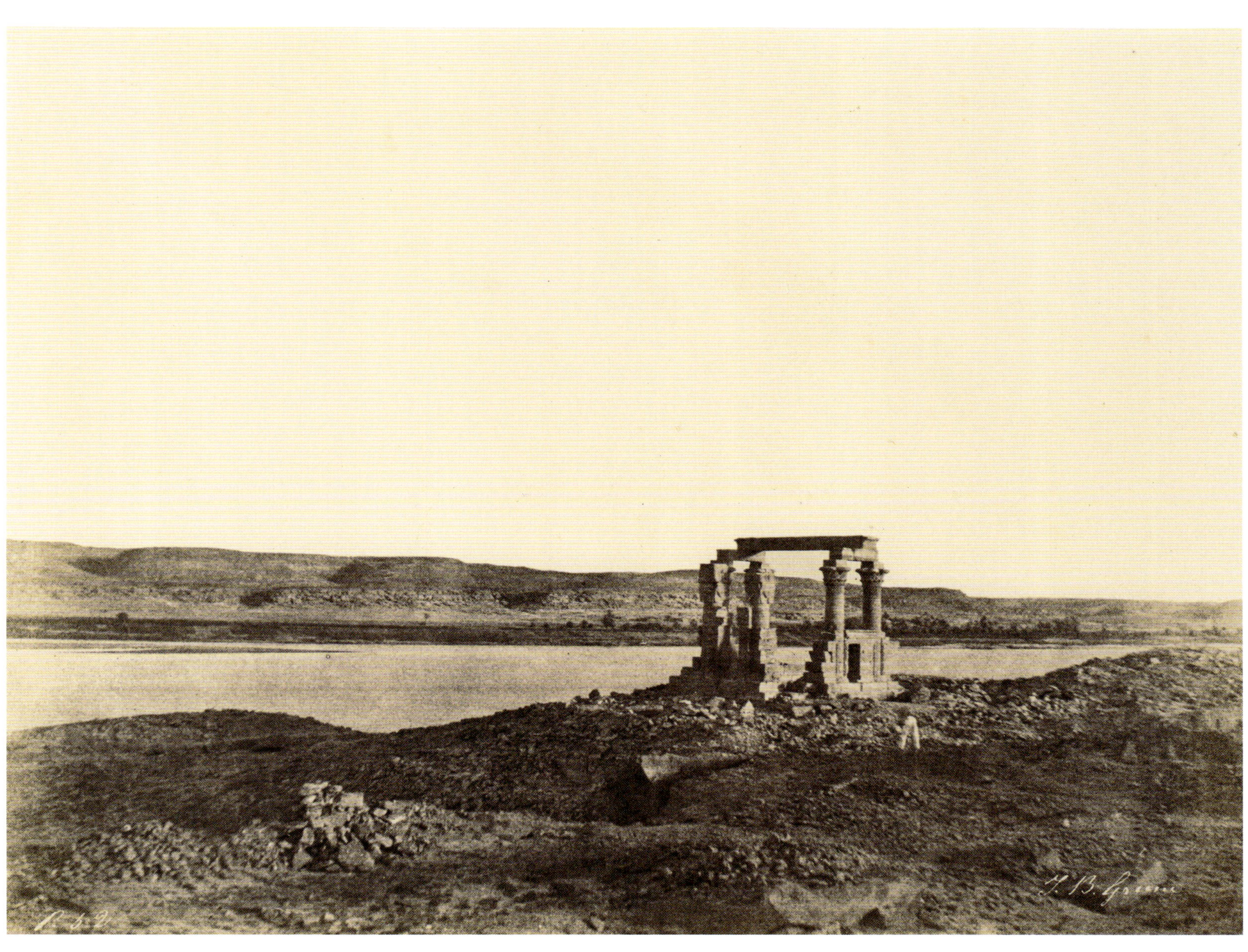

PLATE 30 *Qartas. Temple (Quertassi. Temple)*, 1854

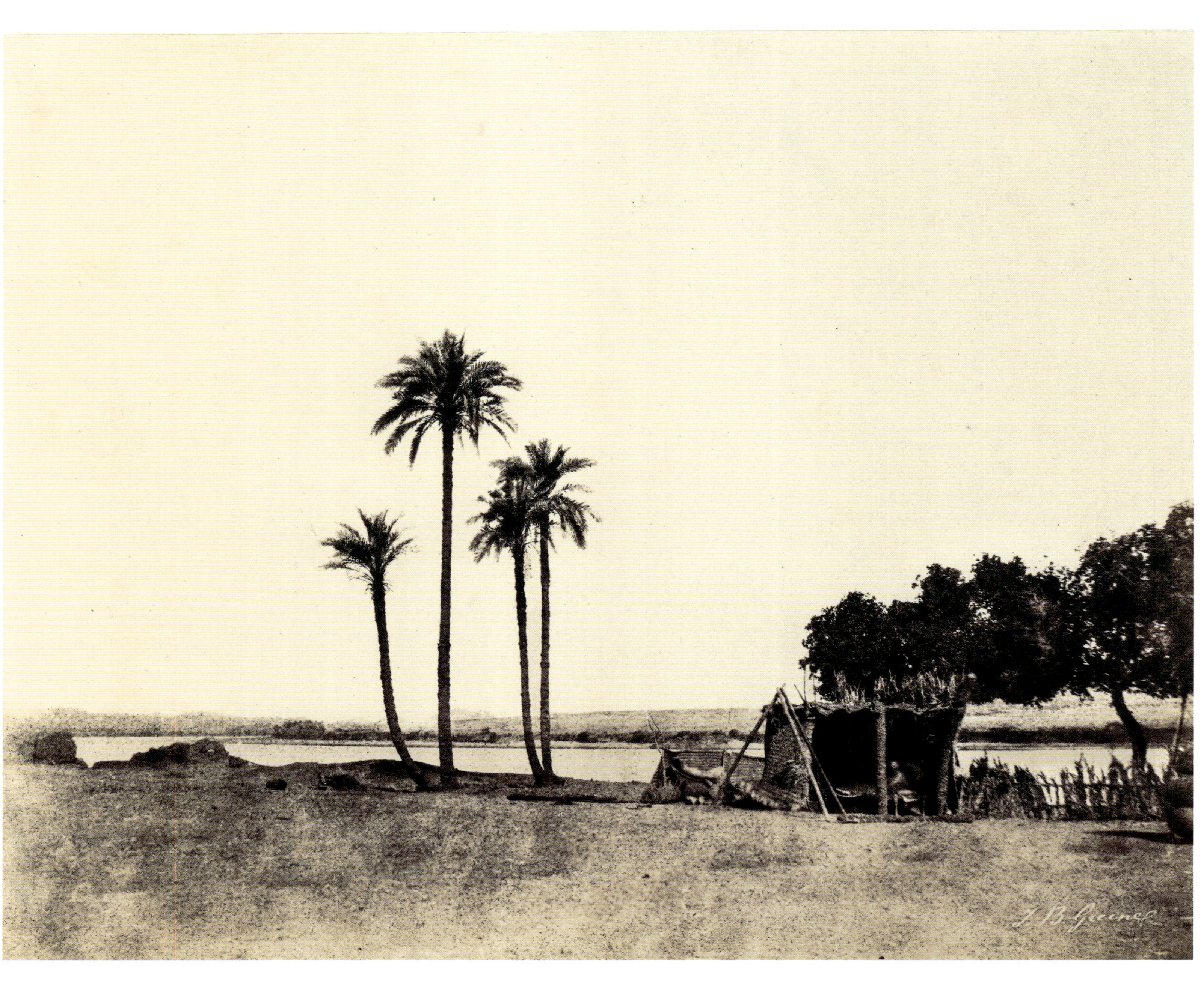

PLATE 31 *Études de dattiers (Studies of date palms)*, 1854

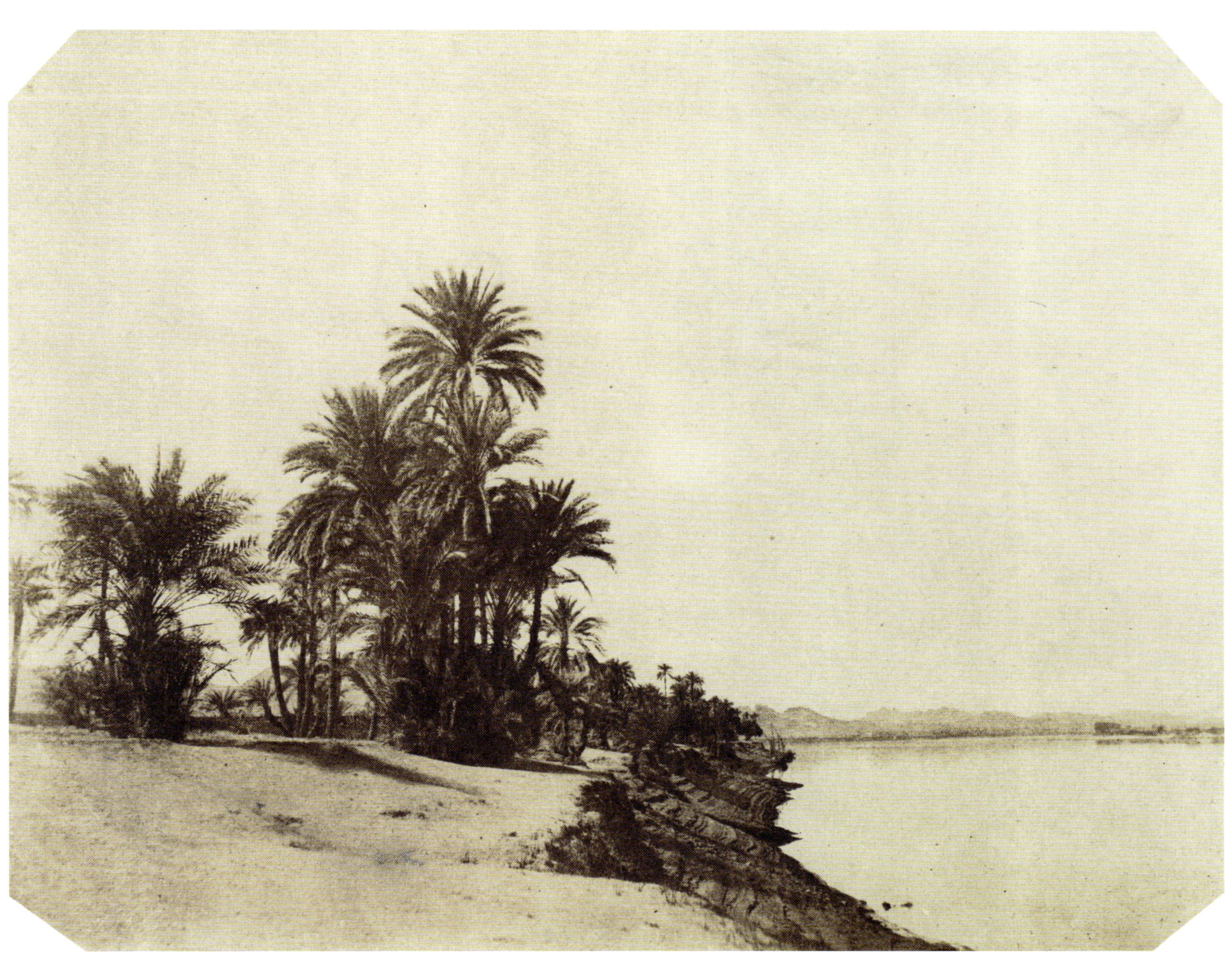

PLATE 32 *Études de dattiers (Studies of date palms)*, 1854

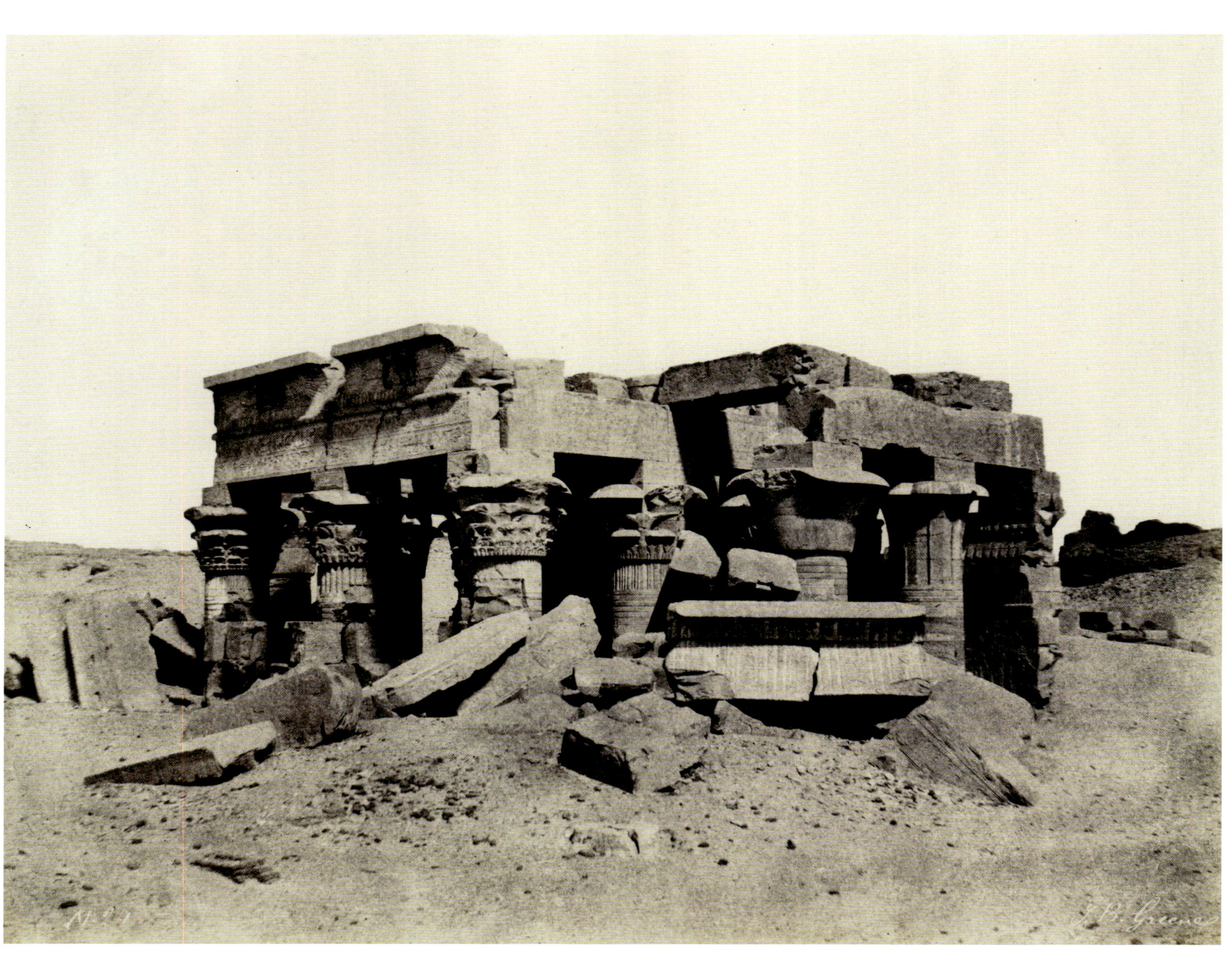

PLATE 33 *Ombos. Temple (Kom Ombo. Temple)*, 1854

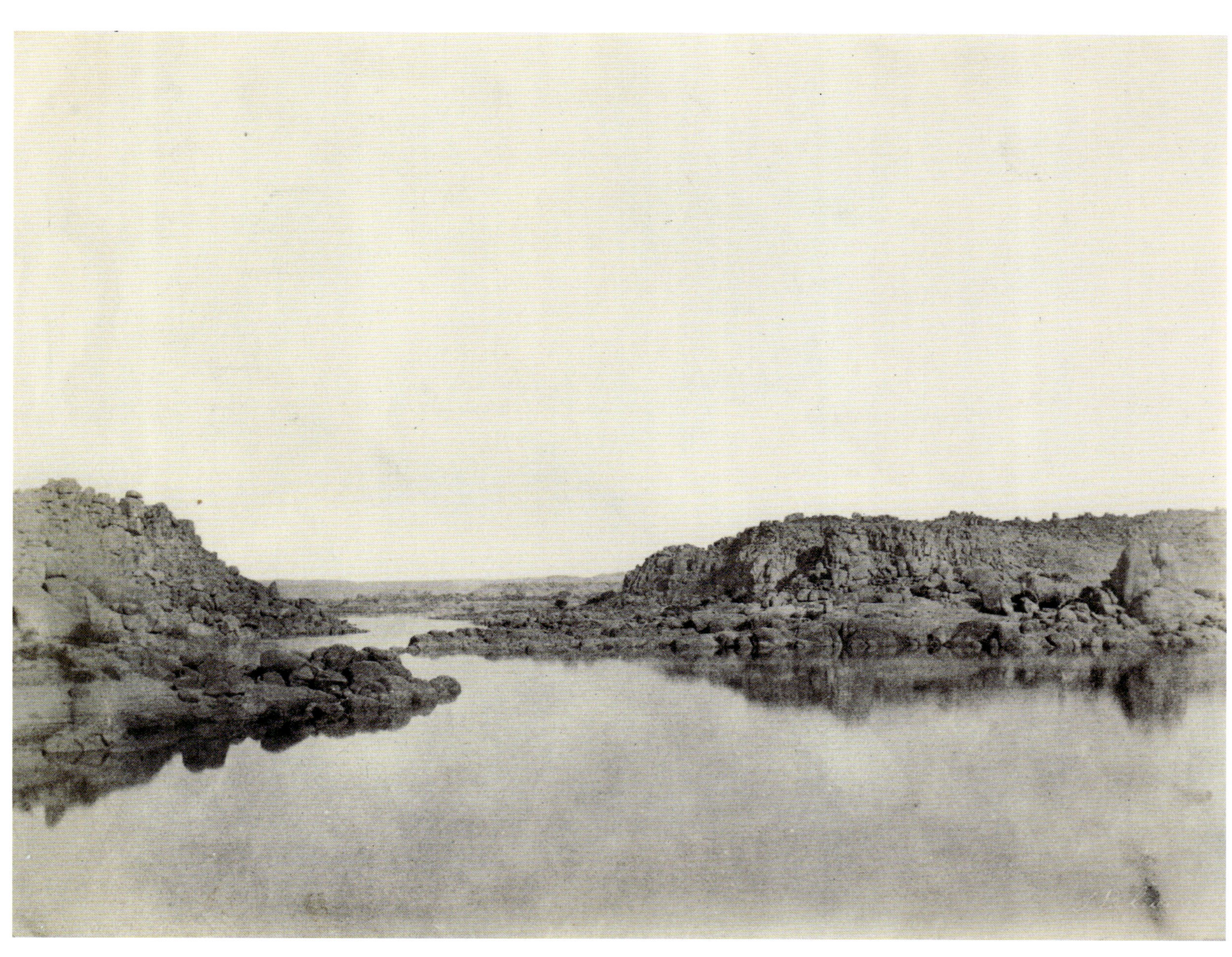

PLATE 34 *Première cataracte, Ile de Philae (First Cataract, Island of Philae)*, 1854

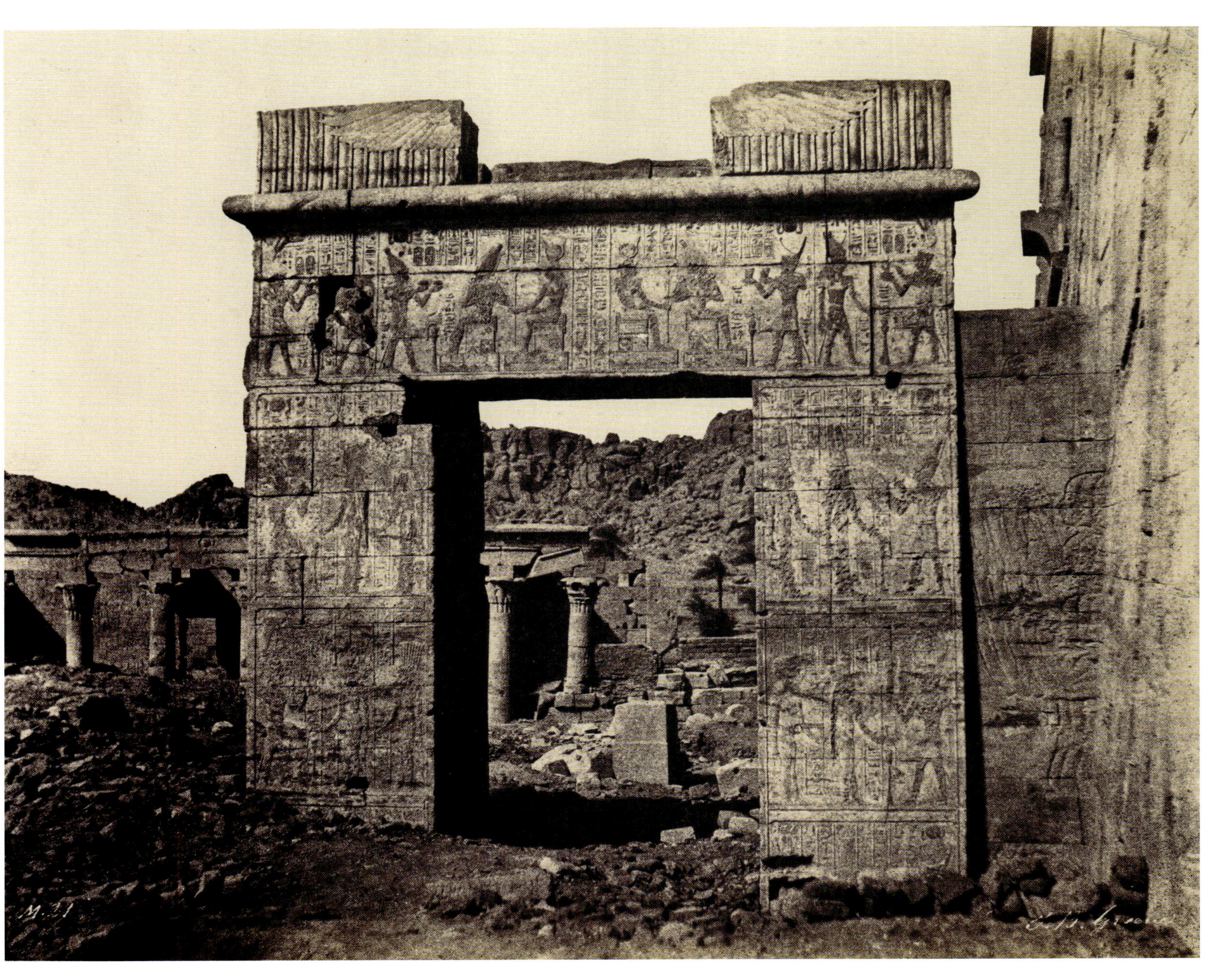

PLATE 35 *Ile de Philae. Porte auprès du grand Temple (Island of Philae. Portal near the Great Temple)*, 1854

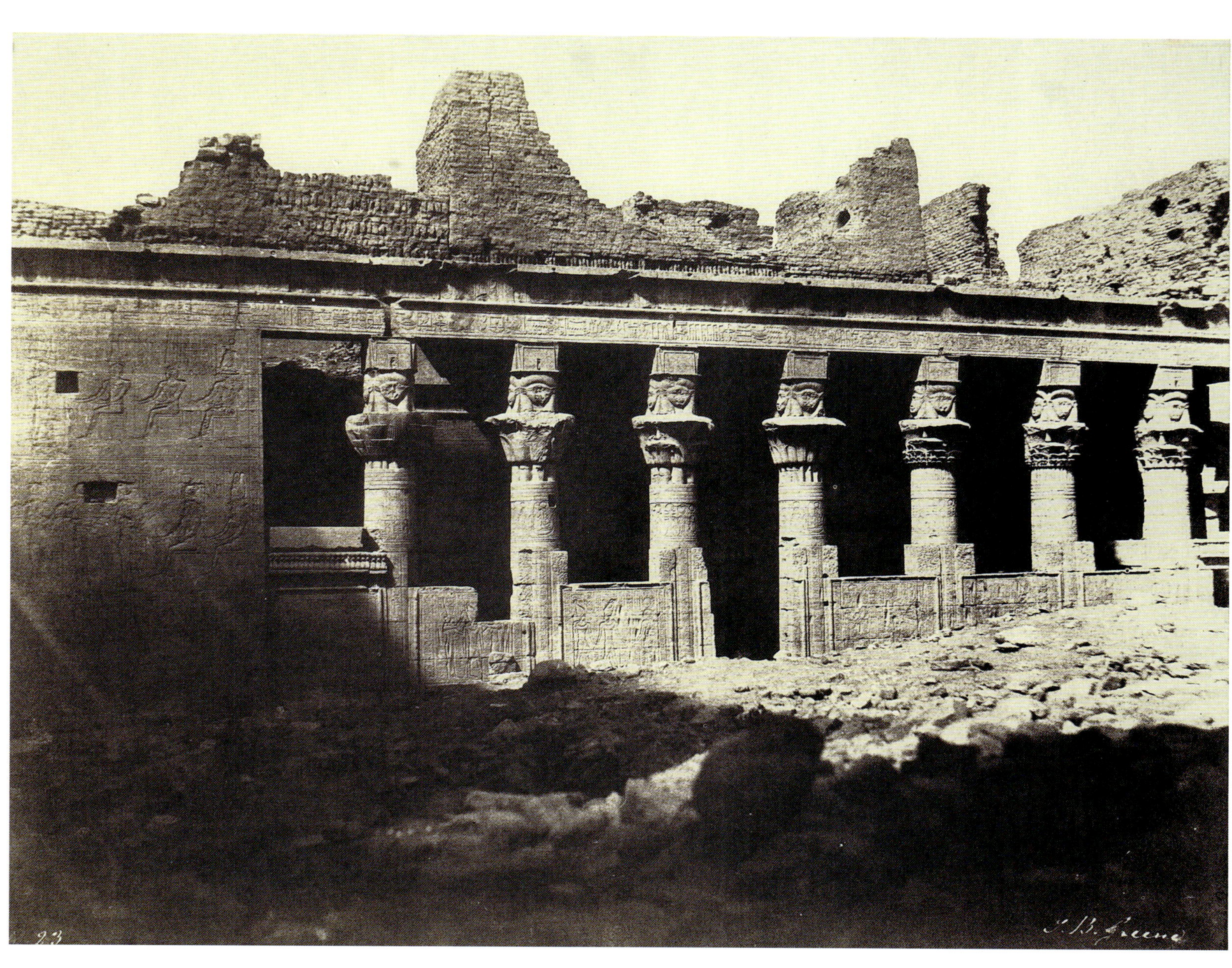

PLATE 36 *Ile de Philae. Grand Temple; côté gauche de la cour (Island of Philae. Great Temple; left side of the court)*, 1854

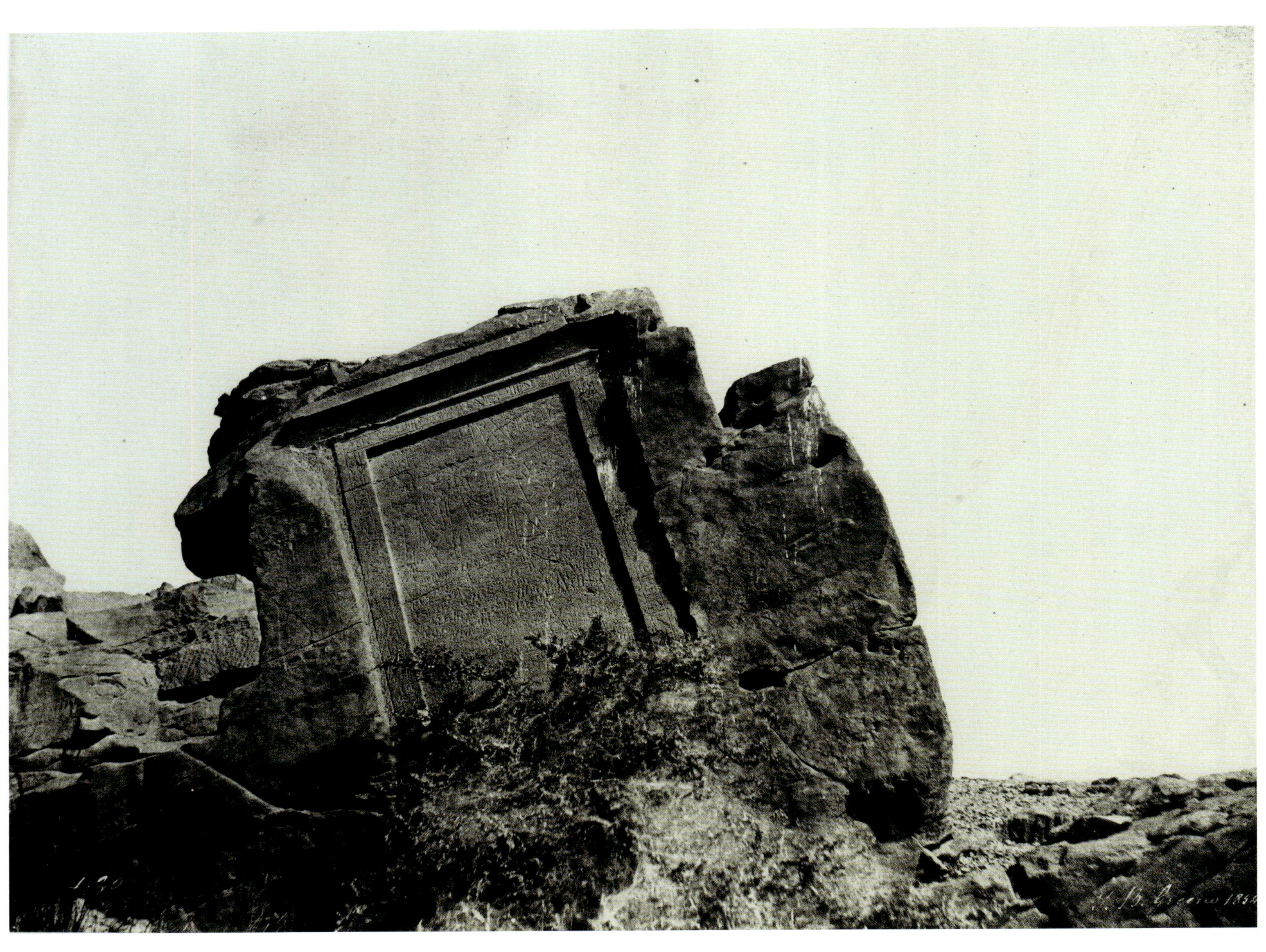

PLATE 37 *Silsilis. Stèle. (Silsilis. Stela)*, 1854

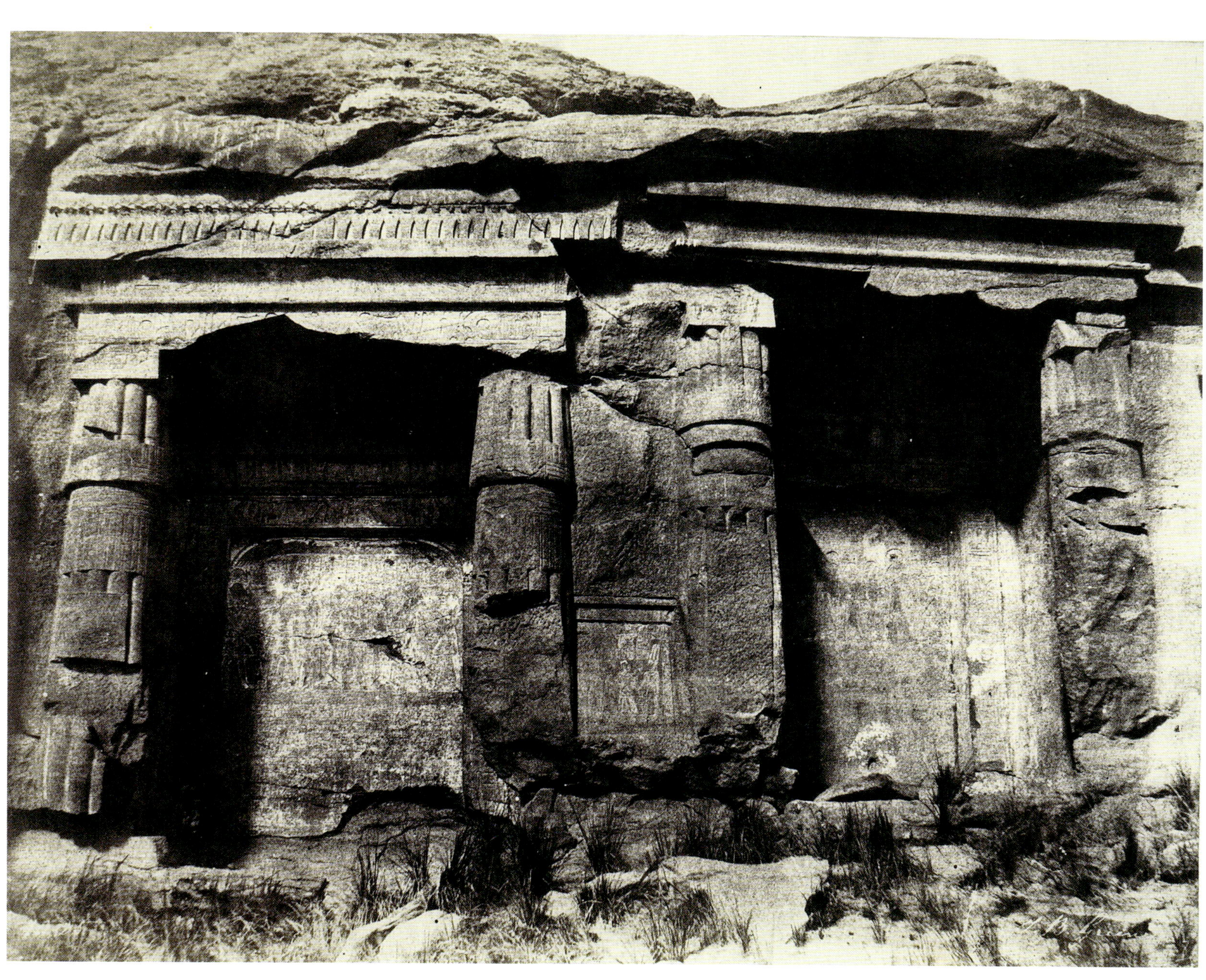

PLATE 38 *Silsilis. Stèles (Silsilis. Stelae)*, 1854

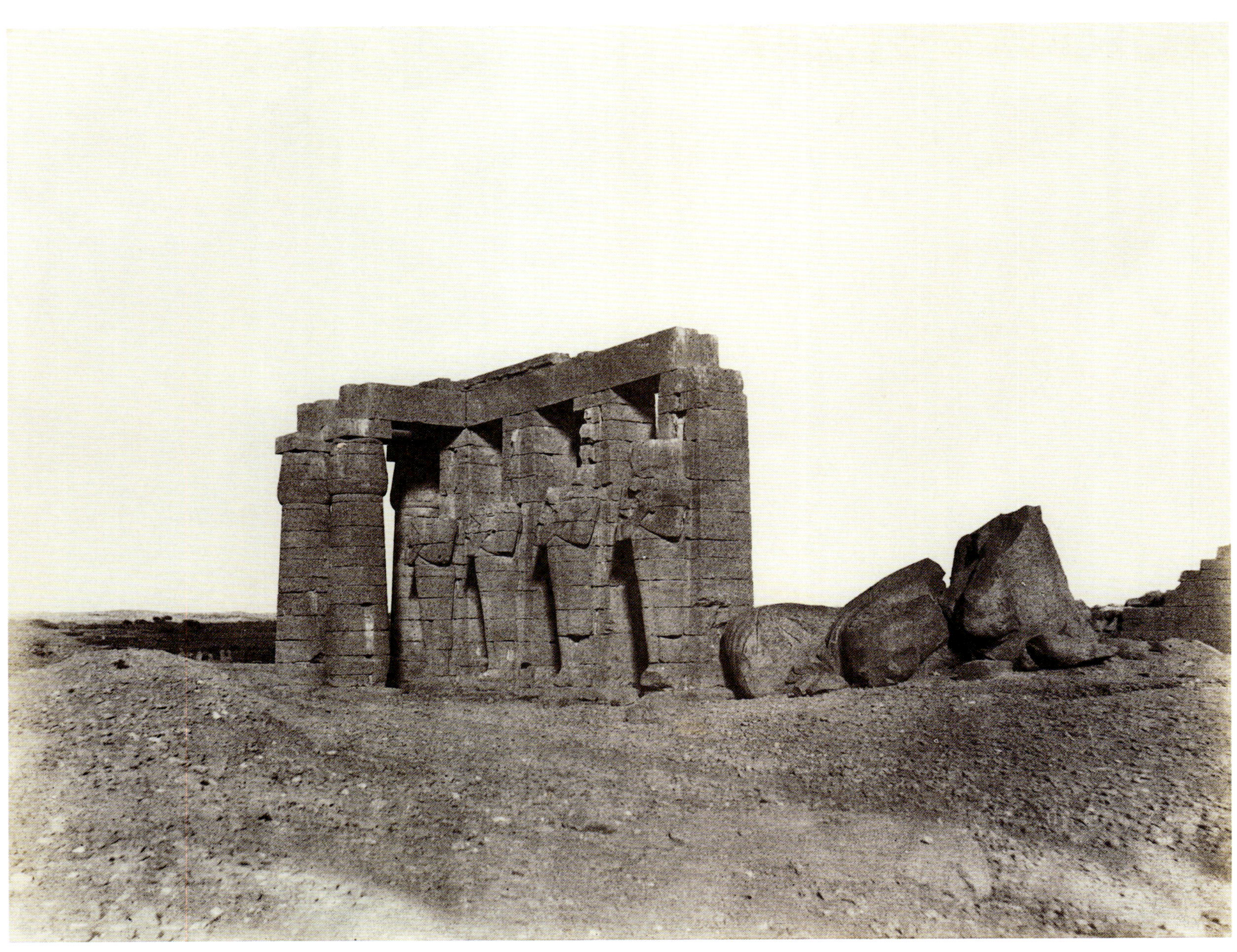

PLATE 39 *Thèbes. Colosses du Memnonium; massif de droite (Thebes. Colossi of Memnon; right side)*, 1854

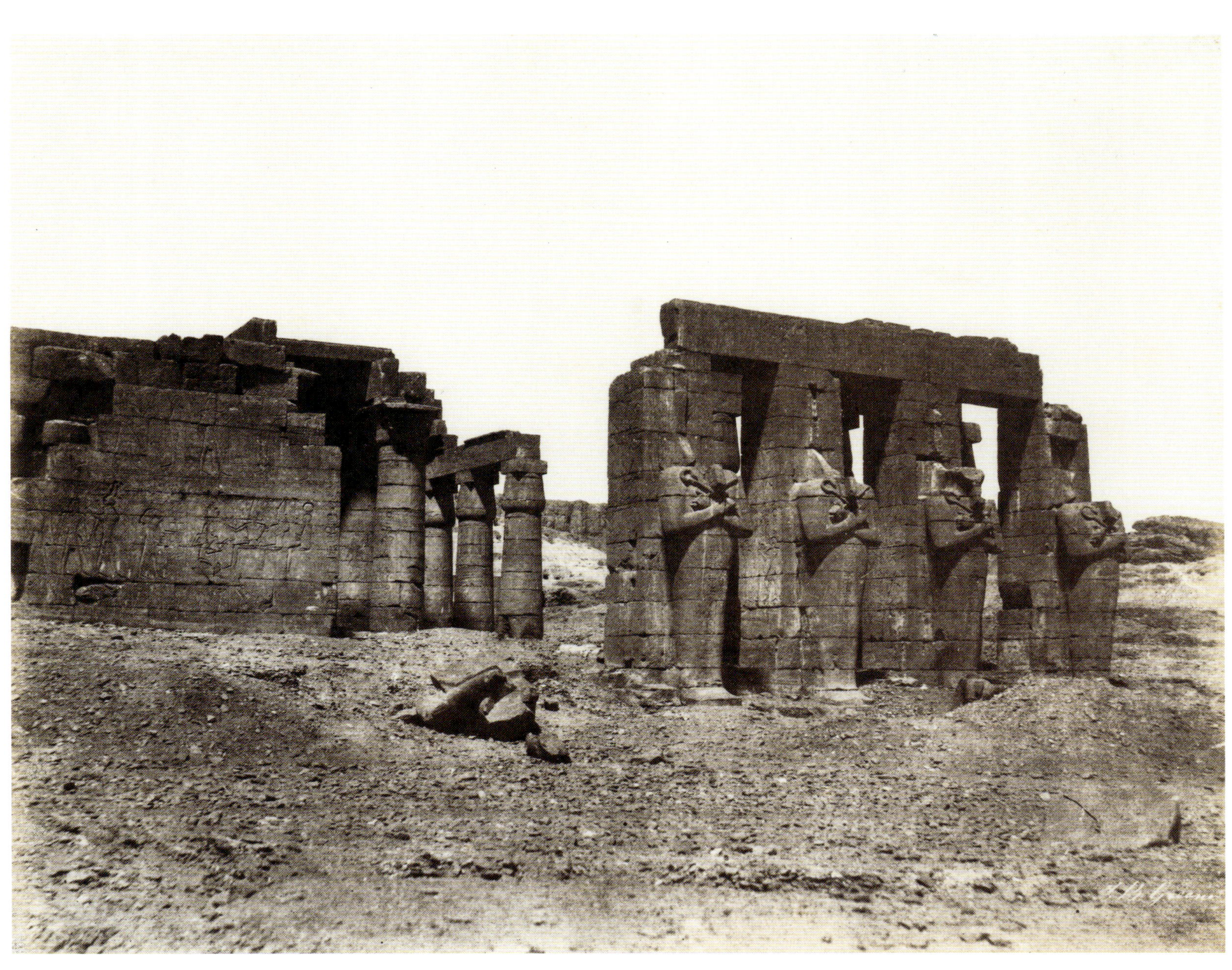

PLATE 40 *Thèbes. Colosses du Memnonium; massif de gauche (Thebes. Colossi of Memnon; left side)*, 1854

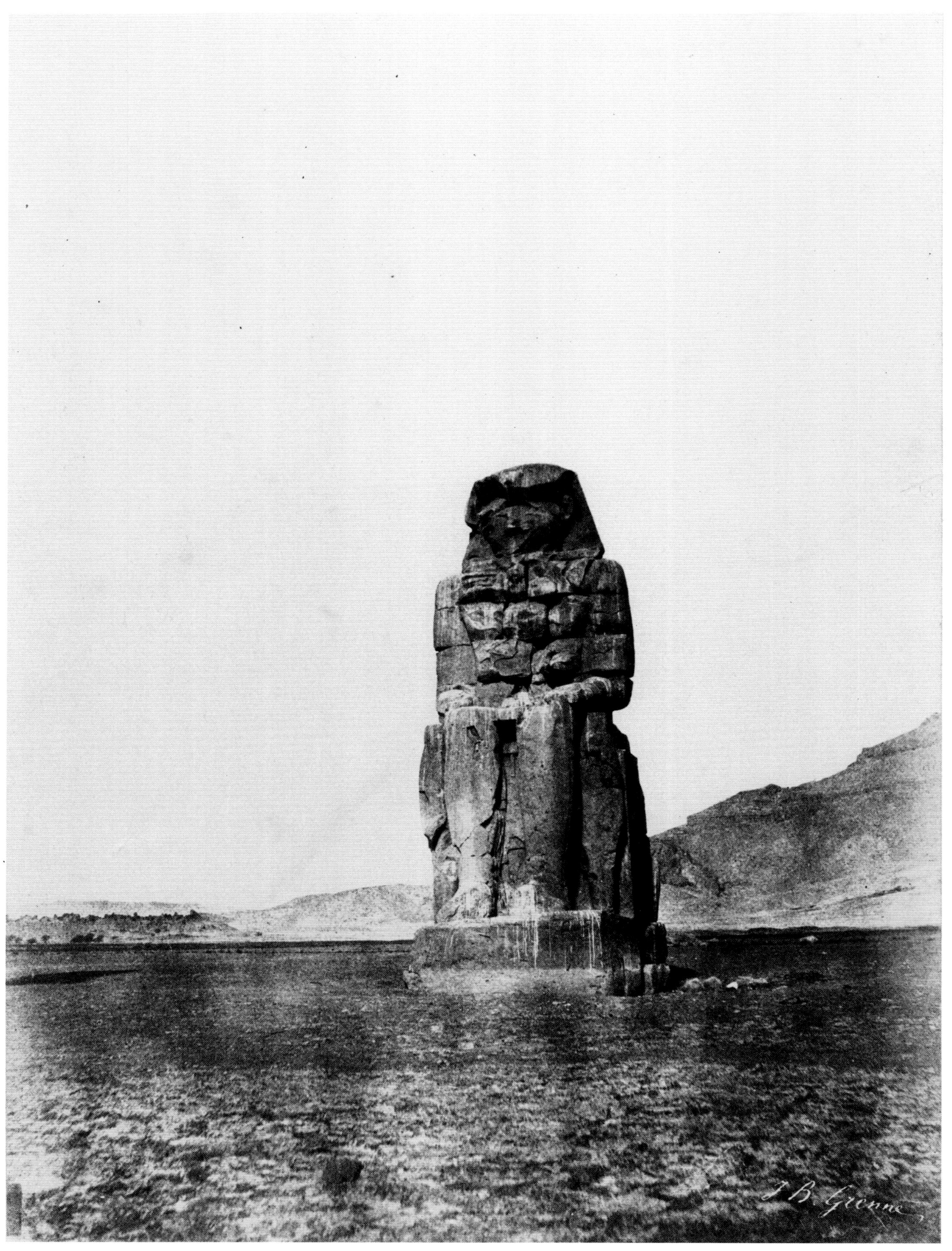

PLATE 41 *Thèbes. Colosse de droite (Thebes. Right colossus)*, 1854

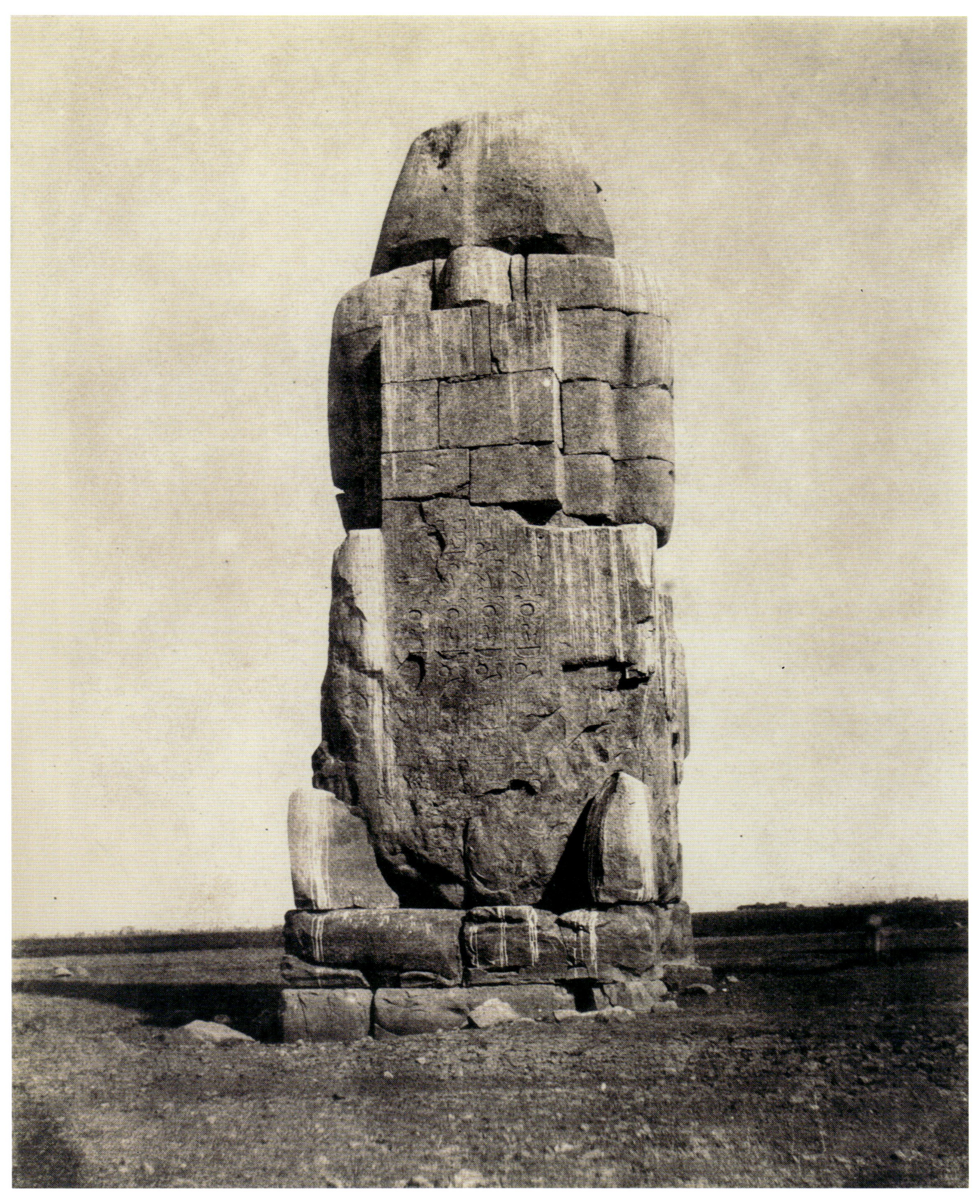

PLATE 42 *Thèbes. Colosse de droite, face postérieure (Thebes. Right colossus, back side)*, 1854

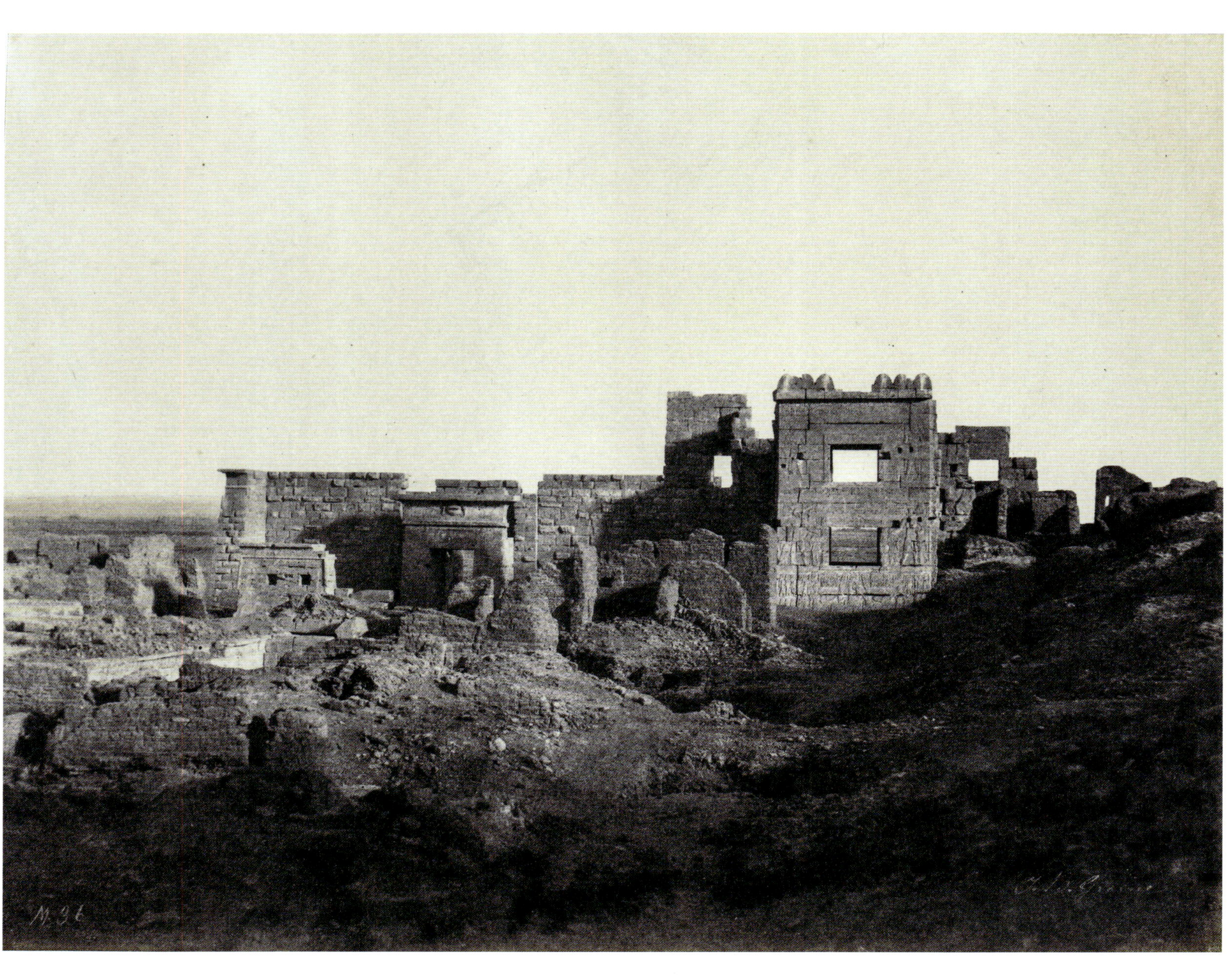

PLATE 43 *Thèbes. Médinet-Habou; vue prise de l'entrée du Palais de Ramsès-Méïamoun (Thebes. Medinet Habu. View from the entrance to the Palace of Ramesses III)*, 1854

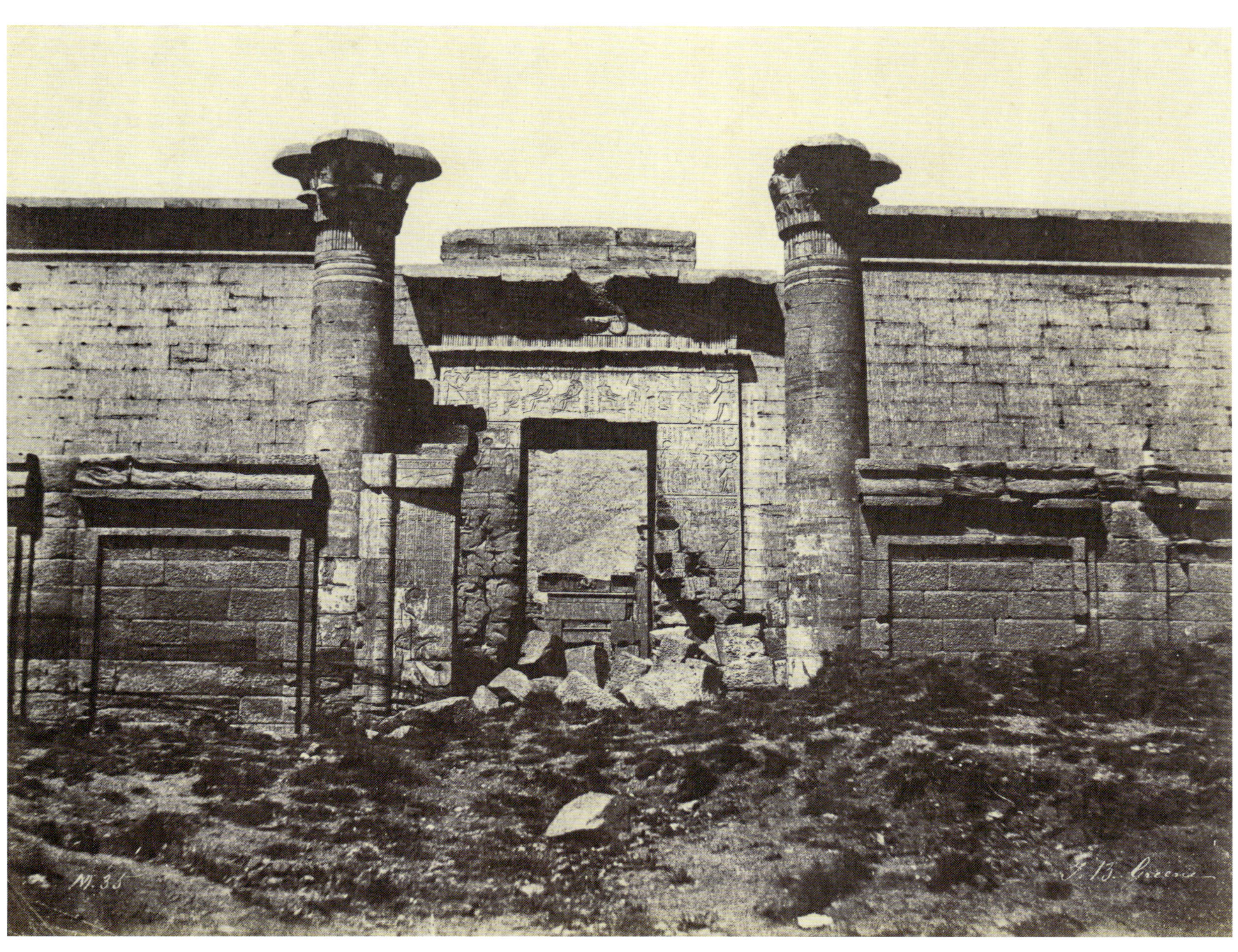

PLATE 44 *Thèbes. Médinet-Habou. Premier Pylône (Thebes. Medinet Habu. First pylon)*, 1854

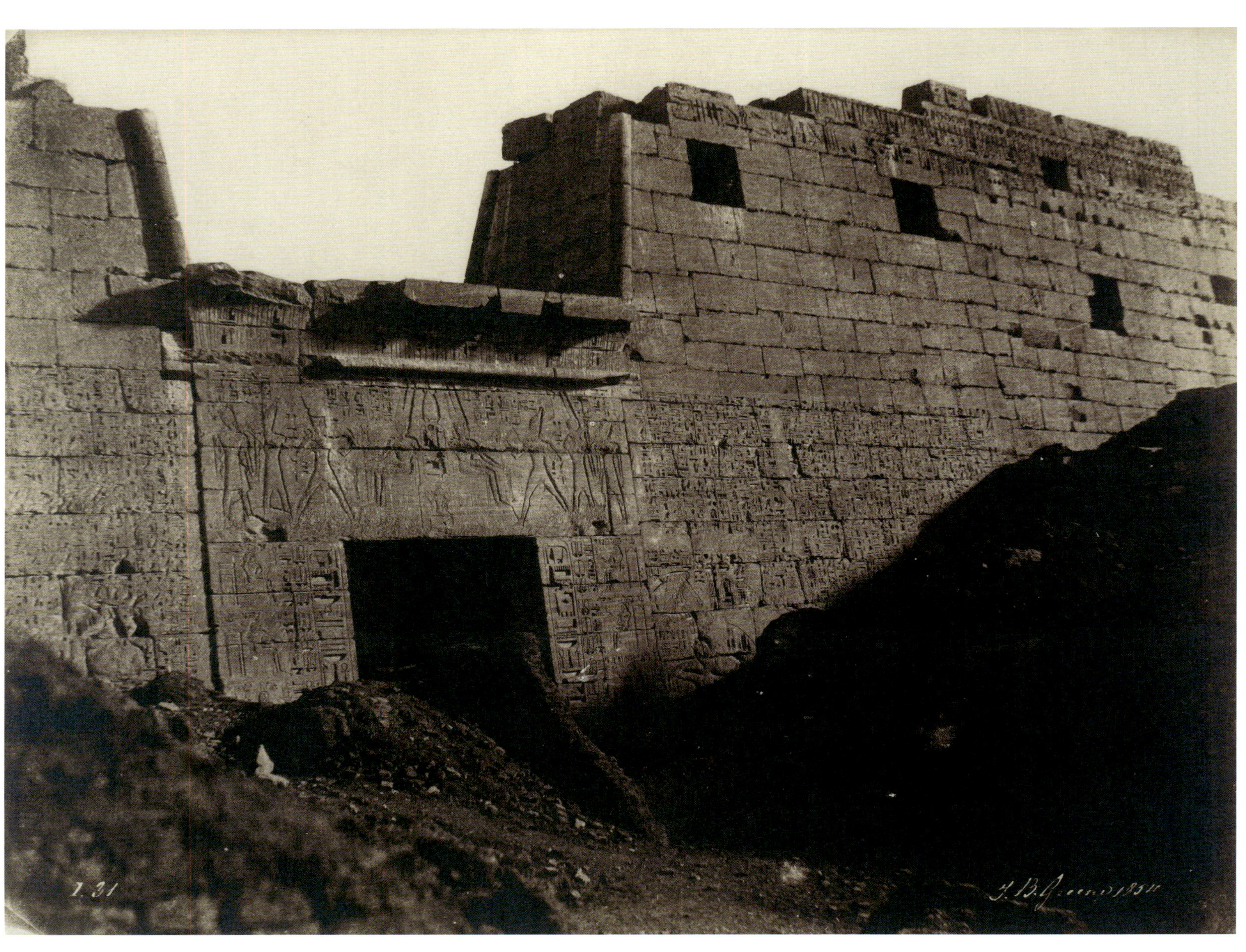

PLATE 45 *Médinet-Habou. Palais de Ramsès-Méïamoun. Premier Pylône. Massif de gauche; face intérieure (Medinet Habu. Palace of Ramesses III. First pylon. Left tower, interior side)*, 1854

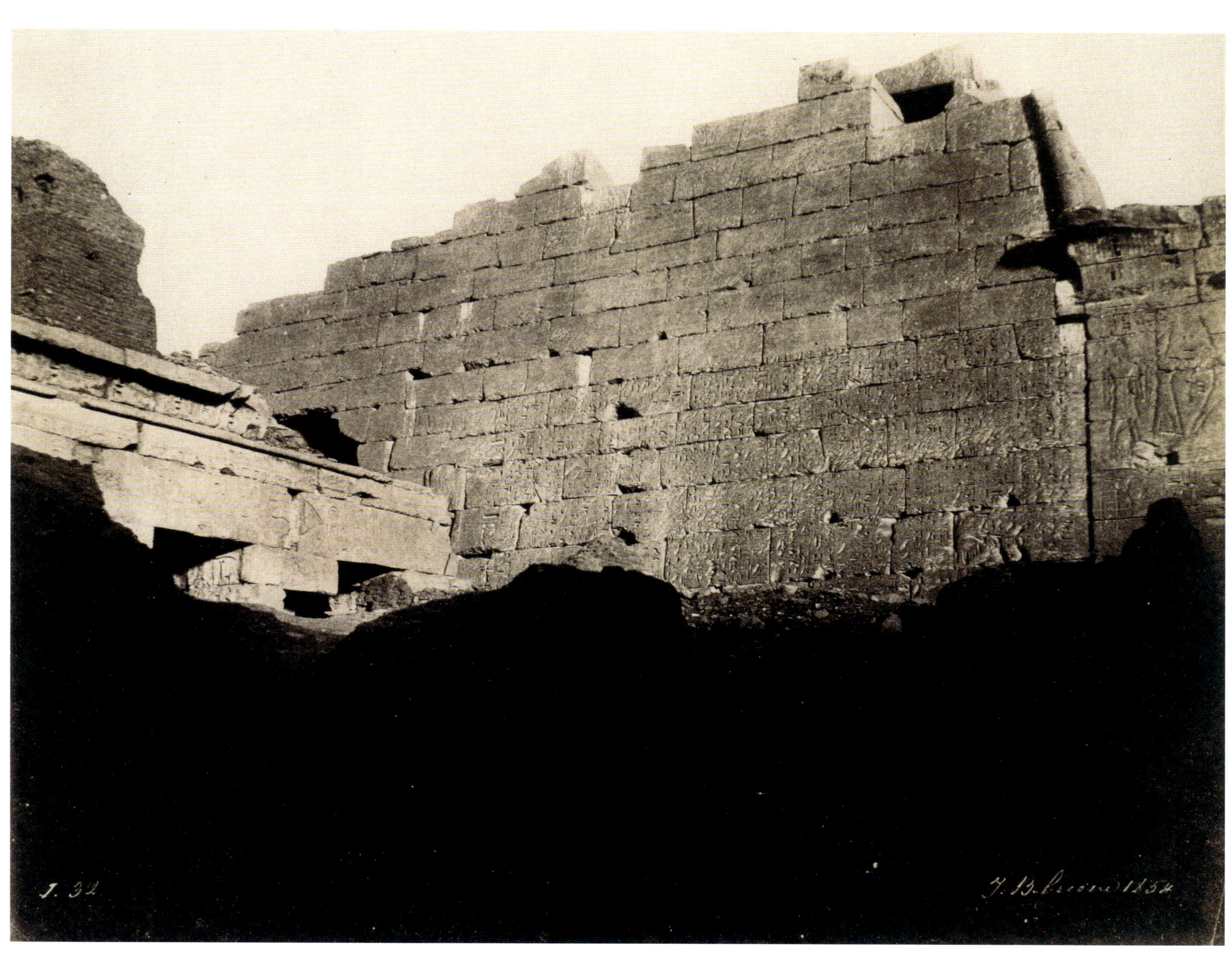

PLATE 46 *Médinet-Habou. Palais de Ramsès-Méïamoun. Premier Pylône. Massif de droite; face intérieure. (Medinet Habu. Palace of Ramesses III. First pylon. Right tower, interior side)*, 1854

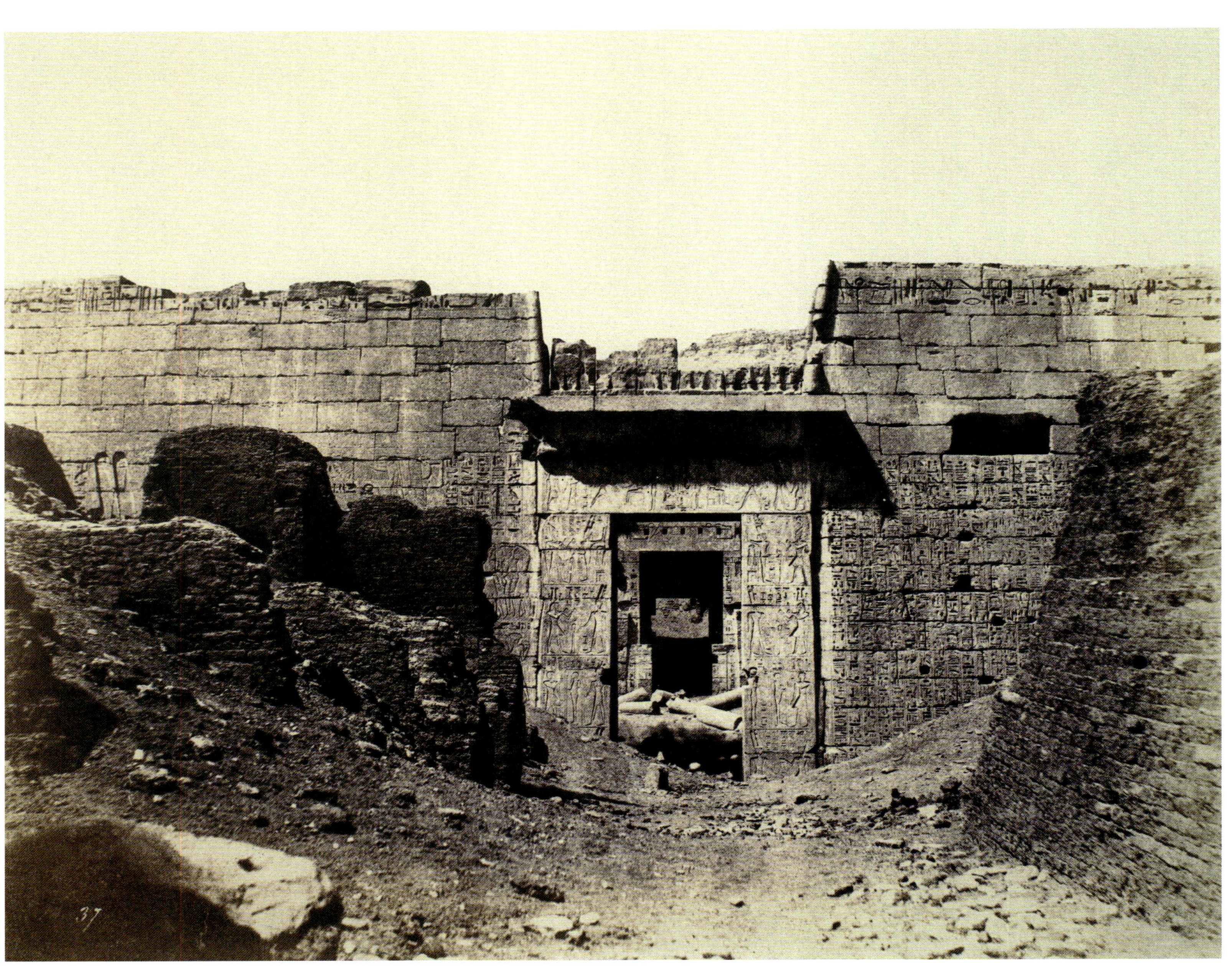

PLATE 47 *Médinet-Habou. Palais de Ramsès-Méïamoun, entrée de la seconde cour (Medinet Habu. Palace of Ramesses III, entry to the second court)*, 1854

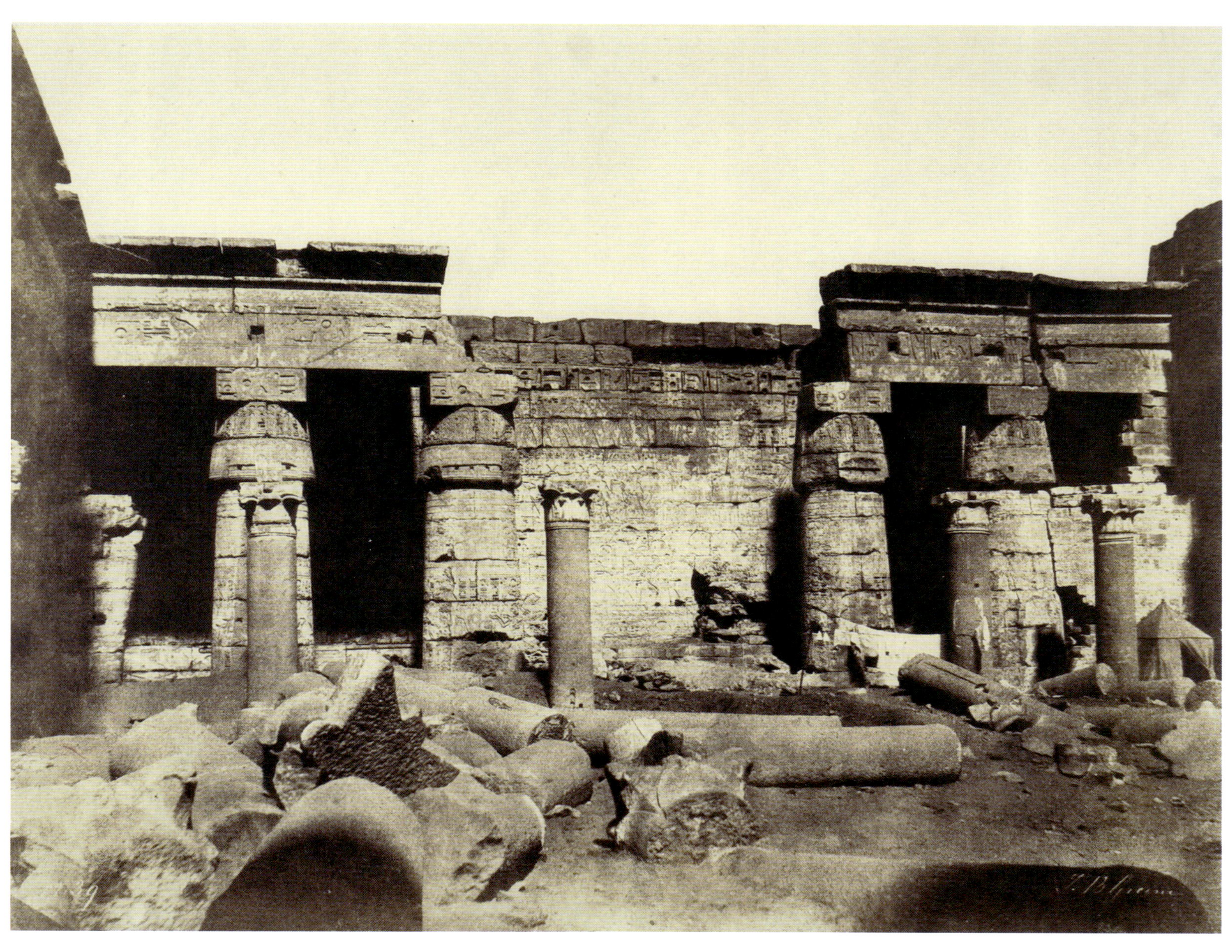

PLATE 48 *Thèbes. Médinet-Habou. Palais de Ramsès III, seconde cour, face nord (Thebes. Medinet Habu. Palace of Ramesses III; second court, north side)*, 1854

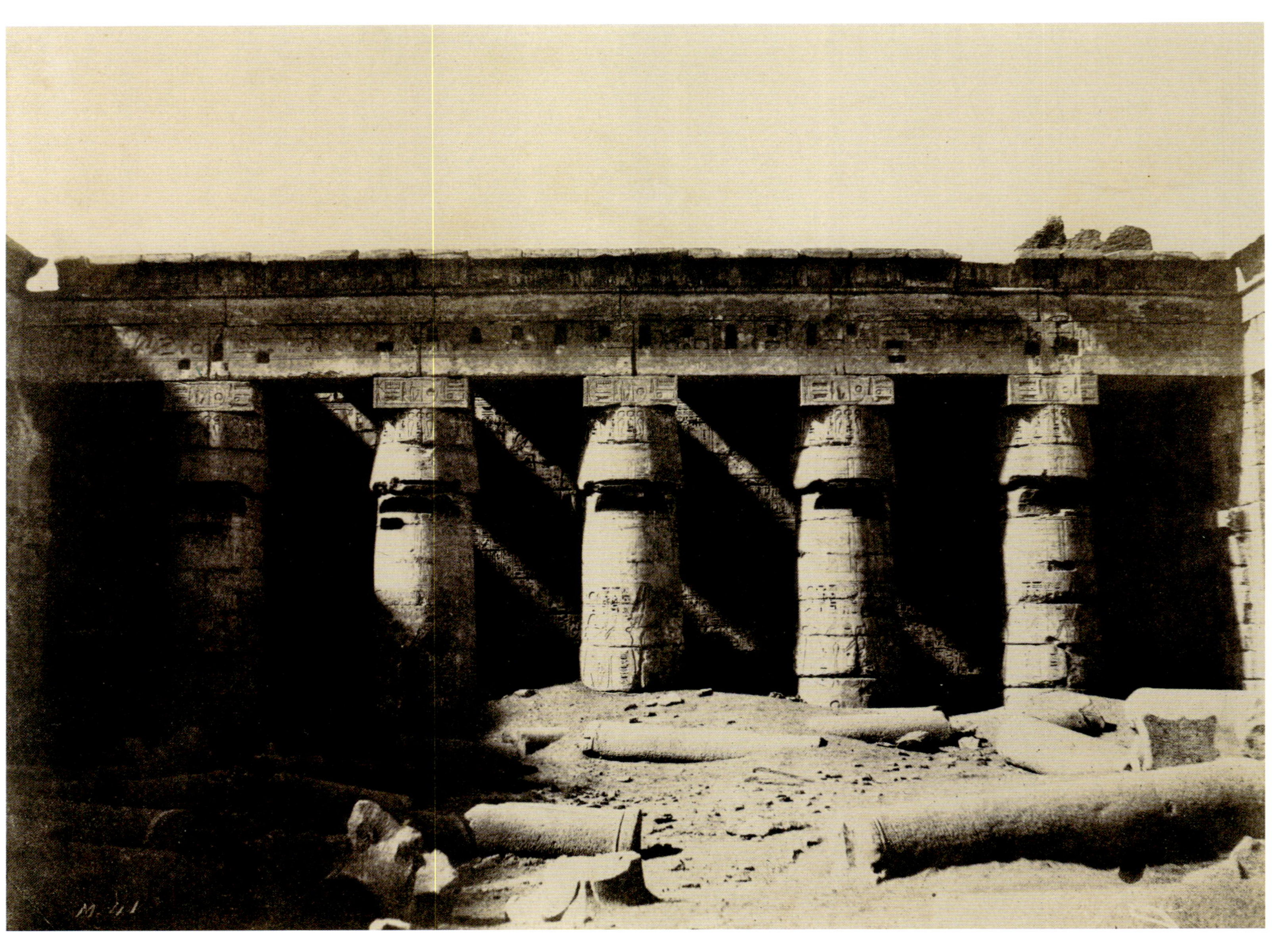

PLATE 49 *Thèbes. Médinet-Habou. Palais de Ramsès-Meïamoun; seconde cour; face sud (Thebes. Medinet Habu. Palace of Ramesses III; second court, south side)*, 1854

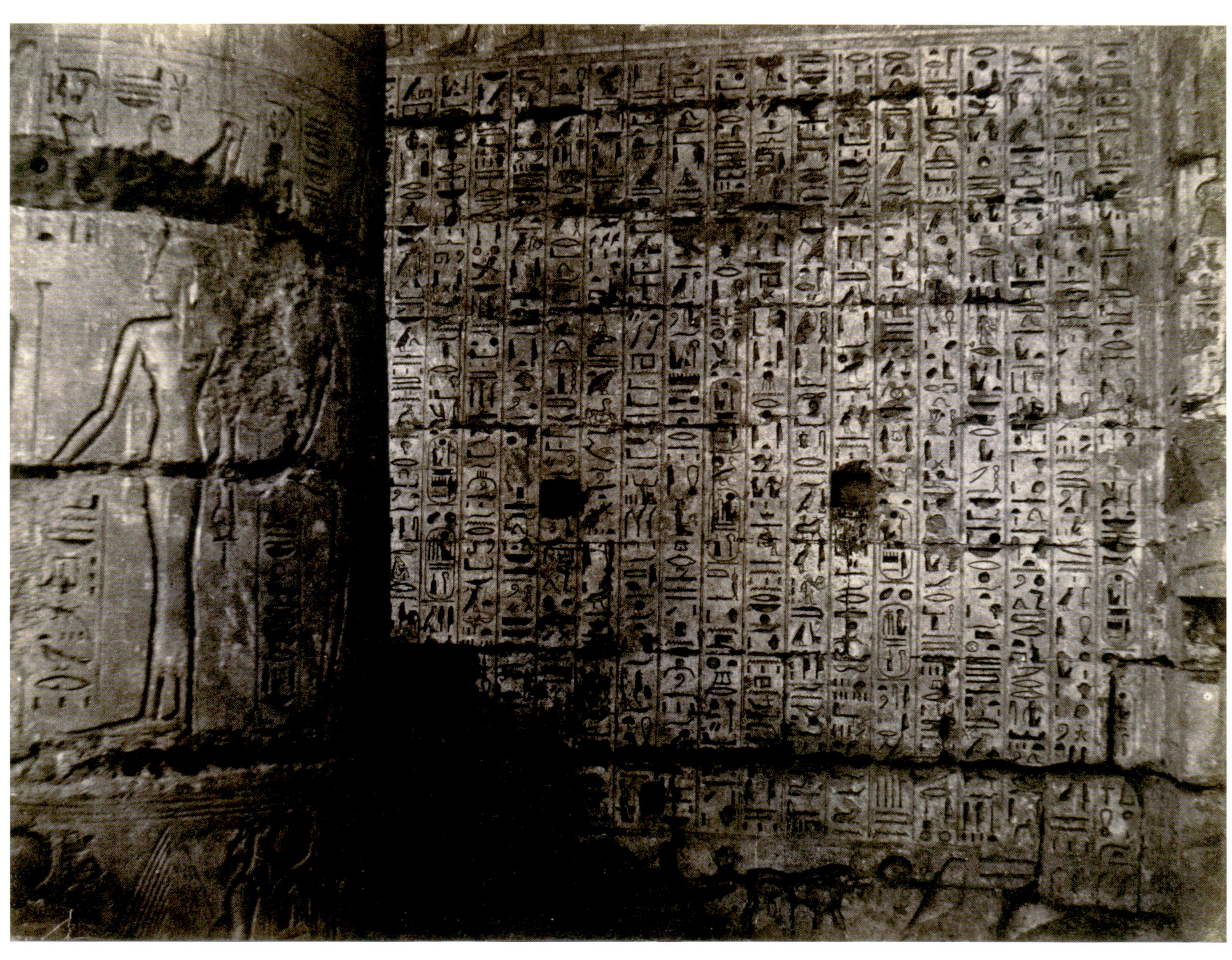

PLATE 50 *Médinet-Habou. Palais de Ramsès-Meïamoun. Seconde Cour. Sculptures et Inscriptions de la paroi gauche. No 1 (Medinet Habu. Palace of Ramesses III. Sculptures and inscriptions of the left inner wall. No. 1)*, 1854

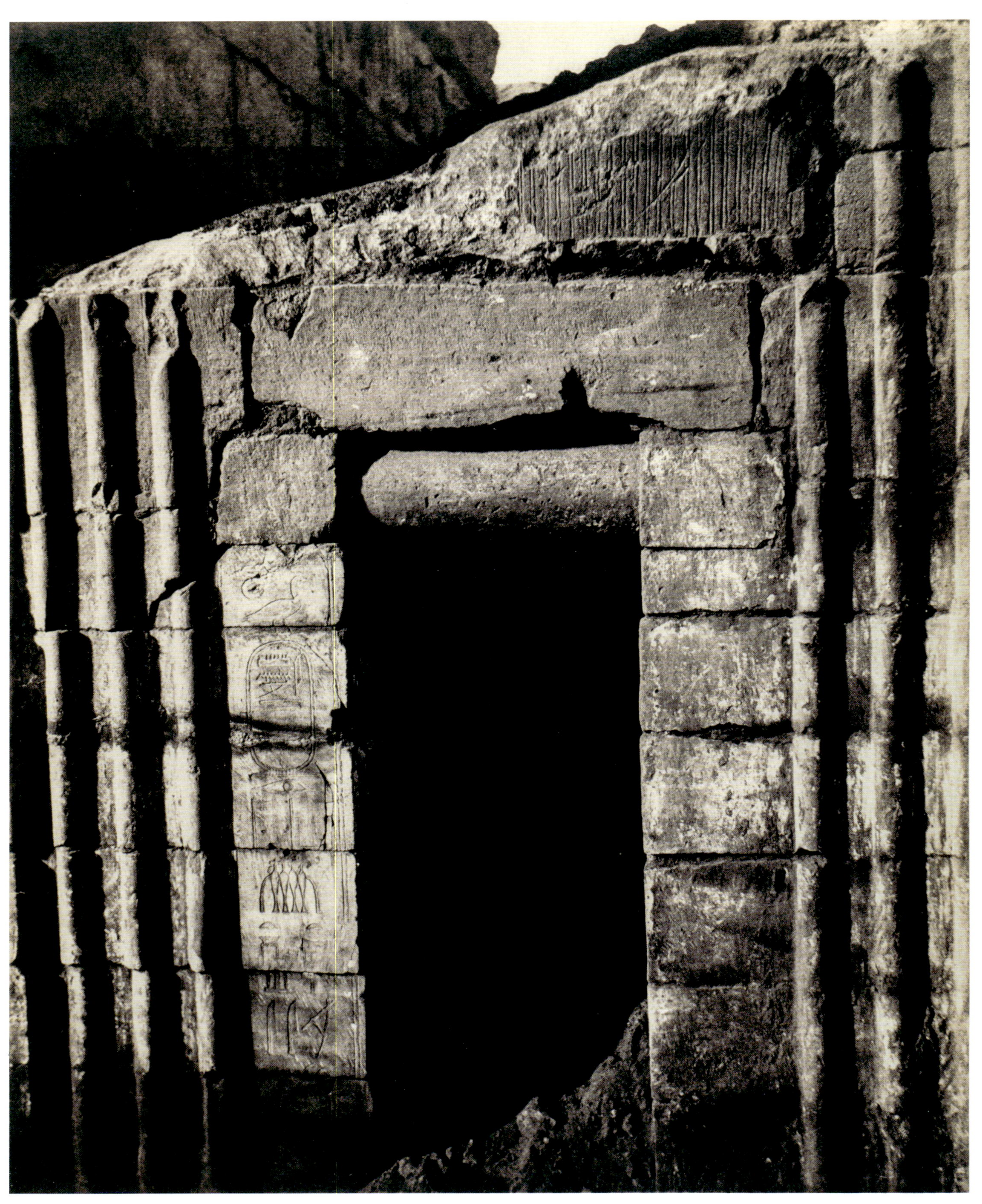

PLATE 51 *Médinet-Habou. Porte découverte près du palais de Thoutmès III (Medinet Habu. Door discovered close to the Palace of Thutmose III)*, 1855

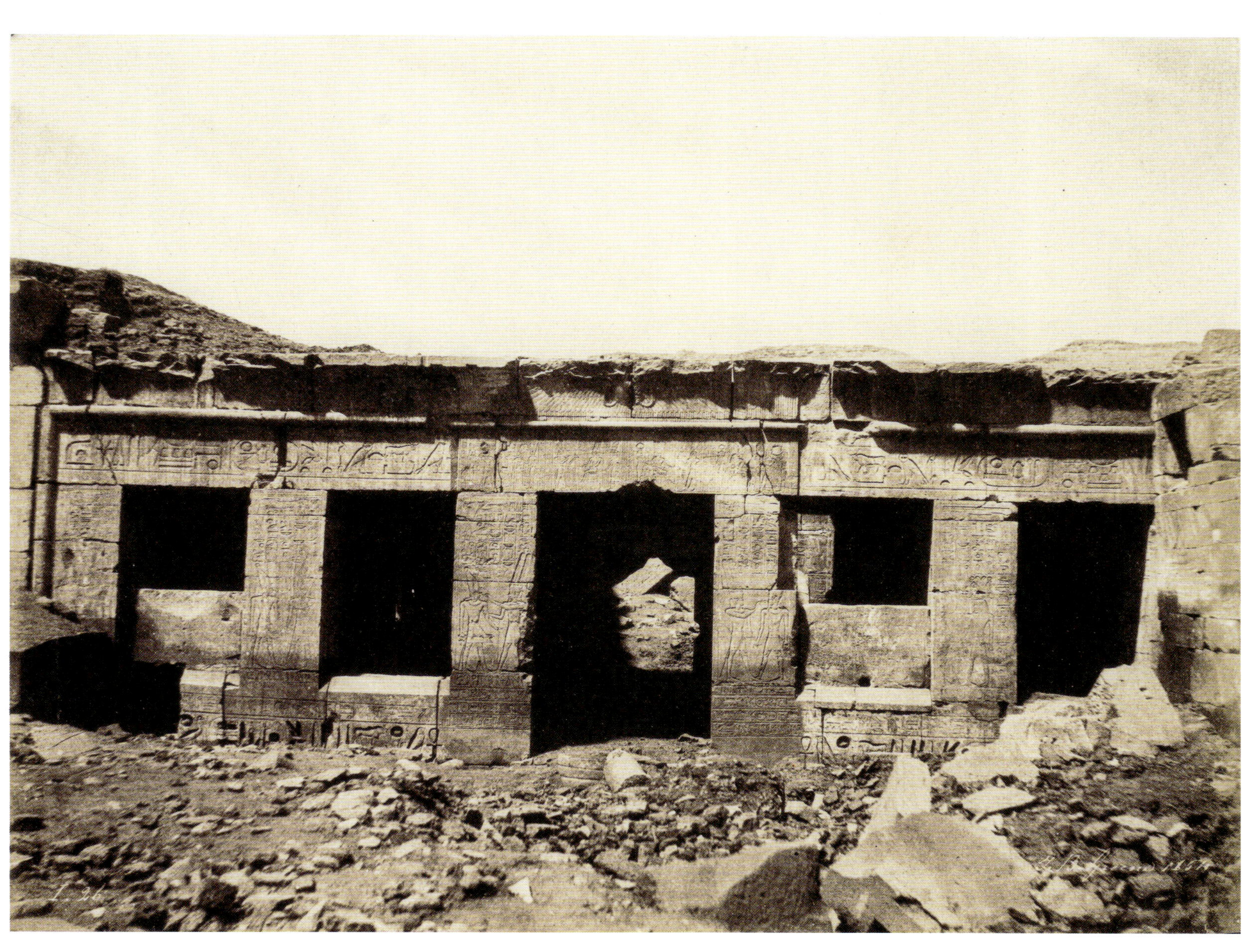

PLATE 52 *Thèbes. Médinet-Habou. Palais de Thoutmosis III (Thebes. Medinet Habu. Palace of Thutmose III)*, 1854

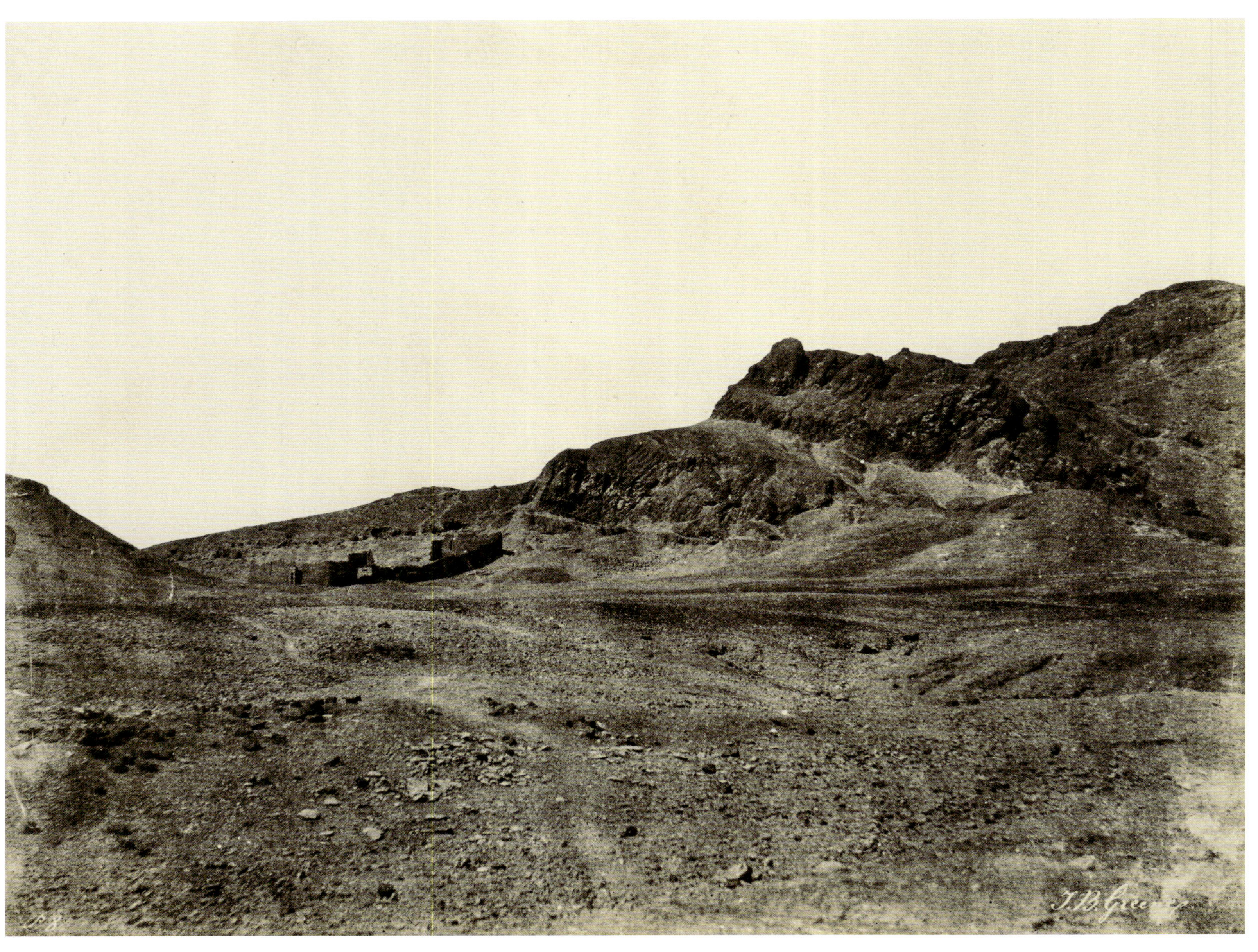

PLATE 53 *Montagne de Thèbes (Mountain of Thebes)*, 1854

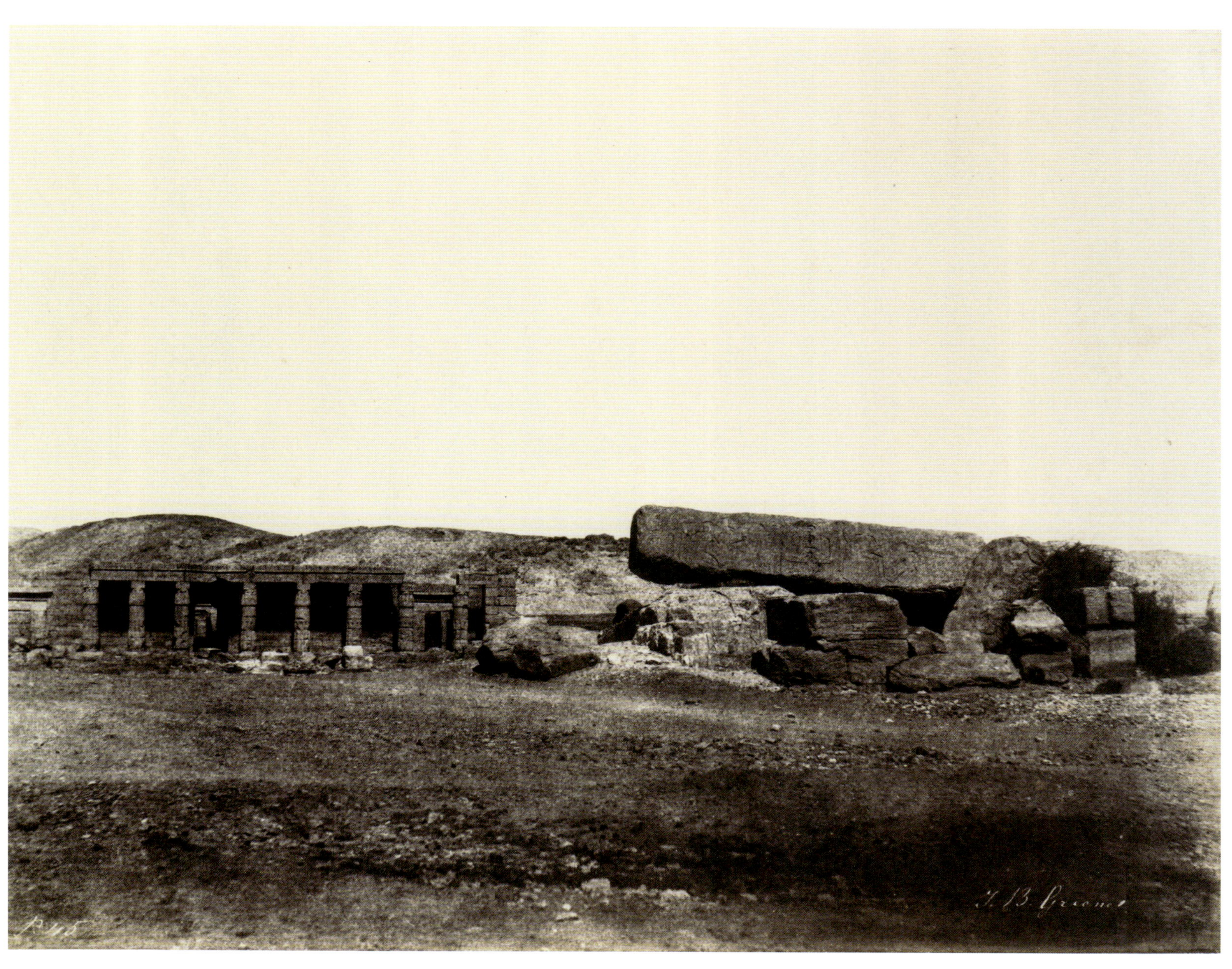

PLATE 54 *Quornah. Temple (Qurna. Temple)*, 1854

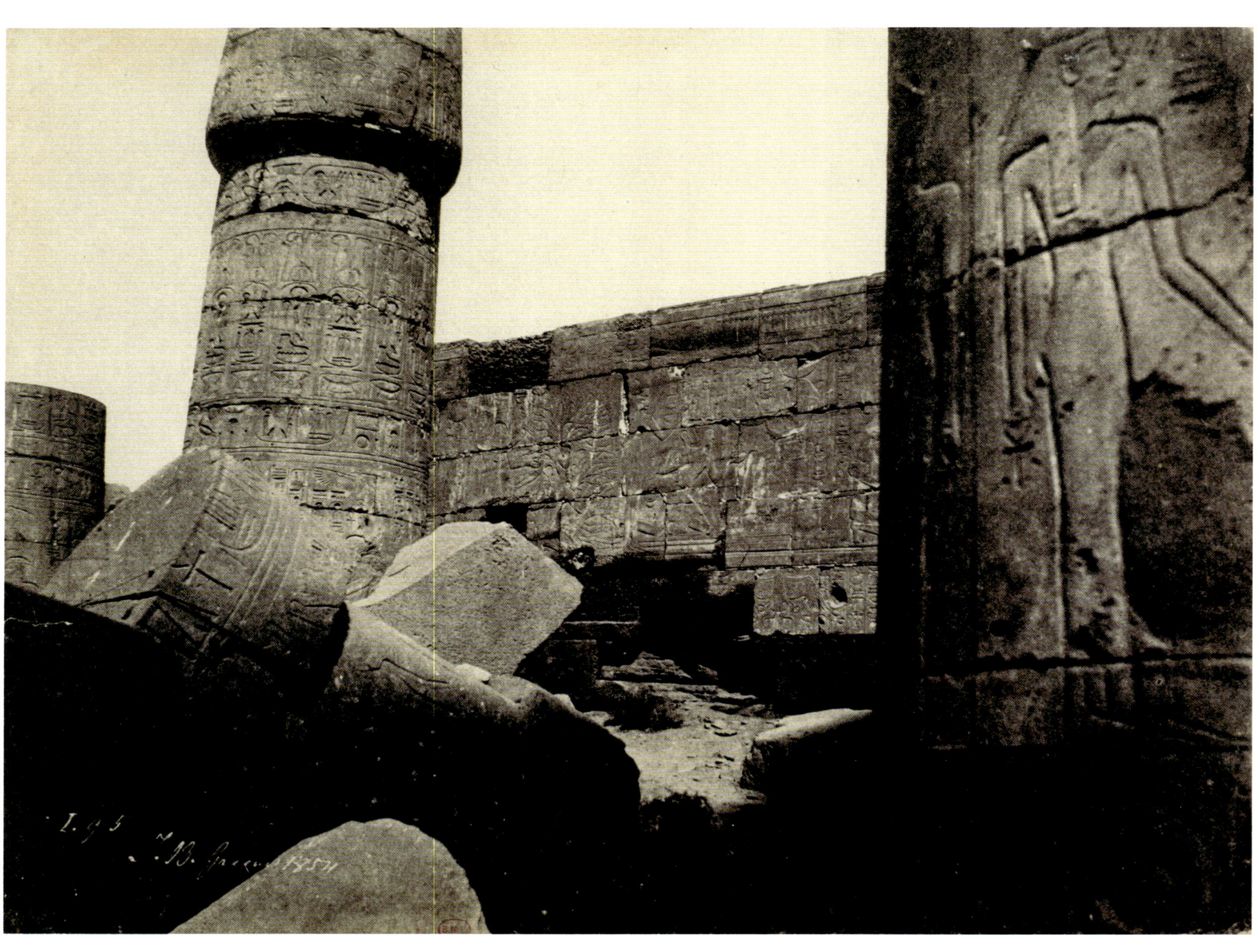

PLATE 55 *Karnac. Salle hypostyle. Mur du Nord. face intérieure. No 3 (Karnak. Hypostyle Hall. Northern wall, interior. No. 3)*, 1854

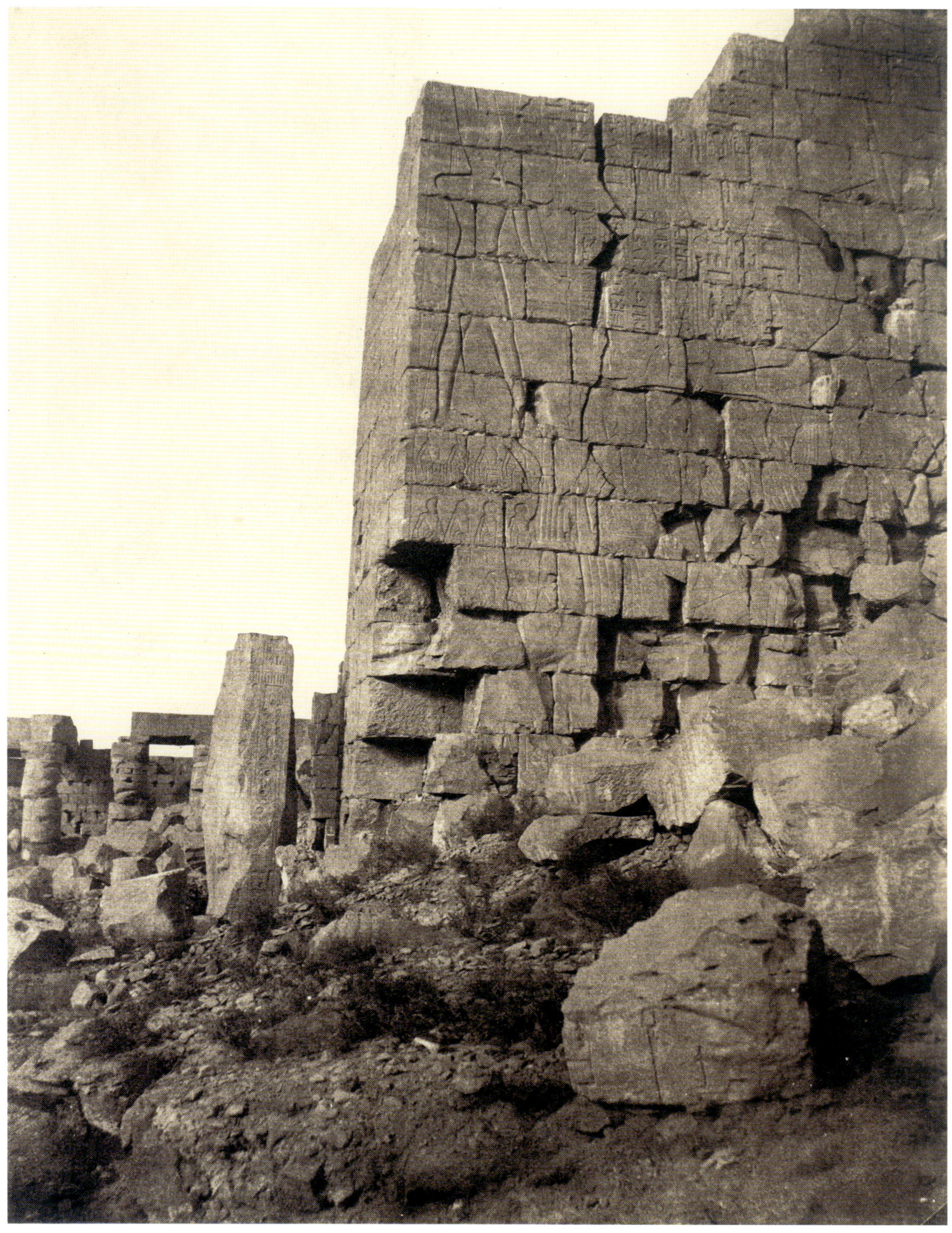

PLATE 56 *Karnac. Mur du Sud. (Karnak. Southern wall)*, 1854

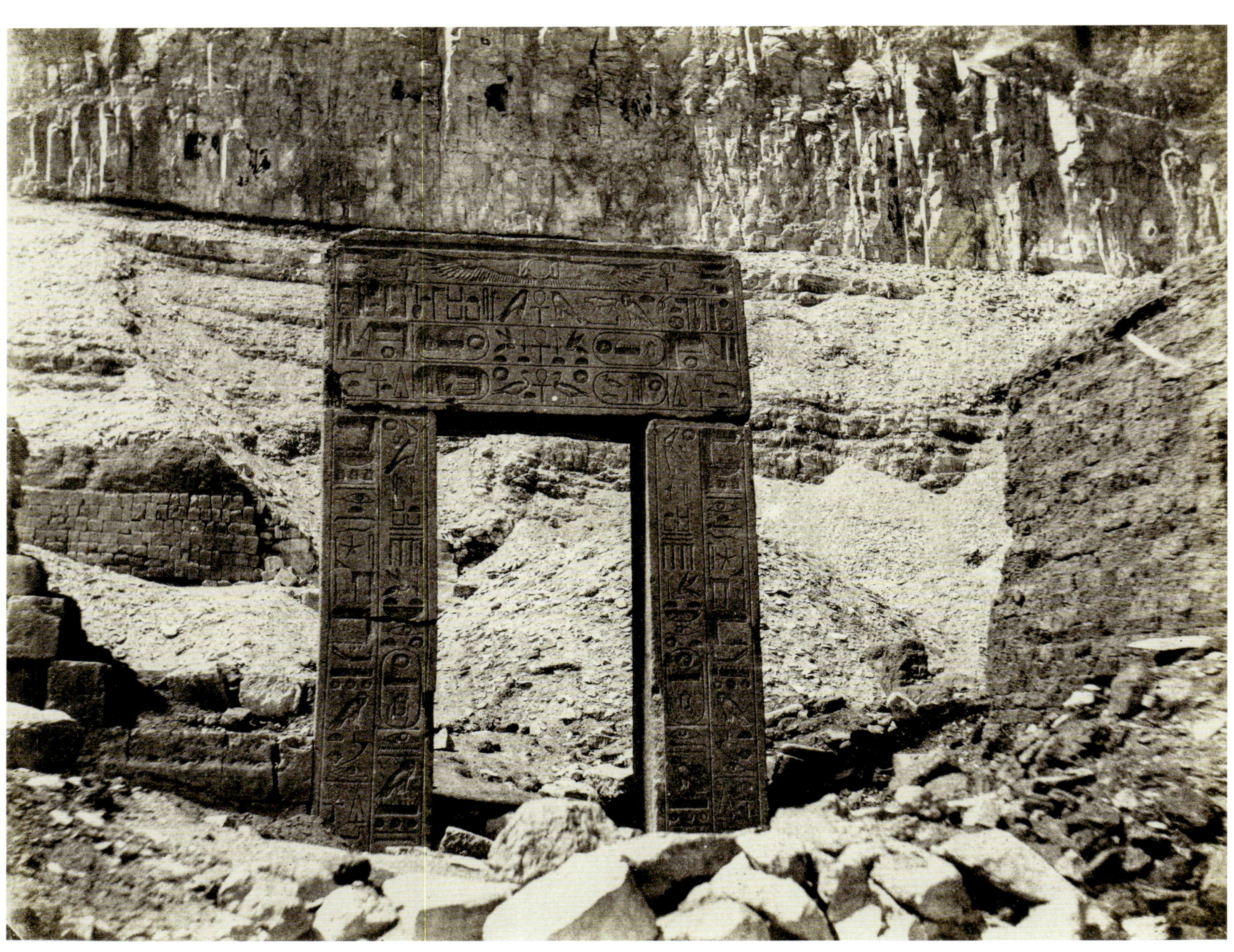

PLATE 57 *El-Assasif. Porte de granit rose, No. 1 (El-Assasif. Portal made of pink granite, No. 1)*, 1854

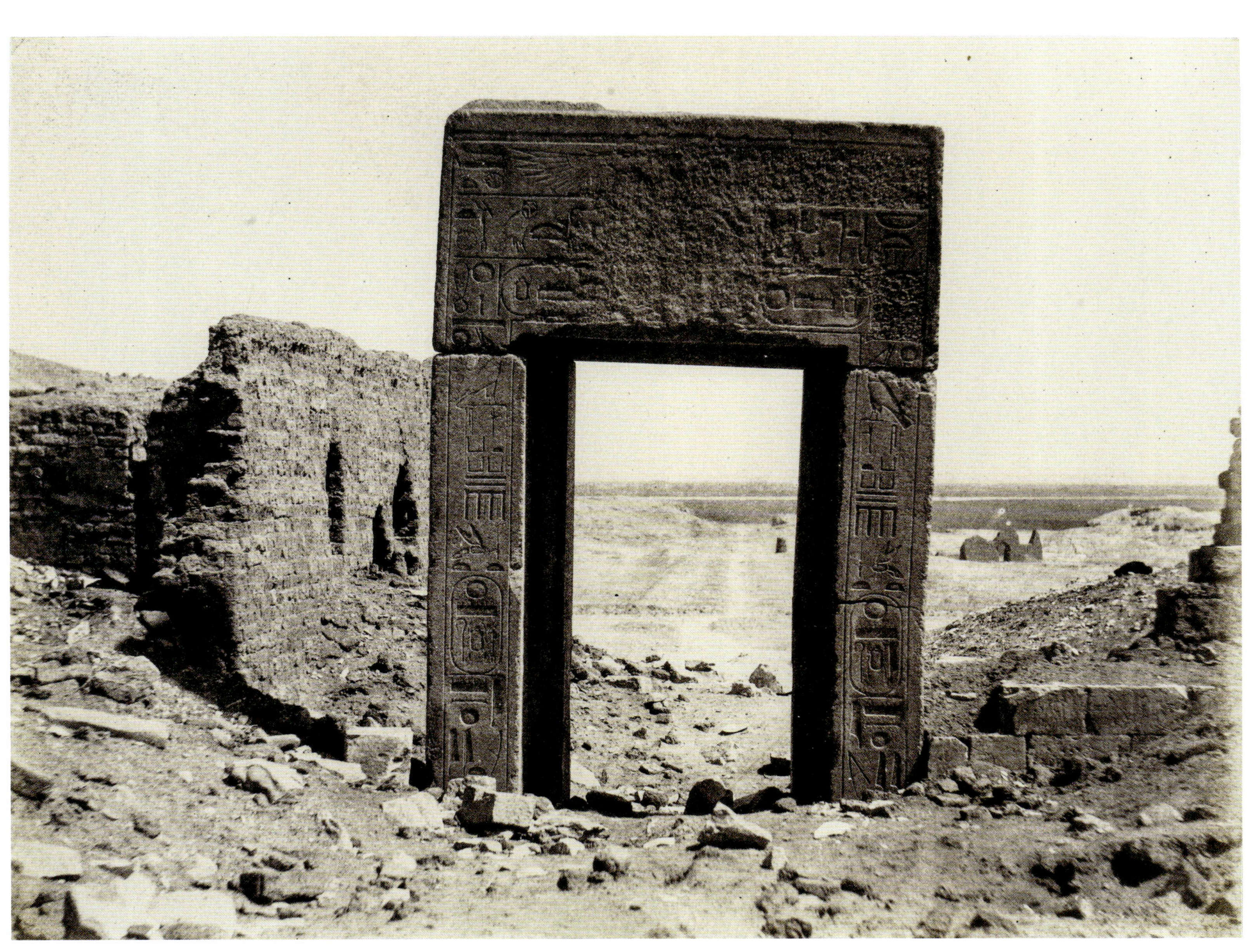

PLATE 58 *El-Assasif. Porte de granit rose. No. 2 (El-Assasif. Portal made of pink granite, No. 2)*, 1854

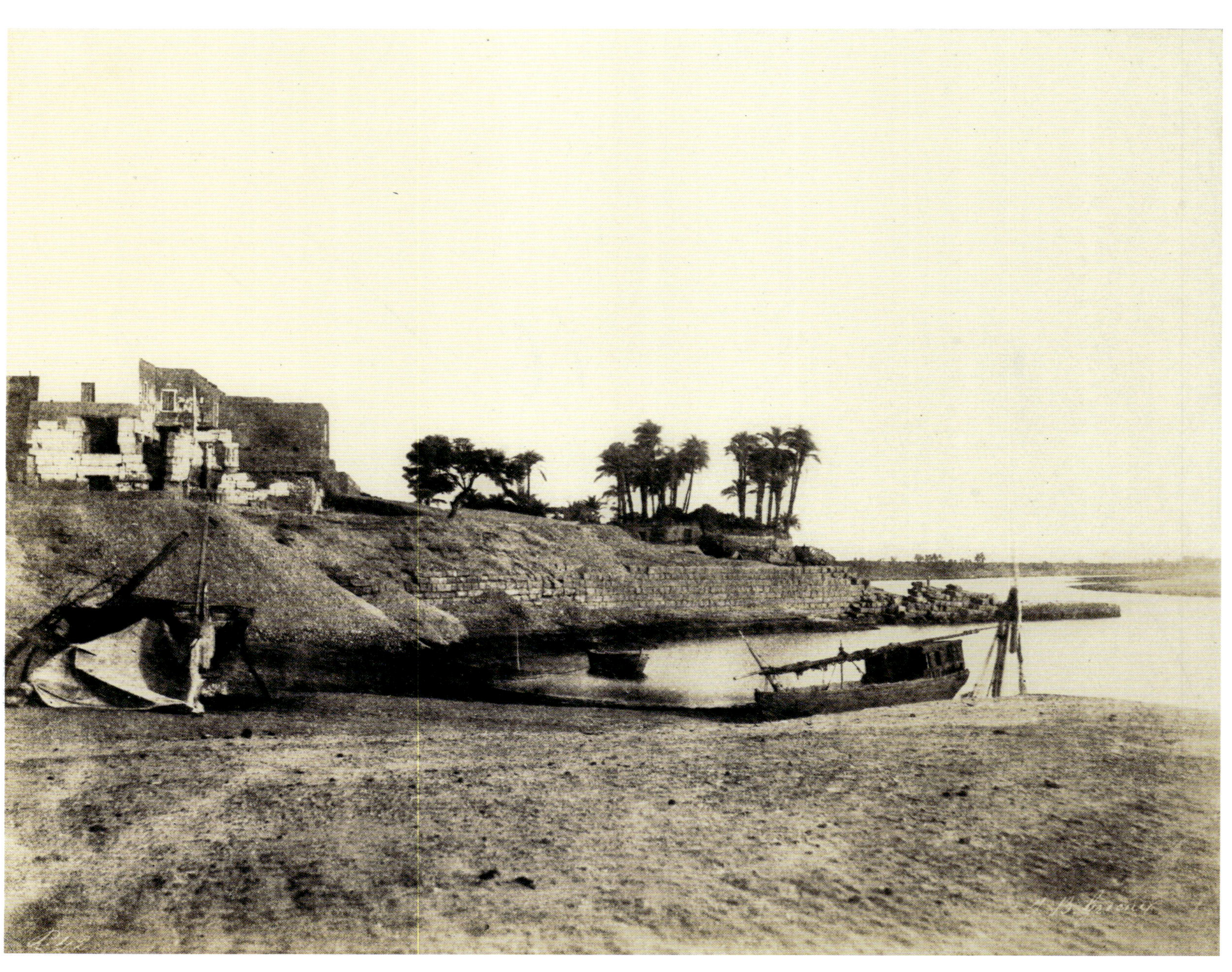

PLATE 59 *Château de France; Louqsor (Château de France, Luxor)*, 1854

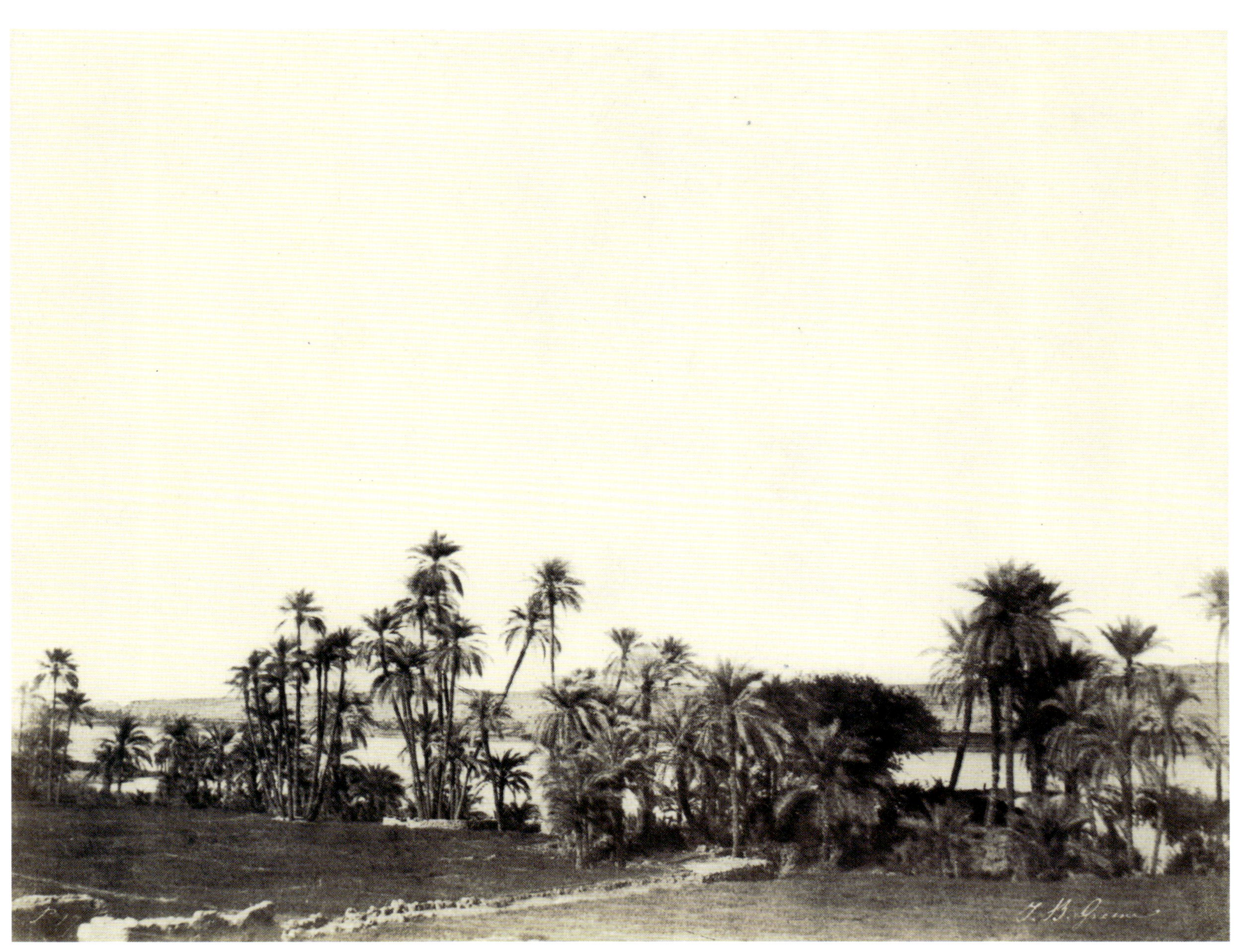

PLATE 60 *Bords du Nil. Kalabschi (Banks of the Nile. Kalabsha)*, 1854

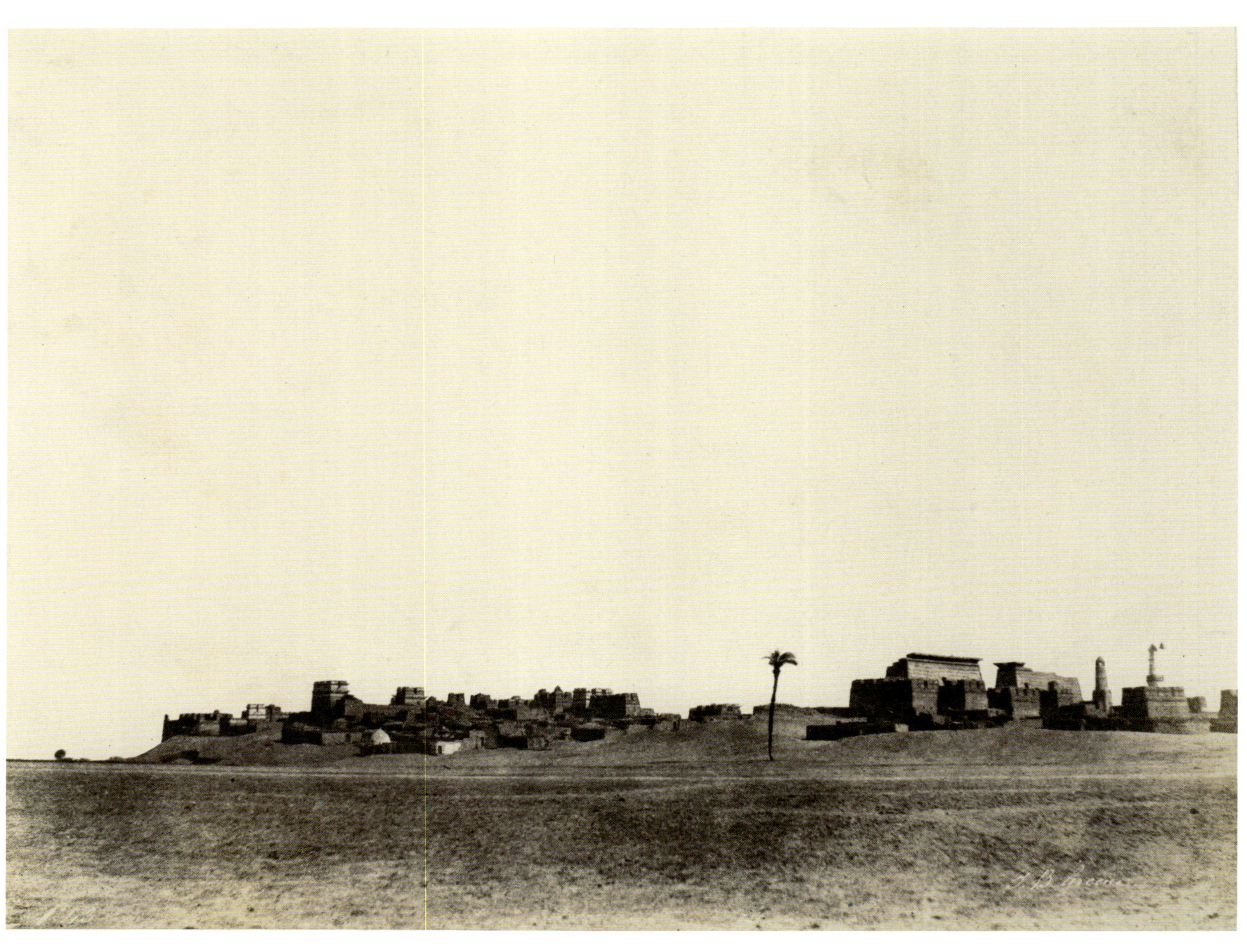

PLATE 61 *Louqsor (Luxor)*, 1854

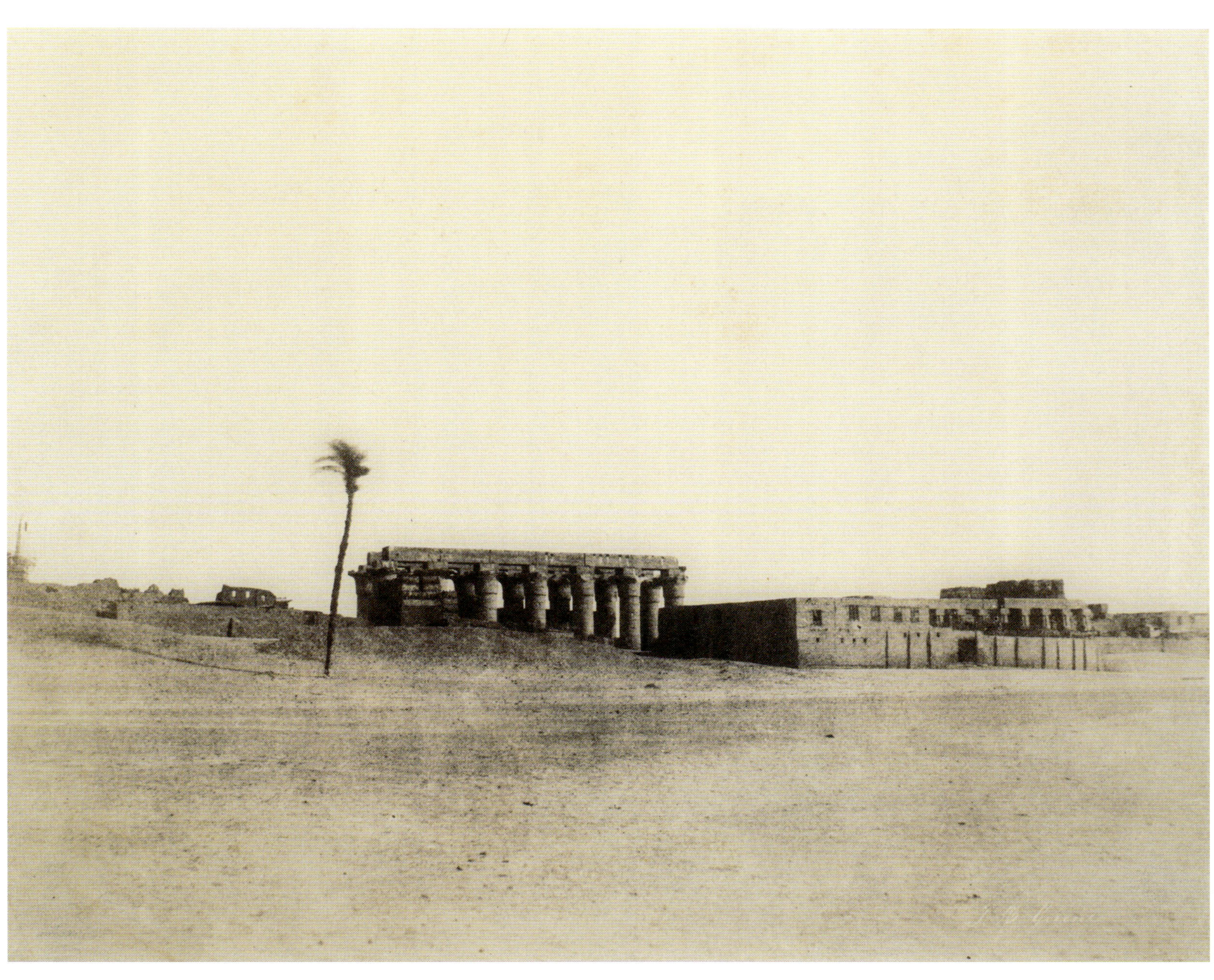

PLATE 62 *Louqsor. Portique (Luxor. Portico)*, 1854

PLATE 63 *Bords du Nil à Thèbes (Banks of the Nile at Thebes)*, 1854

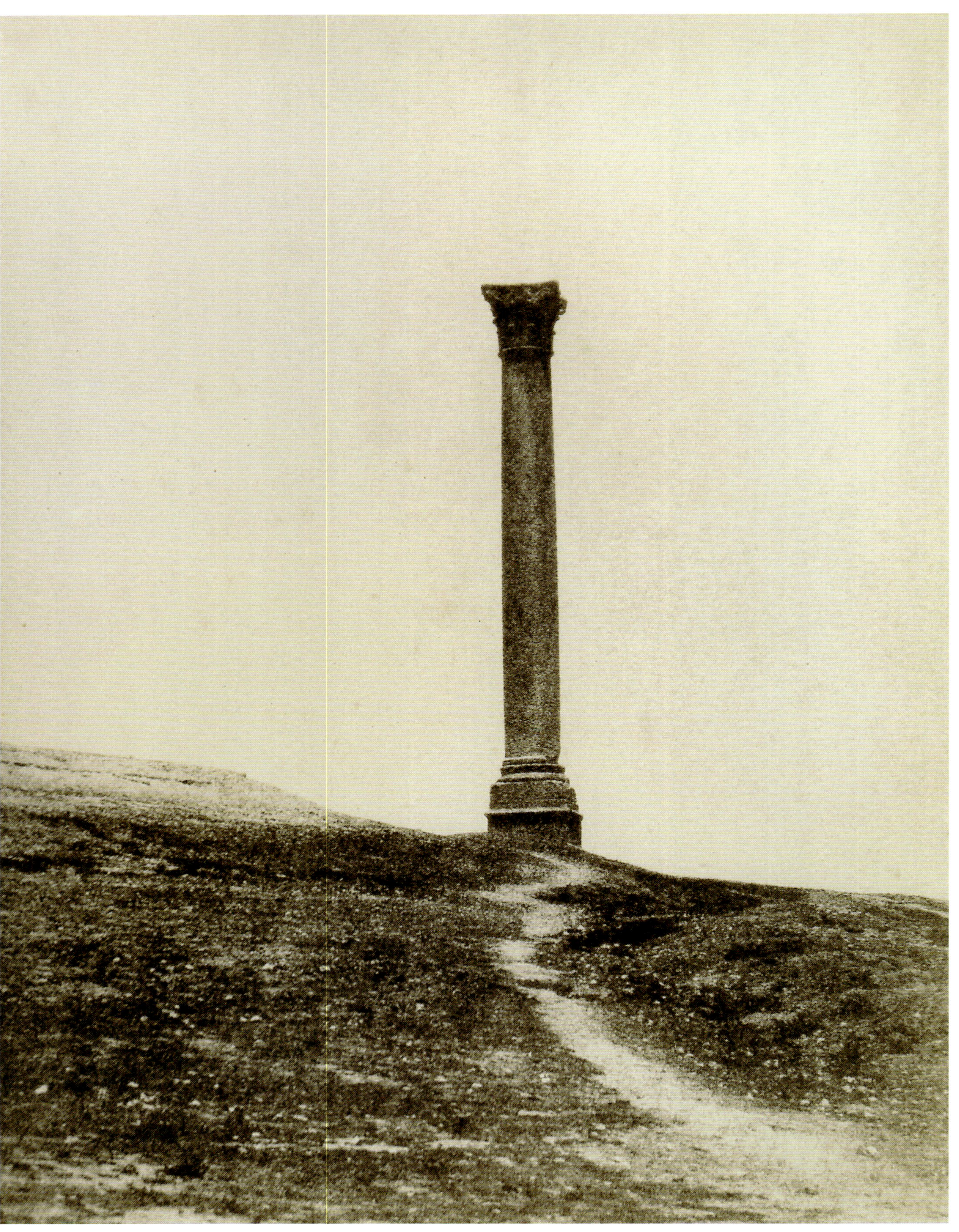

PLATE 64 [Pompey's Pillar], 1854–55

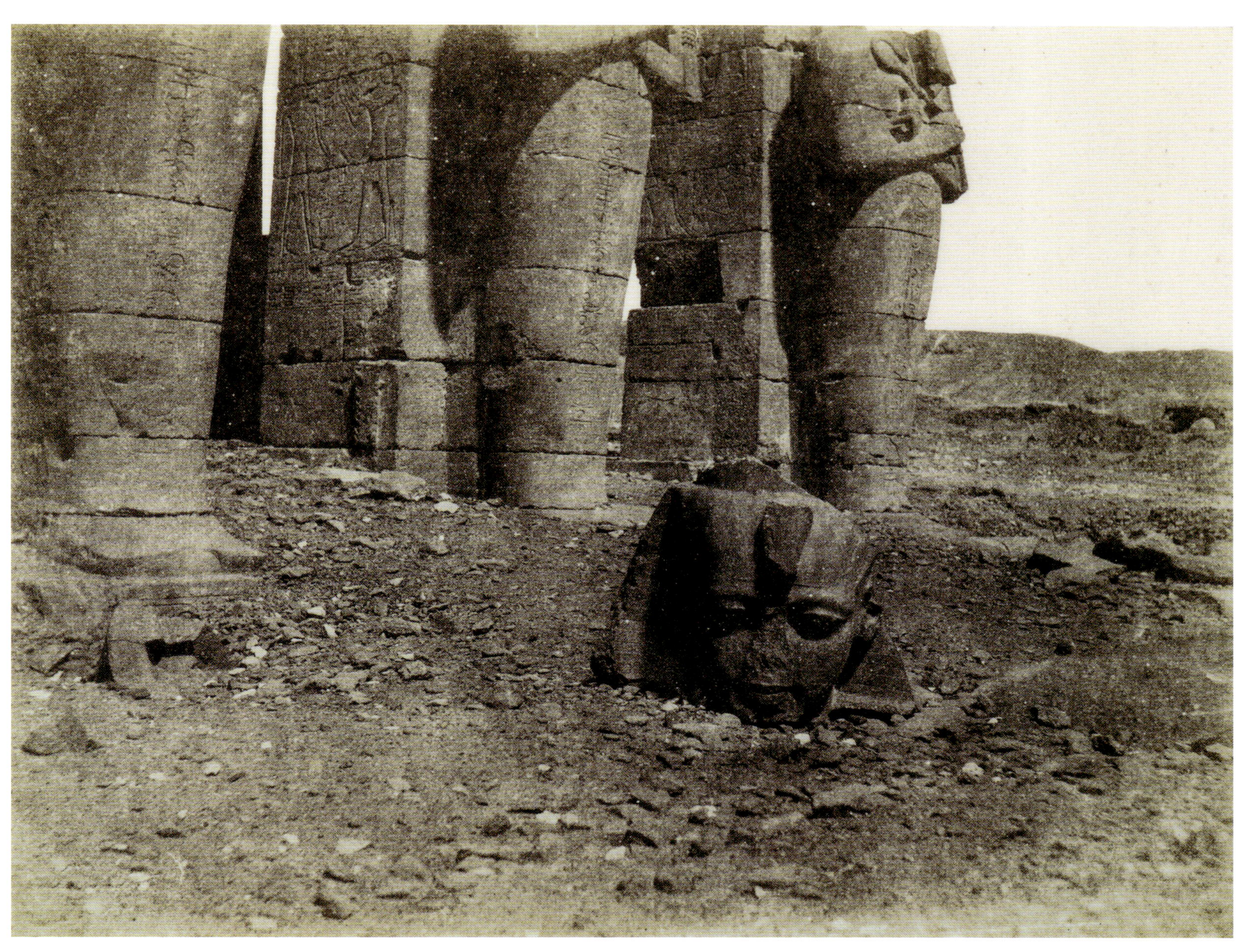

PLATE 65 [Ramesseum, with the head from a colossus of Ramesses II], 1854–55

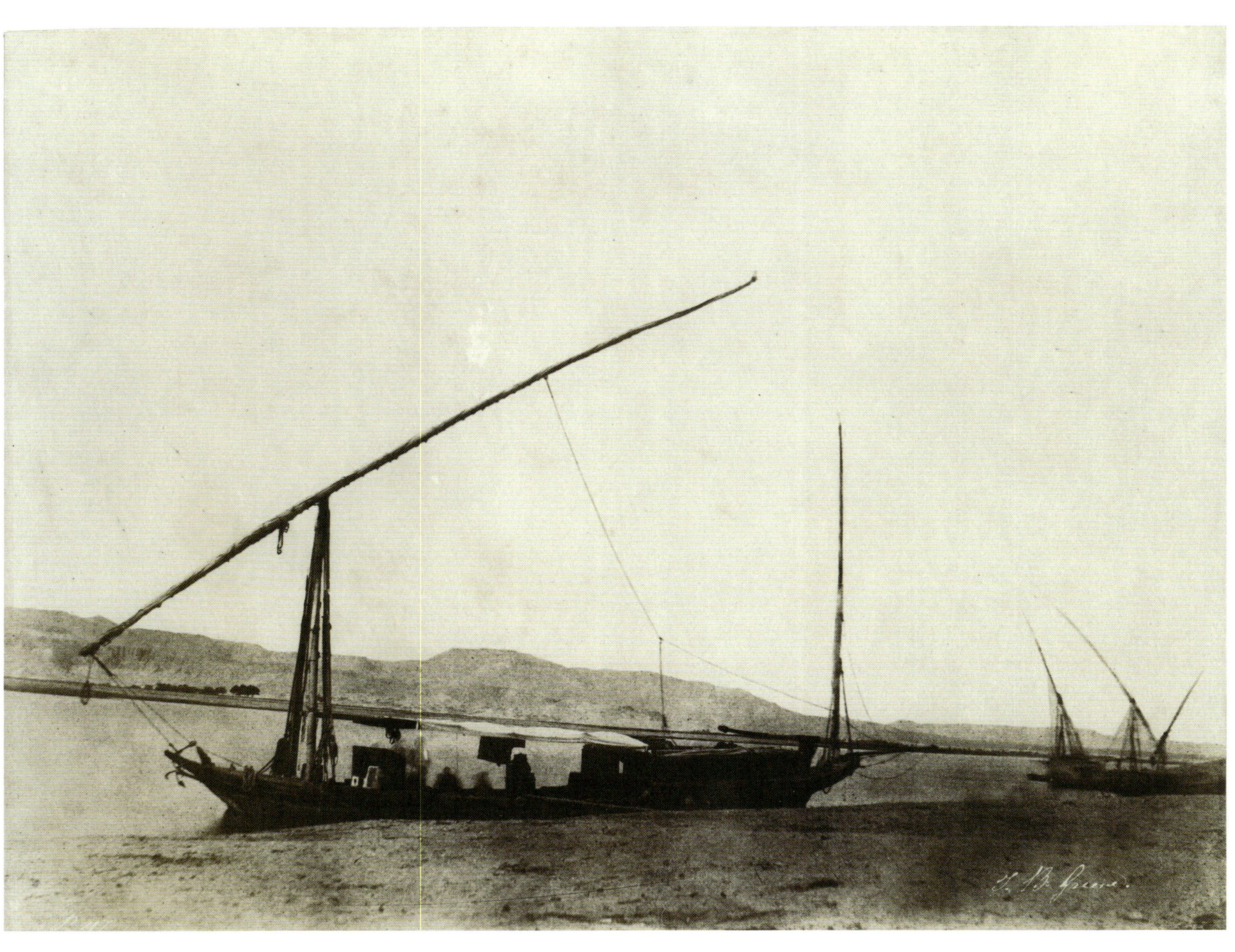

PLATE 66 [Boat on the Nile], 1855

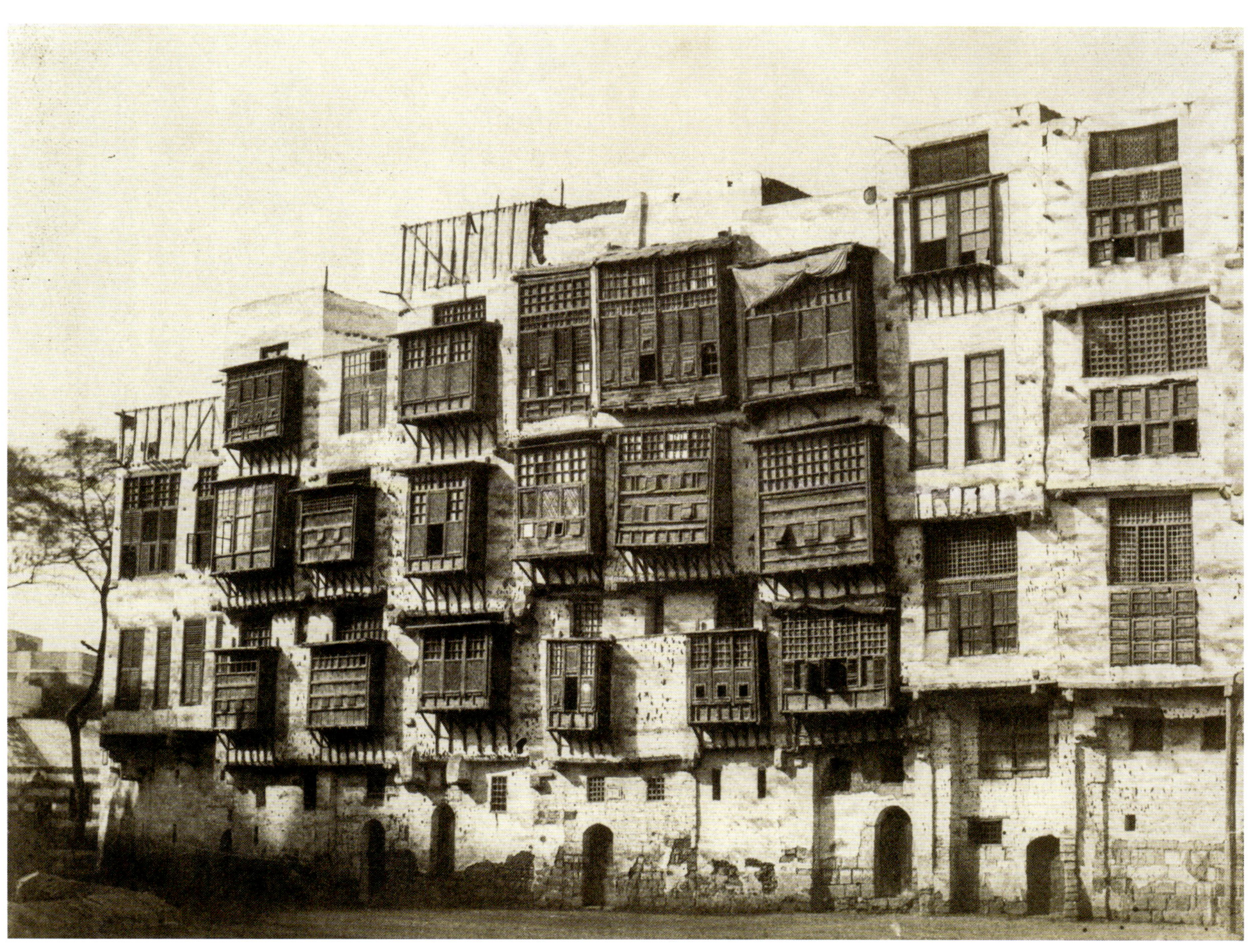

PLATE 67 [View of houses in Cairo], 1854–55

ALGERIA

In late 1855, Greene traveled to the French colony of Algeria. North Africa was exceptionally rich in antiquities and an active site for archaeology during the decades immediately following the 1830 French conquest of the Ottoman regency of Algeria, so it is perhaps not surprising that he was drawn to the Maghreb. While in Algeria, he worked on two archaeological efforts: he documented the initial excavations of a first-century BCE burial mound and wrote an article on a fragment of an Egyptian sculpture in the Cherchell museum of antiquities. However, as he had done on his first trip to Egypt, he also made evocative landscape views that seem unrelated to any scientific program. Though the textual records around his trip to Egypt are sparse, for Algeria they are almost nonexistent: no requests for instructions to the Académie des Inscriptions et Belles-Lettres, no letters to colleagues, that might help us to fully understand the circumstances of his trip.

Nor is his precise itinerary in Algeria known, though we can sketch its broad outline. Greene traveled by steamer from Marseilles to Algiers; by the mid-1850s, there was safe and regular service between the two ports. He photographed in three locations in Algeria: the archaeological site known as the Tombeau de la Chrétienne (Tomb of the Christian Woman) near Tipaza, which lies just west of Algiers; the inland clifftop city of Constantine; and the coastal city of Cherchell (some 60 miles west of Algiers, built on the site of the ancient Carthaginian city Iol, which later became Caesarea under Roman rule).[100] We know for certain that he was at the first excavation of the Tombeau de la Chrétienne by January 1, 1856, and stayed until at least January 5, and that he returned to the site for the second excavation in late March or very early April 1856. He departed for Cherchell on April 6 and arrived home in Paris by May 22, 1856.[101] It appears that he returned briefly to France between the two excavations at the Tombeau de la Chrétienne, and that he likely spent the rest of this interim period in Constantine.[102]

Greene's conviction in photography's utility to archaeology is evident in his most focused body of work in Algeria: a series of fourteen pictures documenting the two initial excavations of Kubr-er-Rumia (also spelled Kbor-er-Roumia), the first-century BCE burial mound then widely (and erroneously) known as the Tombeau de la Chrétienne. Built on a hill so that the tomb's top stood some 1,000 feet above a plain, the tumulus was a distinctive but mysterious feature of the northern Algerian landscape. At the time of Greene's visit, there was great debate over the tomb's builder, the identity of the remains housed inside, and the origin of its name. Even its true form was in question, hidden as much of it was by fallen stones and overgrowth: the tomb had been severely damaged over time, by the sixteenth-century Pasha of Algiers, who attempted to pull it down, and later by the occupying French forces, who used it for target practice. Later excavations would confirm that the tomb was built in 3 BCE by the Numidian king of Mauretania Juba II and his wife Cleopatra Selene II (daughter of

Egyptian queen Cleopatra and Marc Antony), and that its peculiar name derived either from the assumption that a cruciform decoration visible on one of the tomb's four false doors indicated a Christian grave, or from a mistranslation of the Arab word "Rumia," or Roman. It had a cylindrical base some 200 feet in diameter and was originally surrounded by sixty columns supporting a cornice. False doors marked each of the cardinal points of the compass, and the whole was topped by a quasi-pyramidal mound. Yet none of this was known until the 1860s. Nearly impossible to access due to the inhospitable terrain, and the subject of more lore and historical speculation than fact, the Tombeau de la Chrétienne offered a tantalizing mystery to archaeologists.[103]

Adrien Berbrugger, director of the library and museum of Algiers as well as the editor of the scholarly journal *Révue Africaine*, was determined to unlock its secrets. Over the course of several decades, he undertook a series of excavations at the site. In his capacity as secretary to the military commander of the French forces in Algeria, Berbrugger first visited the burial mound in 1835, the day after the French reached the site for the first time. He returned at least two more times during the 1840s, but was unable to dig due to lack of funds and official support.[104] In 1855, he received from the colony's governor-general a pittance of a financial award and an allocation of fifty Zouaves to undertake a first excavation. Berbrugger used his Christmas and Easter vacations from the museum to conduct two explorations of the tomb, one from December 19, 1855, to January 5, 1856, and the second from March 23 to April 5, 1856. These excavations had three goals: to discover the entrance to the monument, research the tomb's original form, and determine the approximate date of its construction.[105] He was not successful in any of these, hampered in part by poor financing, worse weather, and an inadequate workforce. Though Berbrugger's team was able to clear enough of the rubble to partly expose the shape of the tomb, as well as to uncover one of the tomb's four false doors, he was thwarted in his ultimate goal to locate the entrance.[106] At the end of the April 1856 excavation, the tomb remained impenetrable.

Greene joined Berbrugger as a photographer on both expeditions, though how he came to do so is unclear.[107] Some scholars have speculated that he was already in Algeria and joined Berbrugger out of interest in his work, and others that it was the possibility of discovering Egyptian remains within the Tombeau that brought him there.[108] In his report to the Académie des Inscriptions et Belles-Lettres, Berbrugger does not elaborate: "Mr. Greene, who is already known in the scholarly world for the remarkable work he executed in Egypt over three [*sic*] consecutive winters, kindly accompanied me to the Tombeau de la Chrétienne, of which he took several photographic views."[109] It is clear, however, that Berbrugger saw Greene's reputation in Egypt as an asset to his own project. He refers to Greene on at least one occasion as his "traveling companion," which would indicate he considered Greene a peer and not merely a photographer for hire.[110]

Greene's pictures of the Tombeau de la Chrétienne vary between long views of the monument and close-up details. They are strictly faithful to Berbrugger's excavation program, documenting the progress of the dig and highlighting the architectural details Berbrugger found significant. Moving in a circle around the tomb, Greene began with four views that show its general condition on the first expedition as seen from the north, south, east, and west. In each, he set the camera low so that the shape of the mound disengages from the horizon and is silhouetted against the sky; its irregular humped form, dotted with bushes and scraggly overgrowth, is grounded at the bottom of the frame by an out-of-focus band of scrubby grass (pl. 68). At the end of the second exploration, on April 5, Greene made another view of the east side of the tomb, in order to demonstrate the dig's progress. Though the comparison between the two is not dramatic, it is evident that Berbrugger's men had made some progress in clearing the large blocks of stone that had tumbled down around the base (pl. 74). Two other photographs show the excavation of the false door from the northern side: a close-up shows the detail of the partially visible door, still blocked by stones (pl. 69); the other, made on April 5, 1856, shows the stone slab in its entirety, after it had been cleared (pl. 70). Other pictures show the enormity of the challenge: Greene's tightly framed views of tumbled blocks demonstrate not only the quantity of stones that needed to be moved, but also give the impression that the field continues well beyond the edges of the frame (pl. 71). Absent any marker of scale, the image dissolves into a study of pure pattern.

Berbrugger sent Greene's photographs from the excavation in two separate groups to the Académie des Inscriptions et Belles-Lettres, which he later assembled into an album, now in the collection of the library of the Institut de France.[111] The fourteen photographs are mounted, and each album page is annotated in what is likely Berbrugger's hand. The prints themselves are mostly signed and dated by the photographer, some in ink on the surface of the print itself and others in the negative.[112] The plates are arranged chronologically, as Greene documented the two phases of excavation in 1856. For Berbrugger, Greene's pictures, "with the unassailable exactitude of photography," had the additional benefit of proving that his excavation had done no further damage to the monument.[113] In addition to the "before-and-after" pictures described above, Greene documented Berbrugger's interest in the evidence of Roman architecture at the tomb. He discovered two kinds of Ionic capitals at the site, thereby enabling him to correct earlier erroneous descriptions.[114] Two pictures in the album depict one of these capitals: in one version, the capital is shown in situ, upside down, as it was discovered, sitting below the grass-fringed horizon, amidst other architectural fragments (fig. 19). The other view of the same fragment was taken from a slightly different angle, and Berbrugger carefully trimmed around its contours—eliminating the background—and pasted it in the album inverted, so that it appears as it would have right-side up (fig. 20). Seen side by side, the two views present a remarkable contrast: one suggests a rather melancholy meditation on the fall of empires, while the other conjures the dispassionate precision of a scientific atlas of architectural specimens.

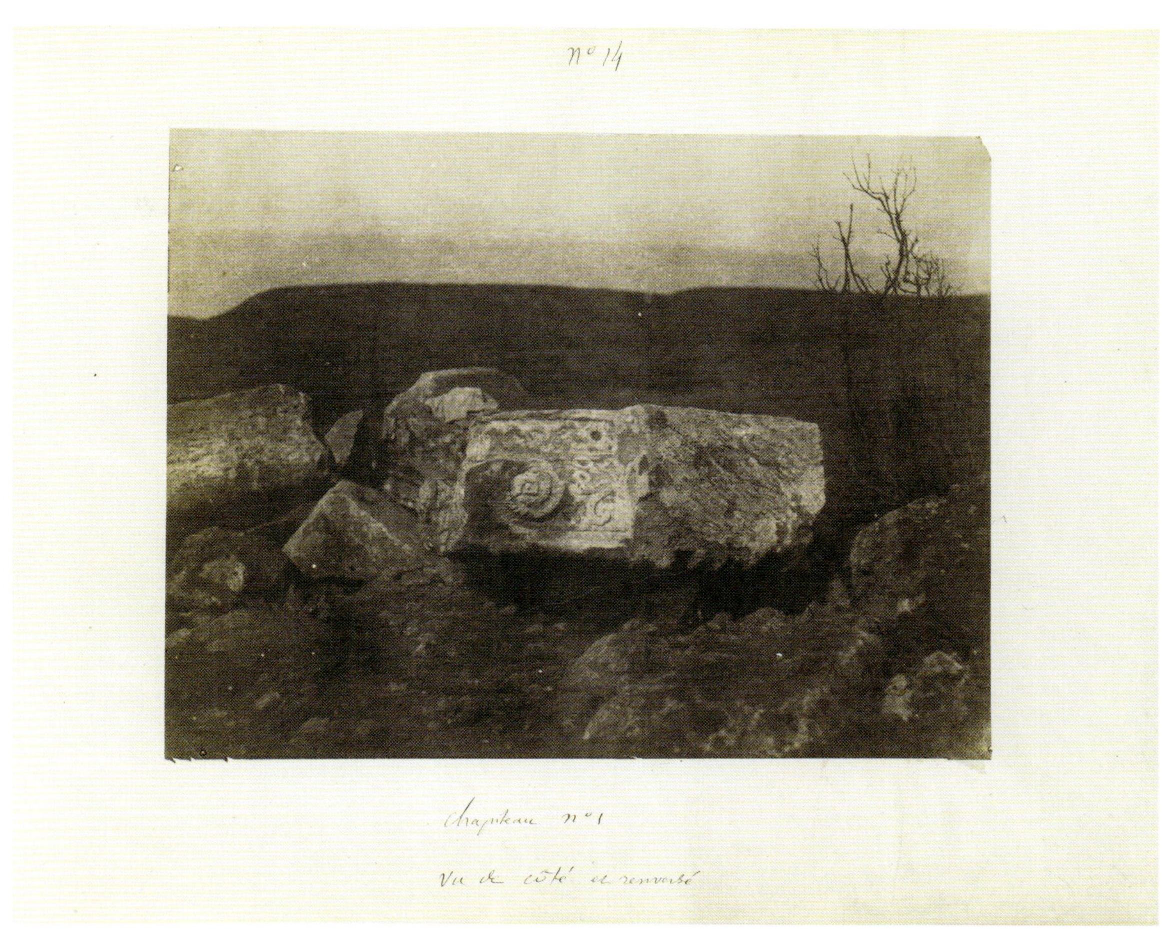

FIG. 19 John Beasley Greene, *Chapiteau no 1 vu de côté et renversé (Capital no. 1, from the side and upside down)*, 1856. Plate 14 of the album *Tombeau de la Chrétienne*. Salted paper print. Bibliothèque de l'Insititut de France, Paris

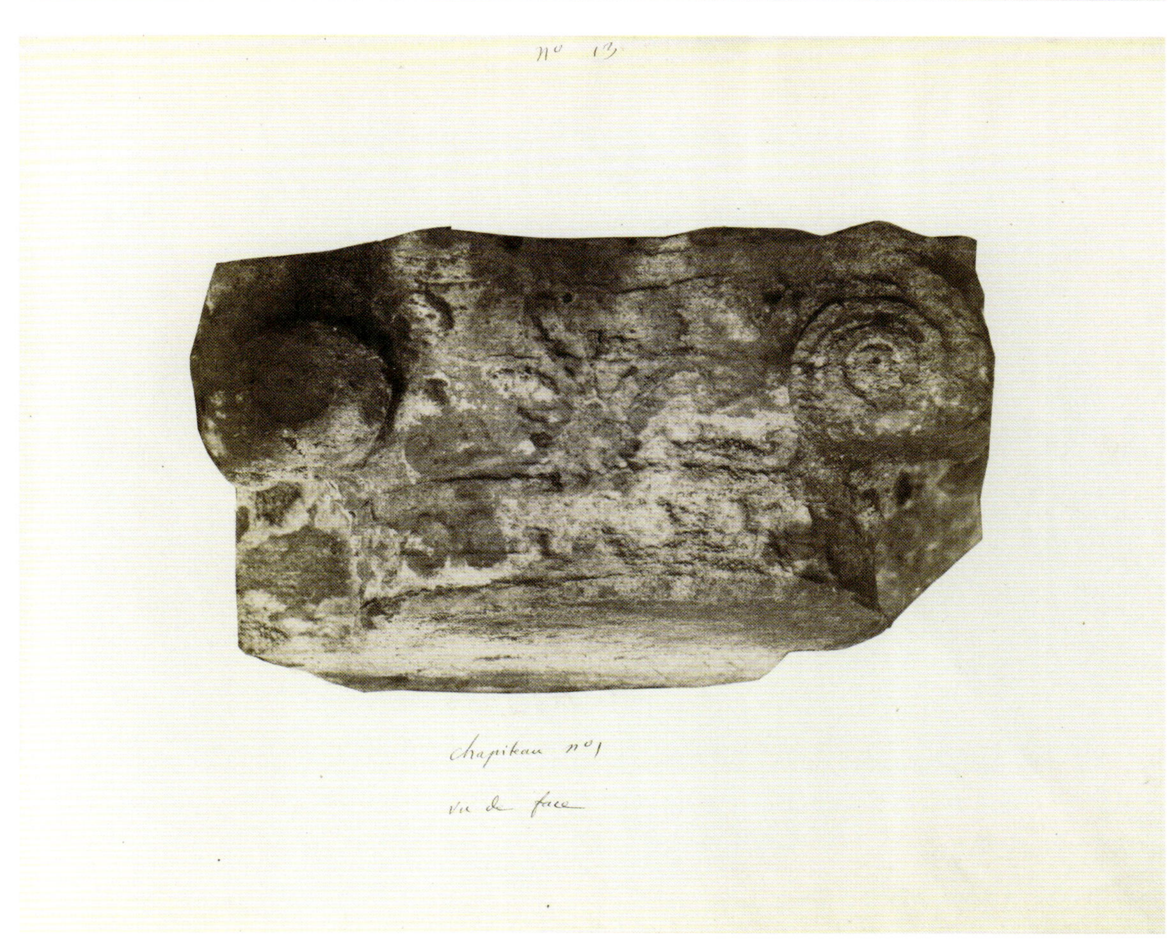

FIG. 20 John Beasley Greene, *Chapiteau no 1 vu de face (Capital no. 1, from the front)*, 1856. Plate 13 of the album *Tombeau de la Chrétienne*. Salted paper print. Bibliothèque de l'Institut de France, Paris

Greene was not the only photographer at the Tombeau de la Chrétienne: at the very end of the April excavations, the team was joined briefly by Félix Moulin, who up until this point was known for his (occasionally scandalous) nude studies. He arrived in Algiers on March 7, 1856, with the aim of making a photographic study of Algeria. No doubt inspired by the success in Europe of photographic albums of other exotic locales, Moulin sought to capitalize on avid French interest in the region. He spent the next eighteen months traveling, resulting in the six-volume photographic study *Souvenirs d'Algérie, ou l'Algérie photographiée*. His 300 views included landscapes, famous monuments, portraits of important individuals (French and Algerian), as well as genre studies and "local color." Moulin reported frequently on his adventures to the photographic journal *La Lumière*, and his breezy accounts paint a colorful picture of French Algeria. Despite his light tone and evident colonialist biases, his letters also give a vivid picture of the challenges a photographer in the region faced. In addition to the adverse weather that limited the hours in which making photographs was even possible (like Berbrugger, he complained bitterly about the rain), Moulin, who used glass negatives and the wet collodion process, was weighed down by nearly a ton of

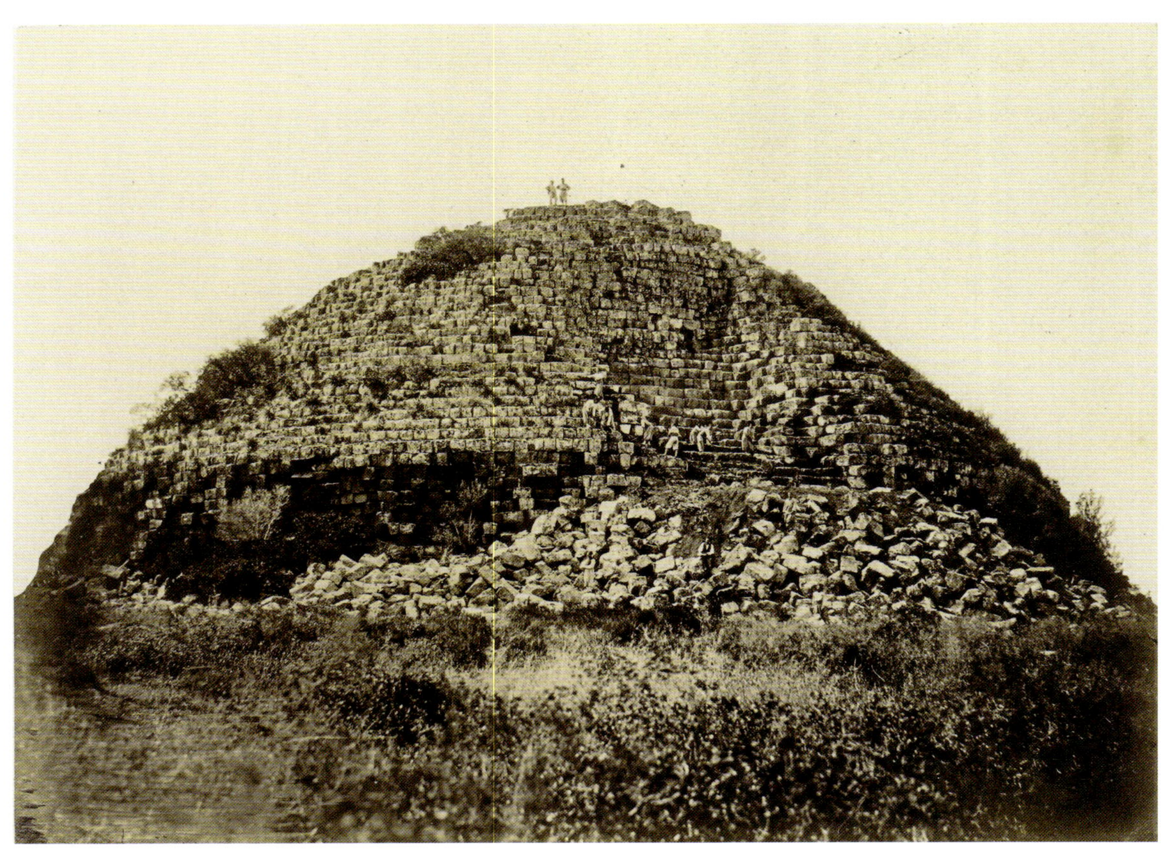

FIG. 21 Félix Moulin (French, 1802–1875), *Kobeur Roumia (Tombeau de la Chrétienne)*. Plate 78 of the album *L'Algérie photographiée: Province d'Alger*, 1856–57. Albumen print. Bibliothèque Nationale de France, Paris

fragile equipment.[115] The roads were frequently in poor condition, and necessary supplies—especially water clean enough for photographic processes—were hard to come by in the field. Greene, who worked with paper negatives, would not have been so heavily freighted, but he would have suffered the same obstacles of transport, weather, and material shortages.

Moulin spent only a brief time photographing at the tomb, and made a mere three views there, but the contrast between his photographs and Greene's is instructive. Unlike Greene, whose pictures hew closely to Berbrugger's research interests, Moulin had little concern for archaeology and approached the tomb much like a tourist. His aim was visual potency rather than scholarly documentation. One of his plates depicts the burial mound in its entirety. Close inspection reveals a number of Zouaves posed at various points with their tools; the mound is topped by two figures, one of whom may be Berbrugger himself (fig. 21). Moulin's glass plates, unlike Greene's paper negatives, were capable of transcribing the smallest details, and their greater light sensitivity meant that he was also able to capture human activity. In an article in the *Revue Africaine*, Berbrugger, after heartily thanking Greene for his work and praising his photographs as invaluable testimony to the stages of the excavation, highlights the difference between the two photographers' works. He notes that Moulin's images give a human face to the excavation and lend a sense of scale: "[one photograph] represents the north face in a moment where the Zouaves were at work; each personage is a perfectly recognizable portrait. One can, thereby, by comparing the workers disseminated across the monument, appreciate the size of the Tombeau de la Chrétienne."[116] Where Greene's rendering of the tomb is solemn, almost elegiac, and seems to exist outside of human scale and time, Moulin's is lively, even celebratory. Indeed, Moulin wrote that he chose to photograph it at that particular time because he knew the presence of the excavators would not only make his sojourn there more pleasant, but that it would allow him to give a more "animated aspect to this inelegant mass."[117] The figures in Moulin's pictures look less like laborers and more like conquerors, and the architecture of the mound seems secondary to the evidence of the human effort exerted. Moulin's other plate of the tomb depicts members of the excavation team surrounding the newly cleared northern false door, including Berbrugger, who leans proprietarily against the stone slab, and a number of Zouaves in their distinctive costumes (fig. 22). Monique Dondin-Payre has pointed out the figure of a very thin man leaning against a rock to the left of the door and suggests that it may be Greene himself, as Berbrugger did not mention anyone in his company besides the Zouaves, and the man depicted is clearly not a laborer.[118] It is an extremely tempting conjecture, for if true, it is the only known portrait of the young photographer.

In addition to providing a pictorial foil to Greene's work, Moulin's captioned and published photographs are also helpful in identifying some of Greene's views in Algeria, which (aside from those in the Tombeau album) were not titled or labeled by the photographer before his death. For example, his depiction of a group of white tents in a dusky field (pl. 73) can be definitively identified as the camp of the excavation team at the tomb, as Moulin made (and labeled) a nearly identical view (fig. 23). Yet the difference in their technical and aesthetic approaches gives their two pictures distinctively different feelings. Moulin shows the camp in full operation—two men are clearly visible in the foreground by a tent with an open flap, one sitting in the tall grass and the other standing, in his exotic Zouave uniform, his figure silhouetted against the white canvas. At the right of his frame, less distinct due to their movement during the exposure, a cluster of men sit on the ground, perhaps having a meal. Moulin's glass plate records every detail. On the other hand, Greene's photograph—which was not included in the prints Berbrugger sent to Paris—is pure mood. The same white tents, here placed well below the horizon, seem to glow against the dark sea of grass. The grassy ridge behind them gives way to a hazy frieze of distant mountains, and finally to a vast expanse of sky. Apart from the tents, there is no evidence of human occupation. As it had no value to the archaeological excavation, Greene's photograph appears to be a purely personal exercise in landscape study. He brings to bear the

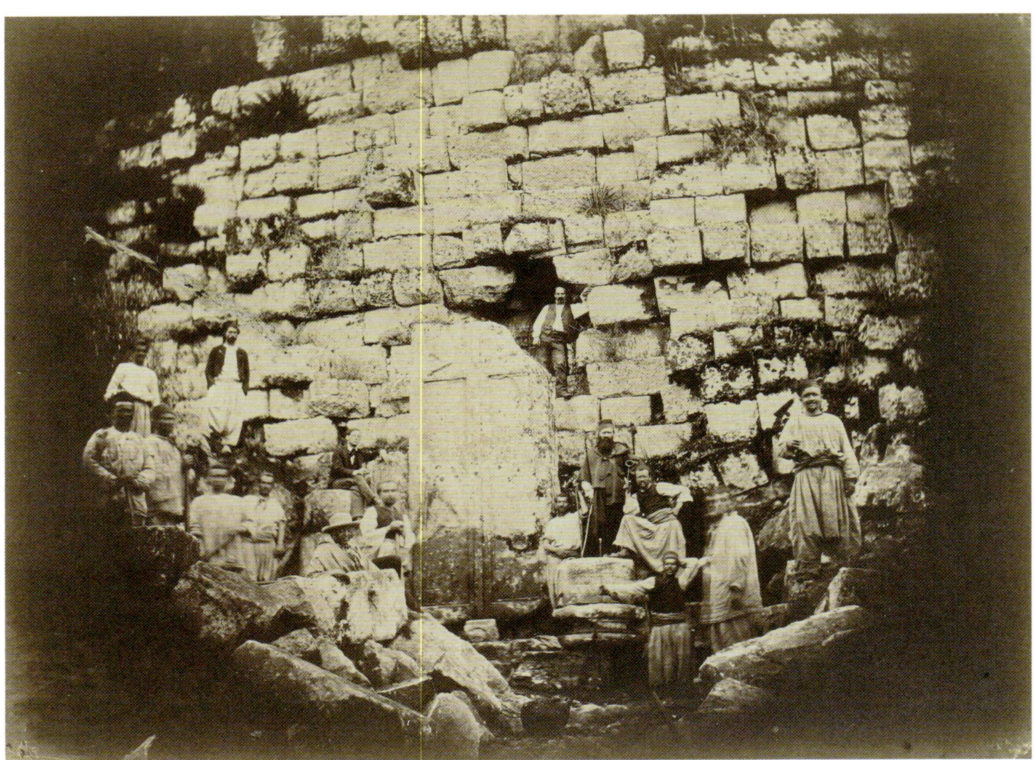

FIG. 22 Félix Moulin (French, 1802–1875), *Partie nord du Tombeau de la Chrétienne. Fouilles faites par un détachement de Zouaves sous la direction de M. Berbrugger (Northern part of the Tombeau de la Chrétienne. Excavations done by a detachment of Zouaves under the direction of Mr. Berbrugger)*. Plate 79 of the album *L'Algérie photographiée: Province d'Alger*, 1856–57. Albumen print. Bibliothèque Nationale de France, Paris

lessons he learned in the vast deserts of Egypt, conjuring a similarly boundless sky. It also recalls (more than a little) the view of tents he made along the road to Chailly in Fontainebleau.

Greene gave full expression to his aptitude for landscape photography in the series of views he made in and around Constantine between the two excavations in Tipaza, though he adapted his approach to better suit the city's unusual and visually striking topography. Constantine, 40 miles inland from the port of Philippeville (now Skikda), is strategically positioned, perched on a plateau some 2,000 feet above sea level and surrounded almost all the way round by steep cliffs and the deep gorges of the Rhumel River.[119] It was thus a highly defensible city, and its location in a fertile plain also made it a desirable site, attractive to numerous groups of people over thousands of years. By the third century BCE, it was the capital of Numidia, called Cirta, from the Phoenician word for "city." Cirta was taken over by the Romans as their empire spread through North Africa, and renamed in 311 for the Roman emperor Constantine.[120] Over the next 1,500 years, the city experienced cycles of decline and rejuvenation, as successive groups—Berbers, Arabs, and Turks, among

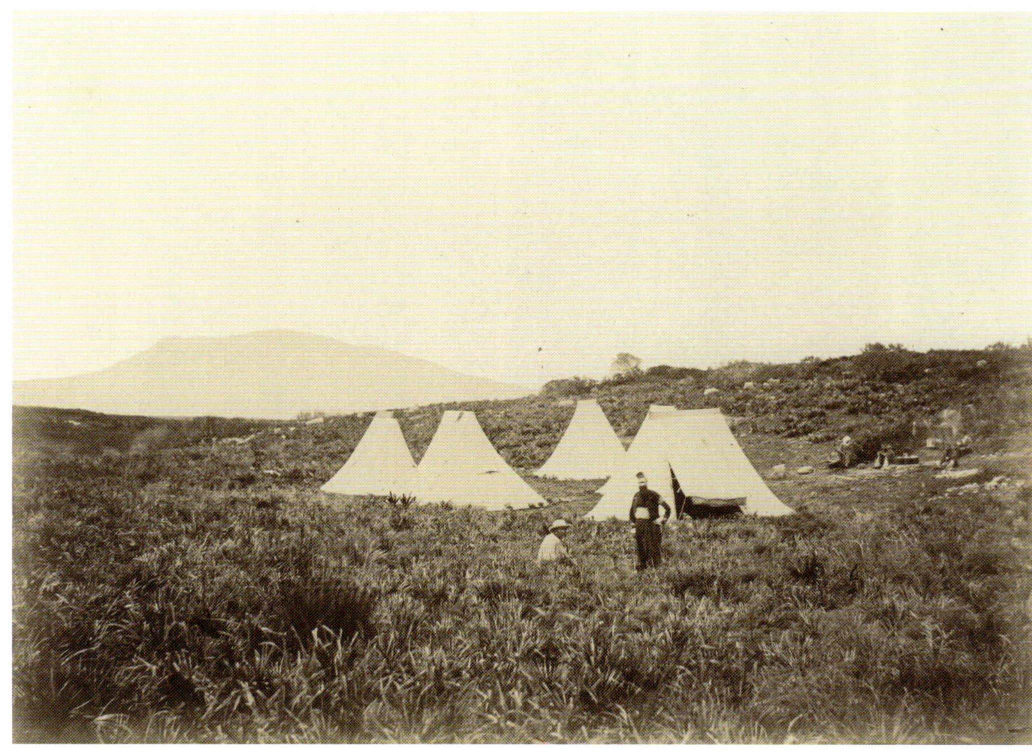

FIG. 23 Félix Moulin (French, 1802–1879), *Campement au Tombeau de la Chrétienne (Encampment at the Tombeau de la Chrétienne)*. Plate 80 of the album *L'Algérie photographiée: Province d'Alger*, 1856–57. Albumen print. Bibliothèque Nationale de France, Paris

others—occupied it. No matter the occupier, the city remained the economic and political center of the region.[121]

Constantine held great symbolic power for the French as well. In 1836, as the colonizers expanded their aspirations beyond the Algerian coast (by then almost entirely under French control), the Armée de l'Afrique moved deeper into the territory, with Constantine in its sights. Initial attempts to take the city were thwarted by the difficulty of access: its walls were heavily fortified, and the winter weather was severe.[122] The following fall, the French launched a successful siege, taking the city in October 1837. It was an especially gruesome victory: hundreds of the native inhabitants, fleeing for their lives, instead plunged to their deaths in the surrounding gorges.[123] In the French colonial imagination, the city came to stand for the perseverance and ultimate triumph of the French, a potent nationalist mythology in which they figured as not only victorious conquerors of the resistant local peoples, but also as inheritors of its glorious Roman past.

Constantine was awash in Roman ruins and artifacts—one of the richest sites for such material in Algeria—and there was an active archaeological society in the city. Yet if Greene made any studies of these Roman antiquities, they have not survived.[124] A handful of depictions of the El-Kantara Bridge—the only point of entry into the city across the deep ravine—show the evidence of Roman engineering, but these views emphasize the startling impression the bridge creates as it slices through the surrounding hills and nimbly skirts the precipice rather than its precision or stability (fig. 24). More of his photographs focus on the natural scenery along the banks of the Rhumel, particularly the lush foliage and rushing waterfalls.[125] In comparison to the aridity of Egypt, Greene's landscapes near Constantine are dense with detail and palpable atmosphere. Nor do his photographs (with few exceptions) dwell on the extensive interventions of the French colonists into the urban fabric. Greene's Constantine offers neither a picture of its French present nor a celebration of its Roman past, but a vivid and visceral sensation of his physical experience of the site.

The photographs made in Constantine provide abundant evidence not only of Greene's keen interest in landscape, but also of his ability to respond nimbly to the particularities of the terrain before his lens. In Egypt, Greene frequently placed the horizon line low in the frame, subsuming the great monuments of man into vast seas of sand, which were in turn dwarfed by boundless skies. In Algeria, he reversed this approach, filling the lower two-thirds of the frame with rocky cliff and squeezing the buildings and the sky into a narrow band at the top. Rather than crowning the cliffs, the buildings appear to merge into their very substance, like layers of sedimentary rock. In other photographs, he used the jagged contours of the cliffs to produce startlingly sharp and geometrical plays of negative and positive space: the triangular shapes formed by water rushing over a rock face are violently counterbalanced by a crisply excised wedge of sky (pl. 82). To accommodate the photographic challenges of the dramatic and vertiginous landscape, Greene also introduced an entirely new

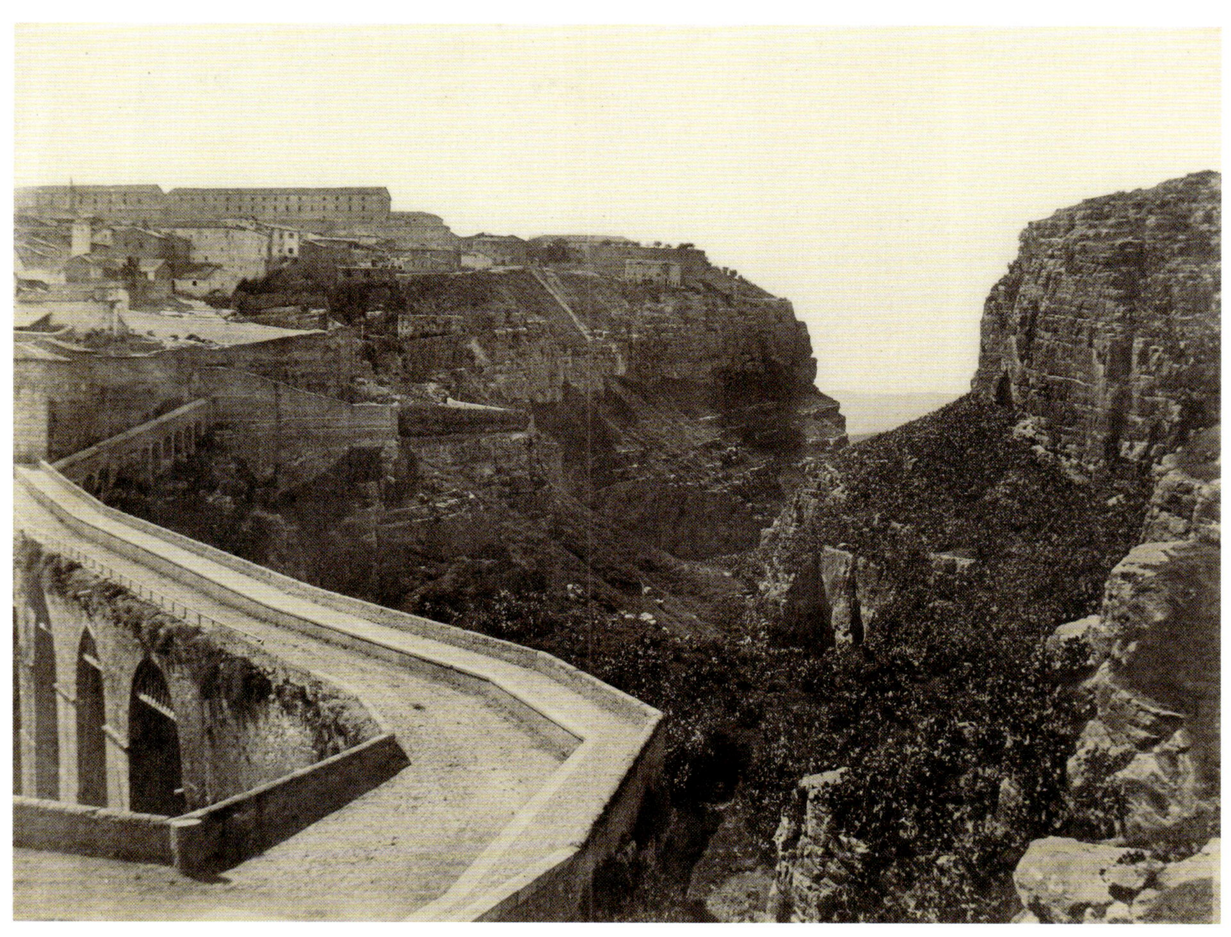

FIG. 24 John Beasley Greene, [El-Kantara Bridge, Constantine], 1856. Salted paper print. The Museum of Modern Art, New York, Gift of Jerome Powell

picture-making strategy into his repertoire: several of his negatives appear to function as components of diptychs or triptychs.[126] Lined up side by side, these photographs provide a wide-angle, panoramic view (pl. 84).[127] Constantine is the only location in which he experimented with this approach. Whereas in Egypt Greene used great expanses of empty space to impart a sense of timeless monumentality, in Algeria he conveyed a similar feeling through an abundance of layered pictorial information.

After Constantine, Greene returned to Tipaza for the second excavation, and at the end of the April 1856 dig, the team dispersed, and Greene headed northwest to Cherchell.[128] Though he made one study of the lighthouse built by the French at Cherchell's Fort Joinville (pl. 90)—his only acknowledgment of the French colonial presence there—and some beautiful landscape views of the ruins of a Roman aqueduct (pl. 86) that are very much in line with his studies in Egypt, Greene's main interest in Cherchell was the museum of antiquities, particularly a fragment of an Egyptian sculpture in its collection. The museum contained a vast array of Roman architectural fragments, sculpture, and tomb inscriptions, as well as other artifacts from the region, most of which were stored in a somewhat haphazard jumble in the museum's courtyard.[129] Greene made three moody studies of fragments of Roman sculptures which form a sort of poetic frieze in the courtyard's somber shadows. His attention, however, was singularly drawn by a black granite Egyptian sculpture of a walking man discovered in 1848, only the lower half of which was still intact (pl. 89). Back in France, he published an article about its possible origins (once again relying on Rougé for translations of the hieroglyphics he transcribed from its base), and his photograph of this object formed the basis for the line drawings that accompanied his text.[130] He must have returned to France almost immediately after his time in Cherchell in order to have published the article so quickly.

Greene made just over forty photographs in Algeria, a fraction of the quantity of work he produced in Egypt.[131] The prints from the Algerian trip are notably different from the Egyptian pictures, which vary wildly in tonality and condition. The Algerian work is far more consistent: with few exceptions, the prints are rich and brown, and show much less evidence of age or fading. (A number of them are also coated with albumen, and a few are albumen silver prints rather than salted paper prints.) It is not clear who printed the last of Greene's photographs: as Blanquart-Evrard's Imprimerie Photographique had closed in 1855, they were either printed by Greene himself or he commissioned someone else to make them. Interestingly, the two known prints of Greene's earliest work from France have a similar look to the albumenized prints from Algeria, suggesting they were made at the same time. Their similar appearance may also account for early confusion about where they were made: a number of institutions originally mislabeled these pictures as tree studies in Algeria, when they in fact were made in Fontainebleau.

In the fall of 1856, Greene once again traveled to Egypt, but this time he did not return. Apparently ill when he left Paris, he went to Cairo with the hope that "he would recover his health in the climate that had already cured him once before."[132] He died on November 29 at the age of twenty-four.

CONCLUSION: A PHOTOGRAPHER OF HIS TIME

This essay opened by considering the way the Rosetta Stone transformed archaeology in the early nineteenth century by providing a point of access into a past that, up to that point, had seemed so remote as to be unrecoverable. Though the gap between the current moment and that of John Beasley Greene is considerably smaller than the millenniums-wide chasm faced by early Egyptologists, the conceptual distance between the frameworks we use for understanding photography today and the ones deployed in the middle of the nineteenth century is nonetheless consequential. Greene's work first came to contemporary attention in the 1980s at a time when the history of photography began to coalesce as a discipline both in the university and in the art museum, alongside a concurrent, and not entirely coincidental, emergence of a photographic market. Many of the histories of photography written during this period sought to assimilate the medium's early years into an aesthetic prehistory of photographic modernism and largely smoothed over (or simply ignored) the ontological and epistemological confusions and inherent contradictions that characterized so much of the discourse shaping the medium in its earliest decades. In a series of essays, Abigail Solomon-Godeau, one of this enterprise's most vocal critics, warned of the intellectual dangers of such retroactive canon formation: "The relentless pursuit of the aesthetic—at the expense of any other consideration of the uses, functions, and discourses of nineteenth-century photography—inevitably leads to distortion and error as well as to significant omission."[133] Taking as an example the photographs made by Auguste Salzmann in Jerusalem in 1855 as evidence of Louis Félicien de Saulcy's dubious archaeological theories, Solomon-Godeau noted that we are inclined to misread his focused, close-up studies of stones as examples of a radical or protomodernist aesthetic rather than as scientific documentation: "So powerful has been the impulse toward reification of the photographic image that the overriding tendency is to assess the photographs of the past in the terms of the present."[134] In recent decades, numerous scholars have sought to broaden and complicate the interpretive framework set out by the early scholars of nineteenth-century photography, to consider why nineteenth-century photographs look the way they do, and to reinsert them into the complex and powerful nexus of social, economic, political, scientific, philosophical—and aesthetic—discursive forces from which the medium emerged.[135] Yet Greene has, for the most part, remained immune to such reevaluation, due in large part, no doubt, to the scarcity of information about his life and career, which has in turn fueled a potent mythology that is difficult to dislodge.

One picture, more than any other in his oeuvre, has secured Greene's place in the pantheon of primitive masters of the medium: *Bords du Nil à Thèbes* (pl. 63). By any measure, it is a stunning image: so minimal in its gauzy rendering of the mighty river and its distant fertile banks that it verges on total abstraction, a quality that has only been helped along by the passage of time. As the prints have faded (particularly around the edges as they are naturally wont to do), its details have been further smudged and softened to a shimmering evanescence. This photograph—though in truth without peer or parallel in Greene's oeuvre—is cited in nearly every assessment of his work as exemplary of his prowess as a picture maker and of his forward-looking aesthetic. There is nothing to suggest, however, that Greene himself thought it particularly remarkable: he did not include it, for example, in the photographs he submitted to the Académie des Inscriptions et Belles-Lettres, the audience to which he seemed to give the most weight; nor did he give it to the grand duke as part of his gift. The only album in which this work is included is *Le Nil*, whose ultimate public and total number are unknown. Slightly more copies of this image are known to have survived than have prints of Greene's other images, but it seems likely that this is as much a measure of its desirability to contemporary collectors as of its importance to its maker.[136]

Born into wealth and privilege, Greene was in a position to finance his own expeditions and had no need to make money from his photographic work. He was an amateur in the true sense of the word, bound neither by economic necessity nor the demands of commissioners or markets, and therefore quite free to experiment. But we have seen that at every turn, he sought official approbation for his scholarship and tailored his photographs and albums to the specific needs or interests of his intended viewers. We do not need to discount the extraordinary beauty of many of his photographs in order to look more closely at the instrumental, evidentiary, even utilitarian motives that underpinned them. Indeed, had Greene only made the photographs of hieroglyphics that compose the first album *Sculptures et inscriptions*, we might not be talking about his work today—much to the detriment of our understanding and appreciation of his undertaking and of the early history of the medium in general. The unexcavated temples depicted in Greene's photographs offer an apt metaphor for the work itself: buried in the sand, shrouded in history, they retain the promise of mysteries concealed. Once dug up and exposed to scrutiny, however, they require we be ready to reassess the narratives we construct to explain them.

1. Champollion outlined his findings in 1822 in a letter to the Académie des Inscriptions et Belles-Lettres, published as *Lettre à M. Dacier, relative à l'alphabet des hiéroglyphes phonétiques, employés par les Égyptiens pour inscrire sur leurs monuments les titres, les noms et les surnoms des souverains grecs et romains* (Paris: Firmin Didot, 1822). Thomas Young in England also made significant contributions toward the decoding of the hieroglyphs, and historians feel his role has been underplayed in the heroicization of Champollion.
2. By the time Greene arrived in Egypt, dozens of the monuments recorded by Napoleon's expedition in 1798–1801 had already disappeared, some dismantled by archaeologists and relocated (often illegally) to the museums in their respective countries, and others used for building materials by the local government. A great many artifacts were "excavated" and sold on the private market as well. See Jason Thompson, *Wonderful Things: A History of Egyptology* (Cairo: American University in Cairo Press, 2015), vol. 1, pp. 209–22.
3. The first known photographs made in the service of archaeology were taken by Gabriel Tranchard at the excavations of Khorsabad (ancient Assyria, present-day Iraq) by Victor Place in 1852.
4. Beaumont Newhall, "John B. Greene," in *Discovery & Recognition*, ed. James Alinder (Carmel, Calif.: Friends of Photography, 1981), p. 33.
5. Ibid.
6. Kathleen Stewart Howe, in her excellent dissertation on early photography in Egypt, similarly argues that not only do such responses obscure our understanding of Greene's enterprise, but that some of these reactions represent a fundamental misreading of particular pictures: "Careful examination of Greene's photographic record warns us away from the late twentieth-century trap of aestheticizing images which seem eccentric and 'non-documentary,' and encourages an attempt to place those problematic images into the context of their making." Kathleen Stewart Howe, "Egypt Recovered: The Photographic Surveys of Maxime Du Camp, Félix Teynard, and John Beasley Greene, and the Development of Egyptology," PhD diss., University of New Mexico, 1996, p. 19.
7. In Newhall's defense, so little was known about Greene at the time that he may have been unaware of his activities in archaeology. Nonetheless, these early resuscitations of his work are almost exclusively framed in aesthetic terms.
8. A 1981 article by Bruno Jammes represents the first substantial scholarship on the

photographer and remains a reliable and important source today. His discovery of several documents in the library and archives of the Institut de France allowed for the first serious analysis of Greene's career. See Bruno Jammes, "John B. Greene, an American Calotypist," *History of Photography* 5, no. 4 (October 1981), pp. 305–24. Until recently, there had been very little further scholarship on Greene. William F. Stapp has conducted substantial research, from which this catalogue profits in the excellent chronology he has compiled. One unpublished master's thesis and two unpublished dissertations also address Greene at length. I have found Kathleen Stewart Howe's superbly lucid dissertation (see note 6) particularly useful for its extensive analysis of Greene's work in the context of early photography and the nascent field of archaeology in Egypt. Anne Lacoste's 2008 dissertation, "La photographie et les sciences de l'antiquité en Orient dans la seconde moitié du XIXe siècle d'après l'étude des fonds photographiques de la Bibliothèque de l'Institut de France" (Université Paris IV–Sorbonne), focuses on the use of photography in archaeology through the lens of the intellectual program of the Institut de France, and also offers a very useful inventory of the Institut's photographic holdings (including Greene's work) as well as reproductions of numerous primary sources.

9. The name is likely a tribute to Reuben Gaunt Beasley, American consul in Le Havre, business associate of the Greenes, and father of the first wife of John Bulkley Greene (Greene's father).

10. This research has greatly benefited from the widespread interest in genealogy and the resulting availability of digitized historical records. Some of this familial history would have been essentially inaccessible even five years ago. While there are still many gaps in Greene's story, especially once in France, it is possible to construct a multigenerational family tree of the New Hampshire and Boston Greenes to well before the Revolutionary War. Stapp's contribution at the end of this book provides a detailed chronology of Greene's life, the product of decades of meticulous research. I am also grateful to Daniel Catan, who located the record of Greene's birth in Ingouville in the digitized civil records of the department of Seine-et-Maritime, and generously shared those findings, along with many other archival records he located in the Archives Nationales. Following his leads, I was able to locate the record of the marriage of Greene's parents in Le Havre as well as of the births of his two sisters there. As the archives of the City of Paris were largely destroyed by fire in 1870, many of the civil records have had to be reconstructed and are therefore less detailed than the ones from the provinces.

11. His birth certificate lists him as a citizen of the state of Massachusetts.

12. For a brief history of the bank, see Walter Barrett, *The Old Merchants of New York City* (New York: Carleton, 1885), vol. 1, pp. 125–28. For a more in-depth analysis of the activities of Welles & Company and Welles & Greene, see Charles P. Kindleberger, "Origins of United States Direct Investment in France," *Working Papers, Department of Economics, Massachusetts Institute of Technology*, no. 105 (March 1973), pp. 2–5.

13. For a social, economic, and political analysis of Ingouville in the mid-nineteenth century, see John M. Merriman, *The Margins of City Life: Explorations on the French Urban Frontier, 1815–1851* (New York: Oxford University Press, 1991), pp. 210–17.

14. Jacob Venedey, *Excursions in Normandy*, vol. 1 (London: H. Colburn, 1841), n.p., cited in Merriman, *The Margins of City Life*, p. 211.

15. The arrondissements of Paris were renumbered in 1860 after Haussmann's redesign of the city.

16. Dr. Jonathan Warren, an American visitor to Paris, recalls the Welles' hospitality in Howard Payson Arnold, *Memoir of Jonathan Mason Warren* (Boston, 1886), pp. 147–48.

17. Catherine Clinton Howland Hunt, "Unpublished Biography of Richard Morris Hunt," 1895, American Institute of Architects/American Architectural Foundation Collection, Library of Congress (RMH Biography, vol. v–vi), p. 10 (hereafter Hunt Biography). By 1854, sometime after the death of his father, Greene, his mother, and his then-unmarried sister had moved to 10, rue de la Grange Batelière, in the same arrondissement. The new occupant of 28, Place Saint-Georges was Esther Lachmann, known as "La Païva." One of the most famous courtesans of nineteenth-century Paris, she lived there until her luxurious mansion on the Champs Élysées was completed several years later.

18. A significant trove of John Bulkley Greene's banking records are housed at the Archives Nationales in the files of his notary, Alexis Achille Delaunay. But they shed little light on the family's personal situation. I am indebted to Daniel Catan for sharing his research in the archives. About the lives of Americans living in Paris in the nineteenth century, see David McCullough, *The Greater Journey: Americans in Paris* (New York: Simon & Schuster, 2011).

19. For a comprehensive examination of Le Gray's activities as a teacher, see Sylvie Aubenas, "Barrière de Clichy: A 'University' of Photography," in *Gustave Le Gray, 1820–1884* (Los Angeles: J. Paul Getty Museum, 2002), pp. 31–86.

20. Ibid., p. 38.

21. Léon Maufras, "Étude biographique," *Le Monte-Cristo* (January 5, 1860), pp. 594–98, reproduced in translation in Aubenas, *Gustave Le Gray*, p. 338.

22. Aubenas notes that at least three other unattributed photographs of *The Marseillaise* were published in 1852, in two separate albums, so it is impossible to conclusively assign the camera pictured in Greene's negative to Le Gray, though it seems likely. Aubenas, *Gustave Le Gray*, p. 56.

23. For an excellent study of the art and artists of Fontainebleau, see Kimberly Jones, ed., *In the Forest of Fontainebleau: Painters and Photographers from Corot to Monet* (Washington, D.C.: National Gallery of Art, 2008).

24. Photographing with even a portable daguerreotype kit was unwieldy. The wet collodion process, on the other hand, was cumbersome, delicate, and required the photographer to carry chemistry and a dark tent to both sensitize and process the still-damp negatives in the field. For an excellent article about early French photography in the forest, see Sarah Kennel, "An Infinite Museum: Photography in the Forest of Fontainebleau," in Jones, ed., *In the Forest of Fontainebleau*, pp. 154–68.

25. Aubenas (*Gustave Le Gray*, p. 46) notes that Eugenia Parry Janis first spotted the camera in her study of Le Gray's photography. See also Kennel, "An Infinite Museum," p. 156.

26. Gustave Le Gray, *Photographie: Traité nouveau, théorique et pratique . . .* (1854), p. 2, cited in André Jammes and Eugenia Parry Janis, *The Art of French Calotype* (Princeton: Princeton University Press, 1983), p. 98.

27. See, for example, Francis Wey, "De l'influence de l'héliographie sur les beaux arts," *La Lumière* 1, no. 1 (February 9, 1851), pp. 2–3; 1, no. 2 (February 16, 1851), pp. 6–7.

28. It has been argued that Greene's rooftop studies were made on the roof of his father's bank, though there is no evidence to either support or reject that theory. However, it seems more likely that he was working on the roof of Le Gray's studio.
29. Charles Nègre made a study of what appears to be an identical statuette around 1849, at the same time he began learning Le Gray's waxed paper negative process. Perhaps Le Gray kept the figurine in the studio as a prop for teaching. Nègre's version (positive and negative) is reproduced in Karen Hellman, *Real/Ideal: Photography in Mid-Nineteenth-Century France* (Los Angeles: J. Paul Getty Museum, 2016), pls. 10, 11.
30. There is substantial scholarly literature on the affinities between photography and sculpture in the medium's early years. See, for example, Patrizia di Bello, "Photography and Sculpture: A Light Touch," in *Art, History, and the Senses: 1830 to the Present*, ed. Patrizia di Bello and Gabriel Koureas (London: Routledge, 2017).
31. William Henry Fox Talbot, *The Pencil of Nature* (London: Longman, Brown, Green and Longmans, 1844), pp. 23–24, pl. 5.
32. For a discussion of photography's relationship to printmaking and mid-nineteenth century discourses around the reproduction of art, see Stephen Bann, *Parallel Lines: Printmakers, Painters and Photographers in Nineteenth-Century France* (New Haven: Yale University Press, 2001), esp. chapter 3: "Inventions of Photography."
33. Gustave Le Gray, *Photographie: Traité nouveau, théorique et pratique, des procédés et manipulations sur papier sec,—humide, et sur verre au collodion,—à l'albumine* (Paris: Lerebours et Secretan, 1852), p. 1.
34. For a lively discussion of the Venus de Milo throughout art history, see Jane Ursula Harris, "The Role of the Copy," *The Believer* (August 4, 2016), at https://believermag.com/logger/2016-08-04-the-role-of-the-copy-2/.
35. Archives de l'Académie des Inscriptions et Belles-Lettres (hereafter AAIBL), pièce E 371. Translated and quoted in Jammes, "John B. Greene, an American Calotypist," p. 307. It is not clear what Greene meant by engraving.
36. AAIBL, pièce E 84, p. 43, quoted in Jammes, "John B. Greene, an American Calotypist," p. 309.
37. While traveling on the Nile, Richard Morris Hunt made the following entry in his journal on February 9, 1853: "Met John Green [*sic*] who has been upset, had his crew flogged &c. Passed Mr. Jones of New York with other gentleman . . . Slow tugging. Passed my day blacking my bocchimo with Elliott." As Greene was the son of the Hunt family banker, and the Hunts had been to the Greenes' home in Paris, they would have known each other. In a second entry, Hunt makes clear that the John Green he has encountered is both young and American: "Thursday, 24th Feb. Had a word or two with our Scotch friends this morning. At about 3 P.M. met Amelican (as our sailors call it) boat, young Mr. Green & 2 others on board, had a glass together & learned from them that our dragoman was an infernal rascal. Why did Mr. Peck & Mr. Gandel give so good a recommendation when they knew it?" Hunt Biography, pp. 27, 32.
38. Howe, "Egypt Recovered," p. 233. While Du Camp, like Greene, learned photography from Le Gray, Howe argues elsewhere that Teynard either taught himself photography through widely available instructional manuals or possibly studied with Le Gray himself, but that it seems clear from his correspondence with the Académie des Sciences he was not yet a photographer when he proposed his trip to Egypt. See Howe, *Félix Teynard: Calotypes of Egypt: A Catalogue Raisonné* (New York: Hans P. Kraus Jr., 1992), pp. 135–37.
39. Teynard did continue to be engaged with photography from a technical perspective, but did not make more photographs himself.
40. Howe, "Egypt Recovered," p. 233.
41. Chabas' voluminous correspondence, of which hieroglyphics is almost invariably the subject, is preserved at the Archives of the Bibliothèque de l'Institut de France. It is clear from Greene's letters to Chabas that the two men knew each other.
42. Sometime after Greene's death, the majority of his Egyptian negatives as well as more than 200 prints came into Devéria's possession, though we do not have any further information about how this came to pass. After Devéria's death in 1871, his widow sold his archive, including Greene's photographs, to the Louvre. In 1986, much of the Louvre's nineteenth-century photography collection was transferred to the Musée d'Orsay, where the negatives and prints now reside.
43. I thank Elsa Rickal of the Bibliothèque de l'Égyptologie at the Collège de France, Paris, for her research assistance on this question.
44. His introduction and admission to the Société Asiatique was announced in "Procès-verbal de la séance du 14 octobre 1853," *Journal Asiatique* 5, no. 2 (1853), p. 529.
45. Howe, "Egypt Recovered," pp. 243–44. Mariette allowed Greene to photograph his excavations, which also seems to indicate they had a friendly relationship. Other, less professional, travelers who encountered Mariette were not extended the same kind of welcome. As Hunt wrote in his diary on April 1, 1853: "The Frenchman, Mr. Marietta [*sic*] is the damnedest ill begotten b.f.s. unperdent [*sic*] rascal blackguard I have ever seen since in this barbarous country. Visited a tomb . . . then visited a couple of the pyramids, a most terrible south wind blowing the dust in our faces & through our clothes. Mr. M. didn't give us shelter even in his stable. I had been told to expect this (a striking example of French civility). Got into the tomb in spite of him, saw a great many sarcophagi, large & beautifully polished, visited ibis mummy pits, broke 1/2 dozen of pots, rifled the mummys [*sic*] &c., returned covered with dust, washed. We all got growling & were happy to have got through with the Egyptian trip." Hunt Biography, p. 40.
46. Greene made several photographs of such boats, two of which fly American flags. This has led many to conclude that the boats were his since he was an American citizen, despite having been born and spent his entire life in France. On the other hand, a surprising number of Americans journeyed on the Nile at that time, by some counts well over a hundred each year in the mid-1850s. See Andrew Oliver, *American Travelers on the Nile: Early U.S. Visitors to Egypt, 1774–1839* (Cairo: American University in Cairo Press, 2014), p. 314.
47. For a typical Egyptian travel experience, including recommendations for timetable and itinerary, as well as an alarmingly extensive packing list, see Sir John Gardner Wilkinson, *Hand-book for Travellers in Egypt, including descriptions of the course of the Nile to the second cataract, Alexandria, Cairo, the pyramids, and Thebes . . .* (London: J. Murray, 1847), esp. pp. 1–8.
48. Not all of the negatives are lettered and numbered. Most of the negatives for the prints included in the albums *Monuments et paysages* and *Le Nil* are numbered, as are many in the album *Sculptures et inscriptions*. Some negatives are also signed, and some

signed and dated. None of the negatives from his second trip in 1854–55 are numbered, signed, or dated.

49. It has been asserted that this table of contents is in Greene's handwriting, but to my eye, it does not match his penmanship and appears to be the handiwork of a professional calligrapher.

50. Both Howe and Lacoste offer insightful analyses of Du Camp's instructions in their respective dissertations and similarly observe parallels between those instructions and Greene's photographic program. See Howe, "Egypt Recovered," p. 116, and Lacoste, "La photographie et les sciences de l'antiquité en Orient," pp. 00. Lacoste (pp. 532–33) also usefully reproduces the original document almost in its entirety: "Extrait des 'Instructions de l'Académie—Rapport de la Commission nommée par l'Académie des Inscriptions pour rédiger les instructions du voyage de M. Maxime Du Camp,'" Procès verbal de la séance du vendredi 7 september 1849, Bibliothèque de l'Institut de France, Ms 3720, fols. 19–22 (pièces 18 and 19).

51. Letter from John B. Greene to Charles Lenormant, July 21, 1854, AAIBL, pièce E 373.

52. "Instructions de l'Académie," reproduced in Lacoste, "La photographie et les sciences de l'antiquité en Orient," p. 532. Translation mine.

53. Dominique François Arago, "Report" (1839), in *Classic Essays on Photography*, ed. Alan Trachtenberg (New Haven: Leete's Island Books, 1980), p. 17.

54. "Instructions de l'Académie," reproduced in Lacoste, "La photographie et les sciences de l'antiquité en Orient," p. 532. Translation mine.

55. Translated and cited in Howe, "Egypt Recovered," pp. 101–2. I have modified the translation slightly.

56. Translated and cited in ibid., p. 108.

57. Letter from John B. Greene to Charles Lenormant, July 21, 1854, AAIBL, pièce E 373. Translation mine.

58. Ibid.

59. In a letter published in the *Bulletin de la Société Française de Photographie*, Greene recommended photographers in Egypt work in the early morning or late afternoon, avoiding the harsh overhead sun at midday.

60. Louis Désiré Blanquart-Evrard, "Des Monuments," in *Traité de photographie sur papier* (Paris: Librairie Encyclopédique de Roret, 1851), pp. 36–37, cited and translated in Jammes and Janis, *The Art of French Calotype*, p. 56.

61. As was customary, Greene sent a description of his process in a sealed envelope along with his letter to the Académie. Apparently, his letter was misinterpreted to mean that he had discovered a new way of increasing the sensitivity of the negatives, and was excitedly reported in the photographic press (*La Lumière* 4, no. 7 [July 8, 1854], p. 105). He hastily corrected the misunderstanding in a letter to the journal, asked the Académie to unseal his envelope, and apologized for the confusion (*La Lumière* 4, no. 29 [July 22, 1854], p. 115).

62. On the mount of Du Camp's photograph *Nubie. Ibsamboul. Colosse occidentale du Spéos de Phré*, 1852, in the collection of the Musée d'Orsay (PHO 1985 123 107), a note reads "Blanchi par les essais de moulage d'un touriste anglais" (Whitened by an English tourist's attempts at mold-making).

63. John B. Greene, "Procédé pour la reproduction par la photographie des bas-reliefs et inscriptions peu ou point éclairés," Archives de l'Académie des Sciences, Communication du 3 juillet 1854. Translation mine.

64. See Patricia A. Rosenmeyer, *The Language of Ruins: Greek and Latin Inscriptions on the Memnon Colossus* (Oxford: Oxford University Press, 2018).

65. The appearance of this particular temple must have been startling; Félix Teynard made a view of el-Sebua that is remarkably similar to Greene's in terms of both framing and sensibility.

66. Gustave Flaubert, *Flaubert in Egypt: A Sensibility on Tour*, trans. and ed. Francis Steegmuller (New York: Penguin Books, 1996), p. 159.

67. James Augustus St. John, *Egypt and Nubia with Illustrations* (London: Chapman and Hall, 1845), p. 472.

68. Francis Wey, "Comment le soleil est devenu peintre: Histoire du daguerréotype et de la photographie," *Musée des Familles* 20 (July 1853), p. 294.

69. Flaubert, *Flaubert in Egypt*, p. 159.

70. It is interesting to consider that if he did in fact travel to Egypt in the winter of 1852–53, the photographs he made in 1853–54 may have benefited from his earlier exposure to the country's sights and terrain.

71. For an analysis of the visual politics at work in the *Description de l'Égypte*, see Anne Godlewska, "Map, Text and Image. The Mentality of Enlightened Conquerors: A New Look at the *Description de l'Égypte*," *Transactions of the Institute of British Geographers* 20, no. 1 (1995), pp. 5–28.

72. See Douglas R. Nickel, *Francis Frith in Egypt and Palestine: A Victorian Photographer Abroad* (Princeton: Princeton University Press, 2003), pp. 85–88.

73. Ibid., pp. 67–68.

74. Maxime Du Camp, *Le Nil*, cited in Julia Ballerini, *The Stillness of Hajj Ishmael: Maxime Du Camp's 1850 Photographic Encounters* (New York: iUniverse, 2010), p. 120. Ballerini has also analyzed the complex Orientalist impulses at play in Du Camp's deployment of Ishmael's native body in his photographs, including Du Camp's compulsion of Ishmael's participation by telling him the camera lens was a cannon that would shoot him if he moved during the exposure. Ibid., p. 121.

75. Isabelle Jammes, in her dissertation on Blanquart-Evrard, states that "of the known copies, that of the Bibliothèque Nationale is the most complete." It is possible that at the time of her writing, there were other copies of the book that have since been broken up for sale, but I have been unable to locate any other groups of prints that suggest they comprise a copy of the album. See Jammes, *Blanquart-Evrard et les origines de l'édition photographique française* (Geneva: Librairie Droz, 1981), p. 103.

76. There may have been plans for another album. An article in *The Photographic and Fine Art Journal* from October 1854 states that Greene had immediate plans to publish a sixty-plate album with Goupil, but this album does not appear to have materialized. However, there is some evidence to suggest that Greene planned another album: most of the plates he donated to the Société Française de Photographie are systematically numbered and titled in an identical style on the mount in pencil (though it does not look like Greene's hand). The numbers on the mount largely correspond to the negative numbers, though they are not divided by category. We can ascertain that the inscriptions on the mount were done at the same time, as at least one reproduces a spelling error on multiple mounts. A great many of the Egyptian works that made their way into the open market since the 1980s are mounted on identically numbered and hand-titled boards, which suggest that they were

produced and labeled in some quantity; in several cases, there are at least seven known mounted and labeled prints of a single image. There are not, however, sixty such mounted images, so it is not clear if this was the beginning of the ultimately unrealized Goupil project, or a separate undertaking.

77. For a discussion of both the revenues and reviews generated by Du Camp's album, see Jammes, *Blanquart-Evrard et les origines de l'édition photographique française*, pp. 87–91.
78. The 102 photographs that make up *Sculptures et inscriptions égyptiennes* appear exclusively in that album (with only the two exceptions that are included in *Le Nil*), and while there are unbound prints of these works, the vast majority of these are in the collection of the Musée d'Orsay, from the large group acquired from Théodule Devéria. Very few of the photographs from this series made their way to the open market or are found in other collections, which indicates that Greene did not print many of them or intend them for a broad audience beyond the scholarly community.
79. Despite the attraction this particular photograph exerts on contemporary viewers, Greene only included it in the album *Le Nil*.
80. The numbering of the negatives follows the sequence of *Monuments et paysages*: the first plate, *Ibsamboul. Spéos de Phré*, is numbered "M.1" in the negative. The rest of the plates bear ascending "M" numbers, though there are several gaps in the sequence, indicating that Greene made other negatives in this series that he did not include in the album. Not all of the negatives are numbered, either. The plate numbers and the negative numbers therefore do not always align. The Paysages section similarly begins with "P.1," *Études de terrain près de Gebel Abousir; 2e cataracte*. The number in the negative is difficult to read, but logic and the rest of the sequence dictates that it is P.1. Gaps in sequence also appear in the numbering of the "P" works.
81. Ballerini, *The Stillness of Hajj Ishmael*, p. 127.
82. Teynard made only one version of his album *Égypte et Nubie*; like Du Camp's scholarly publication, it begins with Giza and concludes with Abu Simbel.
83. Given Greene's chronic health issues, it is possible he spent time in Baden-Baden, a renowned spa, "taking the cure," and that they met there.
84. W. F. Cumming, *Notes of a Wanderer in Search of Health, through Italy, Egypt, Greece, Turkey, up the Danube, and down the Rhine* (London: Saunders and Otley, 1839), p. 201.
85. The obelisk visible in Greene's pictures has stood in New York's Central Park since 1881, behind The Metropolitan Museum of Art. The second obelisk, not visible because it lay fallen on the ground, was moved to London in 1877.
86. "Fouilles exécutées en Égypte par M. Greene," *L'Athenaeum Français* 4, no. 32 (August 11, 1855), p. 689. It is not clear how Greene knew Lesseps, but the former diplomat had also helped Auguste Mariette return to Egypt in 1857 after Mariette's excavations and substantial (and unauthorized) removal of artifacts to France made him *persona non grata* with Egyptian ruler Abbas Pasha. Mariette's activities also made it more difficult for subsequent archaeologists to obtain firmans. Lesseps was well connected to the court of Napoleon III and had a strong relationship with Sa'id Pasha, Abbas Pasha's brother and successor after Abbas' death in 1854, and apparently Lesseps intervened on Greene's behalf. Later that same year, Lesseps secured from Sa'id Pasha the concession for the Suez Canal. See Thompson, *Wonderful Things*, vol. 1, pp. 227–29.
87. Uvo Hölscher, *The Mortuary Temple of Ramses III, Part 1* (Chicago: University of Chicago Press, 1941), p. 4.
88. William J. Murnane, *United with Eternity: A Concise Guide to the Monuments of Medinet Habu* (Cairo: American University in Cairo Press, 1980), p. 28.
89. Ibid., p. 29.
90. Jean-François Champollion, "Dix-huitième lettre: Thèbes (Médinet-Habou), le 30 juin 1829," in *Lettres de M. Champollion le jeune, écrites pendant son voyage en Égypte, en 1828 et 1829* (Paris: Firmin Didot, 1829), at https://gallica.bnf.fr/ark:/12148/bpt6k5772928d/f164.item.r=champollion.zoom.
91. In the latter half of the nineteenth century, some excavations were made by the Department of Antiquities between 1859 and 1899, but it would not be until 1924 that a major excavation was undertaken by James Henry Breasted of the Oriental Institute of the University of Chicago, in order to fully explore and publish the ancient monuments before they deteriorated further. Murnane, *United with Eternity*, p. 4.
92. Greene's excavations are described in two articles in *L'Athenaeum Français*. Though only the second article's author is identified as Emmanuel de Rougé, it is presumed that he wrote both. See "Fouilles exécutées en Égypte par M. Greene," *L'Athenaeum Français* 4, no. 32 (August 11, 1855), p. 689, and "Notice sur quelques textes hiéroglyphiques nouvellement publiés par M. Greene," *L'Athenaeum Français* 4, no. 44 (November 3, 1855), pp. 956–61.
93. Two other copies of this album exist, with slight variations in sequence but identical images. One copy is held at the Bibliothèque de l'Égyptologie at the Collège de France, Paris, and bears a handwritten dedication from Greene to Vicomte Emmanuel de Rougé. Rougé later donated it to the Collège, where he began teaching in 1860. The only other known copy was at Chicago House in Luxor (headquarters for the Epigraphic Survey of the University of Chicago's Oriental Institute), but is now at the Oriental Institute in Chicago. This copy was donated to Chicago House in 1931 by Herbert E. Winlock, eminent Egyptologist and former director of The Metropolitan Museum of Art (1932–39), before he left Egypt (where he was excavating at Deir el-Bahri), but how Winlock acquired the album is unknown. A pencil inscription on the inside cover of the album reads "très rare." Outside these two albums, there are only a handful of known loose prints from this body of work. I thank Elsa Rickal at the Collège de France for her research assistance and Anne Lacoste for alerting me to the album owned by Chicago House. I am also grateful to Brett McClain and Foy Scalf at the Oriental Institute for their generous collegiality.
94. The Epigraphic Survey, *Medinet Habu 3: The Calendar, the "Slaughterhouse," and Minor Records of Ramses III* (Chicago: University of Chicago Press, 1934), p. vii.
95. Ibid.
96. At least two dozen copies of this tract survive in institutional and private collections, indicating that it was printed in some quantity.
97. Rougé republished his portions of the text in two separate articles in *L'Athenaeum Francais* (see note 92), enabling us to parse the authorship of the individual contributions, which are not clearly indicated in Greene's tract. One reviewer of *Fouilles* stops just shy of accusing Greene of deliberately failing to clearly attribute the text and translation to

Rougé and giving the impression that he himself authored all of it. He concludes in a somewhat gentler tone, saying that though one might see ego and plagiarism, the writer prefers to imagine unthinking carelessness. Victor Langlois, "Fouilles exécutées à Thèbes dans l'année 1855, par J. B. Greene," *Revue Archéologique* 12, no. 2 (October 1855–March 1856), pp. 571–72.

98. I am not aware of any extant photographs or publications from this excavation.
99. James Henry Breasted, "Foreword," in *Medinet Habu 1924–28: Part 1: The Epigraphic Survey of the Great Temple of Medinet Habu (Seasons 1924–25 to 1927–28)* (Chicago: University of Chicago Press, 1929), p. ix.
100. One of his views of the waterfalls outside Constantine has been frequently labeled as the *Cascades d'El-Ourit in Tlemcen*. After comparing Greene's waterfall pictures to images of the cascades of El-Ourit and the very distinctive topography of the waterfalls outside Constantine, it seems to me that they were in fact taken in Constantine. Though it is not impossible that Greene visited Tlemcen, it is well to the west of Cherchell, outside his known itinerary, and there is no evidence, photographic or otherwise, that he traveled there. Given Greene's interests, it would not have been a particularly compelling destination: Tlemcen was well known for its Islamic architecture, but by 1856 many of the Roman antiquities had either been appropriated as building materials or destroyed by the occupying French forces. See Michael Greenhalgh, *The Military and Colonial Destruction of the Roman Landscape of North Africa, 1830–1900* (Leiden: Brill, 2014), p. 142.
101. Greene's photographs at the Tombeau de la Chrétienne are dated by year in his own hand; some are dated even more precisely by Adrien Berbrugger in the album at the Bibliothèque de l'Institut de France. On May 22, 1856, Greene wrote to hieroglyphics expert François Chabas, informing him that he had just returned to Paris. Letter from John Beasley Greene to François Chabas, Manuscrits de la Bibliothèque de l'Institut de France, MS 2572, Letter 183.
102. See Stapp's chronology in this volume, p. 00.
103. For a thorough history of the archaeology of the Tombeau de la Chrétienne in English, see Bonnie Effros, *Incidental Archaeologists: French Officers and the Rediscovery of Roman North Africa* (Ithaca, N.Y.: Cornell University Press, 2018), pp. 238–47.
104. Two excellent articles by Monique Dondin-Payre outline Berbrugger's interest in and excavations of the Tombeau de la Chrétienne and also analyze the archaeological value of Greene's photographs. See "Le premier reportage photographique archéologique en Afrique du Nord: Les fouilles du Tombeau de la Chrétienne en 1855–56," *L'Africa Romana* 14 (2002), pp. 2119–46; and "L'Académie des Inscriptions et Belles-Lettres et la photographie: Les fouilles du Tombeau de la Chrétienne au XIXe siècle," *Comptes Rendus des Séances de l'Académie des Inscriptions et Belles-Lettres* 147, no. 3 (2003), pp. 1139–57.
105. Adrien Berbrugger, "Explorations du Tombeau de la Chrétienne," *Revue Africaine: Journal des Travaux de la Société Historique Algérienne* 1, no. 1 (1856), p. 33: "Celui-ci embrassait trois objets: la recherche de l'entrée du monument, celle de sa véritable forme architecturale et de la date approximative de sa construction."
106. Undeterred, in 1865 he convinced Napoleon III to fund another excavation. This time, he was able to locate the opening concealed behind the eastern false door and gain entry. His approach, which involved drilling and, finally, resorting to military explosives, is indicative of his determination and also of the state of archaeological methodology at that time. See Effros, *Incidental Archaeologists*, pp. 243–44.
107. It is assumed that Greene was not hired by Berbrugger, but volunteered his services due to his position of fortune, but there is no way to confirm this.
108. Dondin-Payre ("L'Académie des inscriptions," p. 1141) asserts that Greene noted the possible presence of the remains of Cleopatra Selene in the Tombeau de la Chrétienne as motivation to go to Algeria, citing a passage in his tract *Fouilles executées à Thèbes* (1855) as evidence of his prior interest. Certainly, Greene's interest in Egyptian history led him to seek out evidence of its impact in North Africa, but despite an otherwise excellent article, Dondin-Payre made an error in her source, and the citation she uses as evidence of his motive is not in the 1855 text, but in an article Greene wrote *after* his time in Algeria in 1856. See Greene, "Note sur un fragment de statue égyptienne du musée de Cherchel," *Bulletin Archéologique de l'Athenaeum Français* 2, no. 5 (May 1856), p. 39. While it is still possible—even likely—that her assertion is correct, there is no clear substantiation one way or the other.
109. AAIBL, Rapports, 1856, pièce E 375. Translation mine. Cited in Dondin-Payre, "Le premier reportage photographique," p. 2122.
110. Elsewhere, photographer Félix Moulin refers to Greene as a "young amateur photographer," but this description is probably less of an indication of whether Greene was paid for his work and rather more likely Moulin's attempt to elevate his own status and to distinguish himself from Greene.
111. It had long been assumed that Greene assembled and submitted the album, but as noted by Howe ("Egypt Recovered," p. 281), it does not appear on the library's inventory until 1857 and looks very different from Greene's other albums. However, Dondin-Payre has demonstrated that it was assembled not by Greene but by Berbrugger, which explains the differences in format and handwriting as well as the lack of a dedicatory inscription.
112. The whereabouts of the negatives for these images are unknown, nor is it clear how many prints of each were made. Though there are no other images of the tomb besides those in the album itself, there are usually at least one or two other prints of each image, primarily in North American collections. Aside from the Tombeau de la Chrétienne album at the Institut de France, none of Greene's Algerian pictures were deposited by Berbrugger or Greene in French institutions. This is quite possibly a result of Greene's untimely death less than six months after returning from Algeria; he may not have had time to place his work as he had with his Egyptian photographs. A sizable group of Algerian photographs made their way onto the private market in the 1980s, most through the American dealer Harry Lunn. The one Algerian work in the collection of the Musée d'Orsay was not acquired through Devéria as Greene's other works were, but was rather a gift from Lunn.
113. Adrien Berbrugger, "Chronique," *Revue Africaine: Journal des Travaux de la Société Historique Algérienne* 7, no. 41 (September 1856), p. 394. Berbrugger describes Greene's photographs that he had sent to the Académie: "These views, made during our two explorations by our traveling companion Mr. John Green [*sic*], are the first that have been made of this monument. They indicate, with the unassailable exactitude

of photography, the primitive state of the monument, then the successive modifications made by our labors, according to a program of which the principal tenet, conscientiously observed, was to demolish nothing, but only to clear away."

114. Berbrugger, "Explorations du Tombeau de la Chrétienne," p. 33; Berbrugger, *Le Tombeau de la Chrétienne: Mausolée des rois mauritaniens de la dernière dynastie* (Algiers: Bastide, 1867), p. 56.
115. The conditions for archaeologists were hardly more hospitable: Berbrugger described swarms of wasps, flies, mosquitoes, and midges that congregated in the morning around the monument, buzzing around and biting the excavators. Berbrugger, *Le Tombeau de la Chrétienne*, pp. 10–11.
116. Berbrugger, "Explorations du Tombeau de la Chrétienne," p. 38.
117. Félix Moulin, "La photographie en Algérie," *La Lumière* 6, no. 25 (June 21, 1856), p. 97.
118. Dondin-Payre, "Le premier reportage photographique," p. 2126.
119. Though Constantine was some 200 miles from the Tombeau de la Chrétienne, it was essentially impossible to travel there directly. Most likely, Greene went from Tipaza to Algiers by land, and then to Philippeville by sea, and then again by road to Constantine. During the summer, a daily stagecoach traveled this important commercial route (Philippeville–Constantine), but passage was more difficult in the rainy season. There would not be a railroad in Algeria until the following decade. For a description of the traveler's experience in Algeria in the mid-1850s, see Rev. Joseph Williams Blakesley, *Four Months in Algeria, with a Visit to Carthage* (Cambridge: Macmillan, 1859).
120. Benjamin E. Thomas, "Fortress City of Constantine, Algeria," *The Scientific Monthly* 81, no. 3 (September 1955), p. 130.
121. Ibid.
122. See Effros, *Incidental Archaeologists*, p. 66.
123. Ibid., p. 67.
124. With the exception of three photographs of statuary in the Musée de Cherchell, Greene appears to have had little interest in Roman antiquities. His archaeological interests were apparently confined to Egyptology.
125. Now known as the City of Bridges for its numerous spans across the ravine, at the time Greene photographed, there was a single point of access to Constantine: the stone El-Kantara Bridge. On March 18, 1857, the bridge was largely destroyed by a major earthquake; it was replaced in 1863 by the French using the latest techniques in steel engineering. The new bridge was photographed by Édouard Baldus in 1864.
126. Interestingly, Moulin also employed this panoramic technique in Constantine when he traveled there later that year. It may, of course, be coincidence, a natural response to the exigencies of the landscape. It is tempting to imagine that the two photographers had an opportunity to discuss their work while together at the Tombeau de la Chrétienne. Moulin traveled to Constantine sometime in June 1856 or later. See Moulin, "La photographie en Algérie," *La Lumière* 6, no. 26 (June 28, 1856), pp. 101–2. For a discussion of his photographs in Constantine, see John Zarobell, *Empire of Landscape: Space and Ideology in French Colonial Algeria* (University Park: Pennsylvania State University Press, 2010), pp. 103–10.
127. Rachel Topham was perhaps the first to observe that four individual prints in the Museum of Modern Art's collection overlap to form two panoramic images, one of the clifftop houses, and one of the El-Kantara Bridge. See Rachel Topham, "John Beasly Greene," master's thesis, Ryerson University and George Eastman House, 2004, pp. 55–56.
128. As Moulin reported: "At six o'clock in the morning, the signal for our departure was given. The Zouaves headed toward Coléah, M.B. [Berbrugger] toward Blidah, M. Green [*sic*], an American amateur photographer, to Cherchell, and us to Tipoza [*sic*]. The groups heading out by different routes gave our little encampment the look of a tribe scattered by the approach of an enemy." Moulin, "La photographie en Algérie," *La Lumière* 6, no. 25 (June 21, 1856), p. 97.
129. "In the museum, a great variety of fragments are collected, many of which probably belonged to the same building, together with broken statues, tumulary and other inscriptions, capitals and bases of columns, amphorae, etc., and in one corner, amongst a heap of rubbish, are some precious specimens illustrating curious facts connected with the state of industrial arts during the time of the Romans. . . . There is a boat's anchor much corroded, but still perfect in shape, a sundial of curious design, and, most interesting of all, the lower half of a seated Egyptian divinity, in black basalt, with a hieroglyphic inscription. This was found in the bed of the harbour, and may have been sent as a present to the fair Cleopatra, from her native land." Robert L. Playfair, *Travels in the Footsteps of Bruce in Algeria and Tunis* (London: Kegan Paul, 1877), p. 29.
130. J. B. Greene, "Note sur un fragment," pp. 38–39.
131. As the location of the negatives is unknown, this number is based on extant prints. He may have made more negatives from which prints do not survive.
132. Letter from Théodule Devéria to François Chabas, December 21, 1856, Bibliothèque de l'Institut de France, MS 2572 f. 257. Cited in Jammes, "John B. Greene, an American Calotypist," p. 305. The language of a chronic illness that responded to climate suggests pulmonary tuberculosis (consumption). Tuberculosis was the leading cause of death in nineteenth-century Paris (it was also rampant in Le Havre), and before effective medical treatment for the disease was discovered, a change of climate was often the recommended cure. Southern Europe and Egypt were popular destinations. See David S. Barnes, *The Making of a Social Disease: Tuberculosis in Nineteenth-Century France* (Berkeley: University of California Press, 1995).
133. Abigail Solomon-Godeau, "Calotypomania: The Gourmet Guide to Nineteenth-Century Photography," in *Photography at the Dock: Essays on Photographic History, Institutions, and Practices* (Minneapolis: University of Minnesota Press, 1991), p. 23.
134. Abigail Solomon-Godeau, "A Photographer in Jerusalem, 1855: Auguste Salzmann and His Times," in *Photography at the Dock*, p. 166.
135. Examples include Robin Kelsey, *Archive Style: Photographs & Illustrations for U.S. Surveys, 1850–1890* (Berkeley: University of California Press, 2007); Nickel, *Francis Frith in Egypt and Palestine*; and Jordan Bear, *Disillusioned: Victorian Photography and the Discerning Subject* (University Park: Pennsylvania State University Press, 2015).
136. I have counted twelve copies of this particular print, the vast majority of which were acquired by private or institutional collectors in the 1980s or considerably later; most of Greene's other images from *Le Nil* top out at around eight known copies.

ALGERIA

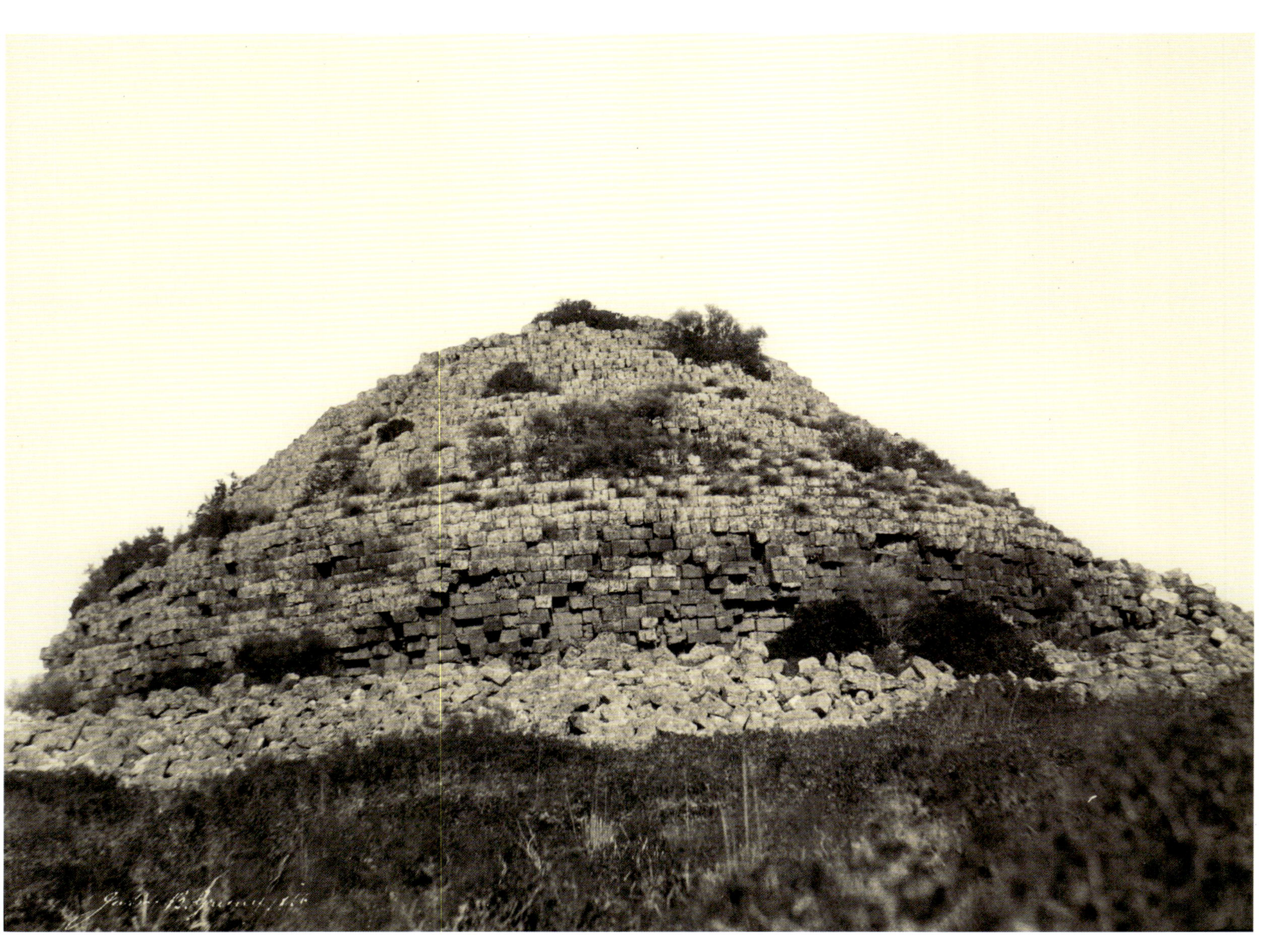

PLATE 68 *Tombeau de la Chrétienne. Côté du sud (Tomb of the Christian Woman. South side)*, 1856

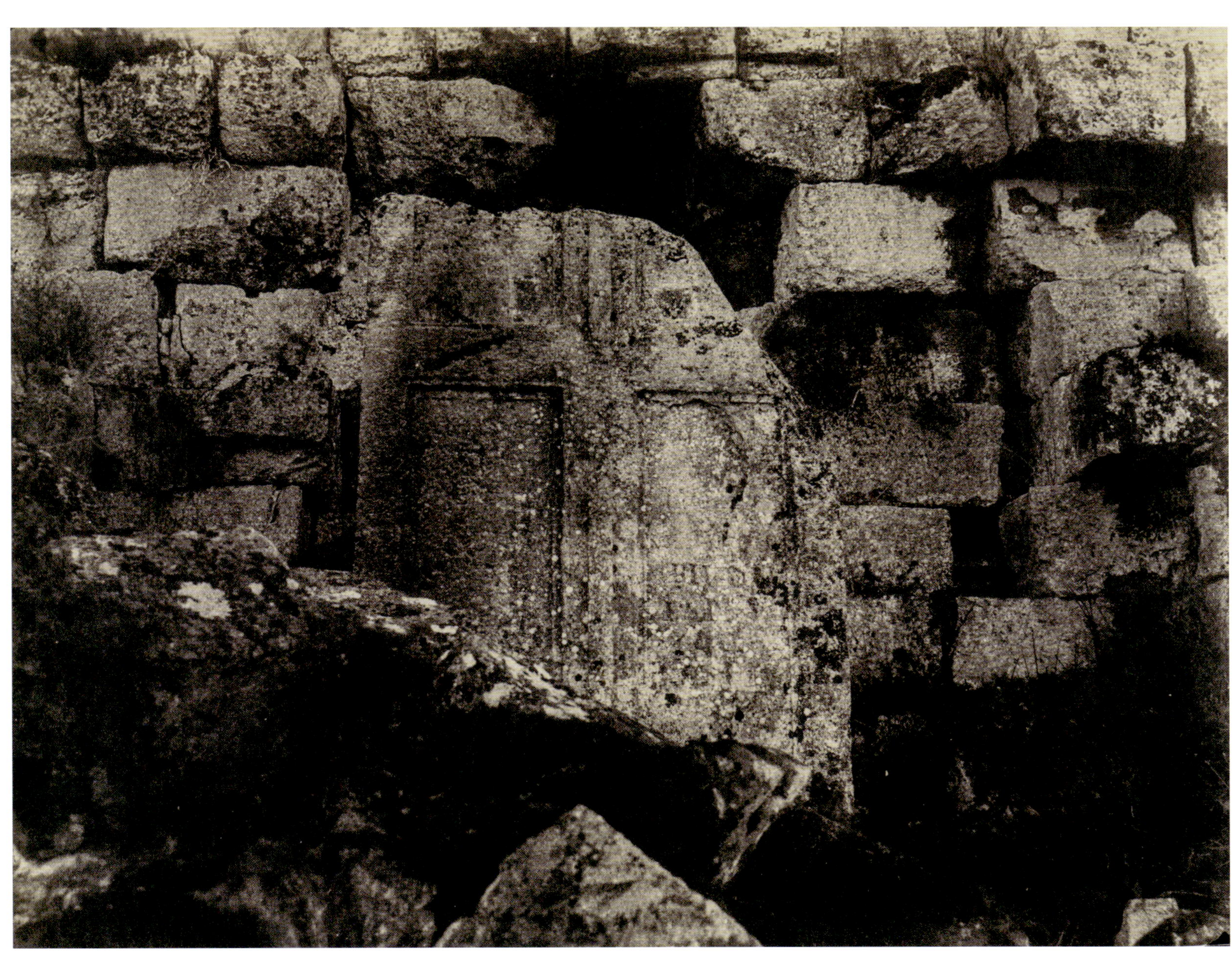

PLATE 69 *Fausse porte, Tombeau de la Chrétienne (False door, Tomb of the Christian Woman)*, 1855

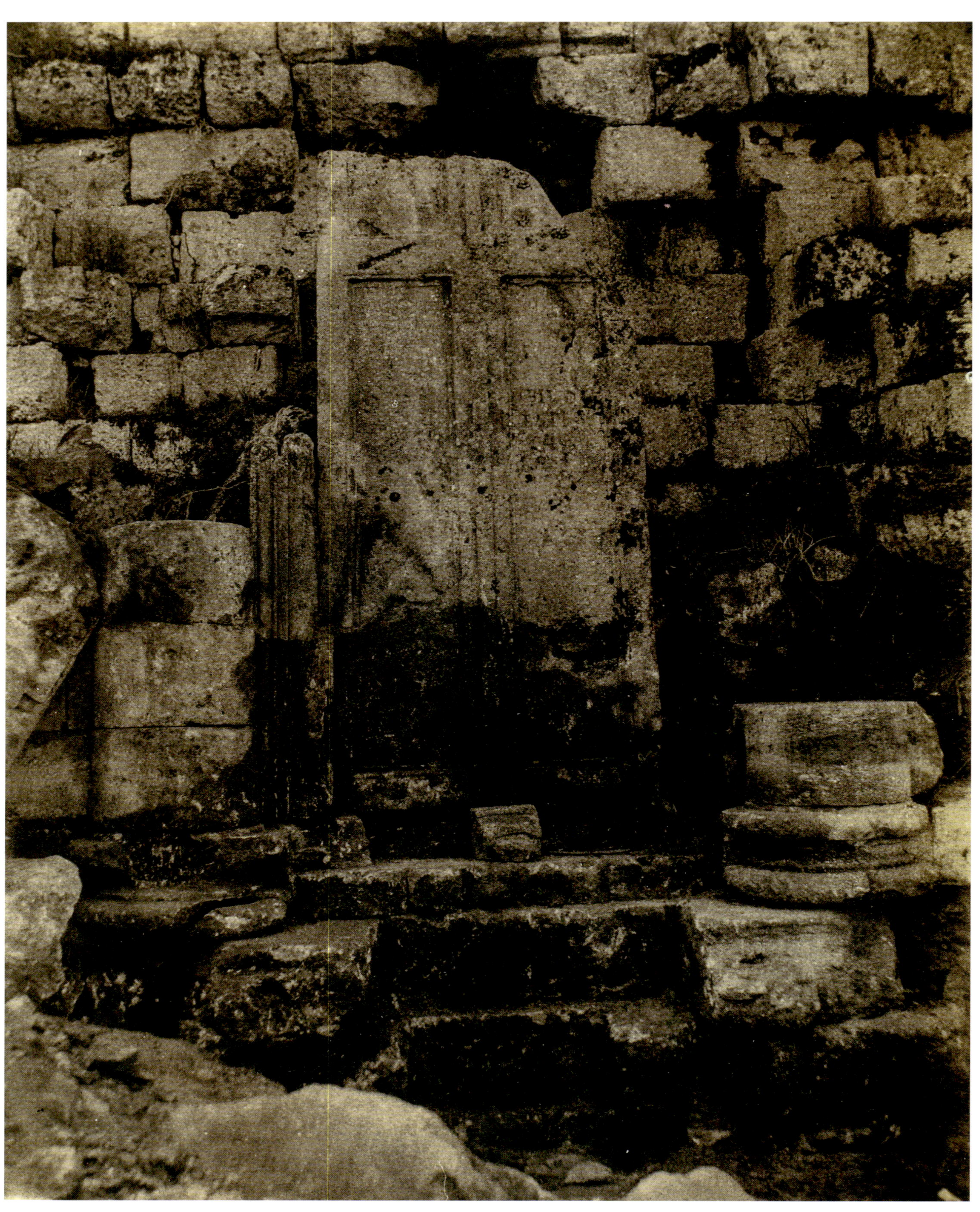

PLATE 70 *Vue de fausse porte du Nord le 5 avril 1856 à la fin des travaux de la 2e exploration (View of the northern false door, April 5, 1856, at the end of the second exploration)*, 1856

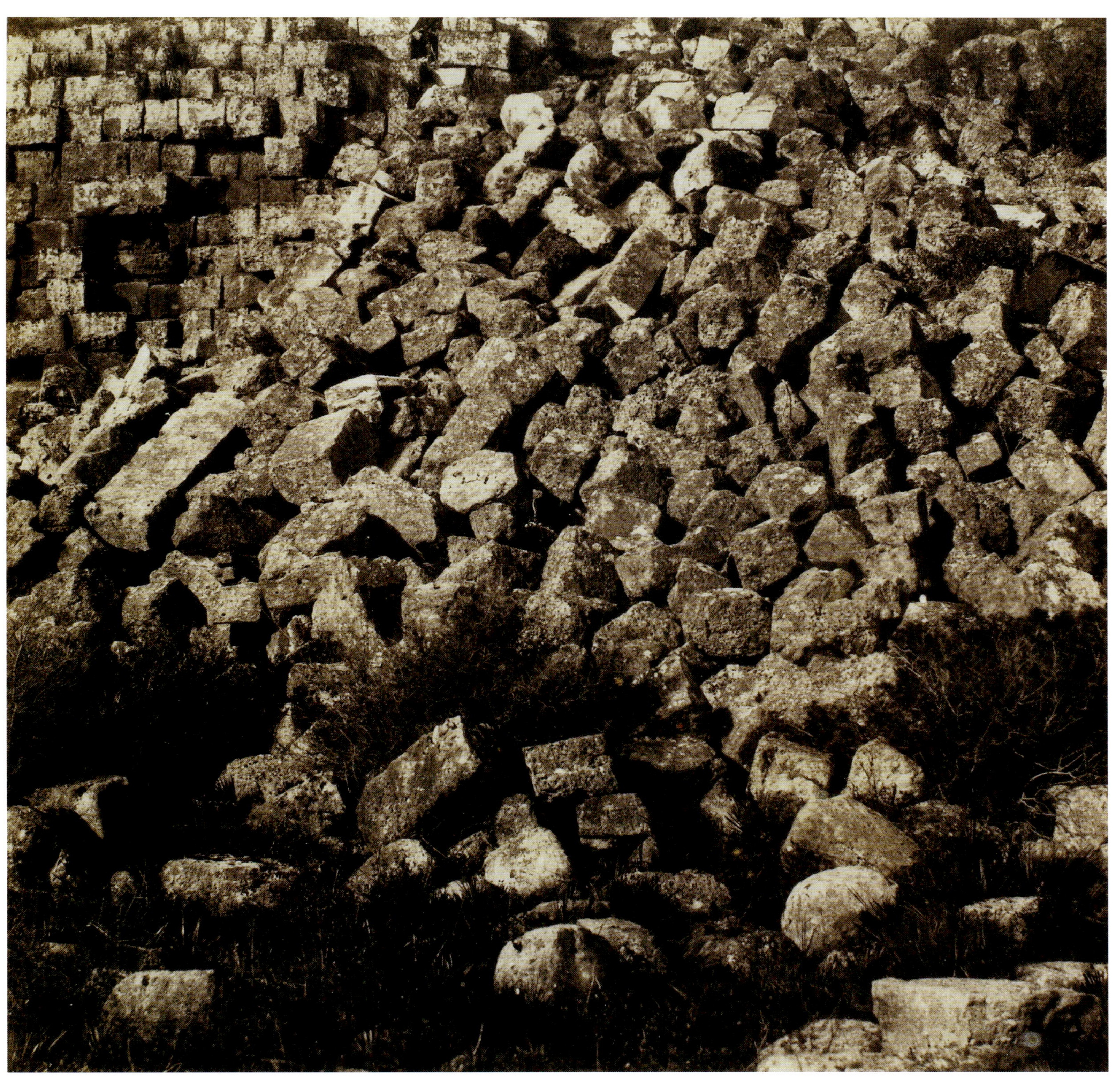

PLATE 71 *Tombeau de la Chrétienne. Etat de l'Eboulement le 1er janvier 1856 après les trois premières journées de travail (Tomb of the Christian Woman. State of the collapsed rock after the first three days of work)*, 1856

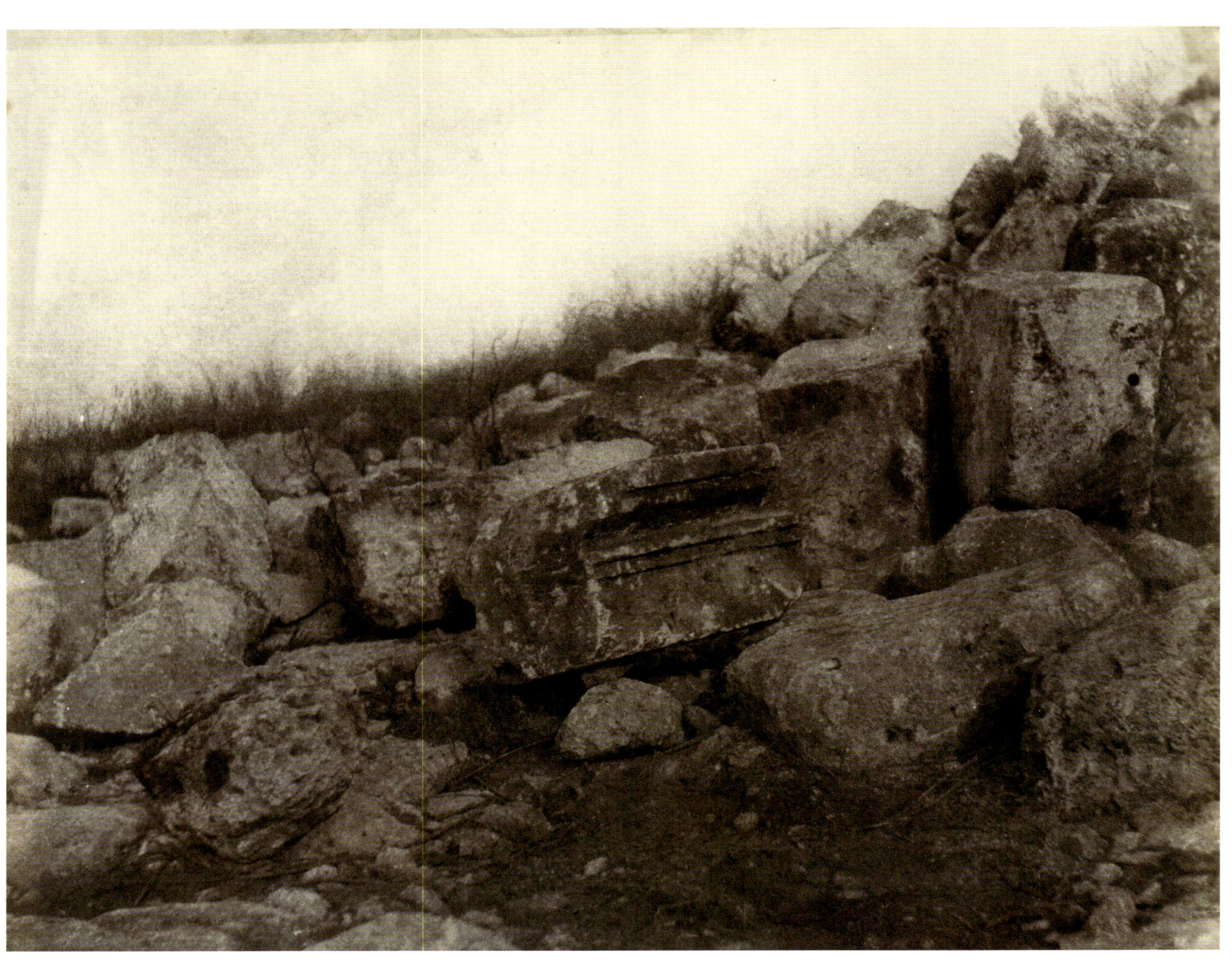

PLATE 72 [Ruins near the Tombeau de la Chrétienne], 1856

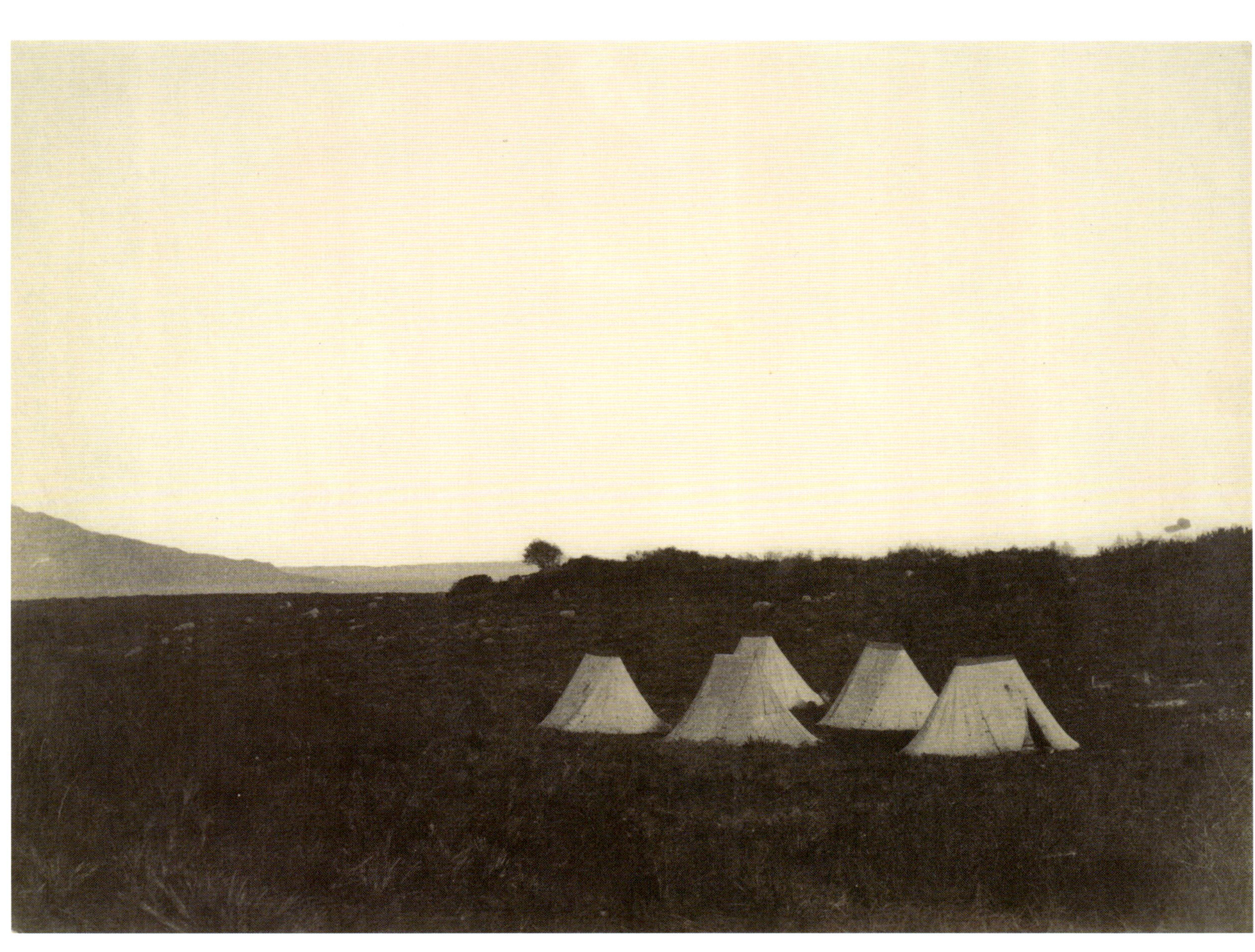

PLATE 73 [Camp by the Tombeau de la Chrétienne], 1856

PLATE 74 *Tombeau de la Chrétienne. Vue du côté Est à la fin des travaux de la 2e exploration (5 avril 1856) (Tomb of the Christian Woman. View of the east side at the end of the second exploration [April 5, 1856])*, 1856

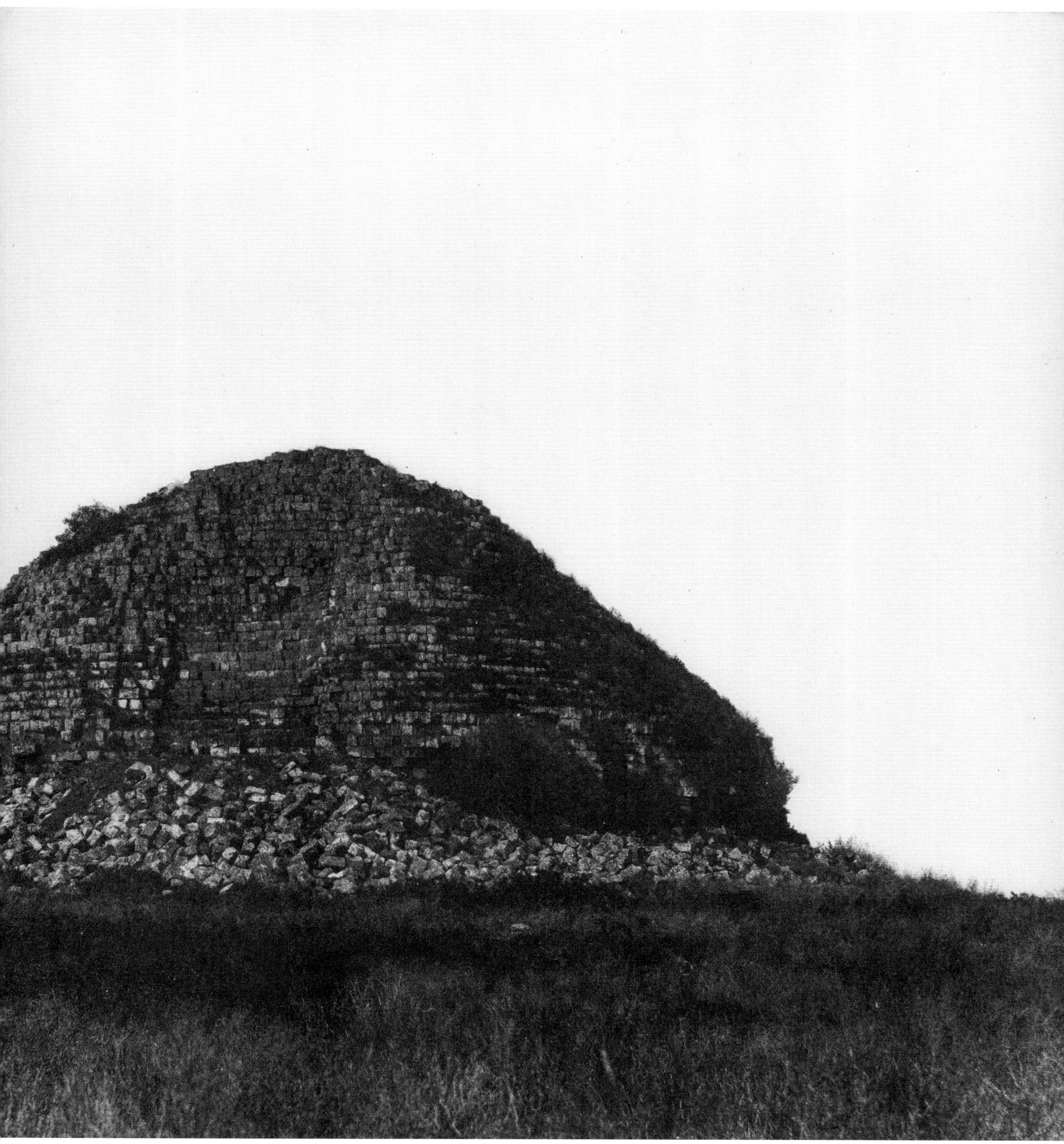

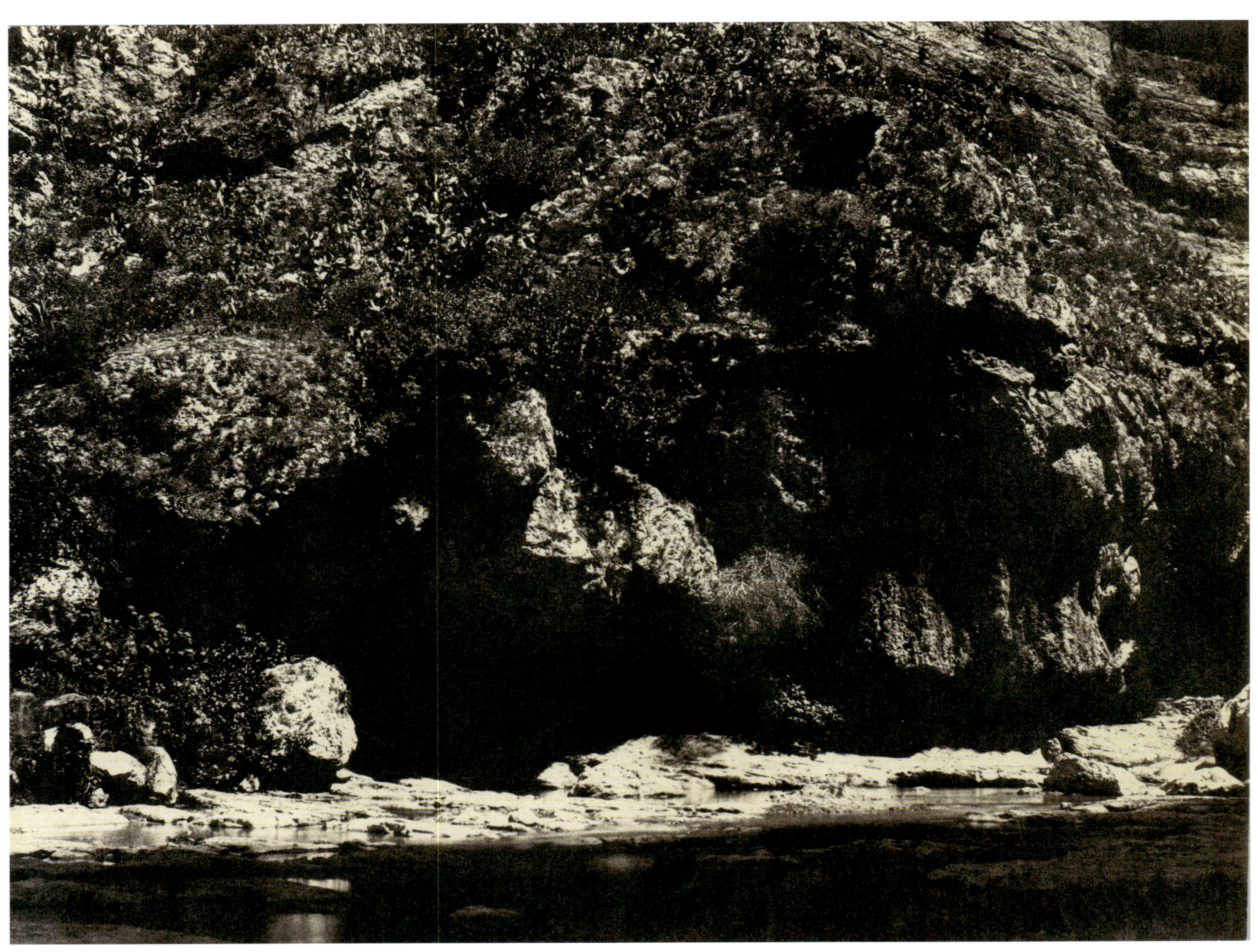

PLATE 75 [Bank of the Rhumel, near Constantine], 1856

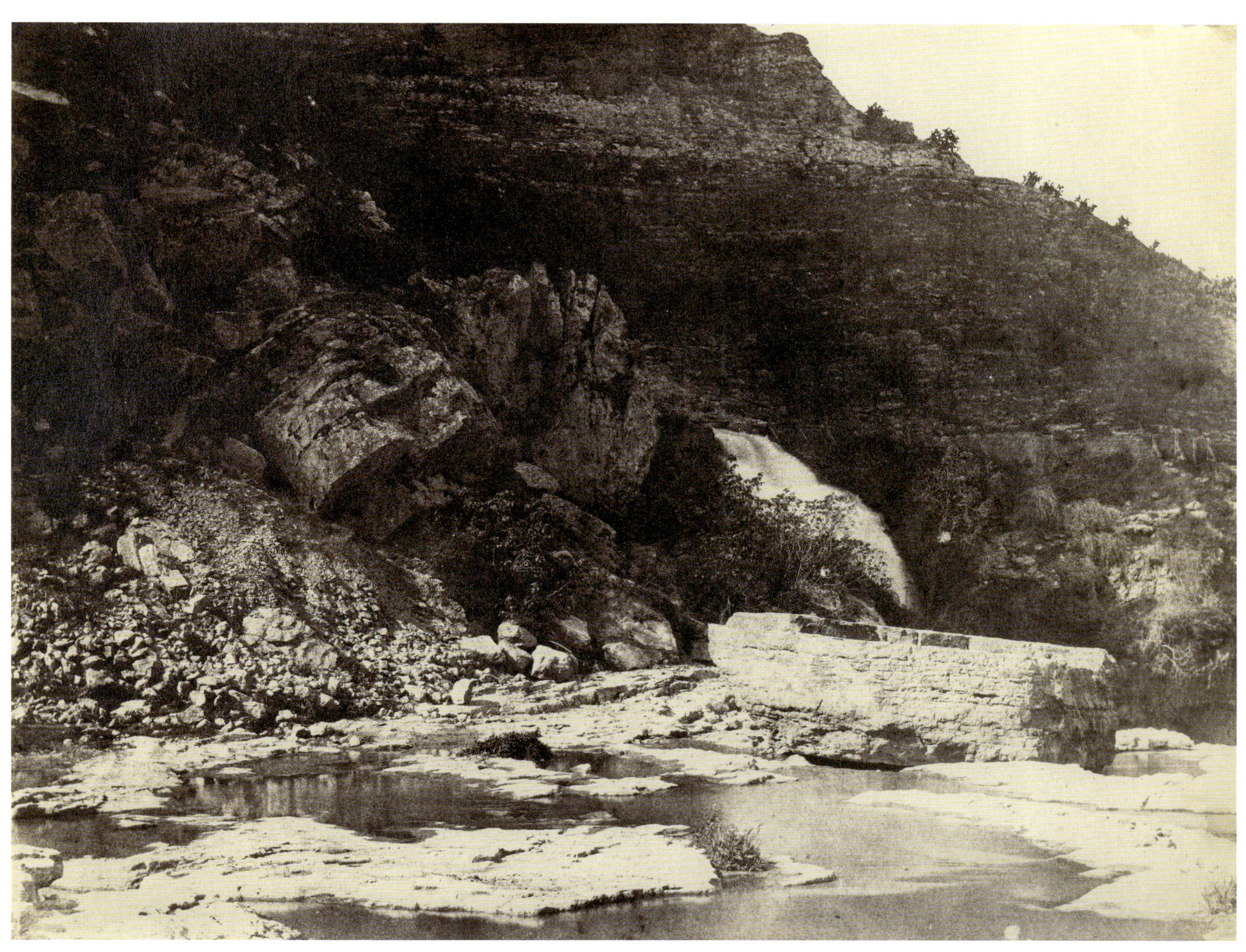

PLATE 76 [Rhumel River], 1856

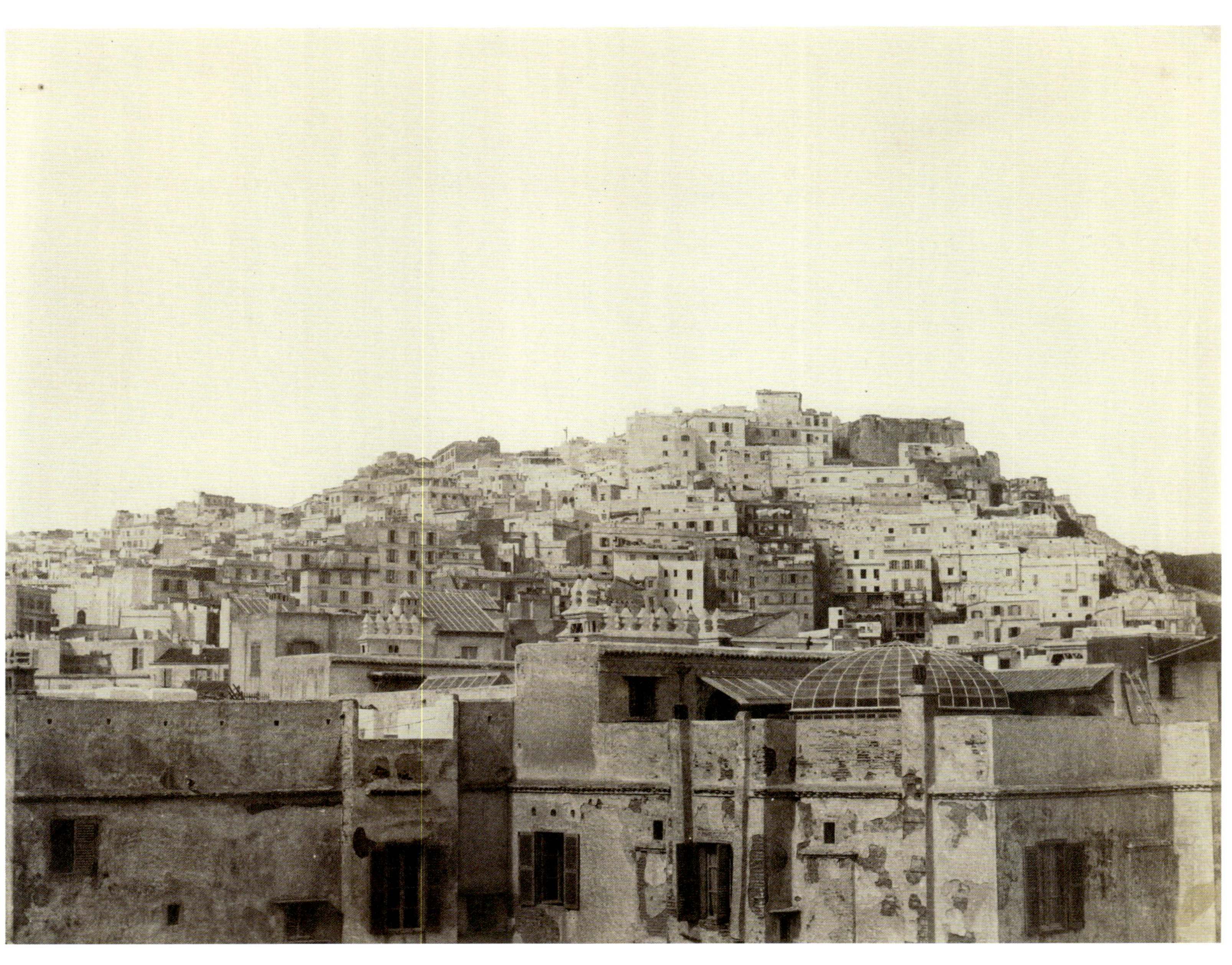

PLATE 77 [Constantine], 1856

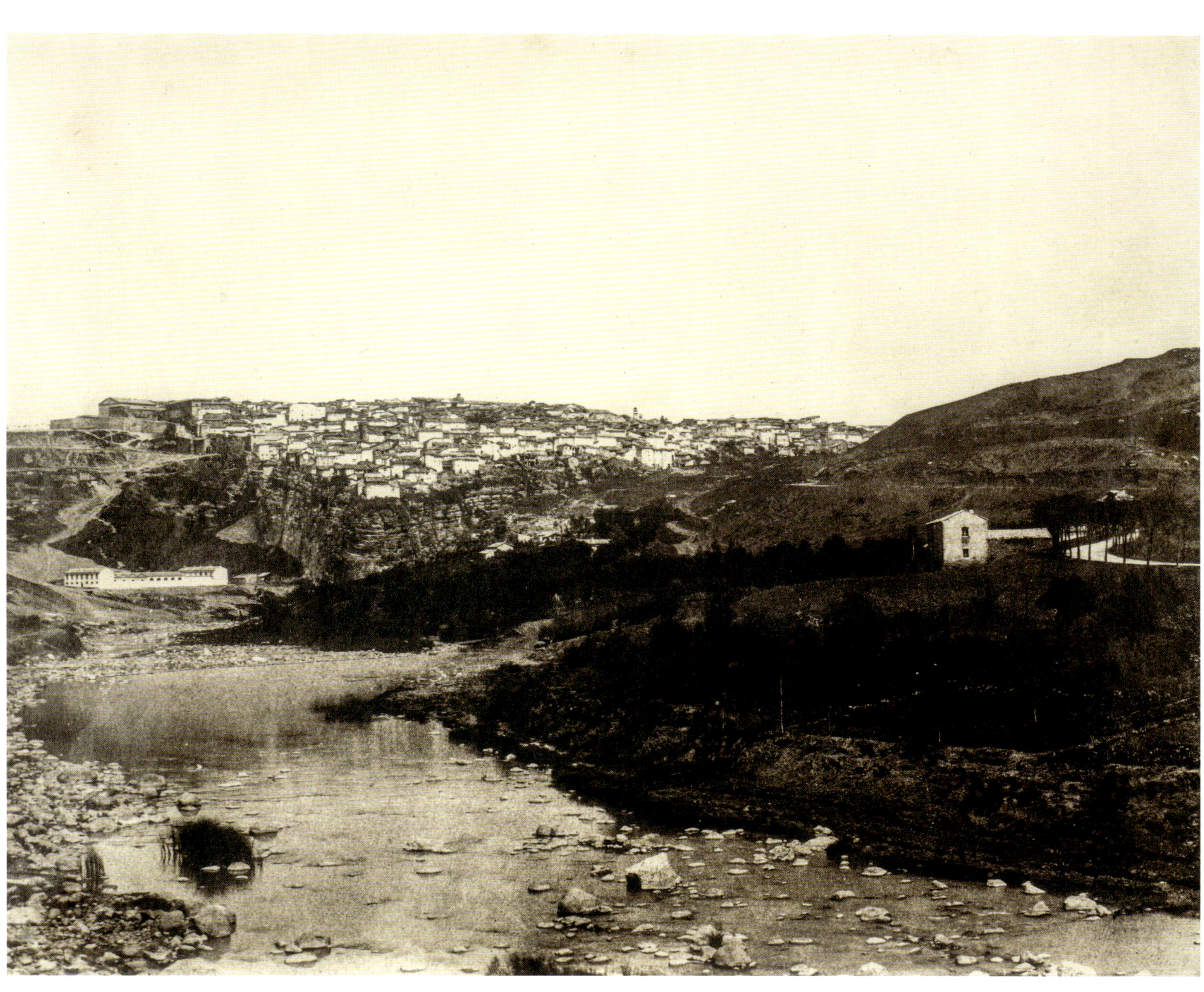

PLATE 78 [Constantine], 1856

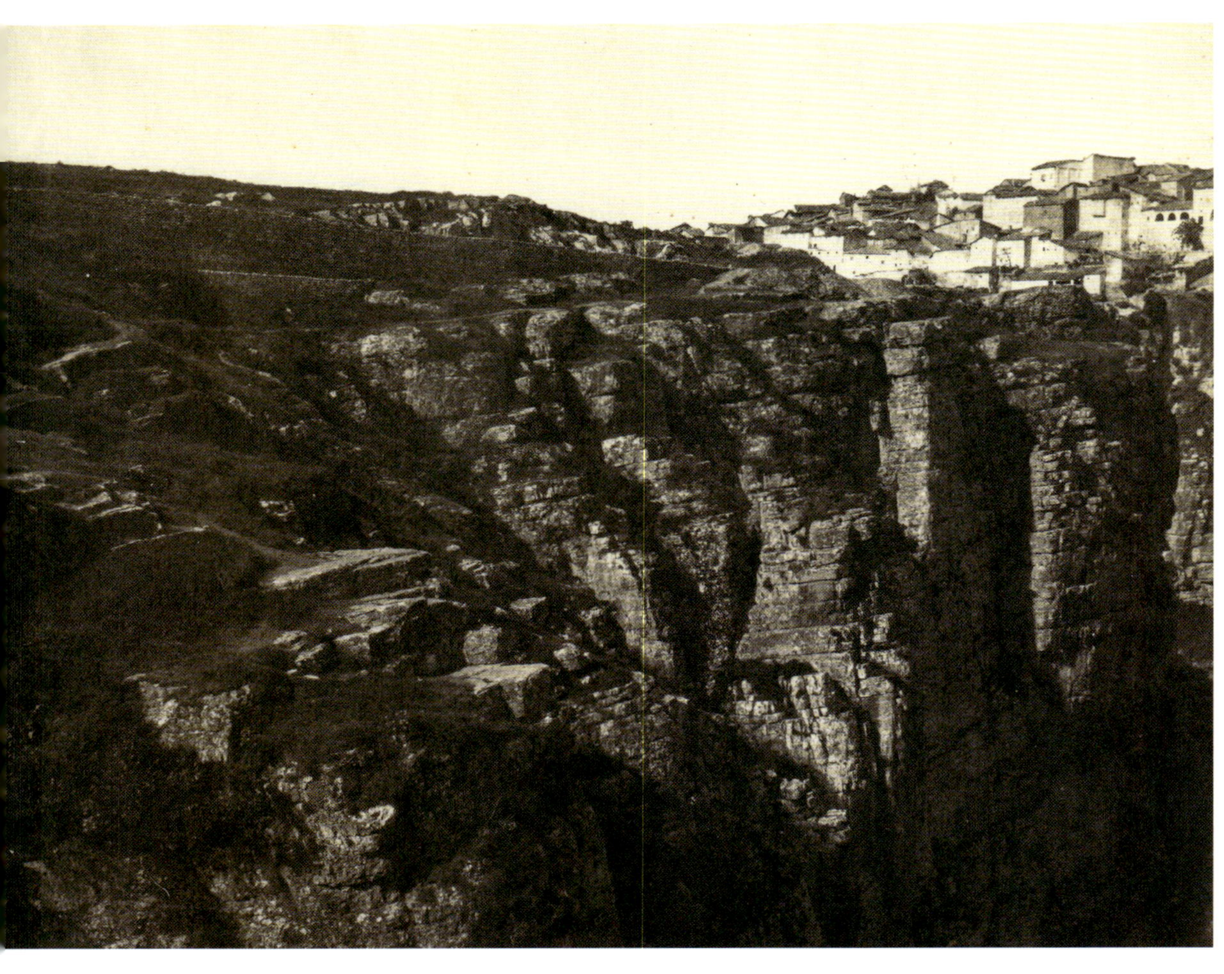
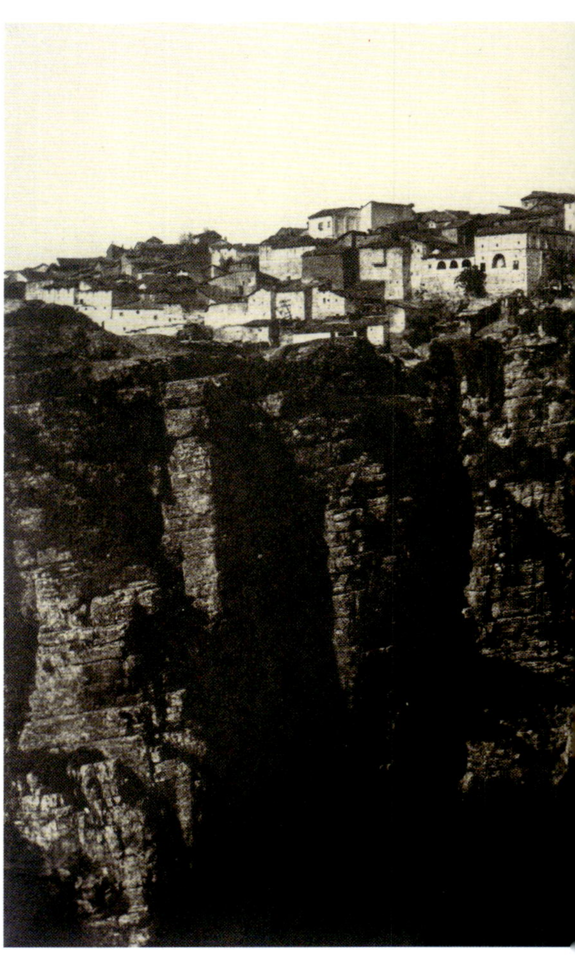

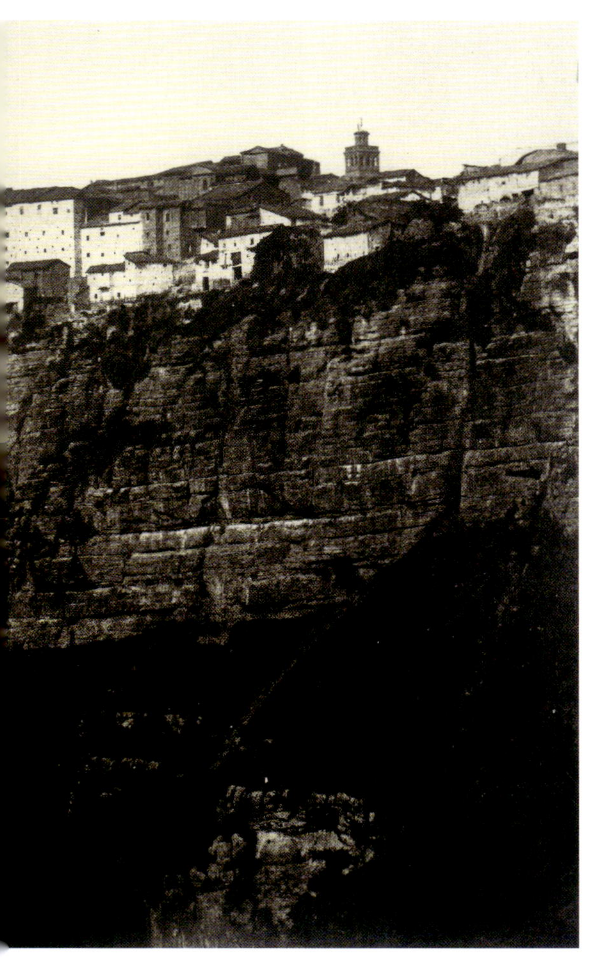

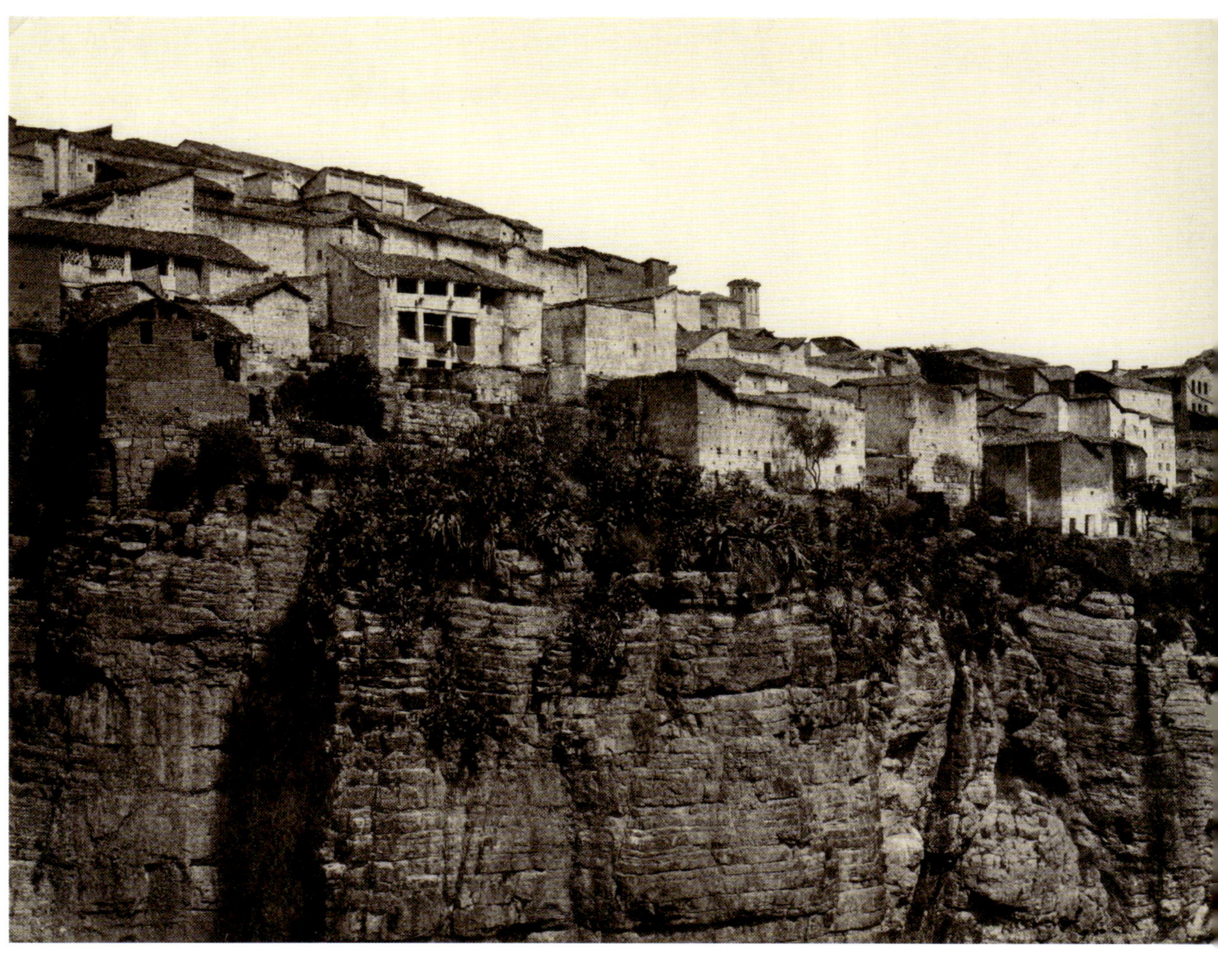

PLATES 79, 80, 81 [Constantine], 1856

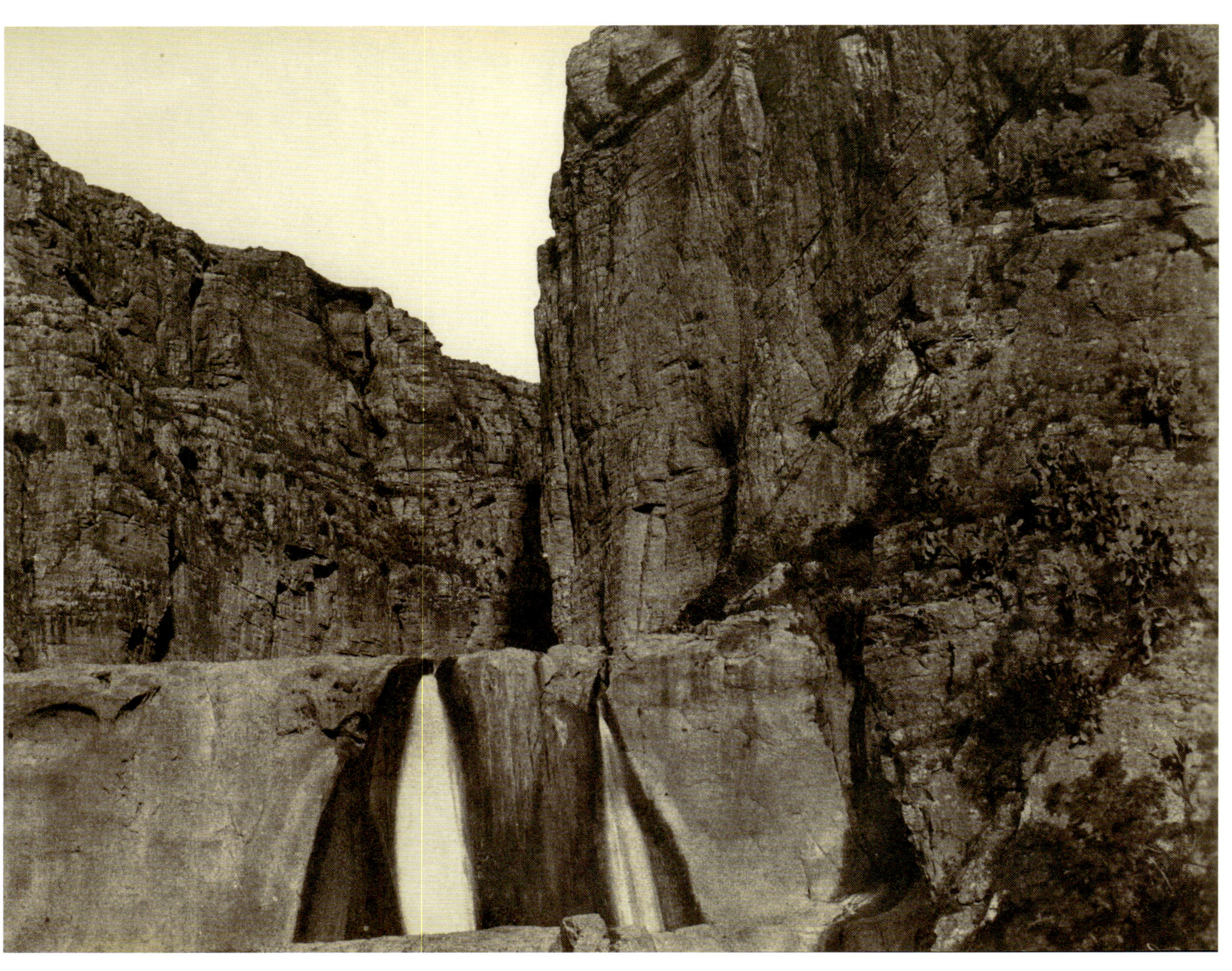

PLATE 82 [Waterfall, Constantine], 1856

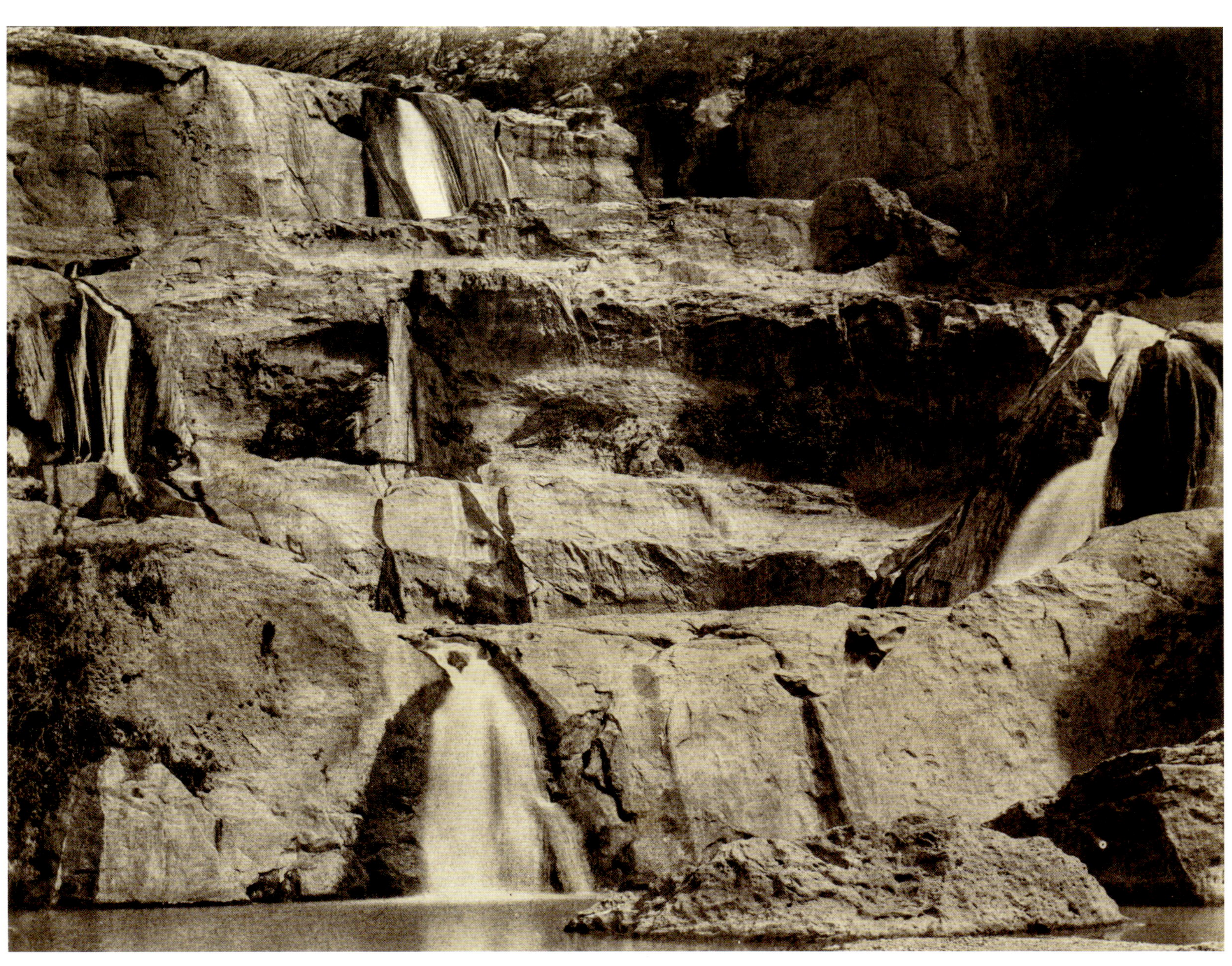

PLATE 83 [Waterfall, Constantine], 1856

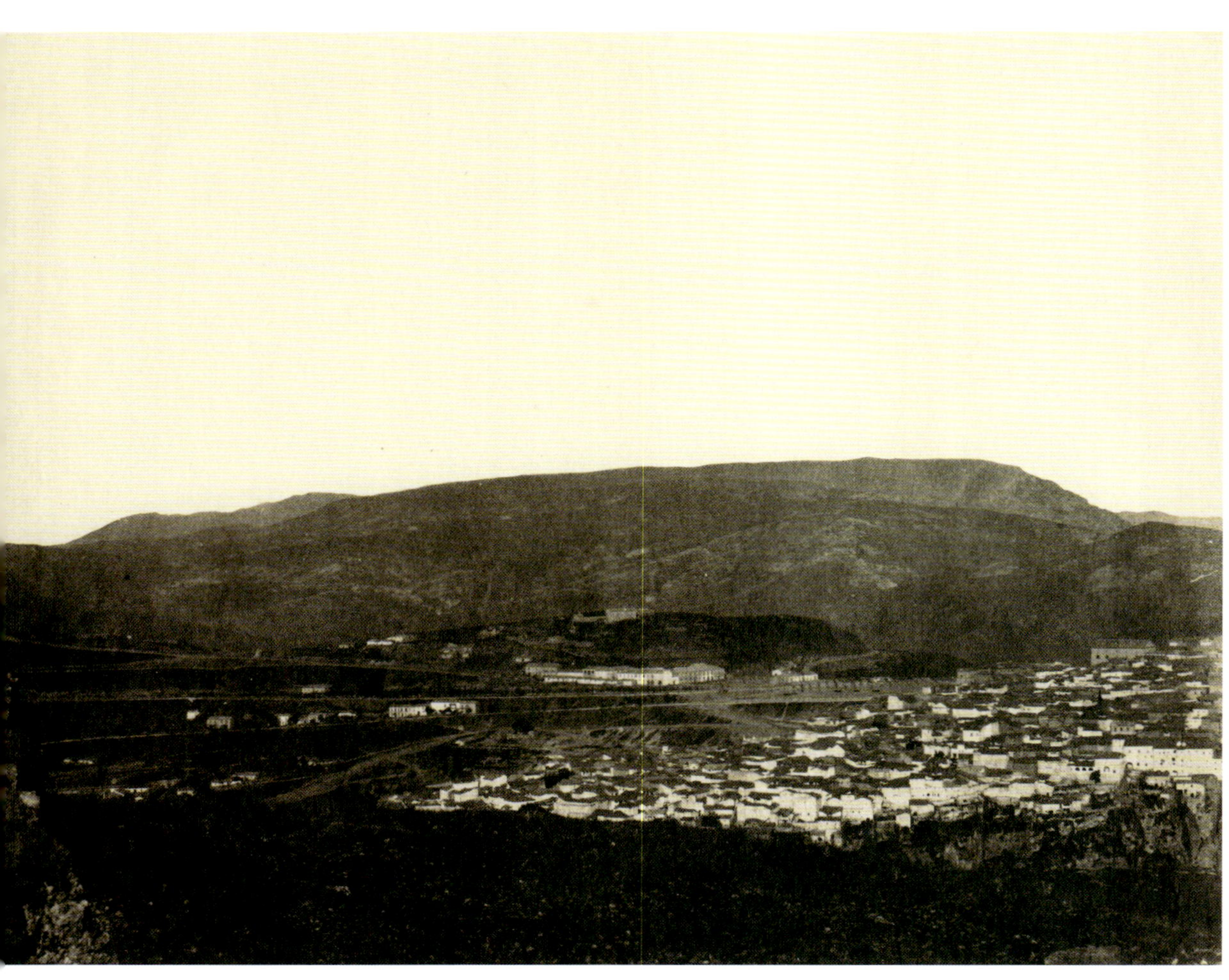
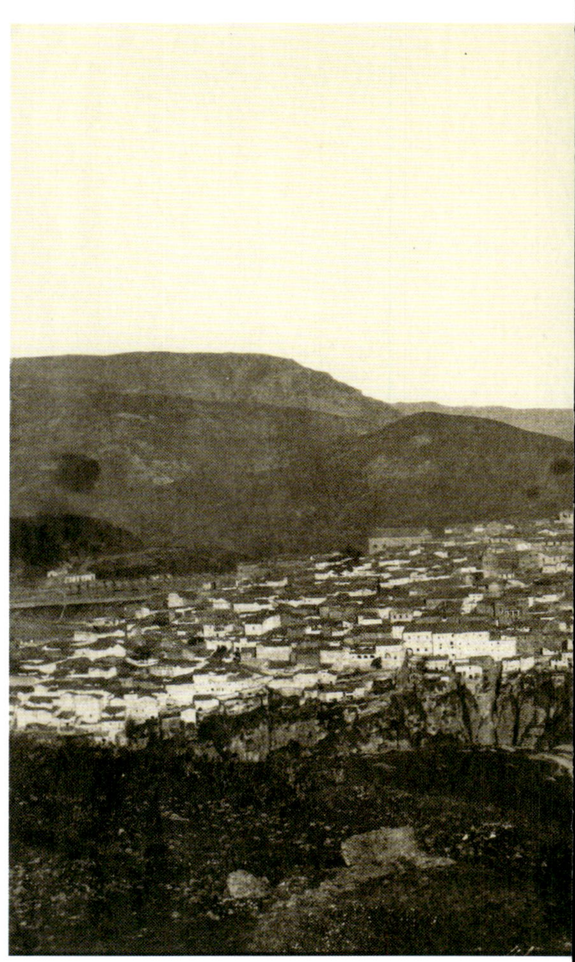

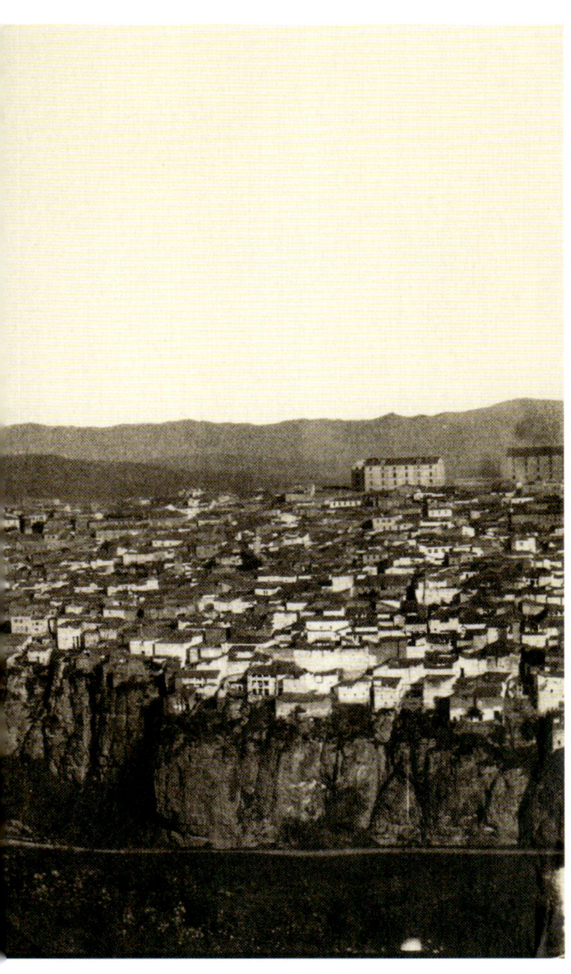
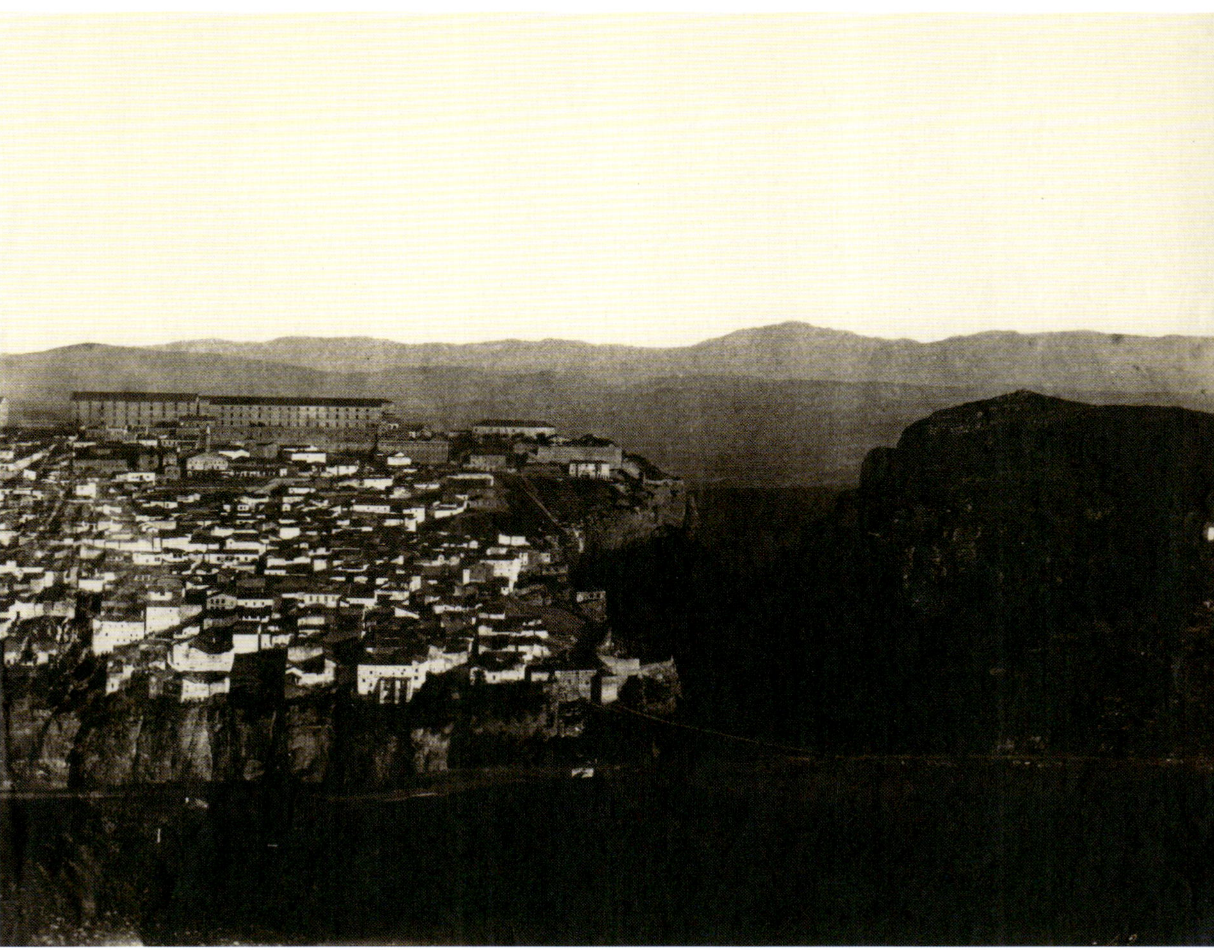

PLATE 84 [Constantine panorama], 1856

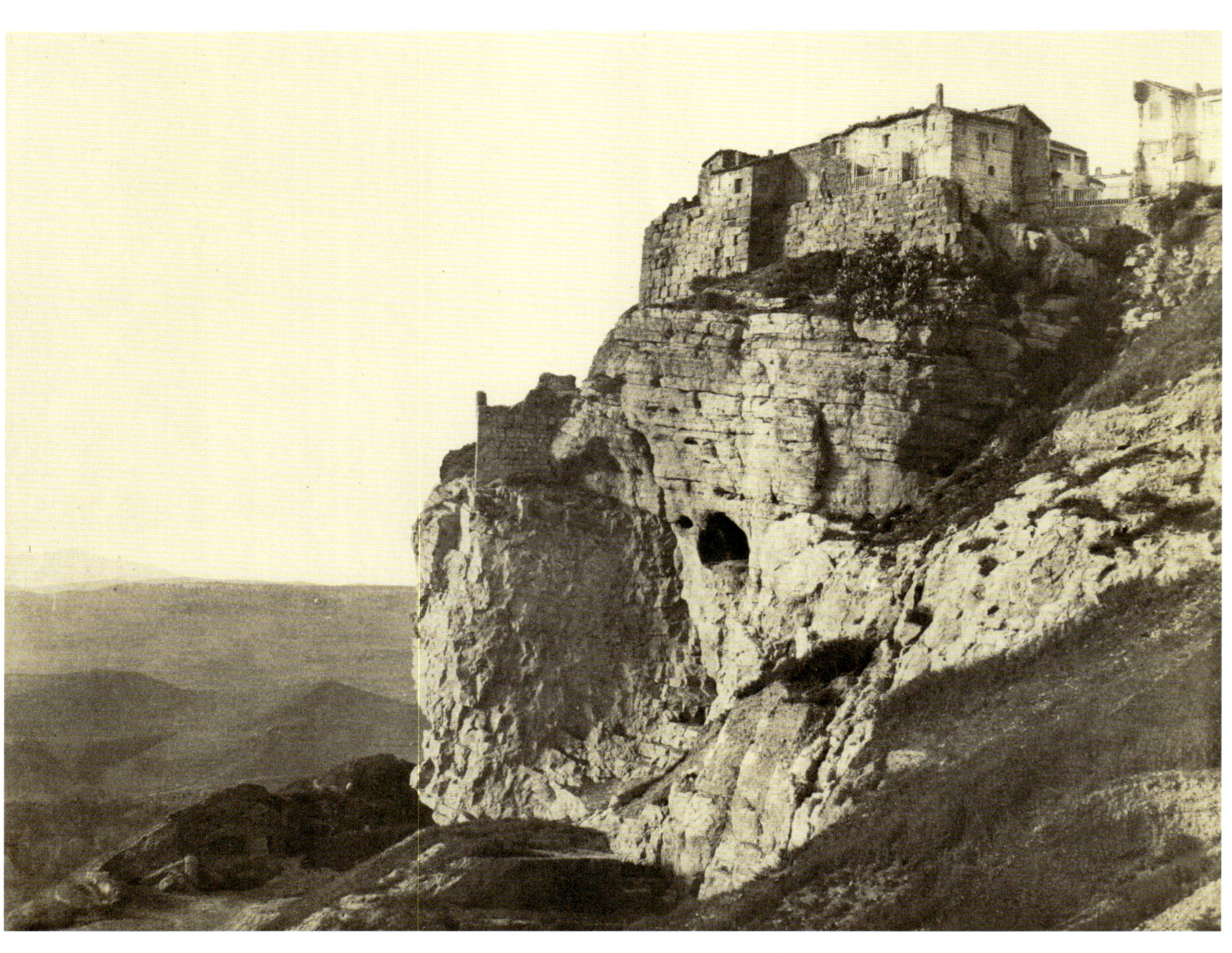

PLATE 85 [Constantine], 1856

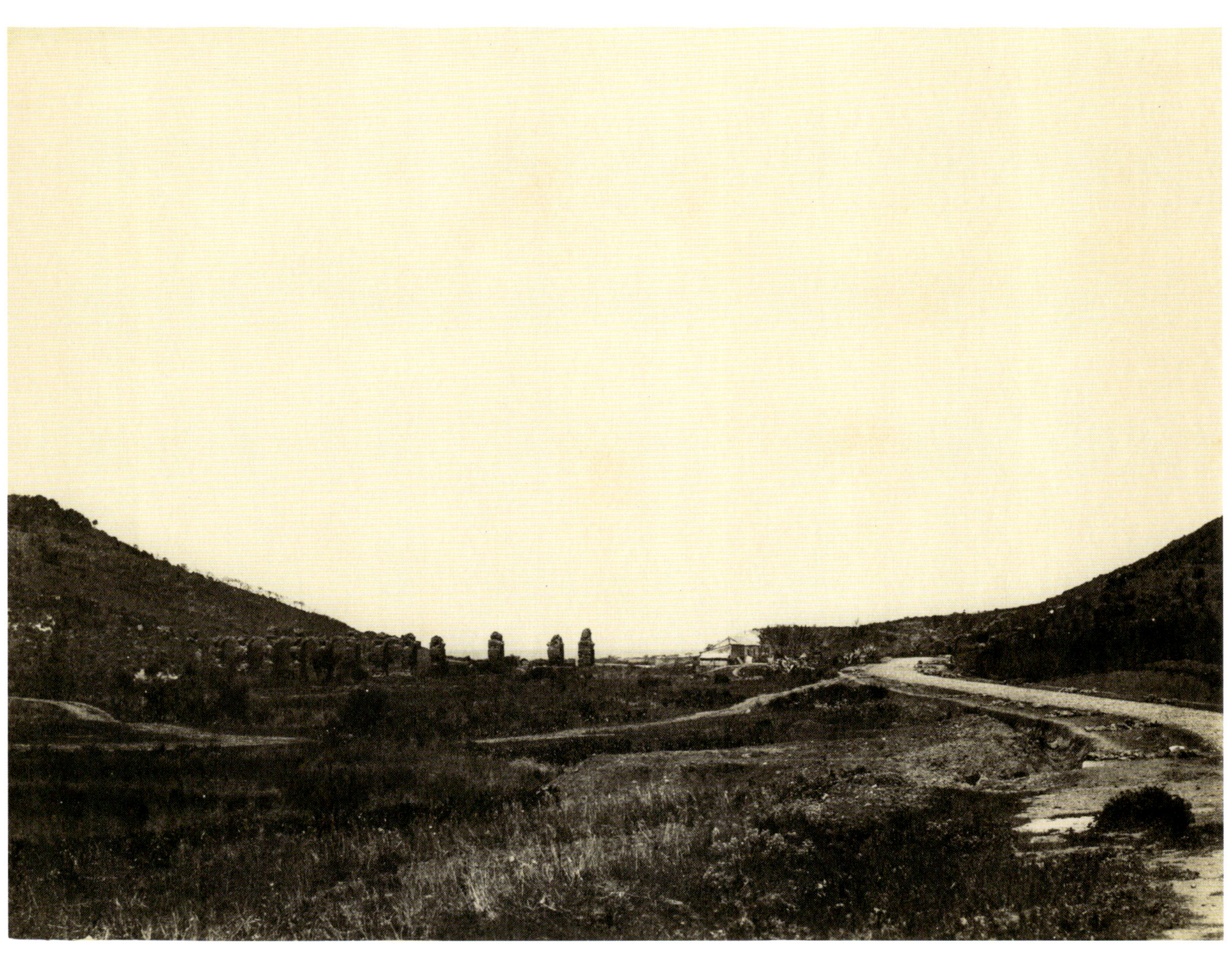

PLATE 86 [Ruins of a Roman aqueduct, Cherchell], 1856

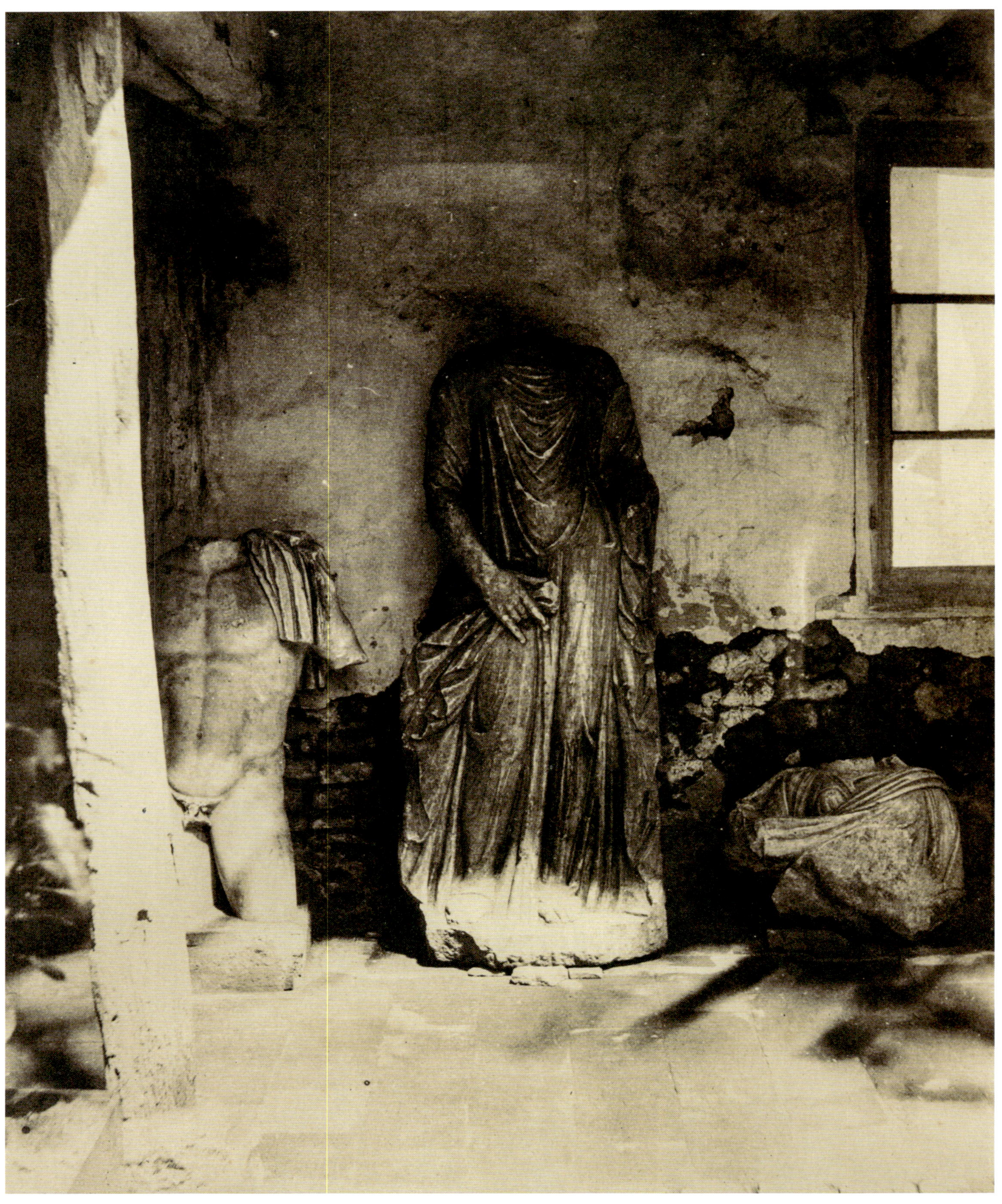

PLATE 87 [Roman sculptures, Cherchell Museum], 1856

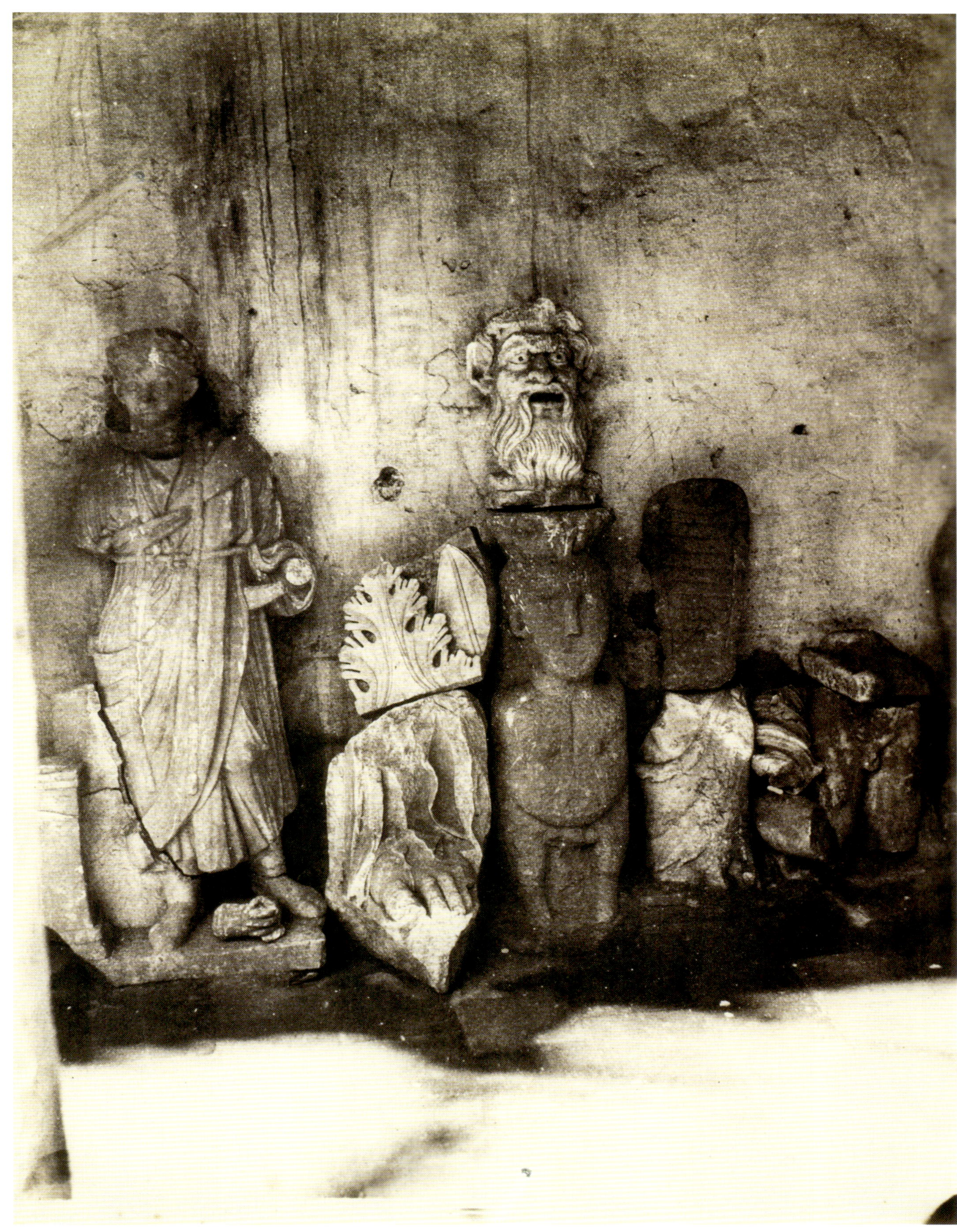

PLATE 88 [Roman sculptures, Cherchell Museum], 1856

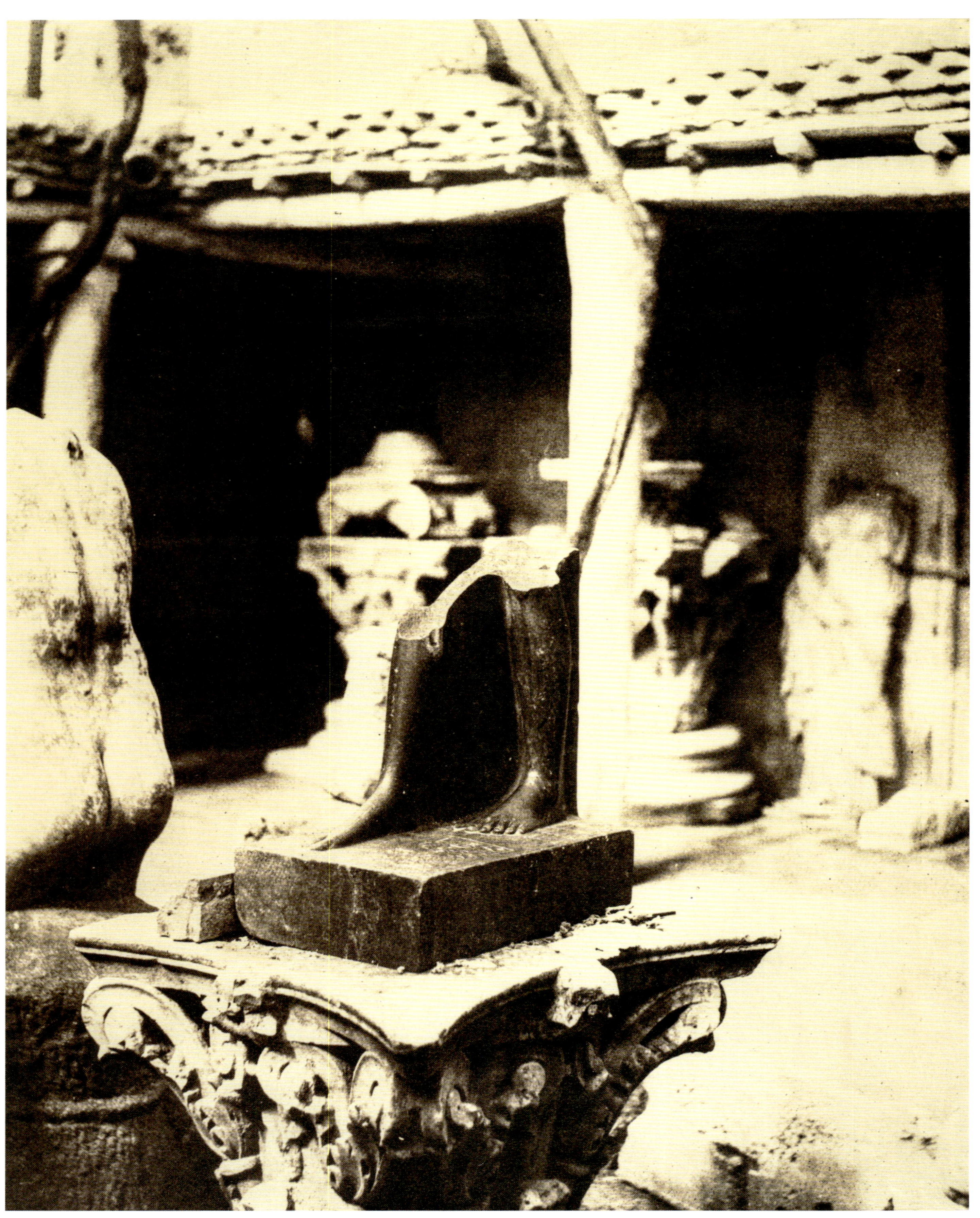

PLATE 89 [Fragment of a statue of King Thutmose I in the Cherchell Museum], 1856

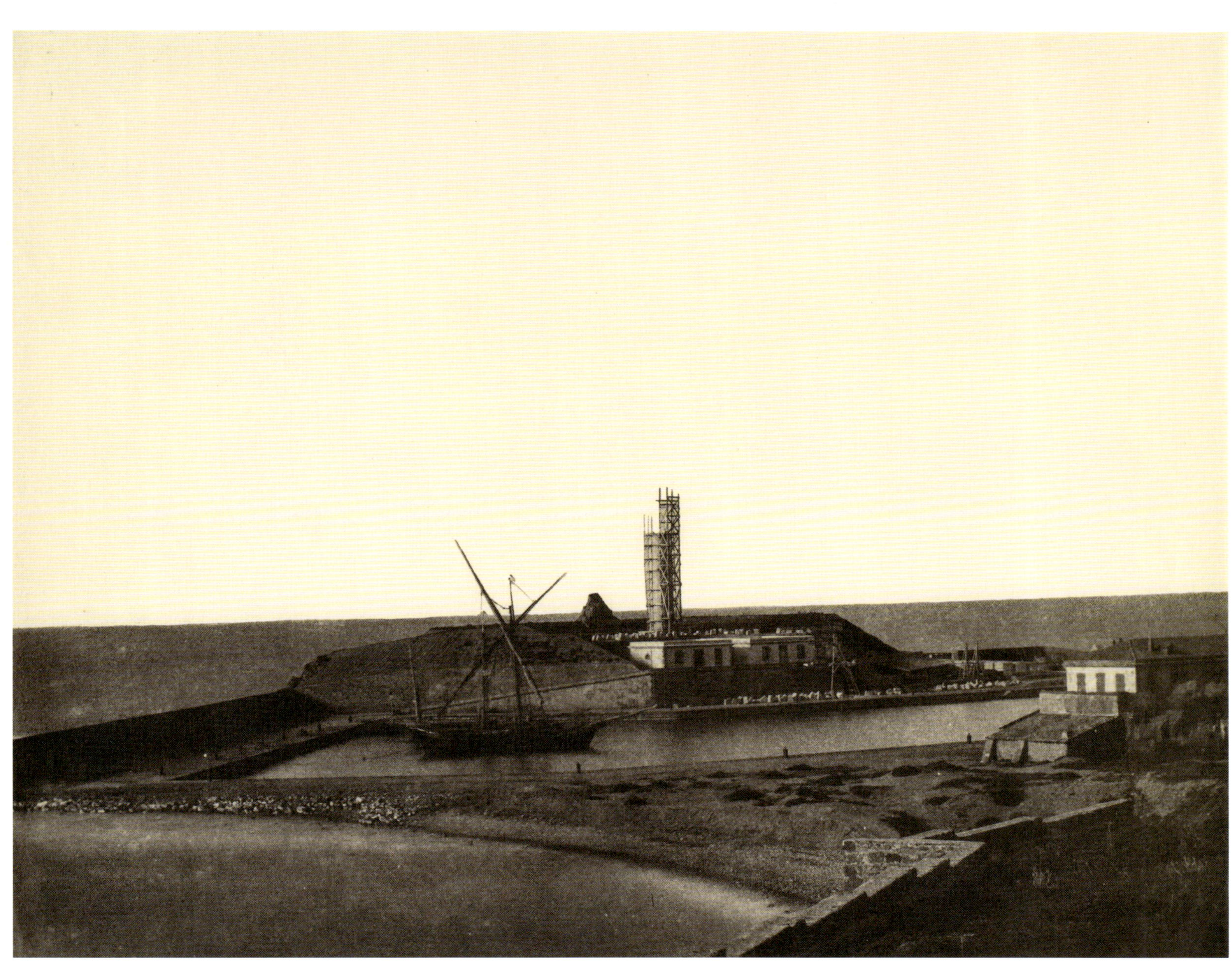

PLATE 90 [Boat in Cherchell harbor], 1855–56

JOHN BEASLEY GREENE CHRONOLOGY

William F. Stapp

1780

OCTOBER 11 John Bulkley Greene, the father of John Beasley Greene, is born in Concord, New Hampshire, the third of six children born to Concord's first lawyer, Peter Greene (1747–1798), and his second wife, née Rebecca Mellen (ca. 1754–1800), whom Peter Greene married in 1775. Bulkley was the maiden name of Peter Greene's first wife, Elizabeth, whom he had married in 1770, and who died in 1774 at the age of twenty-two.

1798

MARCH 27 Death of Peter Greene in Concord, New Hampshire. His widow Rebecca and four minor children (including John Bulkley Greene) move to Boston, where her brother Samuel lives.

1800

MAY 6 When Rebecca Mellen Greene dies, her brother becomes the children's guardian. John Bulkley receives "his mercantile education" in Boston.[1]

1805

APRIL 13 Marie Regina Zélia Dejoye (1805–1872), the mother of John Beasley Greene, is born in Philadelphia to Pierre François Dejoye (1765–1833) and his wife Mary Anastasia Barbe Huet (dates unknown), a French couple from the French West Indies, who may have come to the United States as a result of the Haitian Revolution.

1812

JUNE 18 The United States declares war on Great Britain, marking the beginning of the War of 1812.

1814

John Bulkley Greene departs for England.

1815

FEBRUARY 17 The United States ratifies the Treaty of Ghent, ending the War of 1812.

John Bulkley Greene settles in Le Havre, France, where he becomes a partner in the commission house and bank founded by Massachusetts native Samuel Welles (1778–1841), soon after the end of the Napoleonic wars. When Welles relocates the bank (Welles & Company) to Paris, Greene remains in Le Havre to manage the commission house, known after 1825 as Welles & Greene.

ca. 1819

John Bulkley Greene marries the daughter of Reuben Gaunt Beasley (ca. 1778–1847), who, as the American Agent for Prisoners of War, had been the sole official representative of the American government in Great Britain during the War of 1812. Beasley was appointed the American Consul in Le Havre in 1817, a position he held until the end of his life. Identified only as "Miss Beasley," Greene's first wife's given name and life dates are unknown, but since John Bulkley Greene remarries in 1823, she must have died within three years of their marriage.[2]

1823

APRIL 19 John Bulkley Greene marries Marie Regina Zélia Dejoye (1805–1872) in Le Havre.

1824

FEBRUARY 11 Jeanne Marie Charlotte Zélie Greene, the first child of John Bulkley Greene and Marie Regina Dejoye, is born in Le Havre.

1826

FEBRUARY 4 Rebecca Sophie Charlotte Zélie Greene, the second child of John Bulkley Greene and Marie Regina Dejoye, is born in Le Havre.

1832

JUNE 20 John Beasley Greene, the third child of John Bulkley Greene and Marie Regina Zélia DeJoye and their only son, is born in Ingouville, a suburb of Le Havre.

1835

AUGUST 26 John Beasley Greene is baptized in Le Havre by George M. Jukes, Chaplain.[3]

1839

The first successful photographic processes are publicly introduced: William Henry Fox Talbot's photogenic drawing process in Great Britain and Louis-Jacques-Mandé Daguerre's daguerreotype process in France. Talbot's negative-positive process (patented in Britain in 1841) will be adapted and disseminated in France by Louis Désiré Blanquart-Evrard (1847) and Gustave Le Gray. Talbot's paper negatives are called calotypes (sometimes Talbotypes), though this term is often applied to photographic prints made from paper negatives as well.

1841

Samuel Welles dies in Paris. John Bulkley Greene assumes the directorship of the bank and commission house, now known as Greene & Company, and moves with his family to Paris. The bank's offices and the Greene residence are located initially at 26, Place Saint-Georges (in the present-day ninth arrondissement), then later at 28, Place Saint-Georges.

1847

AUGUST 18 Jeanne Marie Charlotte Zélie Greene, John Beasley Greene's elder sister, marries Jean Fréderic van den Broek (1816–1874), a Belgian-born banker and consul general of the Low Countries in France.

1848

The February Revolution in France forces the abdication of King Louis Philippe and results in the founding of the short-lived Second Republic (1849–52). In June, a bloody but unsuccessful insurrection in Paris against the conservative elected government of the Republic leads to the December election of Louis Napoleon as president of the Second Republic. Four years later, Louis Napoleon suspends the elected National Assembly and proclaims himself Napoleon III, Emperor of the Second French Empire. His reign lasts until 1870, when he abdicates after France's disastrous defeat in the Franco-Prussian War.

1849

SEPTEMBER–OCTOBER Le Gray begins giving photography lessons at his studio at the Barrière de Clichy.

1850

JUNE Le Gray publishes *Traité pratique de photographie sur papier et sur verre* (Practical Treatise on Photography on Paper and Glass), his treatise on the dry waxed paper process.

NOVEMBER 21 After a long illness, John Bulkley Greene dies in Paris and is buried at Père Lachaise. By the time of his death, Greene & Company has become one of the major American banking firms on the Continent and he has amassed a substantial fortune. His son-in-law, Jean Frédéric van den Broek, assumes directorship of the company.[4] John Beasley Greene, his mother, and his sister Rebecca move to 10, rue de la Grange Batelière.

1851

JANUARY The Société Héliographique, the first photographic society, is founded.

FEBRUARY 9 The first issue of *La Lumière*, the Société Héliographique's journal and the first photography periodical, is published.

FEBRUARY 25 Le Gray deposits a sealed envelope containing a description of his waxed paper negative process with the Académie des Sciences in Paris. In July, he publishes *Nouveau traité théoretique et pratique de photographie sur papier et sur verre*, the revised second edition of *Traité pratique de photographie sur papier et sur verre*.

MARCH Blanquart-Evrard founds the photographic printing company Imprimerie Photographique in Lille.

WINTER OF 1851–52 On their grand tour of the Orient, Leavitt Hunt (1831–1907) and his traveling companion Nathan Flint Baker (ca. 1822–1891) become the first Americans to photograph in Egypt and elsewhere in the Middle East. They use the waxed paper process, which they learned in Rome en route to Egypt. Greene, who knows Leavitt Hunt, almost certainly sees his personal album of sixty salted paper prints of the photographs taken in Egypt and beyond on his tour.[5]

1851–52 Civil engineer Félix Teynard (1817–1892) travels to Egypt, where he makes calotype views of the landscape and monuments along the Nile, intended as a photographic complement to the famed multivolume *Déscription de l'Égypte* produced by Napoleon's "scientific army" during the 1798–1802 campaign through Egypt and published between 1809 and 1828. Some 160 of Teynard's calotypes begin to be publicly available in 1853. They are published as an album by Goupil in 1858 under the title *Égypte et Nubie: Sites et monuments les plus intéressants pour l'étude de l'art et de l'histoire*.

1852

Greene takes lessons in the waxed paper process from Le Gray and accompanies him on at least one photographic excursion in the Forest of Fontainebleau, taking several photographs.[6]

Le Gray, Greene, and Henri Le Secq photograph at the Arc de Triomphe in Paris.[7]

MAY Lille publishing house Blanquart-Evrard publishes Maxime Du Camp's *Égypte, Nubie, Palestine et Syrie*, an album of 125 developed-out salted paper prints from the negatives Du Camp made in the Middle East between 1849 and 1851.

SEPTEMBER 24 Greene writes the president of the Académie des Inscriptions et Belles-Lettres announcing that he plans to leave Paris on September 30 and sail from Marseilles on October 4 for Egypt and Syria, where he intends "to collect archaeological, historical, and geographic information of interest" and will try "to record the monuments I come upon by both photography and engraving." He requests "instructions which would allow me to be as useful to research as I can be." The Académie declines to provide any instructions; the planned trip, in any event, does not take place.[8]

OCTOBER 6 Rebecca Sophie Charlotte Greene marries her second cousin, Charles Gordon Greene Jr. (1818–1882), son of the founder, owner, and editor of the *Boston Post* newspaper.[9]

1853

JULY 27 John Beasley Greene and his brothers-in-law Jean Frédéric van den Broek and Charles Gordon Greene form a limited company (*société anonyme*) to own both the commission house in Le Havre and the bank in Paris. Greene & Company, now directed by van den Broek, had prospered under John Bulkley Greene and grown into one of the major banking firms on the Continent. The Greenes are now extremely wealthy, and with his brother-in-law responsible for the bank and with no direct personal involvement in the company, John Beasley Greene is free to pursue his avocations.[10]

OCTOBER 14 Greene is accepted into the Société Asiatique as a foreign member.[11]

NOVEMBER Greene departs for Egypt.

DECEMBER 14 Edwin De Leon, U.S. consul general in Alexandria, reports to U.S. Secretary of State W. S. Marcy that he presented "Mr. Green [*sic*], now resident at Paris" and seven other "American gentlemen" traveling through the country to the viceroy of Egypt.[12]

DECEMBER Greene photographs the pyramids and Auguste Mariette's excavations at Giza.

1854

FEBRUARY 21 Charles Gordon Greene III, the first son of Charles Gordon Jr. and John Beasley Greene's sister, Rebecca Sophie Charlotte Greene, is born in Paris.

Greene travels up the Nile as far as the Second Cataract.[13]

MAY Greene returns to Paris.[14]

JULY 3 Greene submits a photograph of a bas-relief in the tomb of Seti I at Thebes (also known as "Belzoni's Tomb") to the Académie des Sciences, claiming he had used a new technique for photographing sculptures and inscriptions in semidarkness ("dans la pénombre"). When it is discovered that the photograph was, in fact, of a cast of the sculpture Greene had made by pressing water-soaked paper onto the carving, letting it dry, then photographing the resulting mold, he apologizes for his misleading description in a letter to the editor of *La Lumière*, written "to put an end to the misunderstanding which I am the first to regret."[15]

JULY 21 Greene presents the album *Sculptures et inscriptions égyptiennes* to the Académie des Inscriptions et Belles-Lettres. It is a collection of 102 salted paper prints from Greene's waxed paper negatives.[16]

AUGUST 7 Jean Frédéric van den Broek, John Beasley Greene, Charles Gordon Greene, and Marie Regina Zélia Dejoye, the widow Greene, form a corporation (*sociéte anonyme*) that owns and manages both Greene & Company's commercial house in Le Havre and the bank in Paris. The arrangement is retroactive to July 1, 1853, and is supposed to terminate July 1, 1858.[17]

OCTOBER 20 Greene presents the album *Monuments et paysages de la Nubie et de la Haute Égypte* to the Académie des Inscriptions et Belles-Lettres. It is a collection of 83 salted paper prints from Greene's waxed paper negatives, divided into 42 views of Egyptian monuments and 41 landscapes.[18]

1854

Greene commissions Blanquart-Evrard to print his Egyptian negatives, with the apparent intention of publishing an album, *Le Nil: Monuments—Paysages. Explorations photographiques*. The exact publishing history of this album is unclear. Blanquart-Evrard deposited a title page as well as several album pages at the Société Française de Photographie as part of what appears to be a sample album. The only known intact album was purchased by the Bibliothèque Nationale de France in 1946. Though the album cover bears the Blanquart-Evrard crest, the individual pages are not marked with their traditional credit line (as the pages at the Société Française de Photographie are).

NOVEMBER 15 The Société Française de Photographie is founded in Paris. Greene (misspelled as Greenn) is listed as a "premier fondateur" in the first issue of the Société's *Bulletin*.[19]

NOVEMBER/DECEMBER Greene returns to Egypt and, through the influence of Ferdinand de Lesseps, obtains a firman (decree) from Sa'id Pasha, the Ottoman viceroy and *de facto* ruler of Egypt, authorizing him to carry out excavations in Upper Egypt.[20]

1855

Greene assembles a unique album of views from his first trip to Egypt for presentation to the grand duke of Baden. Titled *Collection de photographies prises en Égypte en 1854 offerte à S.A. le Grand Duc de Bade en 1855*,[21] the album contains 26 salted paper prints. The motivation for the gift is unknown. Baden-Baden is one of Germany's most popular health resorts, famous since Roman times for the healing properties of its thermal springs. In the nineteenth century, such spas were popular tourist destinations, for both the healthy and the ill, particularly those suffering from pulmonary conditions such as tuberculosis. Greene's nephew died there, and as Greene himself suffered from some kind of chronic ailment, he may have spent time there as well.

FEBRUARY–APRIL Greene excavates at the Temple of Ramesses III at Medinet Habu, Thebes, where he successfully uncovers an important Egyptian calendar, only a part of which Jean-François Champollion had been able to clear. Greene also excavates two royal tombs at Deir el-Bahri.

MAY–NOVEMBER Fifteen photographs by Greene are exhibited in the U.S. section of the Paris Exposition Universelle. He is awarded a bronze medal, second class, for his Egyptian views. In the Exposition's official catalogue, he is identified as "Green [*sic*] (J. Beasely [*sic*]) à Concord (New Hampshire)."[22]

JUNE 15 Greene gives a selection of representative Egyptian views to the Société Francaise de Photographie. He observes that the morning is the best time to take photographs in the Middle East, depending on how far the day has advanced: after 11:00, the light turns gray. He believes that the best time to make negatives is between 7:00 and 11:00 a.m., and then to wait until 3:00 p.m. to start again.[23]

"Fouilles exécutées en Égypte par M. Green," a report summarizing the results of Greene's expeditions to Egypt in 1853–54 and 1854–55, is published in *L'Athenaeum Français*. The author is unidentified, but is probably Emmanuel de Rougé.[24]

NOVEMBER 9 Greene writes François Joseph Chabas, an Egyptologist, that he is sending him a copy of his report on his excavation at Medinet Habu, Thebes, *Fouilles exécutées en Thèbes dans l'année 1855: Textes hiéroglyphiques et documents inédits*, which is being published by Firmin Didot that week.[25]

NOVEMBER Greene presents *Fouilles exécutées à Thèbes dans l'année 1855*, an album of twelve photographs taken during his excavations at Medinet Habu, to the Académie des Inscriptions et Belles-Lettres.[26]

NOVEMBER Rougé's review of Greene's *Fouilles exécutées en Thèbes* is published in *L'Athenaeum Français*. At the same time, he publishes a slightly revised version of the *Athenaeum* article as a pamphlet. Greene's excavation report receives a mixed review from the eminent French historian Victor Langlois, writing in the *Revue Archéologique*.[27]

DECEMBER 19, 1855–JANUARY 5, 1856 Greene photographs Adrien Berbrugger's first excavation at the Tombeau de la Chrétienne (Tomb of the Christian Woman) in Tipaza Province, Algeria, between Cherchell and Algiers.[28] Greene returns to France at the end of the excavations.

1856

JANUARY 12 Edwin De Leon, U.S. consul general in Alexandria, in a letter to W. S. Marcy, U.S. Secretary of State, refers to J. B. Greene obtaining a firman to excavate at Thebes the previous year, "which resulted in some valuable discoveries, made public at the French Exposition. . . . He has published a book, a copy of which I had the pleasure of presenting the Viceroy a week ago . . ."[29]

FEBRUARY 4 Greene departs Marseilles for Algiers on the *Queen of Clippers*, an American clipper ship chartered by the Algerian government. He arrives in Algiers February 12.[30]

FEBRUARY–MARCH Green photographs in Constantine.[31]

MARCH 24–APRIL 5 Greene photographs Berbrugger's second excavation at the site of the Tombeau de la Chrétienne.[32] When the excavation ends, the members of the expedition disperse: John Beasley Greene departs for Cherchell.[33]

APRIL 17 Edmund Revel Smith, an American traveling in Algeria, writes to J. J. Mahoney, U.S. consul in Algiers, that he had visited the site of the Tombeau de la Chrétienne, and that both Berbrugger "and our compatriot Mr. Green [*sic*] were on the spot, hard at work and in hopes of soon discovering the entrance."[34]

MAY Greene publishes an article in the *Bulletin Archéologique de l'Athenaeum Français* on the fragment of an ancient Egyptian sculpture he discovered in the museum in Cherchell, Algeria. The image of the sculpture illustrating the article is a tracing of Greene's photograph of the piece that was transferred to a lithographic stone for printing.[35]

MAY 22 Greene writes Chabas that he has just returned to Paris from Algeria.[36]

Greene exhibits four photographs taken in Constantine at the Exhibition of Industrial Arts in Brussels, organized by the Association pour l'Encouragement et le Développement des Arts Industriels en Belgique. He is awarded an honorable mention.[37] This is the last public exhibition of Greene's photographs for more than a century.

Berbrugger presents a unique album of fourteen photographs taken by Greene during the excavations at the Tombeau de la Chrétienne at the end of 1855 and over Easter in 1856 to the Académie des Inscriptions et Belles-Lettres.

MID-NOVEMBER Greene, "already seriously ill," returns to Egypt.[38]

NOVEMBER 29 John Beasley Greene dies at age twenty-four of an otherwise unidentified "cruelle maladie" in Cairo, shortly after his arrival. His death is reported in the French and American press and photographic journals.[39] Greene is buried in Cairo, but the location of his grave is not known. His name (misspelled) and dates (incorrect) are inscribed on the family tomb in Père Lachaise in Paris, but the cemetery's burial records for the tomb do not document his interment there.

After Greene's death, a large selection of his Egyptian negatives and prints come into the possession of his friend and fellow Egyptologist Théodule Devéria, who works in the Department of Egyptian Antiquities at the Louvre.[40]

1857

MARCH 27 Greene & Company fails, and the bank suspends payments. According to *The New York Times*, "The cause of this failure is attributed to imprudent advances made on French merchandise dispatched to Nicaragua and other Central or South American countries."[41]

1866

JULY 11 At the request of Greene's family, John G. Nicolay, the American consul in Paris, notifies the French Foreign Ministry that he is legally dead. The document states that Greene died unmarried and intestate and advises the French Foreign Ministry that since he was a citizen of Massachusetts, his estate will be settled according to the laws of that state.[42] The legal recognition of Greene's death allows the family to dissolve Greene & Company, both the commercial house in Le Havre and the bank in Paris.[43]

ca. 1871

The widow of Théodule Devéria (1831–1871) sells his collection and archives to the Department of Egyptian Antiquities of the Louvre. The collection includes a large number of Greene's Egyptian negatives, as well as prints.[44]

1872

APRIL 6 Marie Reine Dejoye, the widow of John Bulkley Greene and John Beasley Greene's mother, dies at home in her apartment in Versailles.[45]

1. "The Late Mr. J. B. Greene," *Boston Daily Advertiser*, December 16, 1850, no. 142.
2. *The Daily Advertiser*, reprinted in *The New Hampshire Patriot & State Gazette*, February 3, 1842.
3. National Archives, London, Foreign and Overseas Registers of British Subjects, 1628–1969, Registrar General 33: *Foreign Registers and Returns, 1627–1960 / Piece 056: Le Havre: Baptisms, Marriages, Burials, 1817–1843*.
4. "Extract from a private letter to the editor of the *Boston Post*, dated Paris, Oct. 23, 1850," *Boston Post*, November 11, 1850, p. 2, col. 2; "Extract from a private letter to the editor of the *Boston Post*, dated Paris, Nov. 27, 1850," *Boston Post*, December 14, 1850; and "The Late Mr. J. B. Greene," *Boston Daily Advertiser*, December 16, 1850, no. 142.
5. The Greenes were friends with the Hunts, members of a distinguished and wealthy Vermont family who had banked with Greene & Company since arriving in Paris in the early 1840s. Catherine Clinton Howland Hunt, "Unpublished Biography of Richard Morris Hunt," 1895, American Institute of Architects/American Architectural Foundation Collection, Library of Congress, p. 10. Hunt's album, one of only two assembled by Hunt and Baker (the other is lost), is in the collection of the Bennington Museum.
6. It is not entirely clear whether Greene photographed in Fontainebleau in 1852 or 1853 or both. A photograph of trees in the Forest of Fontainebleau, signed and dated 1853 in ink by Greene on the print, is in a group of prints donated by Greene to the Société Française de Photographie in 1855. Other work he made in Fontainebleau clearly corresponds to an excursion Le Gray made in 1852. It is possible that he misdated the print at the Société Française de Photographie, or that he went to the forest multiple times.
7. Sylvie Aubenas, ed., *Gustave Le Gray, 1820–1884* (Los Angeles: J. Paul Getty Museum, 2002), pp. 57 and 298, pls. 61, 62, 323; and Eugenia Parry Janis and Josiane Sartre, *Henri Le Secq: Photographe de 1850 à 1860: Catalogue raisonée de la collection de la Bibliothèque des Arts Décoratifs, Paris* (Paris: Flammarion and Union des Arts Décoratifs, 1986), p. 155, nos. 426 and 427.
8. Bruno Jammes, "John B. Greene, an American Calotypist," *History of Photography* 5, no. 4 (October 1981), p. 309.
9. "[no. 237] Greene et Greene, 6 Octobre 1852," in *France, Paris: registres protestants, 1536–1897, Marriages,* L'Oratoire, Paris, p. 108.
10. Archives Départmentales, Paris, D31U3 185, "Prorogation de Société Greene et Cie."
11. "Procès-verbal de la séance du 14 octobre 1853," *Journal Asiatique* 5, no. 2 (1853), p. 529.
12. National Archives and Records Administration, RG59, Dispatches from United States Consuls in Alexandria, Egypt, T45 no. 2.
13. An album cover in a private collection, *Le Nil: Paysages et monuments de la Nubie et de la Haute Égypte photographiés en février et mars 1854 par J. B. Greene,* suggests he made his photographs in February and March; however, the contents of that album are unknown. "Personal and Fine Art Intelligence," *The Photographic and Fine Art Journal* 7, no. 10 (October 1854), p. 320.
14. According to Alfred Maury, "Sociétés Savants. Institut de France. Académies des Inscriptions et Belles Lettres/séances des 28 juillet, 1er, 8 et 15 Septembre," *L'Athenaeum Français* 3 (September 23, 1854), p. 893. Greene's sojourn in Egypt lasted from November 1853 to May 1854.
15. "M. Greene présenté . . .," *Comptes Rendus Hebdomadaires des Séances de l'Académie des Sciences* 39 (July–December 1854), p. 75. A garbled account of Greene's technique, in which he is referred to as "M. J-B Grenne" and the image of the mold of the Egyptian bas-relief that was shown to the Académie des Sciences is described as "representing a bas-relief from an ancient tomb near Athens," was published in *La Lumière* 4, no. 7 (July 8, 1854), p. 105. "Monsieur le Rédacteur," *La Lumière* 4, no. 29 (July 22, 1854), p. 115.
16. Dated inscription in Greene's hand in the album (Réserve Fol. Z129c). The gift is described by Maury, "Sociétés Savants," p. 893.
17. Archives Départementales, Paris, D31U3 185, "Prorogration de Société Greene et Cie."
18. Dated inscription in Greene's hand in the album (Réserve Fol. N142h).
19. "Liste des premiers fondateurs de la Société Française de Photographie," *Bulletin de la Société Française de Photographie* 1 (January 10, 1855), p. 22.
20. J. B. Greene, "Introduction," in *Fouilles exécutées en Thèbes dans l'année 1855: Textes hiéroglyphiques et documents inédits* (Paris: Firmin Didot Frères, 1855), n.p.
21. Collection of Janet Lehr, Inc., New York.
22. *Exposition des produits de l'industrie de toutes les nations à Paris 1855* (Paris, 1855), p. 222; *La Lumière* 5, no. 50 (December 15, 1855), p. 198.
23. "Procès-verbal de la séance du 15 juin 1855," *Bulletin de la Société Française de Photographie* 1, no. 6 (June 15, 1855), p. 165.

24. "Fouilles exécutées en Égypte par M. Greene," *L'Athenaeum Français* 4, no. 32 (August 11, 1855), p. 689.
25. Letter from J. B. Greene to François Joseph Chabas, dated Paris, November 9, 1855, Bibliothèque de l'Institut de France, Correspondance de François Joseph Chabas, vol. 1 (Années 1850–1858, letter 99).
26. Dated inscription in Greene's hand in the album.
27. Emmanuel de Rougé, "Notice sur quelques textes hiéroglyphiques nouvellement publiés par M. Greene," *L'Athenaeum Français* 4, no. 44 (November 3, 1855), pp. 956–61, and 4, no. 50 (December 15, 1855), pp. 1083–88; Emmanuel de Rougé, *Notice de quelques textes hiéroglyphiques récemment publiés par M. Greene* (Paris: E. Thunot, 1855); Victor Langlois, "Fouilles exécutées à Thèbes, dans l'année 1855, par J. B. Greene," *Revue Archéologique* 12, no. 2 (October 1855–March 1856), pp. 571–72.
28. Adrien Berbrugger, "Explorations du Tombeau de la Chrétienne," *Revue Africaine: Journal des Travaux de la Société Historique Algérienne* 1, no. 1 (1856), p. 38. Berbrugger (1801–1869), director of the museum in Algiers, president of the Historical Society of Algeria, and founder and editor of the *Revue Africaine*, led two excavations at the Tombeau de la Chrétienne, in the winter of 1855 and the spring of 1856, for which Greene served as expedition photographer.
29. National Archives and Records Administration, RG59, Dispatches from United States Consuls in Alexandria, Egypt, T45 no. 2.
30. Consular Statement of Official Acts and Fees Received at Algiers from 1st January to 31st March 1856 inclusive. National Archives and Records Administration, Dispatches from United States Consuls in Algiers, Algeria, M23 roll 15, and "Bulletin Maritime," *Le Moniteur Algérien* 1, no. 458 (February 15, 1857), p. 4.
31. The dates of Greene's excursion to Constantine are not documented, but the six weeks between his return to Algeria on February 12 and the resumption of the excavations at the Tombeau de la Chrétienne on March 24 are the only window in his chronology for 1855–56 that would have provided sufficient time to make that trip.
32. Berbrugger, "Explorations du Tombeau de la Chrétienne," p. 38.
33. Letter from the French photographer Félix Moulin from Algeria dated June 9, 1856, published in "La photographie en Algérie," *La Lumière* 6, no. 25 (June 21, 1856), p. 97. Moulin, who met Greene at the site of the Tombeau de la Chrétienne in early June 1856, during Berbrugger's second excavation, refers to him as "M. Green [*sic*] un américain photographe amateur."
34. National Archives and Records Administration, Dispatches from United States Consuls in Algiers, Algeria, M23 roll 15.
35. J. B. Greene, "Note sur un fragment de statue égyptienne du musée de Cherchel," *Bulletin Archéologique de l'Athenaeum Français* 2, no. 5 (May 1856), pp. 38–39.
36. Letter from John Beasley Greene to François Chabas, Bibliothèque de l'Iinstitut de France, MS 2572, Letter 181.
37. *Catalogue de l'exposition instituée par l'Association pour l'Encouragement et le Développement des Arts Industriels en Belgique* (Brussels: Guyot et Stapleaux fils, 1856), cited in Jammes, "John B. Greene, an American Calotypist," p. 316; and "Liste des récompenses," *La Lumière* 6, no. 50 (December 15, 1856).
38. Letter of Greene's friend and fellow Egyptologist Théodule Devéria to François Chabas, dated Paris, December 21, 1856, confirming Greene's death in Cairo. In his letter, Devéria implies that Greene's illness was chronic, and says that during an earlier trip, the Egyptian climate had effected a cure, which suggests a pulmonary disease. Jammes, "John B. Greene, an American Calotypist," p. 305, reproduces and translates the relevant paragraph from Devéria's letter.
39. "Mort de M. Greene," *Revue Photographique* 2, no. 16 (February 5, 1857), p. 246; "Nécrologie," *Le Siècle* (December 18, 1856), p. 3; "Procès-verbal de la séance du 13 février 1857 . . . On annonce le mort de M. John Greene, membre de la Société Asiatique," *Journal Asiatique* 9 (1857), p. 288; "Procès-verbal de la séance du 19 décembre 1857 [*sic*]," *Bulletin de la Société Française de Photographie* 3, no. 1 (January 1857), p. 3; *Galignani's* (December 17, 1856), p. 3; *Journal des Débats Politiques et Littéraires* (December 16, 1856), p. 1. Greene's death in Cairo on November 29 is recorded in a number of French legal documents, including the American consul's official letter of July 9, 1866, notifying the French Ministry of Foreign Affairs that John Beasley Greene has been declared legally dead and that his estate will be settled according to the laws of the Commonwealth of Massachusetts, of which he was a citizen (MC ET-LII-984).
40. Devéria did not acquire any of Greene's Algerian work, and although a number of unmounted prints of his Algerian photographs have appeared on the market since the late 1970s, the whereabouts of the negatives are unknown.
41. "Suspension of an American Banking House in Paris," *The New York Times*, April 16, 1857. See also "Failure of Greene & Company, American Bankers, Paris," *The Bankers' Magazine and Statistical Register* 6, no. 11 (May 1857), pp. 899–900.
42. John G. Nicolay to the French Foreign Ministry, Paris, July 9, 1866 (Archives Nationales, Paris–Centre d'Accueil et de Recherche des Archives Nationales–Minutier Central des Notaires–ET-LII-984).
43. On July 19, 1866, as required by law, the formal announcement of the dissolution of Greene & Company is published by the family's notary in the daily legal papers of the day: *Journal Général d'Affiches*, p. 12; *Le Droit: Journal des Tribunaux, de la Jurisprudence, des Débats Judiciaires et de la Legislation*, p. 16; and the *Journal Général d'Affiches*, no. 19,91.
44. Quentin Bajac, "Deveria [*sic*], Achilles (1800–1857) and Théodule (1831–1871)," in *Encyclopedia of Nineteenth-Century Photography*, ed. John Hannavy (New York: Routledge, 2008), vol. 1, pp. 413–14, and Sylvie Aubenas, "Charles Théodule Devéria," at http://heritage.bnf.fr/bibliothequesorient/en/theodule-deveria.
45. Actes de Décès 422. Greene Vve née Dejoye, 6 avril [1872] / 422 / Dejoye Marie Reine / Vve Greene "décédee hier, dix heures et demie du soir."

SELECTED BIBLIOGRAPHY

BY GREENE

Letters, Articles, and Texts

Greene, J. B. "Correspondance." *La Lumière* 4, no. 29 (July 22, 1854), p. 115.

———. *Fouilles exécutées à Thèbes dans l'année 1855: Textes hiéroglyphiques et documents inédits*. Paris: Firmin Didot Frères, 1855.

———. Letter to François-Joseph Chabas, November 9, 1855. Bibliothèque de l'Institut de France, MS 2572, f 99-100.

———. Letter to the Académie des Inscriptions et Belles-Lettres, September 24, 1852. Archives de l'Académie des Inscriptions et Belles-Lettres, E371, correspondence de particuliers.

———. Letter to the Académie des Inscriptions et Belles-Lettres, July 21, 1854. Archives de l'Académie des Inscriptions et Belles-Lettres, E373, correspondence de particuliers.

———. "Note sur un fragment de statue égyptienne du musée de Cherchel." *Bulletin Archéologique de l'Athenaeum Français* 2, no. 5 (May 1856), pp. 38–39.

Albums in Institutional Collections

Le Nil: Monuments—Paysages. Explorations photographiques par John B. Greene 1854. Lille: Imprimerie Photographique de Blanquart-Evrard, 1854. Collection of the Bibliothèque Nationale de France, Est. Rés. Vh-167-Fol.

Monuments et paysages de la Nubie et de la Haute Égypte. 1854. Unpublished album of 83 photographs. Collection of the Bibliothèque de l'Institut de France, Réserve Fol. N142H.

Sculptures et inscriptions égyptiennes. 1854. Unpublished album of 102 photographs. Collection of the Bibliothèque de l'Institut de France, Réserve Fol. Z 129C.

Fouilles exécutées à Thèbes dans l'année 1855. Unpublished album of 12 photographs. Collection of the Bibliothèque de l'Institut de France, Réserve Fol. A 142D. Copies exist in the collections of the Bibliothèque de l'Égyptologie at the Collège de France, Paris, and at the Oriental Institute, University of Chicago.

Tombeau de la Chrétienne. 1856. Unpublished album of 14 photographs. Bibliothèque de l'Institut de France, Réserve Fol. Z 154D••.

ABOUT GREENE

A.T.L. "Sciences." *La Lumière* 4, no. 27 (July 8, 1854), pp. 105–6.

Delessert, Benjamin, and Louis Ravené. "Documents officiels pour server à l'histoire de la photographie: Extrait des rapports du jury mixte international de l'Exposition universelle." *La Lumière* 7, no. 33 (August 15, 1857), p. 131.

Devéria, Théodule. Letter to François-Joseph Chabas, December 21, 1856. Bibliothèque de l'Institut de France, MS 2572 f 257.

Howe, Kathleen Stewart. "Egypt Recovered: The Photographic Surveys of Maxime Du Camp, Félix Teynard, and John Beasley Greene, and the Development of Egyptology." PhD diss., University of New Mexico, 1996.

Jammes, Bruno. "John B. Greene, an American Calotypist." *History of Photography* 5, no. 4 (October 1981), pp. 305–24.

Lacan, Ernest. "Exposition photographique de Bruxelles." *La Lumière* 6, no. 47 (November 22, 1856), pp. 181–82.

Lacoste, Anne. "La photographie et les sciences de l'antiquité en Orient dans la seconde moitié du XIXe siècle d'après l'étude des fonds photographiques de la Bibliothèque de l'Institut de France." PhD diss., Université Paris IV–Sorbonne, 2008.

Langlois, Victor. "Fouilles exécutées à Thèbes, dans l'année 1855, par J. B. Greene." *Revue Archéologique* 12, no. 2 (October 1855–March 1856), pp. 571–72.

"Liste des premiers fondateurs de la Société Française de Photographie." *Bulletin de la Société Française de Photographie* 1 (January 10, 1855), p. 22.

Méaux, Danièle. "Monuments et paysages de John B. Greene." *History of Photography* 33, no. 3 (August 2009), pp. 262-277.

Newhall, Beaumont. "John B. Greene." In *Discovery & Recognition*, ed. James Alinder, pp. 33–40. Carmel, Calif.: Friends of Photography, 1981.

Parry Janis, Eugenia. *Sun Pictures 23: John Beasley Greene*. New York: Hans P. Kraus Jr., 2016.

"Personal and Fine Art Intelligence." *The Photographic and Fine Art Journal* 7, no. 10 (October 1854), pp. 319–20.

"Procès-verbal de la séance du 15 juin 1855." *Bulletin de la Société Française de Photographie* 1 (June 15, 1855), pp. 149–66.

"Procès-verbal de la séance du 19 octobre 1855." *Bulletin de la Société Française de Photographie* 1 (October 19, 1855), pp. 277–86.

"Procès-verbal de la séance du 19 décembre 1857." *Bulletin de la Société Française de Photographie* 4 (December 19, 1857), pp. 1–15.

Rougé, Emmanuel de. "Fouilles exécutées en Égypte par M. Greene." *L'Athenaeum Français* 4, no. 32 (August 11, 1855), p. 689.

———. "Notice sur quelques textes hiéroglyphiques nouvellement publiés par M. Greene." *L'Athenaeum Français* 4, no. 44 (November 3, 1855), pp. 956–61.

Stapp, William F. "Greene, John Beasly (1832–1856)." In *Encyclopedia of Nineteenth-Century Photography*, ed. John Hannavy, vol. 1, pp. 619–22. New York: Routledge, 2008.

Topham, Rachel. "John Beasly Greene." Master's thesis, Ryerson University and George Eastman House, 2006.

PRIMARY SOURCES

Berbrugger, Adrien. *L'Algérie historique, pittoresque et monumentale, ou recueil de vues, costumes et portraits faits d'après nature dans les provinces d'Alger, Bone, Constantine et Oran*. 4 vols. Paris: J. Delahaye, 1843.

———. "Chronique." *Revue Africaine: Journal des Travaux de la Société Historique Algérienne* 7, no. 41 (September 1856), pp. 393–400.

———. "Explorations du Tombeau de la Chrétienne." *Revue Africaine: Journal des Travaux de la Société Historique Algérienne* 1, no. 1 (1856), pp. 31–38.

——. *Le Tombeau de la Chrétienne: Mausolée des rois mauritaniens de la dernière dynastie*. Algiers: Bastide, 1867.

Blanquart-Evrard, Louis-Désiré. *Traité de photographie sur papier*. Paris: Librairie Encyclopédique de Roret, 1851.

Blinière, M. de. "Antiquités de la ville de Cherchel (Algérie)." *Revue Archéologique* 5, no. 1 (April 15–September 15, 1848), pp. 344–52.

Commission des sciences et arts d'Égypte: Description de l'Égypte, ou Recueil des observations et des recherches qui ont été faites en Égypte pendant l'expédition de l'armée française, publié par les ordres de sa majesté l'empereur Napoléon le grand. 23 vols. Paris: l'Imprimerie Impériale, 1809–22.

Du Camp, Maxime. *Égypte, Nubie, Palestine et Syrie: Dessins photographiques recueillis pendant les années 1849, 1850, et 1851*. Paris: Gide et Baudry, 1852.

Flaubert, Gustave. *Flaubert in Egypt: A Sensibility on Tour*. Trans. and ed. Francis Steegmuller. Chicago: Academy Chicago, 1979. Reprint, New York: Penguin, 1996.

Giffard, Pierre. *Les Français en Égypte*. Paris: V. Havard, 1883.

Julien, G. "L'Algérie photographiée." *L'Illustration* 787, no. 31 (March 27, 1858), p. 2001.

Lacan, Ernest. "L'Algérie photographiée." *Le Moniteur Universel*, no. 343 (December 9, 1858), p. 1493.

——. "Exposition photographique de Bruxelles." *La Lumière* 6, no. 49 (December 6, 1856), p. 189.

Le Gray, Gustave. *Traité pratique de photographie sur papier et sur verre*. Paris: Baillière, 1850. 2nd ed. *Nouveau traité théoretique et pratique de photographie sur papier et sur verre*. Paris: Lerebours et Secretan, 1851.

_____. *Photographie: Traité nouveau, théorique et pratique, des procédés et manipulations sur papier sec,—humide, et sur verre au collodion,—à l'albumine*. Paris: Lerebours et Secretan, 1852.

——. *Photographie: Traité nouveau, théorique et pratique, des procédés et manipulations sur papier sec—humide, sur verre au collodion—à l'albumine*. New ed. Paris: Lerebours et Secretan, 1854.

Moulin, Félix. "La photographie en Algérie." *La Lumière* 6, no. 12 (March 22, 1856), pp. 45–46.

——. "La photographie en Algérie." *La Lumière* 6, no. 25 (June 21, 1856), pp. 97–98.

Wey, Francis. "Comment le soleil est devenu peintre: Histoire du daguerréotype et de la photographie." *Musée des Familles* 20 (June 1853), pp. 257–65; (July 1853), pp. 289–300.

Ziegler, Jules-Claude. *Compte rendu de la photographie à l'Exposition Universelle de 1855*. Dijon: Douillier, 1855.

SECONDARY SOURCES

Abt, Jeffrey. *American Egyptologist: The Life of James Henry Breasted and the Creation of His Oriental Institute*. Chicago: University of Chicago Press, 2013.

Adès, Marie-Claire, and Pierre Zaragozi. *Photographes en Algérie au XIXe siècle*. Paris: Musée-Galerie de la Seita, 1999.

Aubenas, Sylvie, ed. *Gustave Le Gray, 1820–1884*. Los Angeles: J. Paul Getty Museum, 2002.

——, and Jacques Lacarrière. *Voyage en Orient: Photographies, 1850–1880*. Paris: Hazan and Bibliothèque Nationale de France, 2001.

Ballerini, Julia. "Photography Conscripted: Horace Vernet, Gérard de Nerval, and Maxime du Camp in Egypt." PhD diss., City University of New York, 1987.

——. *The Stillness of Hajj Ishmael: Maxime Du Camp's 1850 Photographic Encounters*. New York: iUniverse, 2010.

Brettel, Richard R., ed. *Paper and Light: The Calotype in France and Great Britain, 1839–1870*. Boston: David R. Godine, 1984.

Buerger, Janet E. *The Era of the French Calotype*. Rochester, N.Y.: International Museum of Photography at George Eastman House, 1982.

Carré, Jean-Marie. *Voyageurs et écrivains français en Égypte*. 2 vols. 2nd ed. Paris: Institut Français d'Archéologie Orientale du Caire, 1988.

Cosgrove, Denis, and Stephen Daniels, eds. *The Iconography of Landscape: Essays on the Symbolic Representation, Design, and Use of Past Environments*. Cambridge: Cambridge University Press, 1988.

Dawson, Warren R., and Eric P. Uphill. *Who Was Who in Egyptology: A Biographical Index of Egyptologists; of Travellers, Explorers and Excavators in Egypt; of Collectors of and Dealers in Egyptian Antiquities; of Consuls, Officials, Authors, Benefactors and Others whose names occur in the literature of Egyptology, from the year 1500 to the present day, but excluding persons now living*. London: Egypt Exploration Society, 1972.

Dondin-Payre, Monique. "L'Académie des Inscriptions et Belles-Lettres et la photographie: Les fouilles du Tombeau de la Chrétienne au XIXe siècle." *Comptes Rendus des Séances de l'Académie des Inscriptions et Belles-Lettres* 147, no. 3 (2003), pp. 1139–57.

——. "Le premier reportage photographique archéologique en Afrique du Nord: Les fouilles du Tombeau de la Chrétienne en 1855–56." *L'Africa Romana* 14 (2002), pp. 2119–46.

Duclos, France. *Les voyageurs photographes et la Société de Géographie, 1850–1910*. Paris: Bibliothèque Nationale de France, 1998.

Effros, Bonnie. *Incidental Archaeologists: French Officers and the Rediscovery of Roman North Africa*. Ithaca, N.Y.: Cornell University Press, 2018.

Feyler, Gabrielle. "Contribution à l'histoire des origines de la photographie archéologique: 1839–1880." *Mélanges de l'École Française de Rome: Antiquité* 99, no 2 (1987), pp. 1019–47.

Gasser, Martin. "Between 'From today, painting is dead' and 'How the sun became a painter': A Close Look at Reactions to Photography in Paris, 1839–1853." *Image* 33, nos. 3–4 (1991), pp. 8–29.

Hanlon, David R. *Illuminating Shadows: The Calotype in Nineteenth-Century America*. Nevada City, Calif.: Carl Mautz, 2013.

Heilbrun, Françoise. "Un album de primitifs de la photographie française." *Revue du Louvre et des Musées de France* 30, no. 1 (1980), pp. 21–37.

Hellman, Karen, ed. *Real/Ideal: Photography in Mid-Nineteenth-Century France*. Los Angeles: J. Paul Getty Museum, 2016.

Howe, Kathleen Stewart. *Excursions along the Nile: The Photographic Discovery of Ancient Egypt*. Santa Barbara: Santa Barbara Museum of Art, 1994.

——. *Félix Teynard: Calotypes of Egypt: A Catalogue Raisonné*. New York: Hans P. Kraus Jr., 1992.

Jammes, André, and Eugenia Parry Janis. *The Art of French Calotype, with a Critical Dictionary of Photographers, 1845–1870*. Princeton: Princeton University Press, 1983.

Jammes, Isabelle. *Blanquart-Evrard et les origines de l'édition photographie française: Catalogue raisonné des albums photographiques édités, 1851–1855*. Geneva: Librairie Droz, 1981.

Jammes, Marie-Thérèse, and André Jammes. *En Égypte au temps de Flaubert, les premiers photographes 1839–1860*. Paris: Kodak-Pathé, 1976.

Jones, Kimberly, ed. *In the Forest of Fontainebleau: Painters and Photographers from Corot to Monet*. Washington, D.C.: National Gallery of Art, 2008.

Julien, Charles-André. *Histoire de l'Algérie contemporaine*, vol. 1, *La conquête et les débuts de*

la colonisation (1827–1871). Paris: Presses Universitaires de France, 1964.
Marbot, Bernard. *Une invention du XIXe siècle. Expression et technique. La photographie: Collections de la Société Française de Photographie*. Paris: Bibliothèque Nationale de France, 1976.
——. *Regards sur la photographie en France au XIXe siècle*. Paris: Berger-Levrault, 1980.
Mondenard, Anne de. "Entre romantisme et réalisme: Francis Wey (1812–1882), critique d'art." *Études Photographiques* 8 (November 2000), pp. 22–43.
——, Marc Pagneux, and Vincent Rouby. *Modernisme ou modernité: Les photographes du cercle de Gustave Le Gray*. Arles: Actes Sud, 2012.
Nickel, Douglas R. *Francis Frith in Egypt and Palestine: A Victorian Photographer Abroad*. Princeton: Princeton University Press, 2003.
Oliver, Andrew. *American Travelers on the Nile: Early U.S. Visitors to Egypt, 1774–1839*. Cairo: American University in Cairo Press, 2014.
Oulebsir, Nabila. *Les usages du patrimoine: Monuments, musées et politique coloniale en Algérie (1830–1930)*. Paris: Éditions de la Maison des Sciences de l'Homme, 2004.
Pare, Richard, ed. *Photography and Architecture, 1839–1939*. Montreal: Centre Canadien d'Architecture, 1982.
Parry Janis, Eugenia. *The Photography of Gustave Le Gray*. Chicago: Art Institute and University of Chicago Press, 1987.
Perez, Nissan N. *Focus East: Early Photography in the Near East, 1839–1885*. New York: Abrams, 1988.
Phillips, Christopher. "A Mnemonic Art? Calotype Aesthetics at Princeton." *October*, no. 26 (Autumn 1983), pp. 34–62.
Rahmani, Zahia, and Jean-Yves Sarazin. *Made in Algeria: Généalogie d'un territoire*. Vanves: Hazan, 2016.
Rouillé, André, ed. *La photographie en France: Textes et controverses. Une anthologie, 1816–1871*. Paris: Macula, 1989.
——. "La photographie française à l'Exposition Universelle de 1855." *Le Mouvement Social* 131 (1985), pp. 87–103.
Salmon, Laura. "Nouvelle Cuisine: The Calotype Aesthetic and Gustave Le Gray." *Afterimage* 16, no. 3 (October 1988), pp. 10–13.
Schwartz, Joan M., and James R. Ryan, eds. *Picturing Place: Photography and the Geographical Imagination*. London: I. B. Tauris, 2003.
Solomon-Godeau, Abigail. "Calotypomania: The Gourmet Guide to Nineteenth-Century Photography." In *Photography at the Dock: Essays on Photographic Histories, Institutions, and Practices*. Minneapolis: University of Minnesota Press, 1991.
——. "A Photographer in Jerusalem, 1855: Auguste Salzmann and His Times." *October*, no. 18 (Autumn 1981), pp. 90–107.
Taylor, Roger. *Impressed by Light: British Photographs from Paper Negatives, 1840–1860*. New York: The Metropolitan Museum of Art, 2007.
Thomas, Benjamin E. "Fortress City of Constantine, Algeria." *The Scientific Monthly* 81, no. 3 (September 1955), pp. 130–37.
Thompson, Jason. *Wonderful Things: A History of Egyptology*, vol. 1, *From Antiquity to 1881*. Cairo: American University in Cairo Press, 2015.
White, Minor, André Jammes, and Robert Sobieszek. *French Primitive Photography*. Millerton, N.Y.: Aperture, 1969.
Zarobell, John. *Empire of Landscape: Space and Ideology in French Colonial Algeria*. University Park: Pennsylvania State University Press, 2010.

WORKS IN THE EXHIBITION

Titles in italics are those assigned by Greene and derive either from the albums at the Académie des Inscriptions et Belles-Lettres, now held in the collection of the Bibliothèque de l'Institut de France, Paris, or, in a few instances, mounts of works Greene deposited at the Société Française de Photographie. Titles indicated in roman are descriptive, as these works were not included in albums and have no recorded titles.

Greene's spelling and nomenclature often reflect the state of the field of Egyptology at that time. The English translations have been adjusted to reflect current spellings.

All works are salted paper prints unless otherwise noted.

FRANCE

Plate 1 [View of Paris rooftops], 1852–53
Waxed paper negative
9 9/16 × 12 5/16 in. (24.3 × 31.2 cm)
Hans P. Kraus Jr., Inc., New York

Plate 2 [*La Marseillaise* by François Rude, Arc de Triomphe, Paris], ca. 1852
Waxed paper negative
12 1/2 × 9 3/4 in. (31.8 × 24.8 cm)
Promised gift of Paul Sack to the Sack Photographic Trust for the San Francisco Museum of Modern Art

Plate 3 [Forest of Fontainebleau], 1852–53
Waxed paper negative
12 5/16 × 9 3/4 in. (31.3 × 24.8 cm)
Hans P. Kraus Jr., Inc., New York

Plate 4 [Road to Chailly, Forest of Fontainebleau], 1852–53
9 × 11 7/8 in. (22.86 × 30.16 cm)
San Francisco Museum of Modern Art, Accessions Committee Fund purchase, 2010

Plate 5 [Forest of Fontainebleau], 1853
9 3/16 × 11 15/16 in. (23.3 × 30.3 cm)
The Museum of Modern Art, New York, Gift of Jerome Powell

Plate 6 [Still life with a statuette of the Venus de Milo], 1852–53
Waxed paper negative
12 3/8 × 9 9/16 in. (31.4 × 24.3 cm)
Hans P. Kraus Jr., Inc., New York

EGYPT

Plate 7 *Pyramides de Giseh. (Travaux de Mr. Mariette). Fouille à la gauche du Sphinx (Pyramids of Giza. [Mr. Mariette's site]. Excavation to the left of the Sphinx)*, 1853
8 3/4 × 11 7/8 in. (22.2 × 30.2 cm)
The Metropolitan Museum of Art, New York, Gilman Collection, Purchase, Ann Tenenbaum and Thomas H. Lee Gift, 2005

Plate 8 *Pyramides de Giseh (Travaux de Mr. Mariette). Stèle au bas du portail du Sphinx deblayée par Mr. Mariette, décembre 1853 (Pyramids of Giza (Mr. Mariette's site). Stela at the base of the Sphinx excavated by Mr. Mariette, December 1853)*, 1853
11 5/8 × 9 in. (29.6 × 22.9 cm)
Musée d'Orsay, Paris

Plate 9 *Giseh. Sphinx (Giza. Sphinx)*, 1853–54
9 × 11 9/16 in. (22.9 × 29.3 cm)
Bibliothèque Nationale de France, Paris

Plate 10 *Giseh. Pyramide de Chéops (Giza. Pyramid of Cheops, or Khufu)*, 1853–54
8 9/16 × 11 13/16 in. (21.8 × 30 cm)
National Gallery of Art, Washington, D.C., Purchased as a Gift of W. Bruce and Delaney H. Lundberg

Plate 11 *Études de terrain près de Gebel Abousir, 2e cataracte (Studies of the landscape near Gebel Abusir, Second Cataract)*, 1854
9 1/8 × 11 7/8 in. (23.18 × 30.16 cm)
San Francisco Museum of Modern Art, Purchase through a gift of Christine and Michael Murray, 2008

Plate 12 *Études de terrain près de Gebel Abousir; 2e cataracte (Studies of the landscape near Gebel Abusir, Second Cataract)*, 1854
9 1/8 × 11 1/4 in. (23.2 × 28.6 cm)
Collection of Richard and Ronay Menschel

Plate 13 *Seconde Cataracte, au dessus de Gebel Abousir (Second Cataract, above Gebel Abusir)*, 1854
9 × 11 11/16 in. (22.8 × 29.7 cm)
Bibliothèque Nationale de France, Paris

Plate 14 *Seconde Cataracte (Second Cataract)*, 1854
9 1/16 × 11 13/16 in. (23 × 30 cm)
Bibliothèque de l'Institut de France, Paris

Plate 15 *Seconde Cataracte (Second Cataract)*, 1854
9 × 11 7/8 in. (22.9 × 30.2 cm)
Collection of Gary B. Sokol

Plate 16 *Ibsamboul. Colosse de l'Est (Abu Simbel. Eastern colossus)*, 1854
11 13/16 × 9 in. (30 × 22.8 cm)
Musée d'Orsay, Paris

Plate 17 *Ibsamboul. Statue de femme (Abu Simbel. Statue of a woman)*, 1854
11 13/16 × 9 in. (30 × 22.8 cm)
Bibliothèque Nationale de France, Paris

Plate 18 *Amada. Pilier du temple (Amada. Temple pillar)*, 1854
9 1/8 × 11 7/8 in. (23.2 × 30.1 cm)
Musée d'Orsay, Paris

Plate 19 *Montagne de Ghirché (Mountain of Wadi Gyrshe)*, 1854
8 3/16 × 11 3/4 in. (20.8 × 29.8 cm)
Collection of Gary B. Sokol

Plate 20 *Ouadi Esseboua. Temple (Wadi es-Sebua. Temple)*, 1854
9 3/16 × 11 5/8 in. (23.3 × 29.6 cm)
Private collection

Plate 21 *Deboud. Temple (Debod. Temple)*, 1854
9¹⁄₁₆ × 11¹³⁄₁₆ in. (23 × 30 cm)
Bibliothèque de l'Institut de France, Paris

Plate 22 *Étude de gommiers (Study of gum trees)*, 1854
12 × 9 in. (30.5 × 22.9 cm)
Collection of Gary B. Sokol

Plate 23 *Étude de sycomores, Korosko (Study of sycamores, Korosko)*, 1854
9⅛ × 11⅞ in. (23.18 × 30.16 cm)
Promised gift of Paul Sack to the Sack Photographic Trust for the San Francisco Museum of Modern Art

Plate 24 *Meharraka. Temple (Meharraka. Temple)*, 1854
8¹¹⁄₁₆ × 11⅜ in. (22.1 × 28.9 cm)
Canadian Centre for Architecture, Montreal

Plate 25 *Meharraka. Temple (Meharraka. Temple)*, 1854
9¹⁄₁₆ × 11¾ in. (23 × 29.8 cm)
J. Paul Getty Museum, Los Angeles

Plate 26 *Dakkeh. Salle méridionale du Temple, No. 6 (Dakka. Southern chamber of the temple, No. 6)*, 1854
9³⁄₁₆ × 11⅞ in. (23.3 × 30.2 cm)
The Metropolitan Museum of Art, New York, Gilman Collection, Purchase, Joseph M. Cohen Gift, 2005

Plate 27 *Dandour. Temple 1 (Dendur. Temple 1)*, 1854
9¹⁄₁₆ × 11¹³⁄₁₆ in. (23 × 30 cm)
Bibliothèque de l'Institut de France, Paris

Plate 28 *Dandour. Temple 2 (Dendur. Temple 2)*, 1854
9 × 12 in. (22.9 × 30.5 cm)
Musée d'Orsay, Paris

Plate 29 *Qartas. Temple (Quertassi. Temple)*, 1854
8¼ × 10⅞ in. (20.9 × 27.7 cm)
Bibliothèque Nationale de France, Paris

Plate 30 *Qartas. Temple (Quertassi. Temple)*, 1854
8⅞ × 11¾ in. (22.6 × 29.8 cm)
Bibliothèque Nationale de France, Paris

Plate 31 *Études de dattiers (Studies of date palms)*, 1854
8⅞ × 11⅛ in. (22.5 × 28.2 cm)
Bibliothèque Nationale de France, Paris

Plate 32 *Études de dattiers (Studies of date palms)*, 1854
9⅛ × 11⅛ in. (23.18 × 28.26 cm)
San Francisco Museum of Modern Art, Fractional gift of Paul Sack, and collection of the Sack Photographic Trust

Plate 33 *Ombos. Temple (Kom Ombo. Temple)*, 1854
9¹⁄₁₆ × 11¹³⁄₁₆ in. (23 × 30 cm)
Bibliothèque de l'Institut de France, Paris

Plate 34 *Première cataracte, Ile de Philae (First Cataract, Island of Philae)*, 1854
9³⁄₁₆ × 11¾ in. (23.3 × 29.8 cm)
The Museum of Modern Art, New York, Gift of Jerome Powell

Plate 35 *Ile de Philae. Porte auprès du grand Temple (Island of Philae. Portal near the Great Temple)*, 1854
9¹⁄₁₆ × 11⅜ in. (23 × 28.9 cm)
Bibliothèque Nationale de France, Paris

Plate 36 *Ile de Philae. Grand Temple; côté gauche de la cour (Island of Philae. Great Temple; left side of the court)*, 1854
9³⁄₁₆ × 11¾ in. (23.3 × 29.9 cm)
Société Française de Photographie, Paris

Plate 37 *Silsilis. Stèle. (Silsilis. Stela)*, 1854
9¹⁄₁₆ × 11¹³⁄₁₆ in. (23 × 30 cm)
Bibliothèque de l'Institut de France, Paris

Plate 38 *Silsilis. Stèles (Silsilis. Stelae)*, 1854
9⁵⁄₁₆ × 11¾ in. (23.7 × 29.8 cm)
Société Française de Photographie, Paris

Plate 39 *Thèbes. Colosses du Memnonium; massif de droite (Thebes. Colossi of Memnon; right side)*, 1854
9 × 11⅝ in. (22.8 × 29.5 cm)
Canadian Centre for Architecture, Montreal

Plate 40 *Thèbes. Colosses du Memnonium; massif de gauche (Thebes. Colossi of Memnon; left side)*, 1854
9³⁄₁₆ × 11¹³⁄₁₆ in. (23.3 × 30 cm)
Canadian Centre for Architecture, Montreal

Plate 41 *Thèbes. Colosse de droite (Thebes. Right colossus)*, 1854
11⁹⁄₁₆ × 8⁷⁄₁₆ in. (29.3 × 21.5 cm)
Bibliothèque Nationale de France, Paris

Plate 42 *Thèbes. Colosse de droite, face postérieure (Thebes. Right colossus, back side)*, 1854
11⅝ × 9³⁄₁₆ in. (29.5 × 23.3 cm)
Collection of Richard and Ronay Menschel

Plate 43 *Thèbes. Médinet-Habou; vue prise de l'entrée du Palais de Ramsès-Méïamoun (Thebes. Medinet Habu. View from the entrance to the Palace of Ramesses III)*, 1854
9¹⁄₁₆ × 11¹³⁄₁₆ in. (23 × 30 cm)
Bibliothèque de l'Institut de France, Paris

Plate 44 *Thèbes. Médinet-Habou. Premier Pylône (Thebes. Medinet Habu. First pylon)*, 1854
9¼ × 12⅛ in. (23.5 × 30.8 cm)
J. Paul Getty Museum, Los Angeles

Plate 45 *Médinet-Habou. Palais de Ramsès-Méïamoun. Premier Pylône. Massif de gauche; face intérieure (Medinet Habu. Palace of Ramesses III. First pylon. Left tower, interior side)*, 1854
9³⁄₁₆ × 11¹⁵⁄₁₆ in. (23.3 × 30.3 cm)
Musée d'Orsay, Paris

Plate 46 *Médinet-Habou. Palais de Ramsès-Méïamoun. Premier Pylône. Massif de droite; face intérieure. (Medinet Habu. Palace of Ramesses III. First pylon. Right tower, interior side)*, 1854
9⅛ × 11¾ in. (23.2 × 29.9 cm)
Musée d'Orsay, Paris

Plate 47 *Médinet-Habou. Palais de Ramsès-Méïamoun, entrée de la seconde cour (Medinet Habu. Palace of Ramesses III, entry to the second court)*, 1854
9¼ × 11⅝ in. (23.5 × 29.5 cm)
Musée d'Orsay, Paris

Plate 48 *Thèbes. Médinet-Habou. Palais de Ramsès III, seconde cour, face nord (Thebes. Medinet Habu. Palace of Ramesses III; second court, north side)*, 1854
9¼ × 11¹⁵⁄₁₆ in. (23.5 × 30.4 cm)
Société Française de Photographie, Paris

Plate 49 *Thèbes. Médinet-Habou. Palais de Ramsès-Méïamoun; seconde cour; face sud (Thebes. Medinet Habu. Palace of Ramesses III; second court, south side)*, 1854
8 15/16 × 11 15/16 in. (22.7 × 30.3 cm)
Bibliothèque Nationale de France, Paris

Plate 50 *Médinet-Habou. Palais de Ramsès-Méïamoun. Seconde Cour. Sculptures et Inscriptions de la paroi gauche. No 1 (Medinet Habu. Palace of Ramesses III. Sculptures and inscriptions of the left inner wall, No. 1)*, 1854
9 3/16 × 11 7/8 in. (23.3 × 30.2 cm)
The Metropolitan Museum of Art, New York, Purchase, The Howard Gilman Foundation Gift, 1989

Plate 51 *Médinet-Habou. Porte découverte près du palais de Thoutmès III (Medinet Habu. Door discovered close to the Palace of Thutmose III)*, 1855
11 13/16 × 9 1/16 in. (30 × 23 cm)
Musée d'Orsay, Paris

Plate 52 *Thèbes. Médinet-Habou. Palais de Thoutmosis III (Thebes. Medinet Habu. Palace of Thutmose III)*, 1854
9 1/16 × 11 15/16 in. (23 × 30.3 cm)
Collection of Gary B. Sokol

Plate 53 *Montagne de Thèbes (Mountain of Thebes)*, 1854
9 3/16 × 12 in. (23.3 × 30.5 cm)
J. Paul Getty Museum, Los Angeles

Plate 54 *Quornah. Temple (Qurna. Temple)*, 1854
9 × 11 7/16 in. (22.9 × 29.1 cm)
Collection of Richard and Ronay Menschel

Plate 55 *Karnac. Salle hypostyle. Mur du Nord. face intérieure. No 3 (Karnak. Hypostyle Hall. Northern wall, interior. No. 3)*, 1854
8 11/16 × 11 7/8 in. (22 × 30.2 cm)
Musée d'Orsay, Paris

Plate 56 *Karnac. Mur du Sud. (Karnak. Southern wall)*, 1854
12 × 9 in. (30.5 × 22.9 cm)
Collection of Gary B. Sokol

Plate 57 *El-Assasif. Porte de granit rose, No. 1 (El-Assasif. Portal made of pink granite, No. 1)*, 1854
9 1/16 × 11 13/16 in. (23 × 30 cm)
Bibliothèque de l'Institut de France, Paris

Plate 58 *El-Assasif. Porte de granit rose. No. 2 (El-Assasif. Portal made of pink granite, No. 2)*, 1854
9 1/16 × 11 13/16 in. (23 × 30 cm)
Bibliothèque de l'Institut de France, Paris

Plate 59 *Château de France; Louqsor (Château de France, Luxor)*, 1854
9 1/8 × 11 9/16 in. (23.2 × 29.4 cm)
Bibliothèque Nationale de France, Paris

Plate 60 *Bords du Nil. Kalabschi (Banks of the Nile. Kalabsha)*, 1854
9 1/4 × 12 in. (23.5 × 30.48 cm)
Promised gift of Paul Sack to the Sack Photographic Trust for the San Francisco Museum of Modern Art

Plate 61 *Louqsor (Luxor)*, 1854
8 15/16 × 11 13/16 in. (22.7 × 30 cm)
Bibliothèque Nationale de France, Paris

Plate 62 *Louqsor. Portique (Luxor. Portico)*, 1854
9 3/16 × 11 7/16 in. (23.3 × 29.1 cm)
Robert Koch Gallery, San Francisco

Plate 63 *Bords du Nil à Thèbes (Banks of the Nile at Thebes)*, 1854
8 3/4 × 11 7/8 in. (22.3 × 30.2 cm)
The Metropolitan Museum of Art, New York, Gilman Collection, Purchase, The Horace W. Goldsmith Foundation Gift, through Joyce and Robert Menschel, 2005

Plate 64 [Pompey's Pillar], 1854–55. Plate 1 from the album *Collection de photographies prises en Égypte en 1854 offerte à S.A. le Grand Duc de Bade en 1855 (Collection of Photographs Taken in Egypt in 1854 Given to His Highness the Grand Duke of Baden in 1855)*
Album of 26 salted paper prints, 1854–55
Janet Lehr, Inc., New York

Plate 65 [Ramesseum, with the head from a colossus of Ramesses II], 1854–55
9 × 11 11/16 in. (22.9 × 29.7 cm)
Collection of Richard and Ronay Menschel

Plate 66 [Boat on the Nile], 1855
9 1/8 × 12 1/8 in. (23.2 × 30.8 cm)
Michael G. and C. Jane Wilson 2007 Trust

Plate 67 [View of houses in Cairo], 1854–55
9 1/16 × 11 13/16 in. (23 × 30 cm)
Canadian Centre for Architecture, Montreal

ALGERIA

Plate 68 *Tombeau de la Chrétienne. Côté du sud (Tomb of the Christian Woman. South side)*, 1856
9 × 12 in. (22.9 × 30.5 cm)
Collection of Gary B. Sokol

Plate 69 *Fausse porte, Tombeau de la Chrétienne (False Door, Tomb of the Christian Woman)*, 1855
9 1/2 × 12 in. (24.13 × 30.48 cm)
San Francisco Museum of Modern Art, Accessions Committee Fund and purchase through the gifts of William S. Fisher and an anonymous donor, 2006

Plate 70 *Vue de fausse porte du Nord le 5 avril 1856 à la fin des travaux de la 2e exploration (View of the northern false door, April 5, 1856, at the end of the second exploration)*, 1856
11 7/8 × 9 3/8 in. (30.2 × 23.8 cm)
National Gallery of Canada, Ottawa, Gift of Ward C. Pitfield, Toronto, 1981

Plate 71 *Tombeau de la Chrétienne. Etat de l'Eboulement le 1er janvier 1856 après les trois premières journées de travail (Tomb of the Christian Woman. State of the collapsed rock after the first three days of work)*, 1856
8 5/8 × 8 3/4 in. (21.9 × 22.2 cm)
National Gallery of Canada, Ottawa, Gift of Ward C. Pitfield, Toronto, 1981

Plate 72 [Ruins near the Tombeau de la Chrétienne], 1856
9 3/16 × 11 11/16 in. (23.3 × 29.7 cm)
The Museum of Modern Art, New York, Gift of Jerome Powell

Plate 73 [Camp by the Tombeau de la Chrétienne], 1856
8 9/16 × 11 3/4 in. (21.7 × 29.8 cm)
The Metropolitan Museum of Art, New York, Gilman Collection, Museum Purchase, 2005

Plate 74 *Tombeau de la Chrétienne. Vue du côté Est à la fin des travaux de la 2e exploration (5 avril 1856) (Tomb of the Christian Woman. View of the east side at the end of the second exploration [April 5, 1856])*, 1856
10⅜ × 12¹⁄₁₆ in. (26.35 × 30.64 cm)
San Francisco Museum of Modern Art, Accessions Committee Fund purchase, 1998

Plate 75 [Bank of the Rhumel, near Constantine], 1856
9⅜ × 12⅛ in. (23.8 × 30.8 cm)
The Metropolitan Museum of Art, New York, Gilman Collection, Museum Purchase, 2005

Plate 76 [Rhumel River], 1856
9⅛ × 11⅞ in. (23.2 × 30.2 cm)
The Museum of Modern Art, New York, Gift of Daniel K. Mayers

Plate 77 [Constantine], 1856
9 × 11¹³⁄₁₆ in. (22.9 × 30 cm)
The Museum of Modern Art, New York, Gift of Jerome Powell

Plate 78 [Constantine], 1856
9¼ × 12 in. (23.5 × 30.48 cm)
San Francisco Museum of Modern Art, Accessions Committee Fund purchase, 2010

Plate 79 [Constantine], 1856
9⅜ × 12 in. (23.81 × 30.48 cm)
Collection of the Sack Photographic Trust for the San Francisco Museum of Modern Art

Plate 80 [Constantine], 1856
9⅛ × 11⅞ in. (23.18 × 30.16 cm)
San Francisco Museum of Modern Art, Accessions Committee Fund purchase, 2010

Plate 81 [Constantine], 1856
9⅛ × 11⅞ in. (23.2 × 30.2 cm)
The Museum of Modern Art, New York, Gift of Jerome Powell

Plate 82 [Waterfall, Constantine], 1856
9³⁄₁₆ × 11⅞ in. (23.3 × 30.2 cm)
The Metropolitan Museum of Art, New York, Purchase, Alfred Stieglitz Society Gifts, Anonymous Foundation Gift, W. Bruce and Delaney H. Lundberg Gift, and Marian and James H. Cohen Gift, in memory of their son, Michael Harrison Cohen, 2004

Plate 83 [Waterfall, Constantine], 1856
9⅜ × 12¹⁄₁₆ in. (23.8 × 30.6 cm)
The Museum of Modern Art, New York, Gift of Jerome Powell

Plate 84 [Constantine panorama], 1856
Three salted paper prints
9⅜ × 12¹⁄₁₆ in. (23.8 × 30.6 cm); 9½ × 12¹⁄₁₆ in. (24.1 × 30.7 cm); 9½ × 12¹⁄₁₆ in. (24 × 30.7 cm)
Michael G. and C. Jane Wilson 2007 Trust

Plate 85 [Constantine], 1856
9¾ × 12½ in. (24.8 × 31.8 cm)
Collection of Paul Sack

Plate 86 [Ruins of a Roman aqueduct, Cherchell], 1856
9³⁄₁₆ × 11¹³⁄₁₆ in. (23.3 × 30 cm)
Collection of Paul Sack

Plate 87 [Roman sculptures, Cherchell Museum], 1856
11³⁄₁₆ × 9 in. (28.4 × 22.9 cm)
The Art Institute of Chicago, Photography Gala Endowment

Plate 88 [Roman sculptures, Cherchell Museum], 1856
12¹⁄₁₆ × 9⅛ in. (30.7 × 23.2 cm)
Canadian Centre for Architecture, Montreal

Plate 89 [Fragment of a statue of King Thutmose I in the Cherchell Museum], 1856
11⅜ × 9¹⁄₁₆ in. (28.9 × 23 cm)
San Francisco Museum of Modern Art, Purchase through a gift of Evelyn D. Haas, 2007

Plate 90 [Boat in Cherchell harbor], 1855–56
8⅞ × 11⅛ in. (22.5 × 28.3 cm)
The Metropolitan Museum of Art, New York, Gilman Collection, Museum Purchase, 2005

This book is published on the occasion of the exhibition *Signs and Wonders: The Photographs of John Beasley Greene* organized by Corey Keller for the San Francisco Museum of Modern Art.

Exhibition itinerary:

San Francisco Museum of Modern Art, August 31, 2019–January 5, 2020

Art Institute of Chicago, February 8–May 31, 2020

Published in 2018 by
DelMonico Books • Prestel

DelMonico Books, an imprint of Prestel, a member of Verlagsgruppe Random House GmbH

Prestel Verlag
Neumarkter Strasse 28
81673 Munich

Prestel Publishing Ltd.
14-17 Wells Street
London W1T 3PD

Prestel Publishing
900 Broadway, Suite 603
New York, NY 10003

www.prestel.com

Editor: Philomena Mariani
Designer: Rebecca Sylvers, Miko McGinty Inc.
Production: Anjali Pala

Printed and bound in China

Cataloging-in-Publication Data is available from the Library of Congress.

ISBN 978-3-7913-5846-8

A CIP catalogue record for this book is available from the British Library.

Frontispiece: Detail of *Médinet-Habou. Palais de Ramsès-Méïamoun. Seconde Cour. Sculptures et Inscriptions de la paroi gauche. No 1 (Medinet Habu. Palace of Ramesses III. Sculptures and inscriptions of the left inner wall. No. 1)*, 1854 (see pl. 50).

Page 4: Detail of [Constantine], 1856 (see pl. 81).

Page 8: Detail of *Thèbes. Colosse de droite (Thebes. Right colossus)*, 1854 (see pl. 41).

Figures

1: Digital image courtesy of the Getty's Open Content Program; **2, 3, 6**: courtesy Hans P. Kraus Jr., Inc., New York; **4, 9, 14**: The Metropolitan Museum of Art, New York / Art Resource, NY; **5, 19, 20**: Bibliothèque de l'Institut de France, Paris; image © RMN-Grand Palais / Art Resource, NY; **7**: courtesy Janet Lehr, Inc., New York; **8, 10**: Musée d'Orsay, Paris; image © RMN-Grand Palais / Art Resource, NY; **11**: New York Public Library Digital Collections; **12, 13, 18**: Don Ross, courtesy the San Francisco Museum of Modern Art; **15**: coll. Société Française de Photographie, Paris; **16, 17**: courtesy of the Oriental Institute of the University of Chicago; **21–23**: Bibliothèque Nationale de France, Paris; **24**: image © The Museum of Modern Art / Licensed by SCALA / Art Resource, NY.

Plates

1, 3, 6, 20, 66, 84–86: courtesy Hans P. Kraus Jr., Inc., New York; **2, 4, 11, 19, 23, 32, 52, 60, 70, 74, 78–80, 89**: Don Ross; courtesy SFMOMA; **5, 34, 72, 76, 77, 81, 83**: image © The Museum of Modern Art, New York / Licensed by SCALA / Art Resource, NY; **7, 26, 50, 63, 73, 75, 82, 90**: The Metropolitan Museum of Art, New York / Art Resource, NY; **8, 16, 18, 45–47, 51, 55**: Musée d'Orsay, Paris; image © RMN-Grand Palais / Art Resource, NY; **9, 13, 17, 29, 30, 31, 35, 41, 49, 59, 61**: Bibliothèque Nationale de France, Paris; **10**: National Gallery of Art, Washington, D.C.; **12, 42, 54, 65**: Jason Mandella; **14, 21, 27, 28, 32, 33, 37, 43, 57, 58**: Bibliothèque de l'Insitut de France, Paris; image © RMN-Grand Palais / Art Resource, NY; **15, 22, 56, 68**: courtesy Gary B. Sokol; **24, 39, 40, 67, 88**: Canadian Centre for Architecture, Montreal; **25, 44, 53**: Digital images courtesy of the Getty's Open Content Program; **36, 38, 48**: coll. Société Française de Photographie, Paris; **62**: Robert Koch Gallery, San Francisco; **64**: Janet Lehr, Inc., New York; **69**: Guy Campbell, courtesy SFMOMA; **70, 71**: National Gallery of Canada, Ottawa; **87**: The Art Institute of Chicago / Art Resource, NY.